BY-ELECTIONS IN BRITISH POLITICS

By-Elections in British Politics

Edited by

CHRIS COOK
Director, Historical Records Project,
London School of Economics

and

JOHN RAMSDEN
Lecturer in History, Queen Mary College,
University of London

With an Introduction by

DAVID BUTLER
Fellow of Nuffield College, Oxford

MACMILLAN

First published 1973 by

THE MACMILLAN PRESS LTD

London and Basingstoke
Associated companies in New York
Dublin Melbourne Johannesburg and Madras

SBN 333 14325 6

Printed in Great Britain by
R. AND R. CLARK LTD
Edinburgh

To the Warden and Fellows

of Nuffield College, Oxford

Contents

Introduction and Acknowledgements

The idea which lies behind this book originated in discussions between a number of Fellows and Students of Nuffield College in the autumn of 1971. It was further discussed and defined at a conference held at Nuffield College in the December of that year, and attended by, among others, most of the authors of the present volume. It soon became clear that the interpretation of by-elections in their historical and political contexts would require a wide variety of approaches. Just as no measure of electoral change is satisfactory for the whole period covered by the book, so no single method of description or analysis was felt to be possible – or indeed desirable – for the by-elections which we wished to describe and analyse. For Newport or St George's, concentration on the naturally dramatic events of a single campaign was felt to be valid; for East Fulham, it was felt that a comparative approach was more appropriate; for 1924, the Second World War and the late 1960s, it was felt that only by approaching a whole series of contests could any sense be made of an otherwise confusing pattern. However, even the widest of perspectives cannot bring all the diverse campaigns of over fifty years within a single framework of regimented chapters: it would be misleading to ignore the relatively unimpressive and unexciting by-elections of the 1950s, but it would be equally misleading to treat them as comparable to East Fulham or to Orpington. We have therefore provided editorial passages to cover periods which are not dealt with in specific chapters. We have also included three chapters which look at general issues rather than specific contests. Every contest is at the least a source of psephological information and, because of their small number, each result was significant at least in the short term. By-elections, with all their short-comings as indicators, continue to be more influential than opinion polls or local government elections, continue to arouse a relatively high level of participation among voters, and continue to excite newspapers and television, politicians and historians.

It will be clear from the above that the editors owe a considerable debt to the Warden and Fellows of Nuffield College, whose generosity made the planning and writing of this book possible. They would also like to thank Dr P. G. Pulzer and Mr F. W. S. Craig for assistance at the planning stage, and Professor M. Beloff, Mr P. J. Forsyth, Dr G. C. L. Hazlehurst, Mr A. Hunt, Mr A. J. P. Taylor and Mr G. K. Wilson for general assistance and criticisms of the text. Although authors are responsible only for the sections of the book which appear under their own names, most of them have assisted the editors and each other very considerably. The diversity of the book and its unity owe much to the fact that it is the work of a team. Both diversity and unity are also due to the nature of by-elections themselves.

July, 1973   C. C.
                                                           J. R.

The editors and publishers are grateful to the First Beaverbrook Foundation for the extracts from the Beaverbrook Papers; to the Hon. Mrs. V. E. Butler for the extract from her father's diary; and to George Weidenfeld & Nicolson Ltd for the extract from *Baldwin: A Biography* by K. Middlemas and J. Barnes. The cartoon by John Reynolds on p. 97, from the *Morning Post*, 19 March 1931, is reproduced by permission of the *Daily Telegraph*.

Notes on the Contributors

PAUL ADDISON. Born 1943; educated at Pembroke College, Oxford; Student of Nuffield College, 1965–7; Lecturer at Pembroke College, Oxford, 1966–7; Research Assistant to the late Randolph S. Churchill; Lecturer in Modern History at the University of Edinburgh since 1967.

DAVID BUTLER. Born 1924; educated at New College, Oxford; Student, Research Fellow and Official Fellow at Nuffield College since 1949. Consultant to the BBC on elections; author and co-author of Nuffield College general election studies since 1951; author of *The Study of Political Behaviour* and *The Electoral System in Britain*; co-author of *Political Change in Britain*; editor of *Elections Abroad* and co-editor of *British Political Facts*.

MARTIN CEADEL. Born 1948; educated at Corpus Christi College, Oxford; Student of Nuffield College, 1969–72; Research Fellow of Jesus College, Oxford, and Lecturer in Modern History, Corpus Christi College, Oxford, 1972–1973. Lecturer in History, University of Sussex, since 1973.

CHRIS COOK. Born 1945; educated at St Catharine's College, Cambridge, and Oriel College, Oxford. Student of Nuffield College, 1968–70; Lecturer in Politics, Magdalen College, Oxford, 1969–70; Senior Research Officer, Political Archives Investigation, London School of Economics, since 1970; co-editor of *Election '70*, *The Decade of Disillusion* and *European Political Facts, 1918–72*

RICHARD JAY. Born 1946; educated at Brasenose College, Oxford; Student of Nuffield College, 1968–71; Lecturer in Government, University of Essex, since 1971.

DAVID McKIE. Born 1935; educated at Christ's Hospital and Oriel College, Oxford; joined the *Guardian*, becoming Deputy News Editor; on the Polititical Staff since 1972; co-editor of *Election '70* and *The Decade of Disillusion*.

IAIN McLEAN. Born 1946; educated at Christ Church, Oxford; Student and Research Fellow, Nuffield College, 1967–71. Lecturer in Politics at the University of Newcastle since 1971.

MATTHEW OAKESHOTT. Born 1947; educated at University College, Oxford; Economist, Kenya Ministry of Finance and Economic Planning, 1968–70; Student of Nuffield College, 1970–2; Oxford City Councillor since 1972. Joseph Rowntree Political Fellow working for Rt Hon. Roy Jenkins, MP, since 1972.

CLIVE PAYNE. Born 1942; educated at Southampton University and University of Wales, Aberystwyth; Assistant Lecturer in Statistics, Aberystwyth, 1966–8; Lecturer in Computing, University of Strathclyde, 1968–9; Director of Research Services Unit, Nuffield College, since 1969; author of various articles on statistical and computing methods in the social sciences; computing consultant to the BBC for general election coverage since 1969.

GILLIAN PEELE. Born 1949; educated at Durham University and St Anne's College, Oxford; Student of Nuffield College 1971–3; member of Gray's Inn; Lecturer in Politics, St Catherine's College, Oxford, since 1972. Research Fellow, St Antony's College, Oxford, since 1973.

JOHN RAMSDEN. Born 1947; educated at Corpus Christi College, Oxford; Student of Nuffield College, 1969–72; Lecturer in Modern History, Queen Mary College, University of London, since 1972.

STAN TAYLOR. Born 1948; educated at Newcastle University; Student of Nuffield College, 1970–3. Lecturer in Politics, University of Warwick, since 1973.

KEN YOUNG. Born 1943; educated at London School of Economics; Lecturer in Politics, Goldsmiths' College, London, 1968–9; Research Officer, Government Research Division, London School of Economics, since 1969; associate editor of *Policy and Politics*.

1. By-Elections and their Interpretation

by DAVID BUTLER

In the time of Charles II, when Parliaments had no limit to their duration, by-elections were the prime sources of MP recruitment. When John Wilkes was repeatedly returned by the electors of Middlesex in 1769–70, or when Foxite support was tested at Westminster in 1783, national attention was clearly focused on the verdict of by-elections.[1] However, in pre-Reform days there were few constituencies with a broad enough, or free enough, franchise for by-elections to be given much value as pointers to popular opinion. After 1832 the situation began to change (for example, a by-election at Walsall in 1842 seems to have had some significance in the development of the Corn Law struggle), but it was not until the coming of mass politics in the second half of the nineteenth century that by-elections became a frequent source of comment. It was thought, probably incorrectly, that the deceptively favourable outcome of contests at Southwark and Sheffield in February 1880 lured Disraeli into announcing the general election which ended his career.

Certainly, with the advent of a popular press by-elections attracted a new degree of interest, being treated almost as major sporting events. By the end of the century the letters and diaries of politicians contain increasingly frequent observations on their outcome. Perhaps 1904 and 1905 (with seven government defeats in each year) provide the period when by-elections had most significance for British politics. They did not then bring down a government (they never have),[2] but they did

[1] But the actual term 'by-election' did not come into use until the middle of the nineteenth century.

[2] But the possibility remains. For example, the shadow of by-elections hung heavily over the Labour Governments of 1950–1 and 1964–6 (when the majorities ranged from 6 to 3), while the 15 losses Labour suffered in 1966–70 were only endurable by a government which had started the Parliament with a handsome majority.

much to destroy its morale, as well as to preserve the uncertain unity of the opposition. Mass politics were now conducted on a national scale. As long as there were no opinion polls and few local elections that were fought on a party basis, there was nothing to compete with by-elections as indicators of how the political tide was flowing.

However, 1918 constitutes a turning-point in electoral history, marking the biggest leap towards a universal franchise and the arrival of the Labour Party as a nationwide political force. Because the style of politics changed so abruptly at that time, it offers an appropriate moment to begin a study of the role of by-elections in modern politics.

Incidence

The incidence of by-elections has been very uneven. Since 1918 the annual average number, 15, conceals a variation between 39 in 1940 and 2 in 1966. In fact the number of by-elections has fallen. From 1919 to 1939 the annual average was 18, while from mid-1945 to mid-1970 it was 11.[3] Fewer elderly MPs have stayed on to die in harness – the seven septuagenarians in the 1970 House of Commons was the smallest number on record; fewer MPs have resigned in mid-Parliament for business or personal reasons; and fewer have been appointed to government posts – partly because of the end of overseas governorships and of the use of the House as a path to judicial office and partly because, recently, the increased volatility of the electorate has made governments more chary of creating vacancies even in 'safe' seats. The most outstanding government defeats since 1960 – Orpington, Leyton, Dudley, Sutton and Cheam – were all in by-elections that could have been avoided.

Other causes of by-elections have disappeared. Until the passage of the Re-election of Ministers Act in 1926 the holders of certain offices had to offer themselves for re-election upon appointment; between 1918 and 1926 this caused 20 by-elections – and in two of them the incumbent was defeated.

[3] Of course, many of the by-elections in 1918–22 and in 1940–5 had unopposed returns. Since 1950 there have been only 3 uncontested by-elections, all in Northern Ireland. The victor at Armagh in 1954 was the last MP ever to be returned unopposed.

Members of Parliament seem also to have abandoned the practice of seeking re-endorsement from their constituents over an issue of policy or a change of party: there were 9 such by-elections between 1900 and 1914 and 4 in the inter-war years. But from the defeat of the Duchess of Atholl at Kinross and West Perthshire in 1938 until the resignation of Dick Taverne at Lincoln in 1972 there was no such test (although it was only the intervention of the 1955 general election that prevented Sir Richard Acland from fighting a by-election at Gravesend over nuclear weapons).

Successful election petitions, which from 1900 to 1914 resulted in 13 by-elections, have also declined. The only unseatings for electoral offences in the last fifty years were in 1922 and 1923, although in the 1950s there were three by-elections in Northern Ireland when election victors were declared ineligible (one for being a clergyman, one for being a felon and one for being a government contractor).

Succession to the peerage is another cause of by-elections that has diminished. Fewer heirs to titles sit in the House (18 in 1924, 5 in 1970). Moreover, since Anthony Wedgwood Benn's

TABLE 1.1

Reasons for By-elections, 1918–70*

Cause of vacancy	Total	%	Cause of vacancy	Total	%
Death	380	47·6	Decision to seek re-election on changing party allegiance	4	0·5
Resignation	241	30·3	Expulsion from the House of Commons	3	0·4
Elevation to the peerage	110	13·8	Unseated as a result of election petition	2	0·3
Succession to the peerage	29	3·7	Bankruptcy	1	0·1
Re-election of Ministers Act, 1919	20	2·5	Unseated for voting in the House of Commons before taking the Oath	1	0·1
Disqualification as a Member of the House of Commons	4	0·5			

* Taken from F. W. S. Craig, *British Parliamentary Election Statistics 1918–70*, p. 42.

struggle to repudiate his viscountcy (which produced by-elections in 1961 and 1963 as well as the 1963 Peerage Act), they have been able to stay in the House by renouncing their title, like Lord Lambton in 1970.[4]

Timing

When an MP's seat falls vacant there is no statutory obligation to fill the vacancy. By convention it is left to the Whips of the former Member's party to move for a writ to be issued instructing the local returning officer to proceed.

Over the years the Whips have changed their habits and, in conjunction with party headquarters, have given more importance to timing, and to national as opposed to local considerations. In the 1920s by-elections were called more promptly after the vacancy occurred; they were held at times (in August or in Christmas week) which would now be regarded as almost impossible; they were much less consciously grouped together. Throughout the period since 1918 there are examples of by-elections taking place as soon as the vacancy occurred. However, in the 1960s, although by-elections were called in every month of the year, there was much more of a tendency, whatever the delay involved, to group them together on dates in March (after the new register on 15 February), or in May–June (after the local elections), or in October–November (after the summer holidays and party conferences and before the Christmas rush). Sometimes the timing has been affected by local difficulties in candidate selection and sometimes by the desire to wait for a more favourable political climate or to arrange things so that an awkward result may be masked by a better one.[5]

While the moving of a writ has normally been a routine

---

[4] Apart from Lord Lambton, the only MP to inherit a peerage since 1960 was Viscount Hinchingbrooke (now Victor Montagu), whose father died in 1962 before renunciation was possible. By contrast to the two successions in 1961–70, there were 13 in 1931–40.

[5] The grouping of by-elections is now emphasised by the fact that they are all held on Thursdays. Although one has to go back to 1931 for a general election held on another day (Tuesday), parties continued to experiment with by-election days down to the 1960s. The result in Orpington on a Thursday, 14 March 1962, may have been affected by the near-

matter, on occasions it has been moved by another party or has been opposed in protest about delays in holding the by-election or other matters. The war-time opposition used this tactic on several occasions and more recently the Liberals threatened it, notably over the six-month delays in calling the Orpington and Lincoln by-elections.

Function

By-elections are so much discussed as barometers of public opinion that it is easy to ignore their basic function – the replacement of a Member of Parliament. The replacement of Members is not trivial in scale. Since 1918, by the time each Parliament was dissolved it had on average 53 Members (8 per cent) who had come in at by-elections. In most cases this was a routine matter: the former incumbent's party followed ordinary procedures to find a successor, usually much of the same ilk, and he was duly elected. Only 140 (18 per cent) of the 795 by-elections between 1919 and 1970 resulted in a change in party representation (see Table 1.2). But on occasion a by-election was designed to bring into the House a special person to strengthen the government – either defeated Ministers like the MacDonalds in 1936 or Patrick Gordon Walker in 1965, or new talent, like Ernest Bevin and Oliver Lyttelton in 1940 or Frank Cousins in 1965. Oppositions, too, have eagerly used the first by-elections of a Parliament to bring back their more heavyweight casualties – Arthur Henderson in 1923, Arthur Greenwood in 1932, Harold Macmillan in 1945, Anthony Barber in 1965.

By-elections serve other less noticed functions. They offer tryouts for party tactics: they have been used to test innovations in publicity, field organisation and even private polling methods. They offer training-grounds for party agents: the statutory expense returns do not reveal the number of full-time officials who have come in from other constituencies to

---

success of the Liberals in Blackpool North where voting took place a day earlier, on Wednesday. When Roxburgh voted on Wednesday, 24 March 1965, it might have provided the last parliamentary contest to be held on anything but a Thursday, had not an administrative error led to the Manchester Exchange by-election being called for Wednesday, 27 June 1973, instead of Thursday, 28 June.

TABLE 1.2

By-Elections, 1918–70

	Total[a] by-elections	Changes	Con. +	Con. −	Lib. +	Lib. −	Lab. +	Lab. −	Others +	Others −
1918–22	108	27	4	13	5[b]	11[b]	14	1	4	2
1922–3	16	6	1	4	3	1	2	..	..	1
1923–4	10	3	2	1	..	1	1	1	..	..
1924–9	63	20	1	16	6	3	13	1	..	..
1929–31	36	7	4	1	..	1	2	4	1	1
1931–5	62	10	..	9	..	1	10	..	..	..
1935–45	219	30	..	29	..	..	13	1	17	..
1945–50	52	4	3	..	..	..	..	..	..	3
1950–1	16	..	..	..	..	..	..	..	..	..
1951–5	48	1	1	..	..	..	..	1	..	..
1955–9	52	6	1	4	1	1	4	..	..	1
1959–64	62	9	2	7	1	..	6	2	..	..
1964–6	13	2	1	1	1	..	..	1	..	..
1966–70	38	16	12	1	1	..	..	15	3	..

[a] Up to 1918, and to a lesser extent to 1926, the number of by-elections is inflated by the necessity for Ministers to stand for re-election on appointment. In 53 such cases the returns were unopposed.

[b] In 1918–22 Opposition Liberals won 5 seats and lost 2, Coalition Liberals lost 9.

help in the campaign.[6] They provide a platform for speeches that might otherwise be less remarked, an extra opportunity for public education (as distinct from vote-gathering). They even, in the key period 1957–63, supplied an excuse for the broadcasting authorities to learn how to venture much more boldly into the field of political coverage: in 1958 Rochdale provided the first British campaign to be the subject of a television programme while it was going on.

[6] By-election expense returns, which are hard to come by, must be far more misleading than those for general elections. In a key contest the amount of effort put in by party headquarters, including on occasion expensive market research and large numbers of paid agents, could be costed at a substantially higher value than all the local activities duly recorded in the expense return. There are indeed indications that expense returns, which (given the temptations to spend and the absence since 1929 of any petition challenging overspending) are normally so surprisingly accurate, are sometimes less conscientiously compiled after by-elections.

None the less, the main interest in by-elections has undoubtedly lain in what they are thought to reveal about the state of public opinion, both in relation to specific issues and to the likely outcome of the next general election.

By-elections as indicators

The idea that a by-election in one corner of the country can reveal what voters in 600 other constituencies are thinking does, of course, imply some important assumptions about national uniformity. Furthermore, the idea that a by-election at one point of time gives a key to the result of a subsequent general election implies some equally interesting assumptions about the consistency of voting behaviour over time and in different situations.

The assumption of national uniformity is, of course, challenged after every by-election. 'Special local circumstances' can almost always be found to excuse an awkward result – something in the candidate or in the organisation or in the impact of a particular issue. However, it is plain that in general elections, national behaviour is remarkably uniform: in elections since 1950 three constituencies out of four have shown a swing within 2 per cent of the national average. In by-elections the variation has been appreciably greater. Even simultaneous by-elections often yield sharply different swings – and usually it is hard to explain why. The factor that seems most regularly in evidence is the fall in turnout which tends to be much greater in safe seats and in urban seats than in marginal or rural ones. But it is also clear that in by-elections voters are more affected by special factors such as a local grievance or by the personality of the candidate. However, although a graph of by-election swings showing the movement of government popularity can look decidedly jagged, clear trends still emerge. The anti-government swings in 1960 varied between −2 per cent and 3 per cent; in 1963 they varied between 4 per cent and 14 per cent. But on balance the difference between the average swing in 1960 (−1·7 per cent) and in 1963 (8·1 per cent) offers a reasonable indication of the Conservative slump in that period.

The impact of a by-election depends on how it is interpreted.

Undoubtedly now, as always, victory or defeat makes most impact. A government may be more damaged by losing a seat on a 5 per cent swing than by suffering a 15 per cent swing yet just winning some safer constituency. Before psephological sophistication began to creep in during the 1950s, the focus tended to be on absolute figures – the drop in the vote for a party or the change in the majority – even when a general fall in turnout made them very misleading. Now the focus is, perhaps to excess, on the percentage swing. Dependence on one single indicator is likely to be even more deceptive in by-elections than in general elections: turnout, retained vote and presence of third candidates must be taken into consideration before any verdict on the meaning of a by-election result is offered.

But the problem is psychological as much as statistical. Election results have to be set against expectations. The Conservatives in 1962 and the Labour Party in 1969 managed to present as triumphs the fact that they had held on to seats which a few years previously they would never have dreamed of considering vulnerable. The party managers face a pre-election dilemma. If they display optimism in order to encourage the faithful in the constituency, they court a severe verdict in the post-mortem. If they discount the result in advance in order to induce pleasant surprise among observers, they may induce local defeatism and an unnecessarily bad outcome. To some extent they are at the mercy of the press. By-elections do attract extensive, though seldom high-quality, newspaper coverage. The picture of the situation that is built up by reporters does much to condition the reaction to the final outcome. In the 1960s opinion polls too played a major role. If Gallup or NOP chose to cover a by-election, the result was often discounted in advance. The fact that an NOP forecast gave no hint of the overturn in Leyton in January 1965 did much to heighten the shock of that result.

But whatever people may have thought at the time, and whatever their consequences for contemporary political strategy and morale, by-elections do offer historians (particularly those concerned with the pre-1945, pre-opinion-poll, era) guidance on mass reactions that is very difficult to get from any other source. In some cases a detailed look at by-election figures challenges established historical ideas. For example, the myth of Labour's forward march from 1900 onwards receives no support from an examination of the by-elections after 1910: the First World War was to transform the situation, but in July 1914 the Labour Party could look back to four by-election losses and no gains over the past four years. The period before the Second World War offers another example. After the 1945 upheaval it was widely said that an anti-Conservative landslide had long been brewing and that a normal general election held in 1940 would have shown substantial Labour gains. The by-election results run counter to this contention. Although, once the electorate had recovered from the shock of 1931, there appears to have been a very sharp swing in favour of Labour, from 1933 onwards their support seems if anything to have declined. The reason for the belief that Labour was gaining ground presumably lies in the fact that between 1935 and 1939 they won 13 seats from the government. But a study of the votes cast does not suggest any trend in their favour. They might be said to have won by-elections only because they fared so ill in the 1935 general election.[7]

By-elections and general elections

It is plain that by-elections give results that go against the party in power. Between 1922 and 1970 governments gained 3 seats in by-elections and lost 91. Only 9 of the 165 by-elections between 1955 and 1970 could be construed as showing a pro-government swing. By-elections can never be regarded as offering a direct mirror of how the voting would go in a general election. Although the situation in the 1920s was confused, every general election since then, except for 1945 and 1955, has shown a government recovery compared with the by-elections of the previous year and, especially in recent years, a large proportion of the seats which changed hands in by-elections have reverted to their former allegiance. Tables 1.3 and 1.4 offer some measure of this recovery.

[7] See D. E. Butler, *The Electoral System in Britain since 1918*, 2nd ed. (Oxford, 1963) pp. 184–6, for a fuller discussion of this point; see also p. 116 below.

TABLE 1.3

Pro-Government Swing-Back between By-Election Results and Subsequent General Election in the Same Constituencies[a]

	1929	1935	1950	1951	1955	1959	1964	1966	1970
Number of comparable seats	5	6	3	5	6	5	12	6	8
% swing	+3·9	+5·8	(+3)	+4·2	−0·4	+3·4	+2·3	+4·8	+4·7

[a] The time period included varies from six to twelve months before the election. The 1950 figures involve major approximation owing to re-distribution. Comparisons in 1922, 1923 and 1924 are very difficult. In four by-elections in 1922 the Labour opposition won 4·5 per cent more of the vote on average than in the November general election. In two by-elections in 1923 the Conservative Government fared decidedly better, and in two decidedly worse, than in the December general election. In each of five comparable by-elections in 1924 Labour fared better (in four of them decidedly better) than in the October general election. No by-election in 1931 was anything like as bad for Labour as the general election. In 1945 the Conservatives recovered ground in only one of the four seats they had defended in by-elections during the previous twelve months.

Although from 1923 to 1966 examples of the recovery at general elections of by-election losses were not numerous, they included some of the most famous by-election reverses:

1922	1923	1945	1966
Leyton W.	Mitcham	Newcastle N.	Leyton
Widnes		Wallasey	
Wrekin	1929	Skipton	1970
Dartford	Lancaster	Eddisbury	Carmarthen
Dover	N. Midlothian	Motherwell	Hamilton
Woolwich E.	Southwark N.		Pollock
Dudley		1959	Ladywood
Kirkcaldy	1931	Lewisham N.	Dudley
Penistone	Paddington S.	Torrington	Acton
Heywood &		Kelvingrove	Swindon
Radcliffe	1935		Walthamstow W.
Southwark S.E.	Fulham E.	1964	Oldham W.
Clayton	Wavertree	S. Dorset	
Leicester E.	Swindon	Brighouse &	
		Spenborough	

It is easy to build on this pattern of slump and recovery some theory of how voters react to by-elections. They seldom feel very concerned. Usually there is very little national publicity about the contest and such as there is tends to be reserved to the last day or so, too late to build up interest on a general

TABLE 1.4

Subsequent Result in Seats Changing Hands in By-Elections[a]

Parliament	1918–1922	1922–1923	1923–1924	1924–1929	1929–1931	1931–1935	1935–1945	1945–1950	1950–1951	1951–1955	1955–1959	1959–1964	1964–1966	1966–1970	1918–1970
Seats changing hands at by-election	27	6	3	20	7	10	52	2	0	1	5	7	2	16	158
Number won back at next general election	13	1	—	3	1	3	5	—	—	—	3	2	1	9	41

[a] The University by-elections in 1946 and two by-elections in Bristol South-East in 1961 and 1963 are excluded from this table.

election scale. Even the exceptional concentration of volunteer and professional workers from outside the constituency can seldom prevent a large fall in turnout. In all but 19 of the 281 by-elections in 1945–70, participation was below the level of the previous general election – and almost all the exceptions (for example, Torrington in 1958, Kinross and West Perthshire in 1963 or Hamilton in 1967) had special factors and had been built up by the national press. But in addition to the increase in freedom not to vote, there is also the freedom to vote differently. By-elections encourage the citizen to try his luck and vote for the other side although he would not dream of doing so in a general election when his vote might actually change the party in power. Leyton in 1919 and again in 1965, Dudley in 1921 and again in 1968 produced their sensational results not primarily through abstention but through a sizeable number of party loyalists voting for the other side – and the same was true of the Empire Crusade and the Anti-Waste League successes of forty and fifty years ago and of the Nationalist and Liberal successes of the last decade. In 1968, 43 per cent of Scotsmen told NOP interviewers that they would consider supporting the SNP in a by-election; when asked whether they would do so in a general election the figure fell to 20 per cent.

Such tendencies are probably sharper now than ever before. The growing volatility of the electorate makes it increasingly dangerous to apply rules of thumb learned from the past. The Conservatives who lost Orpington in 1962 on a swing that would have cost them every other seat in Britain (save only South Kensington) came to within a hair's breadth of returning to office in 1964; the Labour Government which on a single day in 1968 lost three seats with swings of 15, 18 and 21 per cent managed to go into the 1970 election as odds-on favourites. Politicians have learned to become increasingly blasé about by-elections, at least until the last year of a Parliament. They may offer some guide to the public mood; but who now would dare to give a figure for the likely difference between a by-election result today and what would happen in an immediate general election? And it is much more necessary to hesitate before extrapolating to a general election that is two or three years off.

Conclusion

This book concentrates in the main on by-elections as political events. Newport helped to bring about the fall of Lloyd George in 1922, Westminster St George's saved Baldwin in 1931, East Fulham conditioned the whole rearmament debate of the mid-1930s, Orpington heralded and stimulated the Conservative disarray of 1962–3, and Hamilton in 1967 gave impetus to the Scottish Nationalist upsurge. Although not many others among the 800 contests in the last fifty years can claim such importance, the explosive potential of by-elections is always there. Sudden and solid evidence of the withdrawal or return of support to a government can transform the political mood – and the Prime Minister's strategy in timing the next general election. Independents and minor parties can test whether any groundswell of sympathy exists – although usually they find it is not there. The accident of by-elections undoubtedly shaped the pattern of the Liberal and Nationalist revivals of the 1960s. The Anti-Waste League in 1921, the Empire Crusade in 1930 and the war-time dissidents in 1942–4 used by-elections, with some measure of success, to make themselves a force to be reckoned with. In the post-1945 period, if the special case of nationalism is excluded, no such challenges have been made. Edward Martell on a People's League platform at East Ham North in 1957, Sir Piers Debenham on an anti-Market platform at South Dorset in 1962, and John Creasey calling for an all-party government at Oldham West in 1968 all just saved their deposits, but, until Dick Taverne's triumph at Lincoln, they were the only candidates to have done so since 1945 when fighting both the major parties in an English by-election. It must be much harder today for anyone to get as far as Randolph Churchill did in 1935 when, fighting his father's battle on the India question, he won 24 per cent of the vote at Wavertree. But, as Lincoln showed, the possibility is always there. By-elections continue to supply one of the safety-valves of the British political system.

2. The Newport By-Election and the Fall of the Coalition

by JOHN RAMSDEN

General Election, 1918		(Electorate 40,146)
Haslam (Co. Lib.)	14,080	(*56·4*)
Bowen (Lab.)	10,234	(*41·0*)
Thomas (Ind.)	647	(*2·6*)
Co. Lib. majority	3,846	Turnout 62·2%

By-election, 18 Oct 1922		(Electorate 42,645)
Clarry (Con.)	13,515	(*40·0*)
Bowen (Lab.)	11,425	(*33·8*)
Moore (Lib.)	8,841	(*26·2*)
Con. majority	2,090	Turnout 79·2%

General Election, 1922		(Electorate 42,645)
Clarry (Con.)	19,019	(*54·3*)
Bowen (Lab.)	16,000	(*45·7*)
Con. majority	3,019	Turnout 82·1%

Newport was the only British by-election which brought down a government – such has been claimed and its influence has been widely accepted. Tom Jones noted in his diary:

> Chamberlain's effort to preserve the Coalition under the leadership of the Prime Minister defeated. Vote largely determined by Bonar Law's speech and by the victory of the Conservative candidate at the Newport by-election announced this morning, and partly by Chamberlain's clumsy, unsympathetic, and unhumorous handling of the meeting itself.[1]

[1] Tom Jones, *Whitehall Diary*, I (1969) p. 210.

Newport's influence was thus indirect: a Conservative won the by-election and this helped Conservative MPs to decide at the Carlton Club on the same day to withdraw their support from Lloyd George's Coalition. The *National Review* gave a less moderate account in its November 1922 issue:

> Newport caused a veritable stampede among the Coalitioners of the Carlton Club, who, until that moment had been prepared to swear that black was white or that white was black, according as they were directed by the despot of Downing Street or his deputy in the leadership of the Unionist Party . . . . It instantly transformed the political situation.

These immediate judgements, accepted almost universally at the time, have been followed by most later commentators. In the mythology of the 1920s, Newport is inextricably bound up with the fall of Lloyd George, who never set foot in the constituency during the campaign nor issued any official statement about it. For Liberals, Newport was the Tories' excuse for breaking up the Coalition and conveniently forgetting all that they owed to L. G. and his followers. For Conservatives, Newport was the moment when Conservatism re-established its touch with the grass roots, and received clear instructions to go it alone with Bonar Law and Baldwin.[2]

All such interpretations are the same basic idea when seen from different points in the political spectrum: they all agree that Newport was a vote against the Coalition Government. But all suffer from the flaw that they are unsure of the most basic facts of the campaign itself: it has never been established whether Lynden Moore was an Independent Liberal or Coalition Liberal candidate – a fact crucial to any interpretation. On the very day of declaration, Newport was attributed a false significance which has obscured its real importance ever since. Historians have recognised its influence on the fall of Lloyd George, but have not seen that this was due to a faulty interpretation of the facts. Nor has it been seen that Newport is more valuable for general implications than for any short-term influence. (In any case, the Carlton Club meeting would

---

[2] David Ogg, *Herbert Fisher* (1947) p. 113, and Sir Charles Petrie, see *The Carlton Club* (1955) p. 179, for typical examples.

probably have voted against coalition even without Newport, and Bonar Law decided to go before knowing the Newport result. Newport did not decide the vote, but probably guaranteed an overwhelming majority.) But Newport was the first election in modern circumstances which was fought by the candidates of the three modern parties, all with an apparently equal chance; in some ways it was also the last, because after 19 October 1922 the Liberals were seen to be the third party, whose success – however insubstantial or temporary – would occasion surprise. The special circumstances of the by-election made it a good test of how voters would react to the existence of three parties, and the model of behaviour established at Newport held good for the rest of the inter-war years.

The national background

The background to Newport was the background to the Lloyd George Coalition and the problems of Newport were those of the Coalition. Coalition had first come in May 1915, after nine months of war and party truce. However, it was Lloyd George as Prime Minister (from December 1916) and the prolongation of Liberal–Conservative collaboration after the war that really created internal dissension. Many were opposed to further coalition: a section of the Liberal Party broke away and remained under Asquith, but Conservative opponents of coalition watched frustratedly as their party supported Lloyd George. Loyalty was probably maintained only because of the Conservatives' current fear of Labour: joint action, it was said, was the only way to keep Labour out of power. However, Austen Chamberlain and others went further, in calling for the fusion of Conservatives and Coalition Liberals into one new party. In 1920 both sides unceremoniously rejected fusion, but Chamberlain continued to preach its virtues and believed it to be inevitable. The bitter division of opinion over coalition or independence did not prevent Chamberlain's unopposed succession to the Conservative leadership in March 1921 – nominated by the same man who moved the Carlton Club resolution against him eighteen months later. However, a decision could not be much longer delayed, for the life of the 1918 Parliament was running out: before another election could be held, the Conservative Party and its leader would have to decide whether to back the Lloyd George government for another five years – perhaps for ever – or to ditch it once and for all.

The Lloyd George Coalition had a very bad record in by-elections throughout its post-war term of office, but this has been exaggerated. Its performance must always be compared with the landslide victory which it had won in 1918, and the highly fortuitous nature of that result. In 1918 the electorate was in an unusually radical mood, and yet Lloyd George and his Conservative supporters, by exploiting the patriotic moment that followed the end of the war, persuaded them to fill the House of Commons with Conservatives and Coalition Liberals. It was only to be expected that by-elections would show a great deviation from the 1918 results, not least because the election had been a 'coupon' one, with an electoral pact, a low turnout and an inadequate register. Furthermore, the very size of the victory simply increased discontent inside the government, as different groups struggled for influence and as backbenchers revolted against the Whips almost at will.

Conservative votes had created an overall Conservative majority in the House of Commons, but the Prime Minister and several of the Cabinet were Liberals and much of its legislation had a distinctly Liberal flavour. Conservative activists became increasingly hostile to a government for which they were responsible but with which they seemed to have no influence. Considering all these factors, the Coalition was not dong as badly as it seemed. It had many bad results, but they were never consistently bad, and indeed not consistent at all. Part of this was due to the fact that the 1918 election had produced a crop of unusual contests, unusual parties and unusual results. It would have been most surprising if by-election swings from the 1918 results had shown any regular pattern. For example, on the same day in 1920 the government lost Dartford with one of its worst results and held both seats at Stockport with one of its best. However, these wild fluctuations were little comfort to a government which saw its fortunes apparently varying randomly from bad to catastrophic.

Maurice Cowling described Spen Valley (20 December 1919)

as the government's worst result,[3] and psychologically it certainly was. But Spen Valley was a freak Labour win with under 40 per cent of the vote. Much worse for the government was Bromley (17 December) where Labour polled 47·5 per cent of the vote when standing for the first time, or St Albans (10 December) where Labour nearly won. Spen Valley made its impact because it was the third in this disastrous series, but particularly because Spen Valley actually changed hands. The government defeats which were the worst statistically were both defeats by Liberals in March 1919: Leyton West was lost on a swing of 24·8 per cent and Hull Central on a swing of 32·9 per cent. Labour gained Bothwell and Widnes during the summer of 1919, and government defeats at Louth (twice), Dartford, Dudley and Kirkcaldy continued into the spring of 1921. Thereafter the tide began to turn, and only in the winter of 1921–2 did Labour's fortunes temporarily revive. Government candidates were again doing quite well in the summer of 1922, holding Wolverhampton West and even gaining Hackney South, which they had failed to win in 1918.[4] A similar pattern of massive Coalition defeats in 1919 and 1920 followed by a revival in 1921 and 1922 can be detected in local government elections. It will be as well to suggest some explanations, since results over the last few years seem to have determined what contemporaries expected from Newport.

Firstly, it might be pointed out that coalitions naturally attract bad results in elections which may influence their policy without threatening their survival. By bringing more than one group into government they create internal friction, but also push the opposition parties into temporary unity. The same thing happened to the National Government of the 1930s. Thus, in 1918–22, the Government faced one Liberal or Labour candidate in 44 by-elections and had the advantage of

[3] Maurice Cowling, *The Impact of Labour, 1920–1924* (1971) p. 112.

[4] The only by-election which was genuinely won by the Coalition was the gain of Woolwich East from Labour in March 1921, and was the more interesting in that the defeated Labour candidate was Ramsay MacDonald, the party's ex-leader. He was defeated by Captain R. Gee, VC, a war-hero, ex-miner and twenty-year serving soldier, who managed to fight the campaign entirely on MacDonald's pacifist record. It should perhaps be seen as the last episode of the 1918 general election, and was certainly more 'khaki' than many contests then.

both Liberal *and* Labour candidates against them only 23 times. It was also true that the sheer size of its victory in 1918 made some government defeats inevitable. More important was the fact that the government could afford to lose many seats that it had won in 1918 without any serious risk of losing a general election. This view is borne out by an examination of the seats which actually changed hands. Labour gained 14 seats, only two of which were not to be regularly won by Labour in the inter-war years, and both of these (Spen Valley, and Heywood and Radcliffe) were won on a fortunate split of the vote. It is difficult to see how a government of the Right could have shed many tears over the loss of Pontypridd. When the Coalition could come close to winning Penistone against both Liberal and Labour (March 1921) they had no real reason to worry about their performance.

This touches on the vital point: contemporary observers had no effective tools for the measurement of opinion after the result was declared. 'Swing' was far in the future, and no serious attempt was made to distinguish between different types of constituency. The political organiser who used percentages was still a pioneer. If it seems clear to us that the government should not have worried because Labour won Pontypridd, it was certainly not clear at the time. The commonest measure of electoral performance was the tradition of the constituency. Unconscious of any change which had been brought about by the rise of the Labour Party, the war, or the redistribution of 1918, the comparisons were made not with the last general election but with 1895 and 1900 – the last occasions when the Conservatives had won in peace-time. This naturally failed to take account of the rise of Labour as a party bidding for, working-class votes. It is because he knows of this that the Conservative can today reconcile himself with equanimity to the loss of Pontypridd.[5]

What the by-elections of 1918–22 should have shown observers was a gradual but definite transformation of British politics. The old politics of nineteenth-century Britain were passing away although still to be seen: middle-class Liberals

[5] The syllogism, 'as goes Pontypridd, so go Portsmouth and Preston', he knows to be quite untrue. His predecessor in 1922 did not and indeed could not know it.

optimistically trying to unite radicalism with local vested interests, and a demagogic Conservatism with substantial working-class support, playing the beer issue and banging the Imperial drum. This old model of politics had been long in decline as class and economic factors began to determine voting patterns, but it was only the hostility between Liberals and Labour after the First World War that made its final death possible. As long as the Coalition survived, Liberals and Labour had enough in common in their hostility to it to postpone the death of the old politics a little longer. Liberals and Labour usually managed to avoid fighting each other in by-elections, and both of them gained seats from the government. Labour was steadily winning a solid base of working-class support, but that support was showing distinct regional, social and occupational variations. Contemporaries stressed the support rather than the important limitations and variations, and this goes far towards explaining their mistaken hopes of Newport.

Labour leaders for the first time enjoyed the electoral support which ideology told them they should enjoy, and were in an understandably euphoric mood. However, as post-war boom was followed by inter-war slump in 1921, the revolutionary fervour and the industrial militancy both began to evaporate. Labour therefore began a strategy of concentration on the by-elections which it believed it *should* win in a campaign for power, and began to ignore those seats which might have seemed possible in 1919 but were seen to be hopeless by 1921. None of the seats left uncontested was marginal, and the seats which were contested could now be given additional assistance, funds and speakers.[6] This was the background to Labour's hopes for Newport. It needed only a small turnover of votes for Labour to capture the seat; it was in South Wales, where Labour had been doing particularly well; and it was undeniably a working-class stronghold. Thus, Labour had an explanation

---

[6] By-elections in single-Member seats:

	1919 and 1920	1921 and 1922
Number of by-elections	38	51
Number in Coalition-held seats	31	44
Number in Coalition-held seats contested by Labour	23 (74%)	18 (41%)

of recent electoral trends which led them to see Newport as an inevitable gain. It was, however, only a partial explanation which ignored the regional and local variations shown by the results. As Pontypridd, so Newport – or so they expected.

The governments losses alarmed both Conservative's and Coalition Liberals, and the net effect was a fatalism which led them to expect that Labour would win Newport too. However, Conservatives were not as obsessed with working-class seats as Labour understandably was. They did not like to see Labour winning industrial and mining seats, but most of these, especially in Wales, were lost by Coalition Liberals rather than Conservatives anyway. Dudley was the only traditionally Conservative seat won by Labour, and the shock that this defeat caused was as much due to the unexpected eclipse of a Minister (Sir Arthur Griffith-Boscawen) seeking routine re-election as to the result itself. More serious to most Conservatives was the loss of safe middle-class seats to right-wing Independents, such as the Anti-Waste League. This threat too was receding by 1922, after the 'Geddes axe' had made a great splash of cutting government expenditure. The Conservative gain in August 1922 was Hackney South, which had been won by Horatio Bottomley in 1918. At Newport the party was defending its first working-class seat for seven months, and was fighting only its second Welsh seat in the entire Parliament. The first had been Rhondda West, where on 21 December 1920 the Conservatives had intervened in a seat where Labour had been unopposed in 1918, and scored a respectable 41·5 per cent of the vote in a straight fight with Labour. If the moral was that a Conservative candidate would do better than a Coalition Liberal in a Welsh industrial seat, then it had been forgotten by October 1922. Conservative gloom at a by-election in Newport was thus matched by Labour's justifiable but exaggerated confidence.

The fall of the Coalition in Newport

In 1922 Newport was a moderately large industrial town, which had expanded rapidly in the later nineteenth century. Its economic importance was chiefly as a port, serving the inland Monmouthshire industrial valleys, and so relying on the prosperity of the coal, steel and heavy engineering industries. Since 1536 Monmouthshire had occupied a strangely intermediate status between England and Wales: the administrative phrase was always 'Wales and Monmouthshire', but population censuses still listed it as an English county. Newport's industrial expansion had been largely achieved by attracting immigrants from England, and so it was far from typical of Welsh boroughs. Indeed, nationality had been a political issue, for Conservatives tended to regard Monmouthshire as English, while Liberals stressed its Welshness. For a port which looked across the Bristol Channel, and many of whose inhabitants derived from England, the Welsh culture which nourished Liberalism further west may have been more of a novelty than a source of inspiration.[7]

As in the country at large, the root cause of Newport Conservatives' hostility to the Coalition Government was not anything that it had done but the fact that it existed at all. It must be doubted whether any lasting coalition could ever work on the basis of a secret electoral pact like that of 1918, especially in a country like Britain where the effective control of local parties is in local hands. The Liberal–Labour pact of 1903 had run into similar troubles in 1911–14; perhaps only the weakness of every participating group but the Conservatives saved the National Government of the 1930s from a similar fate. Traditional local rivalries and entrenched personal hostilities can be much too strong to be abandoned at a word from Westminster.

In 1918 the sitting MP for Monmouth Boroughs was Lewis Haslam, a Liberal who was first elected in 1906. Since Monmouth Boroughs had been composed overwhelmingly of

---

[7] The population of Newport County Borough in 1921 was 92,369; it had almost trebled since 1871, and half the inhabitants had been born outside the town. About seven-eighths of the employed population worked in the transport, engineering or iron and steel industries. However, as well as this concentration of heavy industrial workers, Newport also had the third highest proportion of 'middle-class' residents (unoccupied or in non-manual occupations) in Wales. (Information from various Census tables, 1871, 1911 and 1921.)

In 1921 only about 2 per cent of the inhabitants of Newport were able to speak Welsh, compared with an average in Welsh constituencies of 37 per cent. See M. Kinnear, *The British Voter* (1968) p. 136.

the town of Newport, which was given its own MP in the redistribution of 1918, Haslam wished to remain as MP for Newport. Since Haslam was a moderate Liberal who had supported Lloyd George and the war, he was able to get the 'coupon' and stand in 1918 as the official Coalition Government candidate. The Conservatives had little influence over the distribution of coupons in Wales, since most of the sitting MPs were Coalitionist Liberals, and herein lay the cause of the breach of 1922.[8] Welsh Conservatives had an even longer tradition of hating Lloyd George than had their English colleagues, and so they were very disappointed by an electoral pact which turned over almost every seat in Wales to Lloyd George Liberals. However, the allocation of coupons was accompanied by a good deal of moral pressure from Conservative Party managers and Central Office. More seriously, the pressure was only successful when it was promised that the electoral pact would run for one election only: this tactic restrained the diehards from breaking the united front in 1918, but only at the price of trouble later.

An Independent Democratic candidate emerged for the 1918 election in Newport, but the local Conservatives gave full support to Haslam, who was duly re-elected. However, when Conservatives went to him to press for Conservative policies, he naturally failed to give them satisfaction, and they – just as naturally – felt that they had been betrayed. Here too, Newport was typical of many places where Liberal MPs refused to act as Conservatives just because Conservative votes had helped to elect them, or vice versa. A breach finally occurred in 1920 and 1921, with parliamentary discussion of the question of liquor licensing. This arose as a problem because of the restrictions which had been imposed during the war, but some Liberals certainly wished to continue restrictions, and even to extend them, in peace-time. The 1921 Licensing Bill was treated in Parliament as a subject which had a special local

[8] 22 coupons were issued in the 36 Welsh seats: 19 to Liberals, 2 to Conservatives and 1 to the National Democratic Party. In areas like Cardiff, where the local Conservatives were relatively strong, there were no coupons, but where Liberalism was strong it also had the benefit of the coupon. See F. W. S. Craig, *British Parliamentary Election Results, 1918–1949* (1969).

relevance to Newport, for it had to be decided whether Monmouthshire should be included with England or with Wales for licensing purposes; the Bill included it with Wales, and hence threatened Sunday closing. The Conservative MP for Monmouth, Leolin Forestier-Walker, told the Commons of mass protest meetings in Newport. The Marquess of Salisbury and the Earl of Plymouth both tried to amend it in the House of Lords, quoting similar evidence.[9] However, Haslam was a believer in temperance, whose views had never been disguised and had been frequently cited both for and against him at previous elections. Newport Conservatives felt that his partisan support for such a divisive measure justified their withdrawal of support.

It was therefore in the summer of 1921 that the Newport Conservatives began to look for a candidate, having decided to fight the next general election, irrespective of any national agreement or electoral pact. Efforts to find a candidate went on through the winter, and there were disputes both about the principle of breaking with the Coalition and about the choice of a candidate. However, unity was established when a meeting of over 300 members unanimously adopted Reginald Clarry on 26 July 1922. The political situation was such that Clarry began campaigning at once, expecting a general election in the autumn, and he even canvassed in the political clubs before his selection had been confirmed by the general meeting of the association.

Clarry was given official backing by the anti-Coalition right wing of the Conservative Party (officially called the 'Free Conservatives') through their leader, Lord Salisbury, and their mouthpiece, the *Morning Post*. He was also supported by Lord Tredegar, an influential local figure, whose nephew, Leolin Forestier-Walker, sat for neighbouring Monmouth as the only Conservative MP in the county. It must be stressed here that although Clarry was a Conservative who was quite independent of the party's leadership, he was not an Independent Conservative. Duly selected by the local party, he was as much

[9] *Hansard*, House of Commons, 22 July, 2 Aug 1921; House of Lords, 15 Aug 1921. After his victory at Newport, Reginald Clarry tried to get the new Conservative Government to repeal the 1921 Act, but the then Home Secretary, W. C. Bridgeman, refused (House of Commons, 5 July 1923).

the official Conservative candidate for Newport as Austen
Chamberlain was for Birmingham West. Clarry would have
remained official candidate even if Chamberlain had disowned
him in public – which he dare not do. Chamberlain's instruction that Central Office should not help Clarry was a private
one, and while London political correspondents might hint
that Chamberlain was not entirely happy with Clarry's
candidature, in Newport he still appeared as the official
candidate. This was the more important because Clarry was
posing as the apostolic heir of Disraelian Conservatism and was
preaching the party's established principles. A single word of
support from Austen Chamberlain to the Liberal candidate in
Newport – which Chamberlain would have dearly loved to
give – would have wrecked Clarry's campaign completely.
However, as both Chamberlain and Clarry well knew, it
would also have wrecked Austen Chamberlain as party leader.
In effect, Clarry had all the advantages of being independent –
he had nothing to defend – and yet did not have to appear as a
rebel. The rift between Clarry and Austen Chamberlain only
appeared in the last week of the campaign, when Chamberlain
came out finally for a continued coalition and Clarry denounced him as 'sadly out of touch with the industrial population'. Clarry remained official Conservative candidate, and
after the Carlton Club it was Austen Chamberlain who
became the Independent.

The campaign

Lewis Haslam died suddenly on 12 September, his illness
having been reported only on the previous day, and the
by-election campaign began at once. Clarry was already in
the field and Bowen, the Labour candidate, had been officially
in the field since 1918. Only the Liberals were caught
unprepared.

For the next five weeks, until polling on 18 October, the
national press carried regular reports on the progress of the
campaign. However, news from Newport had to fight for its
place on the main news pages, and it can only have been the
expectation of the seat changing hands that kept it there. This
was because the papers were simultaneously occupied with a

series of severe national and international crises (see Table 2.1). Even papers printed in Newport rarely led with news of the by-election, and so the election campaign was conducted against a continuous backdrop of political crisis: headlines like 'War at Chanak?', 'Conservative Party Splits', 'Lloyd George to Resign?', or 'Cabinet to Call General Election' were typical.

With such a background of political speculation, it might be argued that Newport was not really a by-election at all, but was rather a general election fought in one constituency only. Such is the implication of all interpretations which see Newport as causing the fall of Lloyd George. And yet, in reality, the national and international crises were not live issues in the campaign at all. As J. H. Thomas noticed, the attitude of all the candidates practically amounted to the statement, 'For God's sake, don't connect me with the Coalition'.[10] In other words, on the most vital question of all, they simply had no grounds for disagreement. More surprisingly, none of the candidates was able to exploit the fact. Only the Liberal, Lynden Moore, took any stand on Chanak, which was to back up the government's firm action, but he seems to have been inspired more by tradition Liberal dislike of the Turks than by anything intrinsic to the crisis itself. Clarry and Bowen were content to talk about the weakness of the government in general terms, perhaps because the popular reaction was so unpredictable. It was even thought likely that Lloyd George would achieve a lightning victory over the Turks and then hold another 'khaki' election during the rejoicing which followed. This was the more serious for Newport, since it was possible right up to the last week of the campaign that Parliament would be dissolved, the by-election cancelled and another month of campaigning begun. Taking too firm a stand on the issues of the national crisis, which was developing and changing daily, might be giving dangerous hostages to fortune.

Whatever their motives, the Newport candidates hardly reacted to the political crisis at all. Paradoxically, it seems to have been just because there was a national political crisis that national policy issues were ignored throughout the campaign.

[10] *Spectator*, 21 Oct 1922.

TABLE 2.1

News Coverage during the Campaign

Date	National news	Newport news
12 Sep		Death of Haslam
15 Sep	Govt asked the Dominions for military assistance against Turkey	Readoption of Bowen as Labour candidate
17 Sep	Meeting of Ministers at Chequers discussed calling a general election	
19 Sep		Liberals searching for a candidate. Clarry already actively campaigning.
27 Sep		Moore adopted as Liberal candidate
30 Sep	Gen. Harington at Chanak agreed to a conference with the Turks	
7 Oct	Bonar Law's letter to *The Times* about Chanak	
10 Oct	Cabinet decided to call a general election, as a Coalition	Nomination day at Newport. Labour reported as being very confident
12 Oct		5 Conservative MPs campaigning for Clarry
14 Oct	Austen Chamberlain made a pro-Coalition speech at Birmingham	
15 Oct	L.G.'s Manchester speech. Carlton Club meeting called for 19 Oct	Clarry's first open attack on Austen Chamberlain
17 Oct		Henderson in Newport. Lord Salisbury supported Clarry
18 Oct	Bonar Law decided to oppose the Coalition	POLLING DAY AND COUNTING
19 Oct	CARLTON CLUB MEETING AND RESIGNATION OF THE GOVERNMENT	Newport result announced at 2 a.m.

All were against Lloyd George's Coalition, but none could be sure that it was about to fall and none could predict what form of partisan or bipartisan government would replace it. As long as the parties were in this state of flux, it was useless for their local spokesmen to campaign on detailed policy issues since these were more than likely to be abandoned or compromised in some new political grouping. Only Labour could fight with the national party and the local candidate in complete harmony; the Conservatives had no programme outside that of the Coalition which Clarry had rejected, and Moore refused to link his name to either the Coalition Liberal or the Asquithian Liberal programmes. In a very general sense, the campaign was fought over the same ground as every election – which party should govern? – but this could not be reduced to detailed programmes which won or lost votes. The Conservatives may have felt after Newport that they would win a general election, but they would have been hard pressed to explain why. The Newport campaign was thus a useless forum for the testing of party policy – as the Conservatives showed by fighting the following general election with no policy at all. However, it was just because the Newport electors were forced to choose between the parties rather than between their policies that it provided such a useful indicator for the future.

The candidates

The three candidates in the by-election were far from typical of either their parties or their supporters, but, in the absence of issues or policy discussion, much of the campaign was taken up with discussing each other's relative fitness to be MP for Newport.

J. W. Bowen was the most unremarkable of the three, and the most orthodox in his views and presentation. It was difficult for opponents to paint him as a dangerous revolutionary, but it was perhaps equally difficult for his supporters to raise any real enthusiasm for him. He was General Secretary of the Postal Workers' Union and therefore lived and worked in London. Although both he and his wife came from South Wales, and although he had already fought the Newport seat once, he was said to be something of an outsider. He was typical of the worthy but uninspiring trade unionists who filled the ranks of Labour candidates in the 1920s. His experience in trade unionism, friendly societies, health insurance and the Workers' Travel Association witnessed his own personal dedication to the Labour movement, but did not necessarily prove his popularity with the rank and file. There may have been some truth in Clarry's jibe that he was more in touch with the workers of Newport than was Bowen, since he alone visited them in their natural habitat – which to Clarry was the clubs and pubs.

Reginald Clarry was thus a very different sort of candidate, and his qualities and qualifications made a startling contrast with the local party's first and second choices for the candidature. The first choice, W. R. Lysaght, was the largest employer in Newport, and Sir Leonard Llewelyn was also a local worthy who was heavily involved in the coal and steel industries. Both were respected and very wealthy local men, but both were amateurs at the political game. Clarry, a self-made man who had become a successful civil engineer, was undoubtedly a player rather than a gentleman. He was brash, self-confident, forward and prepared to talk to anyone or anybody in order to win votes. Thus, on one day, he held a series of special meetings with local businessmen to discuss the town's industrial problems, spoke at dock and factory meetings, and made his daily round of the clubs and pubs. With a sympathetic press from the *Western Mail* and the *Monmouthshire Evening Post* (both dailies published in Newport) and an experienced agent, he could be sure that his campaign was well publicised. Despite the army of Labour front-benchers who came down to Newport in support of Bowen and the impressive array of local notables who supported Moore, it was Clarry who made the running in the local campaign. Even the Liberal *South Wales News* used up much of its space attacking Clarry rather than giving positive support to Moore. Clarry made the best use of his style by campaigning on old (but suddenly topical) issues like Ireland and beer. Had the campaign required a sober and circumspect Conservative candidate, Clarry would have appeared much less attractive. When Moore described Clarry as typical of the Conservatives as 'the stupid party', or when Bowen said that Clarry represented all that he hated in Conservatism, they were both paying grudging tributes to his success in selling himself. As the campaign descended more and more to personalities, it was Clarry's personality which was most talked about.

However, it was the Liberal candidate whose selection and whose character most affected the outcome. The background of Liberalism in Newport was not unlike the rest of South Wales, but the Newport Liberals' support of Lloyd George in 1918 makes it difficult to assess their real opinions. In con-stituencies where the Liberal Association supported Asquith, Lloyd George had by 1922 tried to set up his own local party, but where the local association supported Lloyd George, the Asquithians offered no opposition. The decision to back Lloyd George may have concealed the fact that many local Liberals preferred Asquith, and the events of 1922 suggest that this was the case. The Liberal Association was as usual dominated by middle-class and professional men, and their first choice to replace Haslam was Sir Garrod Thomas, their own president and the chairman of the Newport Property-Owners' Associa-tion. While the negotiations with Thomas dragged on, there was speculation about the sort of campaign which the Liberals would fight. *The Times* reported that many local Liberals wanted to fight for a free Liberal rather than a Coalitionist, and since they approached Reginald McKenna, Lady Bonham Carter, Lady Rhondda and Sir Harry Webb, as well as Thomas, there may well have been considerable internal dissention. The man eventually selected was a clear com-promise choice, since he immediately refused to tie himself to either wing of the Liberal Party. He was William Lynden Moore, the Newport coroner, and a well-known local solicitor with a family background of long service to the town. He was not an impressive speaker or an approachable candidate, and his worthy but ineffective efforts contrasted badly with Clarry's image as young, thrusting and aggressive. He was an old-world Liberal, who would probably have been happy enough to support the Coalition in 1922 if circumstances had permitted it. Dissension in his own local party was one reason for not doing so, but Clarry's appearance made it impracticable anyway. The very existence of a Conservative candidate made it pointless for Moore to run as a Coalition Liberal, since by doing so he might well have alienated some potential Liberal supporters, without winning Conservative votes to compensate. As Austen Chamberlain informed Sir Malcolm Fraser, of Conservative Central Office: 'Lynden Moore is, of course, a Coalition Liberal and he means to support the Coalition; but since he cannot obtain Conservative support, he is forced so to trim his sails as to get the largest amount of support from other quarters.'[11]

This ignored Moore's difficulties from within the local party, but was basically correct. However, Chamberlain's conclusions from this were not so sound, because he assumed that what he could see was equally visible in Newport. Moore refused to endorse either Lloyd George or Asquith as Liberal leader, and attacked the Coalition at least as often as he supported it. He fought under the slogan of 'reunited Liberalism' and defined his position in this somewhat unenlightening way: 'I am neither a "pro" nor an "anti". I am told that that is taking up an impossible position; I am not a "Mr Facing-both-ways". I am not a revolving tee-totum, nor a whirling dervish. I intend to keep my face in one direction, and that is the direction in which Liberal progress marches.' This concealed a very simple fact – that the Coalition lost Newport not on polling day but on nomination day: 'Whoever gets to the top of the poll, the Government will have lost a supporter', noted *The Times*. The survival of the Coalition, in so far as it depended on Newport at all, depended now on neither Moore nor Clarry winning, but on a Labour victory which would teach Liberals and Conservatives the value of mutual co-operation. Chamberlain summed this up in his letter to Fraser, quoted above:

> Newport is giving us a beautiful illustration of the results of a split . . . but . . . we must not allow Newport to land us in a general engagement all along the line. I should say, therefore, in reply to your enquiry: Do the least that you can without making a breach with our Conservative friends. They are going to be beaten whatever you do or don't do, but I do not want them to attribute their defeat to you. I want you to be in a position to point the moral when the election is over and the seat is lost.

Only a Labour victory could give Chamberlain the evidence he needed, and after nomination day he changed the date of the Carlton Club meeting, so that it would meet after the Newport result was known rather than on polling day as originally planned. A Labour victory *was* widely expected, and

[11] Austen Chamberlain Papers, Birmingham University Library, AC 33/2/32, Chamberlain to Fraser, 6 Oct 1922.

Chamberlain's moral was widely drawn in advance of the result, so that a Carlton Club meeting on 18 October might have taken a rather different decision. However, this negative argument for the Coalition was as irrelevant as the positive ones when considered from the viewpoint of Newport rather than London. It would make sense only if Clarry and Moore were both seen as rebels against the Coalition, but both simply ignored the Coalition. They were not fighting an election to decide the survival of the Coalition, but about which of the many alternatives should succeed it. Chamberlain was unable even to make the Coalition an issue in Newport, and yet he continued to act as if it was the only issue.

Organisation

The organisation of the three parties in Newport provides an interesting contrast but was surely of less importance than was claimed afterwards. Such is always the case, for the real effect of organisation is only slight or negative. It can be taken as an adequate explanation for none of the shock results with which this book deals, but probably contributed to all of them.[12]

Labour's campaign was described by the *Daily Express* as 'an endless procession of national figures', and this distinguished it from both the other parties. Margaret Bondfield, J. R. Clynes, John Hodge, Arthur Henderson, George Lansbury and J. H. Thomas all came to Newport to speak for Bowen, and Labour tried to use the presence of so many heavyweights to create a sense of irresistible impetus for their campaign. The organisation was run by the party's National Agent, as was usual in marginal by-elections, and other outside assistance was drafted in. They were the only party which published canvass figures, which gave further justification for optimism. On 17 October the *Daily Chronicle* reported that Labour's 'complete' canvass had found 45 per cent favourable, 20 per cent doubtful and 35 per cent against. These were excellent results in a three-party

[12] This is the modern view. See, for example, R. T. Holt and J. E. Turner, *Political Parties in Action* (1968) *passim*. Although it was not so before 1914, the larger constituencies and expense limitations imposed in 1918 probably created the modern situation, with the limited role of local organisation. Of course, hardly anyone in 1922 was aware of this.

campaign, but they bore very little relation to the actual result. They undoubtedly believed the figures – on the eve of poll Arthur Henderson said privately that nothing under a 2,000 majority would satisfy him – but they were derived from a canvass that was far from complete. They surely published them in the hope of keeping their bandwagon rolling forwards, after its progress had slackened in the last week. 'Labour's stock has fallen', reported *The Times*, and more extravagant organisational claims were made in reply. In fact, the Labour organisation was neither as good as they claimed when they expected to win nor as bad as they claimed when they lost.

Moore's organisational problems derived from his refusal to link himself to either wing of the old Liberal Party, since either could have given him the resources which he needed. He actually relied on Coalition Liberal help, but only on an undercover basis: the Coalition Liberals' Chief Welsh Agent was in charge of his campaign, and the *Morning Post* triumphantly reported that it had spotted Sir Alfred Mond's agent also working for Moore in Newport. Moore may have received money from Lloyd George, but the bedrock of his organisation must have been the local Newport Liberals. It is hardly surprising that their electoral machine was rather rusty, for they had not fought against Conservative candidates even in local elections since 1913. They had never fought an independent campaign in the redistributed constituency or with the larger, post-1918 electorate. In seven of the nine wards, Liberal ward committees had to be set up during the campaign because no local organisation existed. The lack of a professional, local agent can only have compounded all these problems.

The Conservative campaign was thought to be the weakest, but was probably the best. As the official candidate of the local party, Clarry could call on Raymond Gibbs, the full-time local agent; Gibbs was a great asset for this sort of campaign since he was experienced both as an agent and as a local organiser – he had been Chief Recruiting Officer for Newport during the early years of the war. Austen Chamberlain had cut off some of the Central Office assistance which was usually given for by-elections: money, advice, literature and teams of trained organisers and speakers. It is not clear what was withheld, but certainly Clarry did not lack for any of these, because they were all available elsewhere. When forced to fight his second election campaign in two months, for the general election of 1922, Clarry was still able to spend right up to the legal maximum – and possibly more. If Central Office withheld money for the by-election, then Clarry had enough wealthy backers to provide it for him, but the rather ambiguous relations between Austen Chamberlain and Sir George Younger (party chairman) make it quite likely that Central Office ignored Chamberlain's instructions altogether. Lord Salisbury's Free Conservatives sent down staff from their London office, including Miss Goring Thomas who had been a Central Office district agent. Other local agents came in to assist, and even Lord Curzon asked his friends if they could make their agents available to assist with the campaign; some at least did so. The Free Conservatives also provided some heavyweight speakers of their own, and Salisbury and Colonel John Gretton, MP, both sent telegrams of support which were read at Clarry's meetings. At one meeting five MPs spoke for Clarry, which at least helped him to show that he was not a rebel against his party as his opponents were claiming. Even the lack of front-bench support was not very serious, since convention would have prevented Cabinet Ministers intervening in a by-election anyway. Until this convention was dropped by Baldwin in 1927, only Labour used its sledgehammers to crack walnuts. Before 1927, party leaders sent letters of support to local candidates, but did not usually visit the constituencies to speak or canvass unless they were themselves candidates. Even here, the Labour advantage was more apparent than real, because Labour's national speakers were unacquainted with what was happening in the Newport election. They duly came down to address one mass meeting, delivered a tirade against the Coalition Government and then returned to London, without realising that exactly similar sentiments could have been heard at a meeting addressed by either Clarry or Moore. They added nothing distinctive to the Labour campaign except their names.

At the grass roots, the Conservative machine, pepped up since they decided to look for a candidate the previous summer, and directed by experienced local men, was more than a match for Labour's 'national' approach to the campaign. One more interesting variation occurred which further invalidated Labour's stance: its 'procession' of national speakers all claimed that to vote Labour was the only way to put an end to the Lloyd George government. They were even more out of touch than Chamberlain, for he at least had seen that a Labour victory – and nothing else – could preserve the Coalition. In so far as Newport voters were voting for *or* against Lloyd George and his government, they could not rationally vote Labour.

Issues

On 21 October, Bowen attributed his defeat 'to over-confidence, shortage of motor cars, and the fact that some districts were not canvassed, while national issues were lost in local problems'. In fact, the only issue worthy of the name was drink, which Bowen regarded as a local question which should not be allowed to obscure real, national problems. Indeed, that he felt this way goes far towards explaining his failure at Newport. Clarry had made himself known in the clubs before the by-election, and was backed not only by the six Conservative clubs in Newport but also by the non-political clubs. Nor was this support simply contrived by a clever Conservative campaign, for the Licensed Victuallers' Association organised independent support for Clarry after sending a questionnaire to all the candidates. Moreover, in South Wales both Liberals and Labour had traditional ties with the Nonconformist chapels and the temperance movement, which the Licensing Bill controversy of 1921 and the by-election merely re-established. During the campaign both Labour and Liberals usually met in the Temperance Hall, while Conservatives used theatres or hotels. Many local politicians were also involved in the local campaign which was being run by the Temperance Council of the Christian Churches, and on several mornings the newspapers carried reports of local temperance meetings addressed by Philip Snowden. The embarrassment of Bowen and Moore was well shown by the way in which they reacted to the LVA questionnaire and to questions asked at their meetings. Hedging and refusing to commit themselves, they relied on counter-attacks to show that Clarry was irresponsible to raise the subject at all. So obvious did these tactics become that Clarry was backed by a local temperance leader, W. R. Williams of Cardiff, who had lost patience with Bowen and Moore. In a letter to the press, he characterised Clarry as 'honest' and dismissed the others as 'shifty and evasive'. More typical of Liberals was the reaction of the *South Wales News* to Clarry: 'He belongs to the most stupidly reactionary party in the state, the party which has in the past resisted every liberty won by the people except, perhaps, the liberty to drink as much beer as they could carry without being locked up.' Few genuine believers in temperance can have been converted by the honesty with which Clarry denounced the temperance movement, but there were probably very few genuine believers in temperance in Newport. There were fewer Nonconformists in Monmouthshire than in any other Welsh county, and the demonstrations against the 1921 Licensing Bill were clear evidence of local feeling.

Several reports suggest that Clarry won a large number of working-class votes: 'The men in Lysaght's works voted Conservative practically to a man, and the local agent expressed the view afterwards that "the working classes had never understood the Coalition. They had regarded it rightly or wrongly as a wangle and as an attempt to ally capitalist forces against the worker."'[13] The appearance of a Conservative agent defending the working classes against a capitalist conspiracy only surprises a reader after two generations of class politics. There was a long tradition of working-class Conservatism in Newport, and this had been part of the reason for the local party's hostility to the Coalition. Earlier in 1922, a report on the Association of Conservative Clubs' rally at Swansea included this passage: 'Mr W. Stevens (Docks Conservative Club, Newport) is not one of those who would go to the stake to defend the Coalition – and in effect said so – and many present endorsed his views.'[14] It was also claimed locally that the government had lost Pontypridd to Labour in July only because the Coalition Liberal candidate was a temperance fanatic who could not get working-class support. Perhaps 'as Pontypridd, so Newport' was right after all!

[13] John Green, *Mr Baldwin* (1933) p. 63. There is similar evidence in local newspapers.
[14] *Conservative Clubs' Gazette* (June 1922).

But how much did the drink issue really affect the outcome of the Newport by-election? Only once before had the Conservatives held the seat (Monmouth Boroughs in 1900) and then they had exploited exactly the same issue. However, since the drink issue was just one of many reasons why they regularly polled well among working-class voters, its effect should be seen as continuous rather than sudden. It was this which delayed the polarisation of Newport politics along class lines and made it possible for the Conservatives to come near to winning the seat – which they have never done since 1945. But they won the seat in 1923, 1931 and 1935 without the same advantage of beer as a topical issue. Drink undoubtedly contributed to the Newport result at every election before 1945, but can hardly be said to have been decisive in 1922. Its emergence during the campaign was the re-creation of old antagonisms rather than the creation of new ones, and the Liberals had only themselves to blame, for it was their Licensing Act which had revived them.

Another issue, which the Liberals tried to exploit and which Bowen regarded as equally irrelevant, was local identity. Moore made much of the fact that he alone was a local man, and this was especially turned to advantage against Clarry, who was not only not from Newport but was from Swansea. A local JP, T. H. Mardy, in a leaflet which the Liberals circulated, reminded voters of the services which Moore had given to the town as coroner and as legal adviser on its parliamentary business, especially in cases involving disputes with other Bristol Channel ports. Since Swansea was a direct rival to Newport, the lesson was obvious. However, Mardy's slighting references to 'a gentleman from Swansea' are representative of something deeper: as Liberalism was driven in upon itself after the First World War, it relied more and more on local roots and its revivals have been increasingly the manifestations of local protest movements, less and less related to national politics. As early as 1922 Liberals were proclaiming that only a Newport man was qualified to represent Newport. When we consider the galaxy of national figures who were approached before Moore became their desperation choice, this claim carries rather less conviction. In effect, the only thing to be said in favour of Moore was that he was a local man, so they said it as loudly and as often as possible.

Clarry's best defence – apart from giving all his pamphlets
and messages to electors a letterhead which suggested that he
lived in Newport – was to stress his knowledge of industry and
Newport's reliance on industry. Here again he was fortunate
in the events which accompanied the campaign, for it was
conducted alongside a major strike at Ebbw Vale which was
bad for local trade and employment. It also did great damage
to the Labour campaign because the strike caused inter-union
disputes which spilled over into Newport. The continuing
strike seemed to justify Clarry's demands for trade union
reform to counter the threat of imminent industrial anarchy,
and he received an unsolicited bonus when the South Wales
miners chose the eve of poll to call a coal strike. Bowen could
not be smeared personally – although the *Morning Post* had an
excellent try by way of publicising his involvement in the
Council of Action – but political Labour always suffers for the
actions of industrial militants and, by comparison with Clarry,
Moore would once again appear as weak and ineffectual.

And yet the most important issue in the campaign was none
of these: it was the simple question of who was going to win.
This became an issue rather than just an interesting speculation
because expectations were obviously going to determine the
actual outcome. In a genuinely three-horse race, the voters
must consider not only who they would like to win but also who
they would *not* want to win, and then they must balance these
conflicting aims. During the inter-war years many voters
faced this situation, especially those who had a clear preference
for Conservative or Liberal but whose first priority was the
defeat of Labour. In these circumstances, all the Newport
candidates had to show complete confidence in their own
victory, for any slight acknowledgement of the possibility of
defeat might cause a rush of votes away to other candidates.
They each therefore spoke of their nearest rival as if he had
already come third, in the hope of winning some of his votes.
Analysis of this 'third-party squeeze' is unusually difficult when
there is no obviously *third* party. Moreover, the newspapers –
from which most information on the campaign is derived –
were all aware that their predictions might affect the result.
Thus, the headlines of the *South Wales News* and *South Wales
Argus*, both Liberal, on 14 October were 'No hope for Mr R.

Clarry' and 'Conservative out of the running'. The Conservative *Western Mail* replied on 18 October with 'Don't waste votes on Mr Lynden Moore.' The committed London newspapers also slanted their reports from Newport, with the *Daily Herald* backing Bowen, the *Morning Post* and *Daily Telegraph* backing Clarry, and the *Daily Chronicle* backing Moore; backing meant giving favourable predictions as well as editorial support. *The Times* provides the best example, for its ownership was changing during the campaign, and it became distinctly more favourable to the Conservatives in the last week.[15]

However, some points can be discerned through this fog of press distortion. On the one hand, most observers expected a Labour win in the early part of the campaign but were not so sure by the last week, and most of them realised that the Liberals were fading away at the end. By polling day it was expected that Bowen would win from Clarry with Moore a poor third. The best evidence for this is in the reaction of the Liberals: they indignantly denied that Moore was merely a stopgap candidate who was showing the flag, and they even panicked to the extent of issuing a special leaflet which denied that they had no chance of winning. It quoted Moore as saying: 'My opponents, afraid of the result, are anxious to shake your belief in the solidity of my support, and weaken, as they hope, the chances of my success.' Candidates with solid support do not issue such leaflets: Moore was surely right in his analysis of the situation but incapable of arresting the trend. The most likely explanation of the result is that some middle-class Liberals, fearing a Labour win, voted for Clarry rather than Moore, because Clarry appeared to have a better chance of beating Bowen. Nor was this an unusual phenomenon in the inter-war years; describing a letter to the *Manchester Guardian*, in which Gilbert Murray explained his reasons for voting Conservative in 1931, Malcolm Muggeridge remarked: 'like all good Liberals, he only believed in supporting Conservatives when there was a possibility that they might otherwise be defeated'.[16] Such a joke could not have been made in 1922; the novelty of Newport was that the squeezing of the Liberals took place for the first time. If any one issue determined the outcome

[15] See *History of the Times*, IV (2) (1952) pp. 722–67.
[16] Malcolm Muggeridge, *The Thirties* (Fontana ed., 1971) p. 136.

of the Newport by-election, it was surely the electors' expectations of the result itself.

The result

Immediate reaction to the result was overshadowed by the imminence of the Carlton Club meeting and the realisation that Newport could materially alter its decision. Clarry's victory was announced at 2 a.m., so most newspapers had no more than the figures in stop-press columns and some did not catch it at all. Only the *Morning Post* and *The Times*, in their London editions, gave it full prominence, and only *The Times* backed this up with a leader. Conservative MPs who attended the Carlton Club at 11 a.m. that morning had therefore heard the result only recently, and they were 'buzzing with the sensational news'.[17] It was therefore important that *The Times* – the only informed comment then available – chose to underline heavily what it saw as the significance of the result: 'The Country will see in it a most complete condemnation of the Coalition Government as such and a vindication of those Conservatives throughout the country who have been so determined to preserve their individuality in previous by-election contests. By these the Newport result will be hailed as the emancipation of the party.' The moral was clear, and it was very different from that which Austen Chamberlain had wished to draw. But 'the most exciting boomerang in the long history of British political strategy', as Beaverbrook called it, was entirely of Chamberlain's making.

It was therefore only after the Carlton Club meeting and the resignation of Lloyd George that most politicians and newspapers made their comments on Newport. The *Morning Post* saw it as a vindication of Lord Salisbury, and the *Morning Advertiser* as a victory for 'the trade', but the overwhelming consensus was that Newport had been a vote against the Coalition. It was now that Bowen and Moore brought out the drink issue and organisation to explain their defeat, but they too accepted the anti-Coalition explanation. But this simply does not stand up to examination. The Coalition had no candidate at Newport and it was not even a topic of disagree-

[17] Frank Owen, *Tempestuous Journey* (1954) p. 658.

ment between the candidates who were there. And if the Conservative Party, which was part of the Coalition, could profit from its unpopularity, then why could not Labour which was wholly, and the Liberals who were partly, outside it? By Chamberlain's own argument, a voter could help the Coalition only by voting Labour, and that was nonsense. In effect, the voters who would have supported a Coalition candidate tested Moore and Clarry as anti-Labour candidates and found Clarry to be the most hopeful. Newport was less an anti-Coalition vote than an anti-Labour vote: *The Times* admitted that 'the significance of the Newport election lies in the heavy defeat of Labour expectations', and Bowen complained that 'the campaign appeared to me to wind up in a determination to keep Labour out at any cost'.

It is therefore necessary to explain the consensus view that Newport was an anti-Coalition vote: if it is wholly wrong, why did it gain such wide credence? Labour's and Liberals' reasons are obvious enough: it gave them an alibi for a surprise defeat and also suggested that the Newport result might not be a guide for the coming general election for which the Coalition would not exist. (This self-delusion merely meant that they got the result of the general election wrong as well.) Conservative reasons are more difficult to find. Many of them felt a little guilty for the rebellion against Austen Chamberlain and for stabbing the Coalition Liberals in the back. What better defence than to interpret the Newport result to show that they had acted in accord with the wishes of the electorate? If Newport was an anti-Coalition vote, then it would justify the decision taken at the Carlton Club, although the evidence suggests that they would have taken the same decision without Newport (perhaps by a much smaller majority). It was thus in the interests of everyone except Austen Chamberlain to interpret Newport as an anti-Coalition vote, and he could scarcely now claim that he had been wrong throughout the last month. Newport therefore passed into mythology.

Local evidence was different, and ignored: 'It is a Conservative victory pure and simple; it is not an anti-Coalition victory', said the *Western Mail*. Moreover, this correct interpretation was implicitly accepted when the new Conservative Government called an immediate general election. 'We should not be surprised to find in the end that the electorate is re-presented very much in the proportion in which their votes were cast at the recent Newport election', commented *The Economist*. As Newport, so the nation.

Surprisingly, the Newport constituency turned out to be a very good political indicator for the inter-war years, although nobody could have known it in 1922. It was a critical marginal which the Conservatives needed to win in order to win a parliamentary majority.[18] The 1922 general election in Newport confirmed the verdict of the by-election: Moore stood down and, on a higher poll, his votes split slightly in favour of Clarry. The Conservatives almost lost Newport in 1923, held it easily in 1924, lost in 1929 and won easily in 1931 and 1935. With all its peculiarities, Newport succeeded in representing the marginal political nation. Factors like drink and the squeezing of Liberal voters must all be seen as gradually changing elements which always distorted the relationship between local and national politics in the inter-war years. Before 1914 Newport had been a fairly safe Liberal seat, and since 1945 it has been a safe Labour seat. 1922 showed that the transition from the old politics to the new – from church and club versus chapel and temperance society to class versus class – was under way but far from complete. As Newport, so the nation.

NOTE ON SOURCES

There is an extensive coverage of the national crises which form the background to Newport, but the following are the most useful:

R. T. McKenzie, *British Political Parties*, 2nd ed. (1963).

Maurice Cowling, *The Impact of Labour, 1920–1924* (1971).

David Walder, *The Chanak Affair* (1969).

Sir Charles Petrie, *The Life and Letters of Sir Austen Chamberlain* (1939).

K. O. Morgan, 'Lloyd George's Stage Army', in A. J. P. Taylor (ed.), *Lloyd George: Twelve Essays* (1971).

Lord Beaverbrook, *The Decline and Fall of Lloyd George* (1963).

Robert Rhodes James, *Memoirs of a Conservative* (1969).

Information on the local background is to be found in:

K. O. Morgan, 'Twilight of Welsh Liberalism', *Bulletin of the Board of Celtic Studies*, XXII (1968).

---

[18] This assumes a uniform national swing with few variations. Although many constituencies between the wars varied considerably from the national pattern, Newport did not.

K. O. Morgan, *Wales in British Politics* (1963).
Henry Pelling, *The Social Geography of British Elections, 1885–1910* (1967).
Michael Kinnear, *The British Voter* (1968).

Detailed information on the campaign and the local personalities has come from *The Newport Year Book* (1922 and 1923), *Who's Who in Newport* (1922) and overwhelmingly from local and national newspapers, especially *The Times*, the *Morning Post*, the *Western Mail*, the *South Wales Argus* and the *South Wales News*. There is also a useful collection of leaflets and other contemporary documents in the Newport Central Reference Library. The drink issue can be explored through the *Morning Advertiser* and the *Conservative Clubs' Gazette*. No complete set of the *Monmouthshire Evening Post* seems to have survived.

Michael Kinnear's *The Fall of Lloyd George* (1973) gives the most detailed account of the political background, but has nothing about Newport itself.

3. By-Elections of the First Labour Government

by CHRIS COOK

In the two years from the Newport by-election of October 1922 to the formation of Baldwin's second ministry following the general election of October 1924, British politics underwent a period of rapid transition. These two years saw three general elections and four Prime Ministers. They also saw a transformation of the political scene: Lloyd George fell from power, never to hold office again; the Labour Party formed its first-ever administration, even though still a minority party. But of all the changes, the most lasting was perhaps the fate of the Liberal Party. Reunited and resuscitated, the party had fought the election of 1923 on its favourite fiscal battleground, with a vigour and a sense of purpose it had not known since pre-war days. Ten months later it emerged from the election of 1924 like the army of Napoleon which recrossed the Berezina in 1812, an exhausted, demoralised rabble that could never challenge successfully for supremacy again.

In the immediate wake of the 1922 general election, however, all these events were still in the future. Bonar Law had won on a programme proclaiming 'Tranquillity' and it seemed that the by-elections would not show any dramatic shifting of votes.

Indeed, until a series of by-election reverses for the government early in March 1923, only four fairly unexciting contests had taken place. At Portsmouth South (13 December 1922), in a by-election caused by the resignation of H. R. Cayzer, the sitting Member, the Conservative candidate was opposed only by an Independent. The Liberals, who had fought in 1922, failed to raise sufficient energy to field a candidate. The Conservatives easily retained the seat, with turnout falling from 73·7 per cent to 57·7 per cent. In the Newcastle East by-election, interest was added to the contest when Arthur Henderson was brought forward as Labour candidate (he had been defeated at Widnes in the 1922 general election).

The significance of the result in Newcastle East was the inability of the Liberal candidate to make headway against Labour in a traditionally Liberal industrial seat. Labour was, in fact, able to increase both its vote and its percentage of the poll. The succeeding by-election in Whitechapel produced a similar result. Despite the withdrawal of a Conservative candidate, Labour very substantially increased its hold on this East End seat, raising its share of the total poll from 40·2 per cent to 57·0 per cent. In the Darlington by-election on 28 February 1923 a straight fight took place, although the Liberals had contested the seat at the previous election. The by-election result again demonstrated the ability of Labour to capture a further portion of the former Liberal vote.

In none of these by-elections had seats actually changed hands. This position was rapidly altered by a batch of by-elections held early in March. Partly as a result of talk of government plans to decontrol rents, and partly as a result of an internal Conservative quarrel, the first of these by-elections, at Mitcham, produced a dramatic result. In a constituency in which in 1922 the Conservatives had taken 65 per cent of the poll in a straight fight with the Liberals, in the by-election the seat was sensationally won by Labour. Partly, this was explained, because the official Conservative candidate, Sir Arthur Griffith-Boscawen, was faced by an Independent Conservative supported by Lord Rothermere.[1] The Independent took 12·7 per cent of the poll, a sufficient level of support to let Labour in, with the Liberals trailing a very poor third with 15·2 per cent of the poll.

In every sense, however, Labour's gain was nothing short of spectacular. Mitcham was hardly the seat to set Socialists dreaming of the promised land.[2] Chuter Ede, the Labour candidate, found on his arrival in the division that the local

---

[1] For Rothermere's part in this campaign, see entry dated 2 March 1923 in Lord Bayford's diary, quoted in Maurice Cowling, *The Impact of Labour, 1920–1924* (1971) p. 257.

[2] For the reluctance of the local Labour Party to contest the seat at all, see R. McKibbin, 'Labour: The Evolution of a National Party', unpublished D.Phil. thesis (Oxford, 1971) p. 410.

party consisted of a voluntary secretary and a few scattered trade union branches. This handicap was somewhat reduced by a campaign extremely well organised from headquarters – so well organised, in fact, that the local Conservatives were instructed to imitate it.[3] Particular use was made by Labour of the mass canvass; no doubt this was one factor that caused turnout to rise abruptly from 52·7 per cent to 66·2 per cent.

Labour's triumph in Mitcham was followed by two further Conservative losses. In a straight fight the Liberals gained the surburban Willesden East constituency while Labour captured their first-ever seat in Liverpool, the marginal Edge Hill division which was won largely on Conservative abstentions (turnout fell from 70·5 per cent to 58·1 per cent).

After this flurry of by-election reverses, the next by-elections evoked little excitement. The death of Sir O. Thomas, the sitting Independent Labour Member, enabled a fairly united Liberal Party in Anglesey to recapture a traditional Liberal stronghold; indeed, the co-operation of the two wings of the party in Anglesey and the recapture of the seat spurred moves towards reunion at national level, but very little materialised. The very safe Conservative seat of Ludlow produced no excitement. With no organisation whatsoever, Labour's intervention was rewarded with only 7.8 per cent of the poll. As one leading Labour agent bemoaned after the election, virtually every working-class Labour man still continued to vote for the Liberal.[4]

In the Berwick-upon-Tweed by-election, where the sitting National Liberal had been unseated on petition and his wife subsequently stood as an official Conservative in his place, the voting revealed very little change. The intervention of a Labour candidate again hit the Liberal share of the poll, while the Conservative vote was almost exactly that polled by the National Liberal the previous November – a perfect example, if any were needed, of the extent to which nominal National Liberals were so often Conservatives in all but name. As in Ludlow, Labour intervention was probably the cause of the increase in turnout.

With very little comfort from previous by-elections, the

[3] *Manchester Guardian*, 28 Feb, 1 Mar 1923.
[4] McKibbin, op. cit., p. 273.

Liberals were able to console themselves with a gain in the Tiverton by-election on 21 June 1923. In a very high poll (88·1 per cent), in which the Conservatives also increased their total vote, the Liberals gained victory by 403 votes. Little of significance can really be interpreted from the result, since whereas Labour had contested the division officially in 1922, the same candidate in 1923 was not officially endorsed and polled only 495 votes.

Much more significant of the standing of the Liberals were the by-elections in Morpeth and Leeds Central. In the mining division of Morpeth, which Labour won in 1922 on a minority vote, the Conservatives stood down to give the Liberals a clear run.[5] The result was a Labour triumph, with 60·5 per cent of the vote on an increased turnout. It was yet further evidence that the miners had finally deserted the Liberals. Similarly, in Leeds Central, in a three-cornered contest the Liberal share of the vote in this Conservative-held seat slumped from 22·2 per cent to 11·0 per cent.

The final three contested by-elections (four by-elections were pending at the Dissolution on 16 November 1923) all occurred in safe Conservative territory. A second by-election in Portsmouth South was caused by the appointment of the Rt Hon. L. O. Wilson, the sitting Conservative, as Governor of Bombay. On a very low poll (54·9 per cent), the Conservatives retained the seat against Liberal opposition. The Yeovil by-election, on 30 October 1923, was perhaps most significant as an example of Liberal difficulties in recapturing votes that had been lost to Labour. Not having fought the seat in 1922, the Liberals were unable to dislodge Labour from second place at the by-election.

Whereas at least the Yeovil Liberals were attempting to regain lost ground, no such animation stirred what remained of the ranks of the Rutland and Stamford Liberals. No Liberal had contested the division in 1922 and none appeared at the by-election, despite warnings by senior officers of the Eastern Counties Liberal Federation that such lack of action would cause irreparable damage to the future prospects of the party.[6]

[5] For examples of subsequent Conservative–Liberal co-operation in this and adjacent divisions, see *Yorkshire Post*, 13 Oct 1924.

[6] Eastern Counties Liberal Federation, Minutes, Exec. Comm., 1 Oct 1923.

In a straight fight with Labour, the Conservatives easily retained the seat.

In all, despite the losses suffered by the Conservatives in March, the more recent by-elections had not shown any signs of a major shift of votes against the government. Rather, the significance of the by-elections had been Labour's ability to consolidate and extend its gains in industrial areas – mainly at the expense of the Liberals – and Labour's slow but definite advance in rural areas – again hitting hardest at the Liberals. Certainly, the by-elections gave little indication of the electoral earthquake that was to come with Baldwin's disastrous Tariff Election on 6 December 1923, but they had not, in any case, been fought on the tariff question.

The place of the general election of 1923 in the chronology of the rise of the Labour Party and the downfall of the Liberals lies outside this essay.[7] However, the fact that very few observers expected the Ramsay MacDonald government to survive more than a few months, together with the extreme interest and excitement engendered by the advent of a Labour Government, meant that the by-elections of 1924 were followed with considerable interest.

Labour sought to see in the by-elections confirmation of its new place in the political order. The Conservatives looked eagerly for signs that the débâcle of 1923 was behind them and that frightened, moderate opinion was rallying to the natural party of stability.

Of all the parties, however, the by-elections were perhaps of most significance for the Liberals. Each by-election in fact constituted a problem for the party. Indeed, the by-elections were in fact a microcosm of a larger dilemma. What attitude should the party adopt to the Labour Government that the Liberals had themselves voted into office? What should be the role of the party, vis-à-vis Labour, in Parliament? What should be party policy in the constituencies, in, for example, adopting candidates against sitting Labour Members? And what should be the policy of the party in by-election vacancies?

[7] For two recent discussions on the significance of the 1923 general election, see Maurice Cowling, *The Impact of Labour*, 1920–24, and Chris Cook, 'A Stranger Death of Liberal England', in A. J. P. Taylor (ed.), *Lloyd George: Twelve Essays* (1971).

The Liberals failed to adopt a consistent, or indeed at times *any*, policy towards these three pressing questions. The party, with two leaders but little leadership, drifted from thoughts of co-operation and liaison with Labour towards a sullen, unco-ordinated and unthought-out policy of opposition to the government. It was a policy which led to the vote against MacDonald over the Campbell case and on to the electoral débâcle of October 1924.

It was hardly surprising that the Liberals in 1924 found themselves faced with a dilemma that was to prove insuperable. To begin with, having just fought an election on the essentially negative policy of defending the *status quo* (i.e. free trade), the Liberals had then turned the Conservatives out to install Labour. Even this decision, welcomed though it was by the bulk of Liberal workers in the constituencies and the federations, seems to have been taken only after Asquith had been tempted to do a deal with the Conservatives in order to install a minority Liberal Government. Certainly, the Liberal decision to install Ramsay MacDonald – without so much as a prolonged meeting of the two leaders, much less any terms or agreed areas of *modus vivendi* – was a heavy blow to Liberalism. This decision in itself, though damaging, would not have been disastrous had the Liberals pursued a constructive policy in 1924. This the Liberals never did – although certain Liberals knew what they wanted. Lloyd George was eager for co-operation with Labour to put radical measures on the statute book – at least until the Labour Party adopted a candidate against him in Caernarvon and until the Abbey by-election seemed to show the strength of the anti-Socialist forces. Meanwhile, Churchill, F. E. Guest and the other right-wingers wanted no truck at all with Ramsay MacDonald. Asquith, not for the first time in his life, wanted to wait and see.

'Wait and see', however, was hardly a policy. Just as, at Westminster, Liberals had to decide their policy as issues came before the House (and usually finished by voting in all three possible ways), so by-elections fell vacant in the constituencies.

It was, perhaps, something of a lucky chance for the Liberals that two of the ten by-elections of the first Labour Government fell vacant in seats that posed no problem of policy – Dover and the City of London, both Tory citadels, and both uncontested even in December 1923.

In fact, the Dover by-election (of 12 March 1924) was something of a non-event, having been caused when the sitting Conservative Member (the Hon. J. J. Astor) inadvertently voted in the House before he had taken the Oath. Although there was some inclination among the Labour ranks to bring forward a candidate (the seat had been unopposed in 1923), party headquarters dissuaded them. Of the dormant Liberal Association, nothing was heard.[8]

The first contested by-election, on 1 February 1924, in the double-Member City of London division, could hardly have occurred in a less interesting seat. Unopposed in 1923 (and indeed at every general election between the wars except 1929), the seat was the sort of Conservative citadel in which even a Liberal candidature produced no ruffling on the waters of the moat. In the event, a straight fight ensued between Conservative and Liberal (there was no Labour organisation in the constituency). A touch of comedy was added to the contest by the fact that the Liberal candidate had himself made efforts to secure the Conservative nomination.[9] The result, not indeed unexpected, was a Conservative victory with 70·1 per cent of the poll on a 41·9 per cent turnout.

The first significant by-election, and the first real policy dilemma for the Liberals, occurred with the vacancy at Burnley, caused by the death of the sitting Labour Member. Here, polling took place on 28 February. The contest soon assumed a national interest when Arthur Henderson, who in the previous general election had lost his seat at Newcastle East through a tacit Conservative–Liberal pact, was put forward as Labour candidate.

The seat was only moderately safe for Labour. In the 1923 general election, Labour had polled 16,848 votes, the Conservatives 14,197 and the Liberals a quite strong 13,543. The local Liberals were keen to contest the by-election and indeed had a candidate ready. The issue, however, was hardly this simple. The appearance of a Labour Cabinet Minister as candidate

---

[8] *Dover and County Chronicle*, 8, 15 Mar 1924.

[9] Gladstone Papers, BM Add. MSS 46,474/74, Donald Maclean to Herbert Gladstone.

placed the Liberals in a difficult dilemma. At a time when the Parliamentary Liberal Party had only just voted Labour into power, and when Lloyd George in particular had visions of a lasting Labour–Liberal co-operation towards putting radical measures on the statute book, a vigorous Liberal by-election attack on Henderson, in a seat which Labour held only on a minority vote, was hardly good tactics.

Thus, after correspondence with headquarters, the Burnley Liberals were dissuaded from fielding a candidate. This decision only led to further complications, for while the bulk of the Liberal voters in Burnley could probably be expected to support Labour, the Liberal Executive was much more pro-Conservative (indeed, in municipal elections in the town a fair degree of tacit Conservative–Liberal agreement went on). Thus, somewhat petulantly, the Liberal Executive proclaimed a position of neutrality, and it was left to the Labour and Conservative candidates to woo the 13,500 Liberal votes.

To this extent, Henderson started at an advantage. From the beginning his campaign was almost a model of an orthodox, Nonconformist Liberal candidature. Indeed, in a Lancashire town where Nonconformity was as much a social-cum-political as a purely religious power, Henderson's election address was studded with quotations from the *Methodist Recorder* and the *Wesleyan Recorder*. (Henderson himself was, of course, a Nonconformist.) Not surprisingly, even the *Times* correspondent covering the by-election found that Henderson's campaign speeches could be endorsed by the average Asquithian and that the Labour candidature was 'the next best thing to a regulation Liberal'.[10]

The Conservative campaign, by contrast, was largely an emotional anti-Socialist attack centred on the dangers of a Labour Government. The editorials of the *Burnley Express* tried hard to depict Henderson as a harbinger of the Red Peril. The Labour Party was denounced as anti-Christian and in 'international alliance' with Soviet Russia, while Henderson was linked by association with the 'Socialist Arbeiter Internationale'. It was hardly realistic tactics, considering the studied moderation of Henderson.

A minor sensation during the campaign, again causing

[10] *The Times*, 9, 14 Feb 1924.

consternation in the Liberal ranks, was a letter of support made public by Churchill to Camps, the Conservative candidate. Urging the Liberals in Burnley to support Camps, Churchill argued that 'no difference of principle' now separated Liberalism and Conservatism. Churchill's letter continued: 'All the great issues on which they quarrelled before the war have been settled by agreement . . . Differences exist, no doubt, of mood, of temperament, of degree. But they are not differences of fundamental principle.' It was a strange argument from a politician who two months earlier had been fighting a rival Conservative in the Leicester West constituency. In fact, Churchill's letter was more significant in indicating his own impatience to range himself under the Conservative banner, than in persuading the Liberal vote in Burnley to move right.

The outcome of the polls was a complete vindication of Henderson's tactics. Labour won with 24,571 votes to the 17,534 of the Conservative, a 7,037 majority and a swing to Labour of 5·4 per cent.

The significance of the result was seen by the *Westminster Gazette*. In an editorial headed 'Burnley and the Average Voter', the paper observed that the result indicated in no uncertain terms 'a clear indication of the willingness of the average Liberal to give the Labour Government a square deal'.

Equally, the lesson of the by-election was not lost on Labour organisers. The increased majority in the absence of a Liberal gave added support to the view that not only was the bulk of moderate Liberal opinion willing to give the new Labour Government a chance, but that it was the Liberal Party which had finally to be broken before Labour could really achieve power. Thus, at a time when Lloyd George was contemplating Liberal–Labour co-operation, the Labour hierarchy and organisers were thinking more and more of the destruction of the Liberal Party.

The rash of adoptions of Labour candidates in rural constituencies and in safe middle-class seats after Burnley was a reflection of this new determination. Among the unlikely constituencies in which Labour candidates were adopted within a few weeks of Burnley were Henley, St Marylebone and Bedford.[11]

11 *Daily Herald*, 4, 7, 8 Mar 1924.

Nor was the lesson of the by-election lost on, of all people, Lord Beaverbrook. Writing in the *Sunday Express* on 9 March 1924, under an article headed 'The Necessity for Liberalism', Beaverbrook warned that, if the Liberal Party went under, its voters, as in Burnley, would vote Labour. How many Burnleys, asked Beaverbrook, are there in England today? Clearly, there were too many for the Beaver who, despairing of his rather bizarre attempts to restore Liberalism in mid-1924, went off to Canada.

Beaverbrook, however, was not to leave for his native Canada before the outcome of the by-election which excited most interest and emotion of any in 1924 – the by-election in the Abbey division of Westminster.

Perhaps the most surprising aspect of the by-election in Abbey was that it surprised anyone. The constituency, like the adjacent St George's division which it rather resembled, was a rock-solid Tory stronghold whose main electoral interest in previous contests had taken the form of rival Conservative candidates.

After an unopposed election in Abbey in 1918, a by-election in August 1921 had produced both a strong Anti-Waste League candidate (R. V. K. Applin) and a Liberal to oppose J. S. Nicholson. Nicholson won, but Applin came an easy second with 34·9 per cent of the poll. In the 1922 general election, Nicholson found himself opposed by a token Labour candidature (the Liberals having abandoned the struggle) and yet another Independent Conservative. On this occasion Nicholson won easily, with over 75 per cent of the total poll.

Meanwhile St George's was also producing electoral fun and games. In a by-election in June 1921 in the division, an Anti-Waste League candidate (J. M. M. Erskine) had beaten a strong Conservative opponent in Sir Herbert Jessel. In the 1922 general election, Erskine went on to win against an official Conservative.

When considering the significance of the Abbey by-election, it is particularly important to remember the somewhat maverick electoral behaviour of both Westminster constituencies and their highly untypical electorates.

It was, perhaps, surprising that the Abbey constituency was

so much a Tory playground, for the seat contained a considerable working-class element and much bad housing. Indeed,
the *Daily Herald* had been running articles highlighting
'Wealthy Westminster's Housing Scandal'. The *Times* correspondent spoke quite rightly of 'a considerable working-class
population' in such areas as the Vauxhall Bridge Road and
Soho, together with the Covent Garden Market area and
theatreland.

The fact that Labour had only once put up a token fight in
the constituency, taking 13·6 per cent of the poll in the 1922
general election, was due much more to the difficulties of
maintaining any form of permanent organisation in the seat
than in getting support during a spirited by-election campaign.
Certainly, in 1922 Labour had made only a token canvass.

In such a safe Conservative seat, it remained to be seen who
would succeed in obtaining this plum nomination. Even before
Churchill's announced intention to seek the nomination, there
were indications that yet another internal Tory feud would
mark the by-election. An independent 'Conservative-Demo-
cratic' candidate, Lieutenant-Colonel George Parkinson, had
already announced that he would stand and had opened up
committee rooms in Shaftesbury Avenue. His candidature was
certainly not entirely frivolous, having the support of such
people as J. C. Gould, MP, together with some local backing.

From the start, rumours abounded that Churchill wanted
to stand: indeed, that he had set his sights on the Abbey
division as the official Conservative candidate. From this time
on, considerable intrigue surrounded the selection of the
candidate by the Westminster Abbey Constitutional Association.

The possibility that Churchill would seek to stand in Abbey
threw the Conservative leadership into something of a turmoil.
Baldwin himself was prepared to support Churchill's return to
the Conservative fold, but, having talked it over with Austen
Chamberlain, agreed that it was too early for Winston to come
out as a Conservative with credit to himself. Baldwin's intention was to explain this to Churchill and offer to find him a
safe Conservative seat later on – as Chamberlain observed –
'when he will have been able to develop naturally his new line

and make his entry into our ranks much easier than it would be today'.

Austen Chamberlain's fear, that Winston would try and rush his fences, was fulfilled completely. The exact dealings which Churchill had with the Abbey Constitutional Association are still difficult to determine. It seems that Colonel Jackson lobbied the officials of the association intensely on Churchill's behalf, with the result that Churchill was invited to address them, on condition that he accepted their decision on a candidate as final. Churchill refused. The final decision by the association on their candidate was taken on Monday 3 March, at a private meeting in Caxton Hall. The meeting was far from unanimous. Eventually the association adopted Otho Nicholson, son of Colonel W. G. Nicholson, the MP for Petersfield, and nephew of the late Member. The only other candidate, John Gatti, received 70 votes to Nicholson's 353.[12]

This decision, which caused considerable acrimony in the association, ended Churchill's hopes of the nomination; but it did not end his interest. There were, to Churchill, considerable attractions in standing as an Independent. However, such colleagues as Edward Grigg, Viscount Grey and Sir Hamar Greenwood all attempted to persuade Churchill against this course, arguing that it was a premature action which might spell disaster.[13] Birkenhead, however, urged him on, as did Lords Wargrave and Burnham. The actual decision, by Churchill, to run as an Independent was partly brought on by Parkinson, the other Conservative rival. It would seem that Parkinson offered to withdraw only if Churchill would definitely stand. Parkinson offered Churchill fifteen minutes to make up his mind. According to the *Daily Herald*: 'Mr Churchill then called up two of his friends on the telephone. One was Lord Birkenhead. He returned, struck his chest, and said "I stand. And now let's have a smoke."'

Meanwhile the likelihood of Churchill as a candidate had prompted the Labour Party on 5 March to decide to enter the field. The party chose Fenner Brockway, who in fact entered the contest with few illusions. As he confessed after the declaration of the poll: 'When I was invited to contest this seat,

12 *Westminster Gazette*, 4 Mar 1924.
13 See Maurice Cowling, *The Impact of Labour, 1920–24*, p. 396.

I asked what was the chance of success. I was told none. My purpose was not to gain the seat, but to take up Mr Churchill's challenge to Socialism.'[14]

The story of Liberal intervention in Abbey proved a typical example of indecision and uncertainty. At a meeting of the Abbey Liberal Executive, on 26 February, the Liberals chose Scott Duckers as their prospective candidate, but declared that they would contest the division only if Churchill stood – a fairly illogical position, which did nothing to enhance their subsequent campaign.

The result of all this was that, when nominations closed on 11 March, the by-election had produced four contenders: Nicholson, Churchill, Brockway and Scott Duckers. During the campaign the main centre of attention was Churchill. Indeed, the *Times* correspondent referred to Churchill's campaign as 'a daily variety show'.

From the start of the campaign Churchill, vociferously assisted by Beaverbrook and Rothermere, appeared intent on exploiting internal party differences within the Conservative Party. Indeed, the amount of Liberal support Churchill received was negligible. The bulk of the Parliamentary Liberal Party opposed his candidature. His supporters included only a few Liberal MPs who formed a right-wing 'coterie' within the party – such figures as Colonel England, J. S. Rankin and Austen Hopkinson – all of whom were to range themselves under the 'Constitutionalist' banner in the 1924 general election.

On the Conservative side, however, Churchill's supporters were many. Balfour supported Churchill; the Press Lords were behind him; Birkenhead and the old Coalitionists were there. Neville Chamberlain noted in his diary the welcome of many backbenchers for Churchill's move.[15] Among leading backbenchers prominent in support of Churchill were Sir Philip Sassoon, Sir Arthur Bull, Rear-Admiral Sueter and Commander Burney. Lord Wargrave, in a supporting letter, flattered Churchill as 'the most brilliant recruit since Chamberlain'. It was all rather like the return of an exceptionally prodigal son.

[14] *Daily Herald*, 21 Mar 1924.
[15] Entry dated 17 Mar 1924 in Neville Chamberlain diary, quoted in Maurice Cowling, *The Impact of Labour*, 1920–24, p. 396.

Indeed, far too little emphasis has been given in accounts of Abbey to Churchill's local support. Churchill, at his adoption meeting, was proposed by John Gatti, the defeated candidate for the official Conservative nomination, and was seconded by Captain Lyon Thomson, a member of the Executive Committee of the Abbey Constitutional Association. Another influential local supporter was R. W. Granville Smith, the chairman of the Westminster Constitutional Association. Perhaps more significantly, Churchill had the enthusiastic support of Erskine, MP for St George's.

Against these, however, were those Conservatives who would have no truck with Churchill or any of his works. Leo Amery was among the front-runners here. As he bitterly observed of Churchill's candidature, it was a case of 'true to type'. Amery noted in his diary: 'Winston will desert his Liberal colleagues with the same swift decision that led him to climb over the railings and escape without Haldane and Le Mesurier twenty-five years ago.'[16]

During the campaign there were effectively only three candidates, for Scott Duckers proved to be a contender in name only. His was a ghost campaign, lacking organisation, helpers, enthusiasm and certainly policy. It even lacked speakers. With Asquith ill, Duckers wrote on 12 March to Lloyd George asking him to speak during the campaign. Sylvester replied that Lloyd George had very heavy commitments and could not come.

Certainly, Lloyd George proved to be a man of few words during the by-election. Having refused to speak on Ducker's behalf, Lloyd George played no part in the by-election. As Grigg wrote to Bailey, Lloyd George was watching events, closely and suspiciously, to see if the by-election might lead to a revival of Coalitionism.[17]

Indeed, even apart from Lloyd George, nothing went right for Duckers. His manifesto declared that he was not a Socialist but was in agreement with the aspirations of Labour – hardly a winning battle-cry in Westminster. At the same time, Duckers attacked the 'military opportunism' of the Labour Government – again, not an effective weapon against Fenner

[16] Entry dated 27 Feb 1924 in Leo Amery diary, quoted ibid., p. 398.
[17] Altrincham Papers, Grigg to Bailey, 20 Mar 1924.

Brockway. It was, perhaps, most galling of all that during the campaign no one took any notice of Duckers: Churchill claimed the fight was between himself and Fenner Brockway. Brockway claimed it was between himself and Nicholson. As Lloyd George appropriately remarked in his article on the inquest on Abbey, Scott Duckers had 'contributed nothing to the national need' – forgetting that, during the by-election, Lloyd George himself had contributed nothing to the Liberal need.

With passions in the Conservative ranks running so high, it needed only one spark to set alight a major conflagration. As Baldwin wrote to J. C. C. Davidson: '. . . this incursion of Churchill into Westminster has been a great worry. It is causing trouble in the Party, just as I thought we were pulling together again. Leading the Party is like driving pigs to market.'[18] On 14 March it seemed as if, perhaps, none of the pigs would ever arrive. Baldwin later recounted to Davidson his version of events:

> Last Saturday I had a really worrying day. I got back tired and longing for bed soon after eleven on Friday night . . . . I found a letter which, mercifully, I opened. It contained a letter from Balfour to Winston wishing him success and a note saying he wouldn't send it if I objected. To leap into the car again and drive off to Carlton Gardens was the work of a moment. I stayed with him till after midnight. He was leaving for Cannes in the morning. We had a long and intimate talk and he consented without demur not to send the letter which I kept in my pocket.

Baldwin then slept peacefully, only to be rudely awakened in the morning:

> Next morning I opened my *Times* in bed as is my custom and to my horror set eyes on a letter from Amery to Nicholson. I saw in a moment what that meant.
>
> By ten o'clock a letter came round from A. J. B. saying that Amery's letter had altered everything and that it wasn't fair, etc., and his letter ought to go to Winston but he was leaving at once and left me to do as I thought right.
>
> About eleven, first communication from Austen: of course he was all over the place and if Balfour's letter was bottled

[18] Quoted in K. Middlemas and J. Barnes, *Baldwin: A Biography* (1969).

up he would let fly! I found by lunch time that it was common knowledge that Balfour had written the letter and that I had it. I released it, as I was in honour bound to, after Amery's letter for which I was responsible technically, though I never dreamed he would be such a fool.

All this chaos in the Conservative hierarchy was, of course, music for Beaverbrook's ears. Even before these latest developments, Beaverbrook wrote a long letter to Brisbane giving his account of the Abbey election and of Baldwin in particular:

> The Abbey Division of Westminster, which Churchill is contesting against an official Tory, has been another terrible hash-up on the part of the Conservatives. Most of the leaders of Conservatism wanted him back, but they had not the nerve, or the power, to thrust him on the Local Conservative Association, which is supposed to choose the candidate. Now, whatever happens, there will be bad trouble. If Churchill gets in, he will return 'savaged' against the Conservatives. If he is beaten there will be all kinds of accusations of 'betrayal' against the Tory leaders.[19]

Beaverbrook continued:

> The third possibility is, that the Socialist will slip in between the Official and the Independent Conservative Candidates. In that event the blame for the disaster will be placed upon Baldwin – and justly too. The Ex-Prime Minister is a very well-meaning man, but utterly unfit mentally for high command.

Meanwhile, Beaverbrook gave Brisbane his own version of Baldwin's conversation with Austen Chamberlain about Churchill's candidature:

> The funny side of the position is, that after Baldwin had privately endorsed Churchill's candidature, he went down into the country to secure Austen Chamberlain's help and approval. Chamberlain has, of course, been 'coalescing' with Winston Churchill and Birkenhead for years – so Baldwin naturally counted on his warm approval. Instead of which Chamberlain was very frigid and said he would not support

[19] Beaverbrook Papers, Beaverbrook to Brisbane, Mar 1924.

Churchill for Westminster until he repented in sackcloth and ashes for his Liberal past, and joined the Tories openly as a penitent convert. The Tory right was, of course, delighted with Austen Chamberlain's attitude and have re-instated him in favour – and *they* count most for the moment.

Beaverbrook's scorn at Baldwin and the course of Abbey was not confined to a private letter. In the *Sunday Express* on 16 March, Beaverbrook delivered a blistering attack. In an article entitled 'The Abbey Division – And Mr Baldwin', Beaverbrook attacked Baldwin's leadership as a 'terrible failure' and Nicholson as 'an unknown individual whose main qualification is that he is the late member's nephew'.

Thus, as the short campaign in Abbey drew to a close, the political temperature had risen to boiling-point. Even the normally fairly subdued *Times* correspondent, having observed Churchill being assailed by turnips in Covent Garden, referred to 'the most remarkable election known in Westminster since the Ballot Act did away with the hustings'. Nor did the Labour campaign lack its highlights, with Fenner Brockway canvassing St James's Palace and York House in search of Socialist votes, and with Oswald Mosley supporting his campaign.

The climax of the by-election in fact turned out to be the result itself. Even the announcement was dramatic. After a very close count, it appeared that Churchill had won: Beaverbrook's early edition of the *Evening Standard* on 20 March proclaimed 'Churchill Wins'. The announcement was premature. Nicholson was home, by the shortest of short heads – 43 votes. The full result was:

Nicholson	8,187	(*35·9*)
Churchill	8,144	(*35·8*)
Brockway	6,156	(*27·0*)
Scott Duckers	291	(*1·3*)

Turnout, at 61·6 per cent, was easily the highest in the division at an inter-war election, comparing with 38·5 per cent in the 1921 by-election, 49·0 per cent in 1922 and 58·4 per cent in 1929.

Not surprisingly, the dramatic result in Abbey produced a welter of comment. Lloyd George, who had said nothing during the campaign, formed his own conclusions on the significance of the Abbey poll. In an article headed 'The Lessons of the Abbey Election' which appeared on 22 March in the *Daily Chronicle*, Lloyd George declared that, not only was the Liberal Party now impotent, but its power had been 'shattered and distributed in bits among the other parties'. Lloyd George went on to attack Scott Duckers as 'just the type of candidate who tars Liberalism with the Little England brush'. The next day Duckers rightly retorted that neither Lloyd George nor any other Liberal leader had made the slightest intimation on these lines during the campaign, and accused Lloyd George of starting 'a new campaign of Jingo Imperialism'.

Aside from this personal argument, the real impact of Abbey on Lloyd George was to set him thinking again on the possibilities of a revived Coalition. To Lloyd George, Churchill's vote demonstrated the strength of anti-Socialist Liberalism. The bulk of the press agreed with this interpretation. As the *Observer* commented on 23 March, Liberalism had cut an abject figure, with the party 'going the way to be smashed to pieces at the next election'. All agreed the result was a particularly impressive advance for Labour.

Historians have, by and large, not disagreed with this interpretation. The most recent verdict on the Abbey by-election has been given by Maurice Cowling. According to Cowling, 'the Abbey by-election demonstrated the strength of anti-Socialist Liberalism and the weakness of the Liberal Party'.[20] Though stated by contemporaries, and repeated by historians, this verdict is hardly justifiable. It is based on two quite erroneous assumptions:

(1) that the size of Churchill's vote was due to Liberals voting for Churchill to demonstrate their anti-Socialist tendencies;
(2) that the vote obtained by Scott Duckers was in any sense a meaningful Liberal poll.

Neither of these two factors stands up to examination. To begin with, if *every* Liberal who had cast a vote in the Abbey by-election of 1921 had voted for Churchill in March 1924, Churchill would have polled 2,500 votes. The great bulk of

[20] Maurice Cowling, op. cit.

Churchill's votes must have been *Conservative* votes; to this extent, like Abbey in 1921 or St George's that same year, the by-election of 1924 was a demonstration of the unorthodox Toryism of the two constituencies, not a demonstration of the strength of anti-Socialist Liberalism.

Nor was Scott Duckers's vote a meaningful yardstick to gauge Liberal strength. As we have seen earlier, he only entered the contest to spite Churchill (which he did, since 291 Liberal votes would have seen Churchill home) and he hardly campaigned. This fact was recognised after the result. As J. A. Spender wrote in the *Westminster Gazette*: '. . . no one can suppose that an organised Liberal Party throwing its back into the fight as the other parties did would not have polled a very much larger number of votes than was recorded for Mr Scott Duckers.'[21] Nor was this merely pique on the part of the *Westminster Gazette*; as the paper had written earlier in the campaign, in many ways the only party that could be indifferent to the result was the Liberals.

This, in fact, leads on to the great paradox of Abbey. The by-election which had least to do with the fortunes of the Liberal Party produced most debate and despair about the party. The other by-elections, with very much more evidence of the state of the party, were almost ignored, their lessons not heeded.

The Abbey by-election also produced additional dissatisfaction at Asquith's leadership of the party. Even though, for part of the time, he had been incapacitated by illness, none the less criticism by rank-and-file Liberals was mounting.[22]

After Abbey, no by-election occurred until towards the end of May. Nothing happened in these weeks to revive the dreary fortunes of the Liberals.

Meanwhile, Labour's considerable cause for optimism at the result in Abbey was reinforced by their good performance in the next by-election in the West Toxteth division of Liverpool. This city, like Birmingham, had been stony ground for Labour for many years. Until the Edge Hill by-election of 6 March 1923, Labour had not won a single parliamentary seat within

[21] *Westminster Gazette*, 22 Mar 1924.
[22] For examples of press criticism of Asquith's leadership at this time, see *Birmingham Post*, 24 Mar 1924, and *Newcastle Chronicle*, 24 Mar 1924.

the city. The old religious cleavage still tied the Protestant working class fairly solidly to Alderman Salvidge's well-organised Tory machine.

Edge Hill, in 1923, had indicated a slight shifting in the position; now the West Toxteth by-election provided Labour with a second opportunity. For the Liberals – who had won two seats in Liverpool quite unexpectedly in December 1923 (in Wavertree and West Derby, the latter in the absence of a Labour candidate) – Edge Hill might also have seemed a useful testing-ground. Indeed, the Princess ward within the constituency had something of a Liberal vote.

However, the local Liberal Association viewed the by-election rather differently. No candidate was put forward and indeed the association actually recommended its supporters to vote Labour. This action enraged Salvidge, and was partly a factor in ensuring that there was no Conservative–Liberal co-operation in the 1924 general election in Liverpool.

Meanwhile a possible candidate for the Conservative nomination was again Churchill. Indeed, Churchill had addressed a meeting of the Liverpool Conservative Working-man's Association on 7 May at the instigation of Salvidge, the first Conservative meeting addressed by Churchill for twenty years. However, Churchill's Irish record virtually excluded him from consideration for West Toxteth, especially in view of the critical situation over the Ulster boundary. In the event, Tom White, a leading Orangeman and city councillor, was chosen.[23]

The Conservative campaign was fought largely on religion and Ulster: Salvidge tried hard to keep the issue to the safe-guarding of Ulster's boundaries. Supporting the Conservative candidate, the Liverpool Grand Master of the Orange Order pledged the support of his Orangemen if Ulster had to fight to resist any transfer of its territories in the boundary adjustment. Every effort was made to pull a full Orange vote for the Conservative. The Provincial Grand Secretary of the Liverpool Province of the Loyal Orange Lodges declared that it was 'the bounden duty' of all members to return 'their tried and trusted friend'.

[23] For a useful account of this by-election, and of Liverpool politics during this period, see D. A. Roberts, 'Religion and Politics in Liverpool since 1900', unpublished M.Sc thesis. (London, 1965) pp. 96–8.

Labour, as in Burnley, carefully wooed the Liberal vote, and Snowden's free-trade budget helped in this direction. In the event, Labour won the seat by 2,471 votes on a swing of 4·6 per cent. It proved another useful boost for Labour morale, with Labour organisers claiming to have finally captured the old Liberal vote.[24]

The following day, on 23 May, Labour's morale received a further strong boost from the result of the by-election in the Kelvingrove division of Glasgow. Kelvingrove, indeed, proved to be one of the most significant of the by-elections of 1924. Both the nature of the campaign, and indeed the result itself, foreshadowed the 1924 general election. The by-election was caused by the death of the sitting Conservative Member. In the elections of 1918 and 1922 the seat had been safely Conservative. Indeed, in 1922 Labour had not intervened, leaving a straight fight between Conservative and Liberal. However, Labour's sweeping successes in Glasgow in 1922 led Labour to contest the division in 1923. Labour's standard-bearer was Aitken Ferguson, a founder-member of the Clyde Workers' Committee, a prominent local Communist and a highly popular candidate within the ranks of the local party. However, the National Executive of the Labour Party refused to endorse his candidature, with the net result that he fought the election as an Independent Labour man.

The result was something of a sensation. The Conservative polled 11,025, Ferguson 10,021 and Grieve, the Liberal, 4,662. Labour, only 1,000 votes behind the Conservatives, welcomed the by-election as a chance to secure victory in a highly promising marginal seat. Ferguson was again nominated by his union, the boilermakers, but the Glasgow ILP strongly favoured Patrick Dollan, the leader of the Labour group on the city council. With strong support in the local party for Ferguson, Dollan withdrew to avoid an embarrassing split.[25]

The Liberal nominee was Sir John Pratt, whose campaign was financed adequately by Lloyd George. The decision to fight Kelvingrove was about the only decision the local Liberals did take during the course of the by-election. The

[24] *New Leader*, 30 May 1924; *Liverpool Post*, 23 May 1924.
[25] For a detailed discussion of the campaign, see McKibbin, op. cit., pp. 333–5.

campaign by the Liberals, whose range of policy resembled the stocks of Mother Hubbard's cupboard, was a disaster. As the Liberal admitted sadly after the result, the campaign had been virtually a plebiscite for or against Communism, in which his party had been on the sidelines.[26]

If, as in Abbey, the Liberal candidature was an also-ran, Labour also encountered difficulties caused by the Communist affiliations of their candidate. After Ben Shaw, the Secretary of the Scottish National Executive, had written to Egerton Wake, National Agent of the Labour Party, on 9 May urging that Ferguson be officially endorsed, the National Executive Committee had voted 14–5 in favour of endorsement on 16 May. However, events during the campaign caused second thoughts. An advertisement by the Communist Party appeared in the *Workers Weekly* (16 May) asking for money to finance Ferguson's campaign, and setting out a policy that was markedly more advanced than anything the Labour Government could approve. The result was that Arthur Henderson wrote to Wake urging the National Executive Committee to reconsider its attitude. In the event a peculiar compromise was reached in which endorsement was not withdrawn but no official support was given.

All this had little moderating effect on Ferguson. The *Times* correspondent wrote of 'the astounding boldness of his Communistic, revolutionary and confiscatory avowals'. Certainly, the tone of the campaign was heated and highly emotional. Ferguson happily called for the appointment of a trade unionist nominated by the TUC as Ambassador to Soviet Russia, while the Conservative, having no need of a Zinoviev letter, launched a full assault on the Red Threat and danger of revolution.

In the event the Conservatives retained the seat with an increased vote and an increased majority. The figures were: Conservative, 15,488; Labour, 11,167; Liberals, 1,372. The result was a Liberal disaster: as the *Glasgow Herald* remarked, the outcome was 'amazing evidence of the slump of Liberal stock'. And, as Grigg wrote to Bailey, the result was nothing less than a catastrophe for Sir John Pratt.[27]

Perhaps the result should have come as little surprise to

---

[26] *Glasgow Herald*, 7 June 1924.
[27] Altrincham Papers, Grigg to Bailey, 27 Mar 1924.

Scottish Liberalism, for there had been persistent dreary accounts of the low morale of the party north of the Border during the spring of 1924.[28] Kelvingrove confirmed the worst of these forebodings. The by-election also foreshadowed the outcome of the 1924 general election in Scotland, where, in an emotional campaign, the bulk of the Liberal vote which still remained in 1923 went over to the Conservatives in 1924. Or, expressed differently, by 1923 the rump of the former Scottish Liberal vote was already of a much more right-wing calibre than was general south of the Border.

After the disastrous performance at Kelvingrove, a further blow fell to the Liberals in the Oxford by-election, where a vacancy arose when the election of the sitting Liberal, Frank Gray, was declared null and void after a petition. Oxford, from 1918 onwards, presented a rather sensational electoral history. In the 'coupon' election the historian J. A. R. Marriott had romped home on the Coalition Conservative ticket with 70·7 per cent of the poll in a straight fight with a Liberal. In 1922 the tables had been completely overturned. The Liberal, Frank Gray, won in another straight fight with 59 per cent of the poll and a turn-out of 83·8 per cent.

It was a sensational result. Partly, no doubt, it owed something to the dynamic, if eccentric, tactics of Frank Gray, whose campaign tactics included blocking the exit from Oxford Station to prevent late (and predominantly Conservative) commuters from reaching the polls in time. Such other items as an individual birthday card to each elector eventually led to Gray's downfall on petition. None the less, Liberal politics in Oxford were nothing if not colourful.[29]

There was much more, however, to Liberal strength in Oxford than Frank Gray's personal vivacity. Oxford was one of the few centres in the 1920s where the Liberals were entrenched at municipal elections. Of Oxford's four wards, the South ward was a Liberal monopoly, while the East was

---

[28] For the morale of Scottish Liberalism, see the letter from James Wood to Donald Maclean, 26 Apr 1924, in Gladstone Papers, BM Add. MSS 46, 474/87.

[29] Much the most useful account of Oxford politics in this period is C. Fenby, *The Other Oxford* (1970). See also F. Gray, *Confessions of a Candidate* (1925).

virtually so. Of the 108 councillors elected in Oxford during the years 1919–27, 60 were Liberal (55·6 per cent), 46 Conservative (42·6 per cent) and 2 Labour (1·8 per cent). It would, as can be seen, be quite wrong to attribute Gray's startling electoral victory to purely personal factors.

Certainly, Gray's 1922 victory left the Conservatives in the town demoralised. When the 1923 election campaign was announced, the party was without a candidate. Captain R. C. Bourne was hastily adopted, but Gray easily retained the seat.[30]

The unseating of Gray on petition upset this position rather radically. This time the Conservatives had readopted Bourne early in January; Labour, also, had decided to contest the division for the first time. It was now the Liberals who were on the defensive. Much of the subsequent campaign was occupied with debate over the abolition of the McKenna duties, with its local interest for Oxford.[31] The Liberal campaign rested almost entirely on trying to arouse a sympathy vote for the departed sitting Member. The Conservative machine, on a thorough canvass, estimated the result as Conservative, 12,400, with 12,000 against and 3,000 uncanvassed. It proved a fairly accurate forecast.

In the event, the Liberals lost the seat by 1,842 votes. The Conservatives took 10,079 votes (47·8 per cent), the Liberals 8,237 (39·1 per cent) and Labour 2,769 (13·1 per cent). The real significance of the result lay, not in the Conservative triumph, but in Labour's ability to take sufficient Liberal votes to deny them victory.

Oxford proved to be the only Liberal by-election loss during the first Labour Government, but the lessons of the final three by-elections gave little encouragement to the Liberals.

A vacancy occurred in the safe Conservative seat of Lewes when the sitting Member, W. R. Campion, was appointed Governor of Western Australia. Here was a constituency,

[30] Oxford Conservative Association, Minutes, Exec. Comm., 14 Nov 1923, 9 Jan 1924.
[31] For an alarmist forecast of the increase in unemployment that the abolition of the McKenna duties would entail, see *Daily Telegraph*, 31 May 1924. For other aspects of the campaign, see 'Report on Oxford By-Election', *Conservative Agents' Journal* (July 1924).

predominantly rural and with very little trade union working-class electorate, that would have seemed fertile Liberal territory. The very opposite was the case; no Liberal had contested the division since January 1910. At the three post-war elections, straight fights had ensued between Conservative and Labour, with the exception of 1918 when an Independent also took the field, polling 3·6 per cent of the vote.

With Liberal organisation moribund, Labour had profited considerably, raising their share of the poll to 32 per cent in 1922 and 40·4 per cent in 1923. For the by-election on 9 July, Labour fielded the same candidate as in 1923, B. W. R. Hall. On this occasion the Liberals entered the battle. The result was little less than an insult to the party. Thirteen years without a candidate had had its effect. The party came in a weak third, well behind Labour. The full result, compared to 1923, was:

1923			*By-Election*		
Con.	9,474	(*59·6*)	Con.	9,584	(*52·0*)
Lab.	6,422	(*40·4*)	Lab.	6,112	(*33·2*)
			Lib.	2,718	(*14·8*)

It was, as Cowling has written, a quite irrelevant Liberal vote.[32] Perhaps more significant for the political climate in the country was the success of the Conservative in actually increasing his vote, despite Liberal intervention – as indeed had happened in Oxford despite Labour intervention. In line with the general trend, turnout at Lewes increased from 58·1 per cent in 1923 to 67·3 per cent in the by-election.

The penultimate by-election of the first Labour Government, in the Holland-with-Boston constituency, rather defies analysis. A Labour-held seat in a highly rural Nonconformist constituency was itself highly unusual: in the 1923 election, Labour won only five seats in which the proportion of the electorate engaged in agriculture exceeded 35 per cent. To add to the complication, the sitting Labour Member, W. S. Royce, had in pre-war days been a leading Conservative in the same division. It was Royce's death that occasioned the by-election. The results in Holland-with-Boston since 1918 had been as follows:

[32] Maurice Cowling, *op. cit.*, p. 355.

	1918			*1922*	
Lab.	8,788	*(39·8)*	Lab.	12,489	*(39·1)*
Con.	7,718	*(35·0)*	Con.	11,898	*(37·3)*
Lib.	5,557	*(25·2)*	Lib.	7,535	*(23·6)*

	1923	
Lab.	15,697	*(54·1)*
Con.	13,331	*(45·9)*

The Liberals, having polled almost a quarter of the votes in 1922, had somewhat surprisingly abandoned the contest in 1923. The fact that Royce received a letter of support from Mrs Margaret Wintringham, the Liberal MP in adjacent Louth, and that Labour stayed out of contesting Louth, was probably more than a coincidence. It is certainly reasonable to assume that Labour attracted a fair degree of Liberal support in 1923.

At the by-election on 31 July the Liberals intervened, with a strong candidate in R. P. Winfrey. Labour's standard-bearer was Hugh Dalton. After a very short time, considerable bitterness developed between the Liberals and Labour, with the Liberals indulging in an extremely emotional tirade against the evils of Communism and atheism with which they, like the Tories in Burnley and Kelvingrove, sought to identify Labour.[33]

The result of the Holland by-election, producing the only Labour by-election loss of the Parliament, did nothing to improve Liberal–Labour relations. The full result was:

Con.	12,907	*(39·6)*
Lab.	12,101	*(37·1)*
Lib.	7,596	*(23·3)*

The result had little consolation for the Liberals, whose share of the vote was lower than in 1918 or 1922. With a new candidate who did not have Royce's special connection with the division, Labour had no cause to be too dejected.

Having had no joy from any other by-election, it seemed that the Liberals might at last enjoy a change of luck at Carmarthen, where a safe Liberal seat fell vacant owing to the resignation of the Rt Hon. E. J. Ellis-Griffith. After the various complications of rival Liberal candidates in 1922, together with an Agricultural candidate, the result in 1923 had been more of a return to the traditional order of things:

Lib.	12,988	*(45·1)*
Con.	8,677	*(30·1)*
Lab.	7,139	*(24·8)*

[33] See H. Dalton, *Call Back Yesterday* (1953) pp. 149–50.

Probably the most interesting feature of the 1923 result was the strength of the Labour vote. It was an impressive first attempt with an unknown candidate imported at the eleventh hour from North Wales.

For the by-election, the Liberals adopted Sir Alfred Mond, who had lost his seat in Swansea West the previous December: not that this had dissuaded him from writing to Asquith suggesting he become Chancellor in the event of a Liberal Government being formed.

Mond, who was eventually to join the Conservative Party, effectively fought a Conservative campaign in the Carmarthen by-election. His tactics consisted of a trenchant attack on the insidious dangers of Socialism – Lady Mond declaring that Socialism and Communism would be the downfall of the country – together with insistence on Liberalism as the 'safe middle course'.

For a radical Welsh rural constituency, the by-election was a witness to a changing world. Times had indeed changed when a Conservative candidate could speak to a packed meeting in the Nonconformist chapel at Pencader, and when Liberalism would fight as the 'safe party'. In the event, aided by some 225 cars on polling day (compared with 6 Labour cars and a motor-bike with sidecar), the Liberals retained the seat fairly easily.

Even so, the party had little comfort in the result. The Liberal majority, and the party share of the poll, were both down, if only marginally. Labour had most cause again for comfort, moving into second place and increasing its share of the poll from 24·8 per cent to 28·8 per cent.

Carmarthen proved to be the last by-election before the advent of the Russian Treaty and the Campbell case brought the first MacDonald ministry to an end.

Diverse though these by-elections had been, in the political situation of 1924 these contests lend themselves to a very definite interpretation. The lesson of the by-elections for the Liberal Party should have been clear. In every contest the party had polled a worse vote than in 1923: this was true from such Liberal-held seats as Oxford and Carmarthen through to Kelvingrove. Where the party had intervened (as in Lewes) there had been little impact. Equally disturbing was the ability of Labour to deny the Liberals victory in Oxford, and to advance in areas as diverse as Carmarthen or Abbey.

The by-elections had also revealed the Liberals as a party bereft of policy and leadership. The party had come very near to ridicule, with a local Liberal Association in one area urging supporters to vote Labour, while others campaigned on a 'Red scare' anti-Labour ticket. To cap it all, with Asquith almost impossibly supine, Lloyd George, irritated by a Labour adoption at Caernarvon and fascinated by Churchill's antics in Abbey, could think only of intrigue towards a new Coalition.

Beyond the poor – at times disastrous – showing of the Liberals goes a more fundamental meaning of these by-elections. Three factors combine to demonstrate that these by-elections in many ways foreshadowed the general election of 1924: the ability of Labour to increase its vote even in strongly entrenched Liberal areas (e.g. Carmarthen and Oxford); the ability of the Conservatives to rouse the electorate against the Socialist threat (as at Kelvingrove and Lewes); thirdly, and finally, the extent to which, long before the Russian Treaty and the Zinoviev letter, turnout was increasing and the campaigns becoming increasingly centred on the 'Bolshevist' nature of the Labour Party, even in such areas as Holland-with-Boston. It was significant that turnout *increased* in every by-election except for Burnley and Oxford. Even here, turnout was very high, at 82·4 per cent and 80·3 per cent respectively.

Even though, no doubt, the course of events during the 1924 election campaign accentuated the difficulties facing a sorely tried Liberal Party, long before Campbell or Zinoviev the writing was already on the wall.

Note: 1924 to 1931

By CHRIS COOK and JOHN RAMSDEN

The general election of 1924 returned Baldwin to power with an overwhelming majority. The Labour ranks could muster only 151 MPs; the Liberals managed a mere rump of 40. Against these, the Conservatives numbered 412, with an additional 7 'Constitutionalists' who voted consistently with the government in the lobbies.

Considering the massive realignment of seats and votes that had taken place in 1924, the by-elections in the first years of the new government displayed a fair degree of stability. It was not until the Stockport by-election of 17 September 1925 that Labour made its first gain from the Conservatives since the general election. During 1926 seats began to change hands more rapidly. Labour took Darlington from the Conservatives on 17 February 1926, East Ham North on 29 April and Hammersmith North a month later. Meanwhile the unhappy Liberal Party lost a by-election in the Combined English Universities seat to the Conservatives in March. The Liberals suffered additional humiliation when Commander J. M. Kenworthy, the sitting radical Liberal MP for Hull Central, joined the Labour Party. In the ensuing by-election Kenworthy was re-elected with 52·9 per cent of the poll, the Liberals taking a mere 9·5 per cent.

Two events in 1926 rather changed the political scene in Britain. The first was the defeat of the General Strike. The second was Asquith's retirement, in October, as leader of the Liberal Party.

The accession of Lloyd George as leader of the Liberal Party brought a final attempt at the revival of the party. As so often when Lloyd George was involved, his old dynamism and energy brought a new sense of purpose. Within six months of his return, it seemed that at long last a real recovery was at hand. On 28 March 1927 the Liberals gained Southwark North from Labour.

A series of by-election victories followed: Bosworth was won on 31 May 1927, Lancaster fell on 9 February 1928 and St Ives a month later. On 20 March 1929 Eddisbury fell to the Liberals, and the following day Holland-with-Boston was also gained. All these gains were from Conservatives and, with the partial exception of Bosworth, were in rural, agricultural areas. Had the Liberals been able to follow up their initial victories in Southwark North and Bosworth with a gain in the Westbury by-election of June 1927 (which the Conservatives retained by a mere 149 votes), the revival might have gathered even further momentum.

As it was, in the spring of 1928 optimism ran very high. Lord Rothermere wrote to Lloyd George on 10 April 1928: 'You are back to where the Liberal Party was at the election of 1923 . . . . In my opinion, an election today would give you just about the same number of followers.'[1] Rothermere continued: 'Continue as you are doing and I think you and I will agree . . . that there is almost a certainty that the Liberals will be the second party in the next House. This would give you the Premiership beyond any question.' While Rothermere's political judgement does not have to be taken too seriously, none the less the Liberals were doing undeniably well, as the following figures indicate:[2]

By-Election Contests[a]

	No.	Average Con. %	Lab. %	Lib. %
May 1926–end 1927	10	37·9	33·6	28·5
Jan–Dec 1928	15	39·8	30·5	29·7
1929–Gen. Elec.	5	33·6	44·6	21·8

[a] Three-party contests only.

However, even at the height of Liberal success in 1928, Lloyd George himself realised that Liberal by-election victories would not necessarily mean gains at a general election. He wrote to Garvin of the *Observer* in October 1928: 'I have followed your analysis of the by-election figures. I am convinced that "the triangle" will enable Labour to sweep the industrial

[1] Lloyd George MSS, Rothermere to Lloyd George, 10 Apr 1928, quoted by permission of Beaverbrook Newspapers Ltd.

[2] D. E. Butler, *The Electoral System in Britain since 1918*, 2nd ed. (Oxford, 1963) p. 181.

constituencies next time.'[3] Lloyd George had written in similar vein to Philip Snowden: '. . . owing to the fact that Liberal and Labour candidates are fighting each other, there are 170 seats which will go to the Conservatives which in straight fights would have been either Labour or Liberal.'[4] Lloyd George's judgement was nearer the mark. Even armed with his sweeping land and unemployment policies, reinforced by Samuel's reorganisation of the party, the Liberals could win only 59 seats in the 1929 general election.

As Lloyd George had foreseen, three-cornered contests had let Labour take no fewer than 287 seats. Indeed, even at the height of the Liberal resurgence, Labour was still gaining by-election victories. In February 1927 Labour gained Stourbridge from the Conservatives; in January 1927 Labour won North-ampton, followed by Linlithgowshire in April, Halifax in July (a Liberal seat unopposed in 1924) and Ashton-under-Lyne in October. This last by-election attracted tremendous local interest and turnout reached 89·1 per cent, a record for any by-election. The result was announced to the waiting crowds by the firing of yellow rockets (Labour's colour in Ashton) from the roof of the Town Hall.[5]

Labour completed their successes prior to the 1929 general election by gaining three more seats early in 1929: Midlothian and North Peeblesshire (29 January), Battersea South (7 February) and North Lanarkshire (21 March), all from Conservatives.

In all, the record of the parties at all by-elections between 1924 and 1929 were as follows:

Total by-elections: 63 (2 of these uncontested)
Candidates: 182 (Con. 60; Lab. 56; Lib. 59; Others 7)

Gains and losses (net):
Con. − 15 (1 gain from Lib., 11 losses to Lab., 5 losses to Lib.)
Lab. + 12 (11 gains from Con., 2 from Lib., 1 loss to Lib.)
Lib. + 3 (2 losses to Lab., 1 to Con., 5 gains from Con. and 1 from Lab.)

---

[3] Lloyd George MSS, Lloyd George to Garvin, 31 Oct 1928.

[4] Lloyd George MSS, Lloyd George to Snowden, 3 Oct 1928. Lloyd George estimated that, of these 170 seats, 108 would have been gained by Labour, 62 by Liberals.

[5] F. W. S. Craig, *British Parliamentary Election Statistics, 1918–1970*, 2nd ed. (1971) p. 108.

After the 1929 general election, Labour was again in office but not in power, for although it was the largest party in the House of Commons, it had no overall majority. As in 1923-4, the indecisive result of the general election meant that through-out Labour's time in office, great attention was paid to the results of by-elections (see above, pp. 48–9). If Labour could gain 20 seats over the life of the Parliament, they would reach an overall majority; if the Conservatives could gain 15 seats from Labour, they would be the largest party once again. Much more likely than either of these, the by-elections would show anxious politicians of all parties what the public were thinking. Mac-Donald's minority government, like the Labour Governments with unsafe majorities in 1924, 1950 and 1964, was looking keenly for the right moment to call another general election which would break the parliamentary deadlock. In the mean-time there was a temptation to flirt with the Liberals in order to strengthen Labour's position at Westminster and at by-elections.

Early results, up to the end of 1929, appeared to give Labour grounds for hope: Labour candidates improved their position in every contest, and the parliamentary party ended the year with two more MPs than it had had immediately after the general election. But both these gains were technical rather than real. At Preston, W. A. Jowitt was re-elected after he had crossed over from the Liberals to Labour, but he had been elected originally on Labour votes as well as Liberal, and no Liberal opposed him at the by-election. At Liverpool Scotland the rarest of events occurred, when Labour actually gained the seat unopposed. T. P. O'Connor had held the seat as an Irish Nationalist since 1885, and after his death in 1929 he was succeeded by D. W. Logan, an official Labour candidate with strong Nationalist connections. Both Preston and Liverpool Scotland were seats where Labour was entering into its in-heritance on becoming the major party of the Left – Irish and radical votes. Most such gains had already been made and there was small prospect of progress in this direction. Moreover, both Jowitt and O'Connor had already given regular support to Labour in the division lobbies, so neither gain made much parliamentary difference.

Labour's other early success was at Twickenham, and this too was complicated by special problems of interpretation. The

Conservative candidate, Sir John Ferguson, was the herald of all the difficulties which the party was to suffer through its divisions over tariffs and the Empire. When he announced his conversion to Empire Free Trade, he was abandoned by Central Office and denounced by the party leaders. In the resulting confusion he almost lost a safe Conservative seat to Labour. Since the Liberal vote collapsed, it seems likely that many Liberals voted Labour to vote against tariffs. Twickenham was the forerunner of Bromley, Islington East, Paddington South and Westminster St George's, the by-elections which were to plague Baldwin well into 1931. This aspect is fully considered in Chapter 4 below. However, up to the end of 1929 Labour's record was good. In a more typical contest, at Tamworth, it had reduced the Conservative majority with a swing to Labour since the general election.

Baldwin's severe difficulties in 1930 and 1931 seem to have diverted attention away from Labour's increasingly serious plight. As the slump deepened and unemployment rose, Labour's performance at by-elections began to deteriorate; by 1931 it was doing as badly as any government since 1918. During 1930 and 1931 only one by-election registered a swing to Labour (Pontypridd, 0·5 per cent) while twenty showed a swing to the Conservatives. Many of these swings to the Conservatives were very large, and were more serious for MacDonald than for most Prime Ministers: as leader of a minority government, he had to regard *any* swing away as disastrous, for only a substantial swing to Labour would have justified him in calling a general election. Without a general election to provide a stable parliamentary majority, Labour could not take effective action to combat the economic crisis. Thus, the deterioration of the economy was both a cause of by-election results and was directly affected by them.[6] Different types of contest all showed Labour's poor performance. Where Scottish Nationalists or Communists intervened, Labour seemed to be affected more than proportionately. Even in straight fights with the Conservatives, Labour was suffering swings which, in a general election, would have put Baldwin securely back in Downing Street. The number of straight fights was in fact very small, and the pattern of interventions

[6] This point is discussed on p. 319 below, in relation to 1964–6.

and withdrawals complicates any comparison with 1929. However, six of the constituencies which had by-elections in 1931 had had identical contests in the 1924 general election, and these six were a good cross-section of the electorate.[7] In 1924 the Conservatives had polled 52·7 per cent of the Conservative–Labour vote in these constituencies; in the 1931 by-elections the Conservatives polled 53·7 per cent. Making allowances for interventions and withdrawals, the other by-elections of 1931 also show a pattern which is strikingly similar to that of 1924. It is clear that if Labour had been foolish enough to hold a general election in the summer of 1931, even as a united party, they would merely have returned the Conservatives to power with a large majority. This point is worth stressing because of the natural tendency to explain away the result of the 1931 general election as caused entirely by the events of the late summer, the economic crisis and the Labour split. It is undoubtedly true that Labour did much worse in November than it would have done in June, but only the scale of its defeat would have been different. Of course, without a Labour split and a National Government, there would have been no 1931 general election anyway.[8]

Perhaps because of the setbacks which the government was suffering in by-elections and in economic policy, there were negotiations for a Liberal–Labour pact. Labour would enact electoral reform, which could help only the Liberals, in return for a by-election pact and Liberal support at Westminster. Dark rumours of such a secret pact were certainly current in Conservative newspapers, and these were partly responsible for the Liberal splits in early 1931.[9] However, as an article in

[7] The six constituencies were: Woolwich East, Rutherglen and Manchester Ardwick (Labour-held), Salisbury and Stroud (Conservative-held) and Sunderland (Conservative gain). Doing as well as in 1924, or better, would suggest that the Conservatives were doing very well indeed.

[8] Things were so bad by the summer of 1931 that it was recognised that an alliance with the Liberals was necessary if the government was to survive; see R. Skidelsky, *Politicians and the Slump* (1967) p. 333. Skidelsky believes that the alliance with Lloyd George gave Labour cause for 'cautious optimism'. For an alternative view, see E. Shinwell, *Conflict without Malice* (1955) p. 109.

[9] The Liberal split is described in Roy Douglas, *The History of the Liberal Party, 1895–1970* (1971) pp. 208–32.

the *Conservative Agents' Journal* pointed out, such a 'squalid deal' might work at Westminster, but would never work in the constituencies,[10] Labour withdrew from the Scarborough and Whitby by-election in May 1931, and the Liberals almost gained the seat from the Conservatives. But when Liberals withdrew in favour of Labour candidates, they were unable to deliver the votes. Just as the Parliamentary Liberal Party was deeply split over the prospect of supporting Labour, so the Liberal voters were at least as likely to vote Conservative as Labour, if they were deprived of the chance to vote Liberal.[11] The last five contests of the 1929 Parliament illustrate the point:

> Stroud: Lib. at both elections, swing to Con. 0·6%
> Rutherglen: Lib. & Comm. withdrawal, swing to Con. 6·5%
> Gateshead: Lib. withdrawal, swing to Con. 13·9%.
> Manchester Ardwick: no Lib. 1929 or 1931, swing to Con. 9·8%.
> Liverpool Wavertree: Lib. withdrawal, swing to Con. 11·1%.

If anything, then, the withdrawal of Liberal candidates actually harmed Labour; that is what had happened in the general election of 1924 and that was what was to happen in the general election of 1931. This effectively ruled out any real radical alliance for electoral purposes.

The freak results of the 1929–31 Parliament distort the total picture considerably: technically, Labour had lost four seats but had gained two and the Conservatives had gained four but lost one – an indecisive overall result. However, it does not require much analysis to show that this was misleading, and looking only at the seats which Labour lost to the Conservatives should have been enough. Fulham West and Sunderland would be won by the Conservatives only if they were doing better than Labour nationally, and Shipley had never been won by a Conservative before. Finally, Ashton-under-Lyne had actually been won by Labour in the run-up to the 1929 general election, but was regained by the Conservatives in April 1931. If gains and losses were to be the measurement of performance, then the message should have been clear.

[10] *Conservative Agents' Journal* (July 1931).
[11] This refers to hard-core Liberal voters who could not be 'squeezed' in a three-party contest (see above, p. 39). If the Liberal candidate withdrew, they were faced with the same decision as marginal Liberal voters and seem to have reacted in the same way.

4. St. George's and the Empire Crusade

By GILLIAN PEELE

General Election, 1929		(Electorate 53,914)
Worthington-Evans (Con.)	22,448	*(78·1)*
Butler (Lab.)	6,294	*(21·9)*
Con. majority	16,154	Turnout 53·3%

By-Election, 19 Mar 1931		(Electorate 54,156)
Cooper (Con.)	17,242	*(59·9)*
Petter (Ind. Con.)	11,532	*(40·1)*
Con. majority	5,710	Turnout 53·1%

General Election, 1931
Cooper (Con.) Unopposed

General Election, 1935		(Electorate 54,442)
Cooper (Con.)	25,424	*(84·6)*
Fremantle (Lab.)	4,643	*(15·4)*
Con. majority	20,781	Turnout 55·2%

The St George's division of Westminster does not, at first sight, appear a likely setting for one of the most eagerly awaited by-elections of the inter-war years. Sedate and very prosperous, the constituency included within its boundaries many of London's most fashionable residential districts as well as Hyde Park and Buckingham Palace. Yet here, in March 1931 – watched by the inhabitants of Mayfair and Knightsbridge – was conducted a bitter and abusive election campaign which commentators of the time believed would have an enormous impact on the course of political events. On the outcome of this by-election hung the future of Baldwin, the future of Indian constitutional advance and the future of the Empire Crusade.

Today, when by-election results are generally interpreted as a verdict on the performance of the government, it may seem curious that the central issue of a by-election could have been the adequacy of the Leader of the Opposition. But that was clearly the case at St George's: in the absence of a government candidate (the Labour Party had contested the seat in 1929 for the first time and did not put up a candidate at the by-election), the electors had to choose between Alfred Duff Cooper, the nominee of the local Conservative Association, and Sir Ernest Petter, an Independent Conservative who was backed by the rudimentary Empire Crusade and United Empire Party organisations together with the Beaverbrook and Rothermere press.

It was evident from the beginning that the St George's contest would not be an ordinary by-election, and certainly by the time Petter entered the field everyone thought that this by-election would determine Baldwin's personal fate. In his first press statement the Independent Conservative put the issue thus: 'My candidature is intended to be a definite challenge to Mr Baldwin's leadership of the Conservative Party.' Baldwin at one stage even considered taking up the Empire Free Traders' challenge directly by offering himself as a candidate in Westminster, and although was dissuaded from such a course, this suggestion is some indication of how seriously the by-election was regarded at the time. Lord Beaverbrook had also staked a lot on the outcome of the confrontation. He threw himself into the fight in the belief that a victory in St George's would finally show Central Office that London was solidly in favour of a policy of Empire Free Trade and that Baldwin, with his equivocal position on this issue, would have to go. Opinions about the significance of the result when it was actually announced were somewhat less categorical than these prior speculations might lead us to believe. There is, however, a notable absence of any detailed treatment of the by-election either in terms of its immediate impact on the actors in the drama or in terms of its long-term significance for national politics. Admittedly, St George's did not pass into the political mythology of the 1930s in quite the same way as did East Fulham or Oxford; but it deserves a fuller account than it has hitherto received both because of its intrinsic interest and because of its place in the history of the Empire Free Trade movement.

It is, of course, possible to dismiss the whole Empire Crusade (to say nothing of Rothermere's United Empire Party) as an inherently misconceived venture, and it is perhaps a pity that the most recent major contributor to our knowledge of the movement should take this view.[1] Empire Free Trade as expounded by Lord Beaverbrook demanded the creation of a single economic unit from the variety of territories within the British Empire. The argument was that the Dominions should provide all Britain's food while British industry could provide the rest of the Empire with the manufactured goods it required. All that was needed to put this plan into operation was a single protective tariff; but here the scheme ran into the old difficulties associated with food taxes as well as those associated with the new centrifugal forces which threatened the whole Imperial edifice. But such problems did not deter Beaverbrook. In 1930 he created a somewhat populist movement to convert the Conservative Party to his ideas; and he did not deny that, if the Conservatives proved recalcitrant, he was willing to split their party and possibly supersede it.

The contradictions discernible in the policy of the movement and the Empire Crusade's almost farcical electoral machine may thus lead one to conclude that this was nothing more than a frivolous interlude in Beaverbrook's career and in the pattern of British politics which, as we know it today, is essentially two-party. But if one's primary interest in the Empire Crusade is not because of its role in Beaverbrook's life, then it is possible to make a slightly different assessment. The structure of the country's politics was by no means fixed in the 1920s and 1930s. It was precisely at this time that a new party – especially one of the populist type[2] – might have emerged as a major force on the barren scene of unemployment and economic distress. Beaverbrook was very well placed to spearhead such a

[1] A. J. P. Taylor, *Beaverbrook* (1972). I am greatly indebted to Mr Taylor for his help with my researches into this by-election.

[2] I am aware that the term 'populist' can cause confusion. I think, however, that it is justified both in relation to the style of the Empire Crusade and to its specific policies. For a general discussion of the phenomenon of populism, see Ernest Gellner and Ghita Ionescu, *Populism* (1970) esp. pp. 9–27, 153–250.

development – although to be successful it would obviously have had to construct a very much broader base than the Empire Crusade ever actually achieved; but it is by no means certain that it could not have done so. For what now seems remarkable about the Empire Crusade – and to a lesser extent about its uneasy ally the UEP – is the degree of electoral exposure and success which it obtained during its short life. This success cannot simply be attributed to Lord Beaverbrook's dynamic personality, nor be explained away as a perverse reaction by the electorate to a wholly freakish set of political factors. It will not, unfortunately, be possible to expand all these points at length in relation to St George's; nevertheless, the account of this by-election must be read not against the background of a political movement 'which seems in retrospect a trivial episode hardly worthy of record',[3] but against the background of an embryonic attempt to refashion some elements of the Conservative Party into a new political alliance.

The national background

The years 1929 to 1931 present a picture of mounting dissatisfaction with Baldwin's leadership of the Conservative Party. His inability to take a firm line on the issue of protection, his endorsement of the Labour Government's Indian policy and his general complacency all combined to fan the flames of dissatisfaction within the party. On the sidelines, Beaverbrook, Rothermere and, to some extent, Lloyd George were waiting to exploit the opportunity provided by Tory disarray to their own advantage; and at Westminster the Labour Party rejoiced at the disunity which reigned on the opposition benches. Whether the promotion of Empire Free Trade – a slogan which touched a chord in Tory hearts both within and outside Parliament – or the pro-coalition manoeuvrings of some Conservatives was more dangerous to Baldwin's position than Churchill's marshalling of the diehard forces on the Indian issue is a matter for debate; together these rumblings threatened to destroy the Conservative Party and Baldwin with it.

The Tories had taken the defeat of 1929 very badly indeed.

[3] Taylor, *Beaverbrook*, p. 273.

Criticisms of Baldwin's own role in the débâcle were to some extent deflected by the initiation of an investigation into the relationship between Central Office, the National Union and the leader of the party.[4] Investigations were also conducted at a local level, but here the constituency officials were determined that the blame for the events of May should not be laid upon the shoulders of the extra-parliamentary organisation. Thus the Rochester and Chatham Constitutional Association, whose Member, Lieutenant-Colonel John Moore-Brabazon, had lost his seat at the general election, while admitting a 'certain want of cohesion and teamwork' at the local level, also mentioned 'the want of a couragous live Conservative policy and a lead from Conservative Headquarters, the delay in the issuing of the Prime Minister's Appeal to the Electors and the general apathy in the Party'.[5] The first few months in opposition are usually difficult for Conservative leaders, but the second half of 1929 was particularly troublesome for Baldwin. Beaverbrook's own campaign opened with an article in the *Sunday Express* in June, while the espousal of the doctrine of Empire Free Trade by the candidate at the Twickenham by-election set a pattern which was to be repeated in the following two years. Central Office withdrew its support from the heretic; he nevertheless held the seat – albeit with a much-reduced majority – after several prominent Conservative MPs added their encouragement to that given by Beaverbrook. Then, in October, Baldwin was hurled into another crisis by the Irwin declaration which promised India Dominion status.[6] The year culminated with the conversion of Beaverbrook's personal adherence to a policy of protective tariffs into a mass appeal for funds for a new political movement.

Baldwin's stock had thus been steadily falling throughout the latter half of 1929, but in 1930 it plunged to perhaps its lowest level ever. By March, J. C. C. Davidson (who remained the

[4] See Robert McKenzie, *British Political Parties* (1970) for a full account of this episode.

[5] *Report of the Special Committee of the Rochester and Chatham Constitutional Association* (copy in the Salisbury Papers). See also the correspondence between Frederick Stigant and the Marquess of Salisbury, in the Salisbury Papers.

[6] See K. Middlemas and J. Barnes, *Baldwin: A Biography* (1969) pp. 530–44.

chairman of the party until the middle of the year) was already seriously worried by the Empire Crusade – as Beaverbrook's new movement had christened itself. Although he attested to the stability of the Conservative machine at the top, he thought that this was very like a pie-crust, for, as he said, 'the rank and file were seething with uncertainty and unrest underneath'.[7] The protracted negotiations of the Round Table Conference enabled Baldwin to keep the Indian problem at arm's length for much of 1930, despite the formation of a new backbench committee to keep a watch on the situation and of an Indian Empire Society strongly opposed to any constitutional advance for India beyond the proposals of the Simon Commission. But twice in 1930 Baldwin had to submit himself to what amounted to votes of confidence in his leadership of the party. The second of these party meetings coincided with the first independent electoral success of the Empire Crusade: in a by-election in Paddington South in October, Admiral Taylor beat the official Conservative nominee Sir Herbert Lidiard, after a good deal of wrangling between Central Office and the local association.

This victory gave the Empire Crusade movement further electoral impetus, and at the beginning of 1931 Beaverbrook confessed to Rothermere that their tactics for 1931 should be to fight all possible by-elections. Rothermere agreed with this strategy although he differed from Beaverbrook in believing that India was 'far more vital to the British Empire than Empire Trade'.[8] The diehard camp in fact received a boost to their morale when Churchill finally resigned from the opposition business committee over the tenor of Indian policy, but Beaverbrook, who had originally refused Churchill's plea for them to join forces,[9] only allowed the Empire Crusade to exploit this issue at Rothermere's insistence.[10] Beaverbrook was later to regret this submission to Rothermere's wishes.

An Empire Crusade and United Empire Party candidate

---

[7] See Robert Rhodes James, *Memoirs of a Conservative* (1969) p. 324.

[8] Beaverbrook Papers, Rothermere to Beaverbrook, 14 Jan 1931.

[9] See Beaverbrook Papers, Churchill to Beaverbrook, 23 Sep 1930.

[10] The Beaverbrook Papers contain a number of telegrams from Rothermere to Beaverbrook urging him to concentrate on the Indian issue during the Islington campaign.

entered the contest at Islington East – which was due to poll in mid-February 1931 – while Beaverbrook and Rothermere began to plan intervention in other by-elections and to choose suitable candidates to carry their banner in the event of a general election. On 8 January 1931 F. W. Doidge, the former financial director of the *Daily Express* and the chief organiser of the Empire Crusade, reported that it was unquestionably the intention of the local branch of the United Empire Party to put up a candidate against the former Secretary of State for War, Sir Laming Worthington-Evans, in the St. George's division of Westminster. Beaverbrook thought that Keith Erskine, the son of the constituency's former Member, would make the best candidate in that situation. These speculations were given vital significance when, early in the morning of 14 February 1931, Sir Laming Worthington-Evans suddenly died. The Crusaders and the United Empire Party had another London seat to contest.

The constituency

The constituency of St George's covered an area of 1,479 acres bounded by the Bayswater Road and Oxford Street to the north and by the Thames to the south (see map, p. 103 below). The constituency was divided into five wards which differed in both size and social composition. Victoria – the most populous of the five – was by far the poorest ward; the other wards – Conduit, Hamlet of Knightsbridge, Knightsbridge St George's and Grosvenor – were nearer to each other in their socio-economic characteristics, but they too revealed differences in terms of wealth and political organisation. The outstanding feature of the St George's electorate, however, was the high proportion of women it possessed. 61·4 per cent of the total of 54,156 voters were women – a number rivalled only in five other London constituencies: St Marylebone (61·1 per cent), Paddington South (61·7 per cent), Peckham (62·2 per cent), Hampstead (62·4 per cent) and Kensington South with the astonishingly high total of 69·0 per cent. Many of these women would, of course, be domestic servants 'working below stairs' in the homes of the upper middle classes, and some of them would only have received the vote in 1928. This factor – together with the safeness of the seat – may go a long way to explain the relatively low turnout which St George's experienced even at general elections.

The local Conservative Association benefited from the opulence of the constituency, and its annual income of £2,000 made it self-supporting. It was therefore able to make a relatively generous grant towards the poorer London constituencies – a fact which pleased Central Office but which was not altogether to Worthington-Evans's liking when he was asked to make an annual donation of £300 to the constituency coffers. In the end Worthington-Evans was allowed to give only £100 a year because, as he argued, the tendency to rely on the Member for money was not only 'vicious and pernicious' in itself but also had the effect of encouraging sloth in the local party.[11] Yet although the organisation was healthy and although the character of the constituency was overwhelmingly Conservative, this did not mean that there was always unanimity in St George's. Indeed, its electoral record reveals a surprising pattern of independent behaviour. James Erskine, the division's Member from 1921 to 1929, had been elected at a by-election with the support of the Hanover Square Conservative Association and the Anti-Waste League, despite the fact that the official Conservative candidate was Sir Herbert Jessel. Anti-Semitism was thought to have lost the election for Jessel, but when the former Chief Whip, Leslie Wilson, contested the seat at the general election of 1922 he too was defeated by Erskine. Eventually Erskine's position was accepted and he was returned unopposed in 1923 and 1924, while the two rival Conservative associations which were survivals of the 1918 redistribution were amalgamated in 1924. The fact that Erskine was returned unopposed in 1923 and 1924, and the proximity of the constituency to Whitehall and Westminster, made the seat an ideal one for a busy Cabinet Minister, especially given the failing health of Sir Laming Worthington-Evans. Erskine was induced to retire, was knighted in 1929 and was replaced by the Secretary of State for War. The latter's death after representing St

[11] Worthington-Evans Papers, Worthington-Evans to Brigadier-General Cooper, 11 July 1929. I should like to record my thanks to Dr Cameron Hazlehurst for allowing me to use these papers at an early stage in my research.

George's for less than twenty months meant that a new official Conservative representative would have to be found.

Preparing the ground: the candidates emerge – and recede

When Worthington-Evans died, the campaign in Islington East was still going on. Beaverbrook was naturally anxious to announce the Crusaders' intention of fighting the St George's vacancy before Islington East polled in order to make as much electoral capital as possible from the development. He accordingly telegraphed to Rothermere to ask for authority to make a statement on St George's, and Rothermere replied on 16 February that the decision should be made public on Wednesday (18 February) if Worthington-Evans's funeral had by then taken place. Rothermere also told Beaverbrook that a deputation of the United Empire Party and the Empire Crusade was approaching Esmond Harmsworth to see if he would stand as a candidate at St George's. Beaverbrook still thought that Keith Erskine might be the best man for his purposes, but felt that the Empire Crusade could announce its intention to fight the seat without committing itself to any particular candidate. Thus, when a member of the audience at an election meeting in Islington East on Wednesday asked whether Lord Beaverbrook intended to fight in St George's, Beaverbrook was able to reply that he would.

On the same day as Lord Beaverbrook was addressing the Empire Crusade meeting in Islington East, the St George's Conservative Association convened a special meeting of the executive committee to convey its sympathy to Lady Worthington-Evans and to set in motion the machinery for selecting a new candidate. Although the committee could not have known it at the time, the selection process was to be one of most sensational aspects of the by-election and its difficulties alone were almost to oust Baldwin from the leadership. A selection committee was appointed in the normal way and its members – the officers of the association together with five other powerful figures on the committee, including Lord Howe and Lord Jessel (the former contender for the seat) – began their task of sifting through the list of aspirants for one of the safest constituencies in the country.

Five days later the selection committee met again and Brigadier-General Cooper, the chairman of the association, related the rather surprising details of a meeting he had had with Erskine, the ex-Member. Erskine had apparently intimated that he was willing to be considered for the vacancy, but this was not an offer which the selection committee was likely to welcome without qualification. It was agreed, however, that Erskine should be interviewed again and the committee decided in principle to recommend three names to the executive committee for the final process of selection. Among the list of possible candidates at this stage were Geoffrey Ellis, Sir Edward Grigg (a former Liberal who had served as Lloyd George's secretary), Sir William Ray (a prominent member of the LCC) and Lieutenant-Colonel Moore-Brabazon (a former junior Minister and a distinguished pilot).[12]

Islington East had polled on 19 February and the result had been a disaster for Central Office and something of a triumph for the Rothermere–Beaverbrook axis. Although Brigadier-General Critchley, the Press Lords' candidate, had not actually captured the seat, he had pushed the official Conservative into third place. And the Labour winner, as *The Times* was quick to point out, owed her seat to the fact that the Tory vote had been split. This added a certain edge to the selection proceedings in St George's because it was vital to find a first-rate candidate who could rally loyal Conservatives in the constituency against the Empire Crusade. On Wednesday 25 February the selection committee interviewed the potential runners with great care. As a result of the ballot taken after the interviews, it was decided to submit the names of Moore-Brabazon, Grigg and Ray to the executive committee. Sir James Erskine's name was then added despite the fact that his bid for his old seat seemed likely to put the association in an embarrassing position.

No news of the events in St George's was at this stage given to the press, but two other developments on that Wednesday brought St George's close to the centre of the political stage. In the evening the local branch of the UEP resolved to put

[12] Moore-Brabazon was one of the Members defeated in 1929. Central Office was anxious for his return to Parliament. See Baldwin Papers, memorandum from Sir George Bowyer, 1 Dec 1930.

forward its own candidate at the by-election (there was no local Empire Crusade organisation in the constituency until after the by-election) and, although there were rumours that Brigadier-General Critchley would be asked to stand, Ward Price, an associate of Rothermere's, was chosen.[13] More important, however, from the national viewpoint was the memorandum which Robert Topping, the Principal Agent of the Conservative Party, was preparing to send to Neville Chamberlain.[14] This document was a strongly worded condemnation of Baldwin's handling of Conservative policy and expressed the view that a broad section of opinion in the party now felt sure that it was time for Baldwin to go. Neville Chamberlain was placed in a difficult situation by the memorandum because his position as Baldwin's heir-apparent seriously curtailed his room for manoeuvre as party chairman. The loyalty which the chairman always owes to a leader, together with this delicate personal factor, meant that Neville Chamberlain could not precipitate Baldwin's departure. Baldwin himself knew nothing of the memorandum and Chamberlain resolved to keep its contents from him at least until the Newton Abbot speech – scheduled for 6 March – had been delivered. But Chamberlain's hand was to be forced by the news from St George's.

Until almost the end of February the only candidate to have emerged was Ward Price. On 27 February the scene was radically transformed when Lord Beaverbrook and Lord Rothermere managed to persuade Sir Ernest Petter, the chairman of an engineering firm and a former candidate in Bristol North for both Sir Henry Page Croft's National Party and for the Conservative Party, to stand as an Independent Conservative. In his election address Sir Ernest Petter threw down an explicit challenge to Baldwin's leadership, to the Conservative Party for its mishandling of the tariff issue and to the moderate consensus on Indian affairs. The message on Baldwin was clear: 'I believe the continuance of Mr Baldwin as leader of the Conservative Party is fraught with great mischief to the party and to the nation.' Baldwin, according to

---

[13] Ward Price withdrew from the contest as soon as Petter came forward and helped with the Petter campaign. See *The Times*, 4 Mar 1931.

[14] The memorandum is reprinted in Iain Macleod, *Neville Chamberlain* 961) pp. 139–41.

Sir Ernest Petter, had failed to take any action to avert the ruin of British agriculture when what was needed was an extension of protection to agriculture and the restoration of British arable farming. As far as India was concerned, it was the duty of the Conservative Party to be 'the jealous guardian' of the 'splendid and beneficent rule' which the British had exercised in India for over one hundred and fifty years. Suggestions that the Beaverbrook–Rothermere alliance intended to break up the Conservative Party had abounded in the press in recent months. But, said Sir Ernest Petter: 'It is not my aim or desire to disrupt the Conservative Party, which I believe to be the only agency which, under God, can avert disaster to our country. It is only my profound conviction that under its present leadership that mission will not be fulfilled which induces me to come forward at this time.'

In his press statement, which reached the morning papers on Saturday 28 February, Sir Ernest Petter claimed that he was standing as the candidate of neither the Empire Crusade nor the United Empire Party but simply as an Independent Conservative. He had, according to a number of newspapers, decided to come forward at the request of a number of electors. This explanation of Sir Ernest Petter's candidature and the ostensible independence which was claimed from the Press Lords was certainly a twisted version of the truth. Although the Beaverbrook and Rothermere press announced the decision to support Sir Ernest Petter after he had published his election address, the address itself had been scrutinised by Beaverbrook and some minor amendments made before publication. Moreover, Beaverbrook had planned the 'request' from the electors (who included such friends as Viscountess Chaplin and G. H. Pinckard, the owner of the *Saturday Review*) partly as a means of bringing pressure on Sir Ernest Petter himself and partly perhaps to create the impression of a spontaneous anti-Baldwin movement arising in the constituency.

It had been necessary to bring some pressure to bear on Sir Ernest Petter because he was not at all convinced that he wanted to become involved in a campaign run by what he, like Baldwin, called the 'gutter press'.[15] Yet he had been a

---

[15] I owe this information to Professor E. G. Petter's unpublished essay on the by-election.

lifelong supporter of protection and was seriously worried by the policy which the Labour Government, with Baldwin's support, was pursuing with regard to India. He delayed a decision by reserving the right to withdraw his offer to stand right up until six o'clock on the evening of 27 February. Beaverbrook, who made a secret arrangement with Sir Ernest Petter to pay all his election expenses, put the position to Rothermere thus: 'Petter has reserved the right to decline at 6 o'clock this evening. I think his brother will urge him not to stand. I am told Petter is meeting his brother this afternoon. Even if he decides on his brother's advice not to stand, I think he can be persuaded to come in, with a little assistance.'[16] Eventually Beaverbrook's view prevailed over that of Sir Ernest Petter's twin brother, and the election agent (who had been Admiral Taylor's agent in Paddington South) rushed the election address to the Press Association.

In many ways, Beaverbrook regretted that Baldwin's personality and India rather than Empire Free Trade had become the dominant issues involved in the St George's challenge. But the news of Sir Ernest Petter's intervention was made all the more sensational by the immediate effect which it had on the aspirants for the official Conservative nomination. By this stage Moore-Brabazon was the favourite in the St. George's election stakes, but when he heard that Petter was going to stand on a platform which made it inevitable that any officially backed Tory would have to defend Baldwin's record, he withdrew his name from the list. Moore-Brabazon had been informed of the possibility that Petter would stand and he frantically tried to get in touch with Beaverbrook on 27 February. Three telephone calls to Stornoway House were unsuccessful and it is not clear whether Moore-Brabazon finally made his decision after an interview with Beaverbrook early on the morning of 28 February or whether he had relied simply on his own judgement and the information in the morning newspapers.

Moore-Brabazon's decision was made public in time for it to reach the Saturday evening newspapers and came as a bombshell to Central Office and to Baldwin. It was particularly embarrassing for the Tory leader because Moore-Brabazon had

16 Beaverbrook Papers, Beaverbrook to Rothermere, 27 Feb 1931.

served in Baldwin's government and was no backwoodsman. The reasons for the sudden withdrawal could not be kept secret, and indeed the letter which Moore-Brabazon had sent to the chairman of the St George's Conservative Association made them plain:

> Since I came before you as a potential candidate to fight the cause of Conservatism in the division, there has appeared an independent with similar views to our own, but who questions openly the wisdom of continuing the present leadership of Mr Baldwin. I expressed at the time my misgivings on this matter but hoped that these differences might have been kept within the party to be arranged by ourselves. It is to be otherwise and these questions are now to be matters of public controversy. It will therefore come as no surprise to you to hear from me that I must withdraw my name from the list of candidates, as I cannot allow myself to be manoeuvred into pleading a cause I have not wholly at heart.[17]

Chamberlain realised that he could delay the confrontation with Baldwin no longer; he accordingly made some slight amendments to the Topping memorandum and sent it to Baldwin by hand on Sunday morning. Baldwin was initially prepared to accept retirement, but after consultation with his closest political allies he decided to stay and fight – although the suggestion that he might contest St George's himself was quickly scotched.[18]

On Monday 2 March the St George's Conservative Association – unaware of the weekend manoeuvrings at Central Office – met to discuss the new situation created by Moore-Brabazon's action. The selection proceedings had been thrown into chaos, for not only had the favourite disappeared from the race but the second favourite – Sir William Ray – also looked as though he might withdraw from the list. Although Ray had in fact denied that he was about to follow Moore-Brabazon's example, he had expressed the opinion that the association should examine the position afresh and that, if necessary, he was willing to stand aside. It was clear that Ray did not

[17] See *Daily Mail*, 2 Mar 1931.
[18] See James, *Memoirs of a Conservative*, pp. 357–8.

particularly relish the idea of a fight on the issue of the leadership, and Beaverbrook later undertook to pay £250 towards his election expenses if he secured the nomination in the Wirral.[19] Sir Edward Grigg and Sir James Erskine, the other contenders for the St George's nomination, were no more comforting to the association than Sir William Ray. Sir Edward Grigg's political record would hardly have made him popular in St George's and he was in any case much more concerned at the time with the cause of 'Liberal-Unionist' unity.[20] It therefore came as no surprise when he made a statement to the effect that he would be unlikely to respond to an invitation to stand as the official Conservative candidate in the by-election. Thus the St George's Conservatives were in danger of being left with Sir James Erskine as the only available candidate. Central Office could not, of course, allow this to happen – for Sir James Erskine shared many of the views expressed by Sir Ernest Petter. Indeed, the former Member for St George's had been approached at an earlier stage with a request that he should contest the seat for the Empire Crusade. The suggestion had, however, been vetoed by Sir James Parr, one of Beaverbrook's collaborators in the Crusade organisation, who commented on it thus: 'Yesterday some of my Crusader friends in the George electorate (late Worthington-Evans) came to see me and asked me to use my influence with you in favour of Sir James Erskine as a suitable crusade candidate. But I confess I am not impressed a bit with Erskine. He looks rather too elderly and "moth-eaten". Why not a younger and more striking personality with some "ginger"!'[21] The St George's Conservative Association could really do nothing but postpone the recommendation of any names at all, and the selection committee duly agreed to do this. Sir James Erskine was intensely irritated by the delay because, of course, the time would be used for consultations with Central Office on the choice of a candidate able to fight on the leadership issue; such was the tension in St George's that it did not seem at all strange when Erskine communicated his anger to the press as well as to the chairman of the association.

[19] Beaverbrook Papers, memorandum, 2 Oct 1931.
[20] See *The Times*, 3 Mar 1931.
[21] Beaverbrook Papers, Parr to Beaverbrook, 17 Feb 1931.

Speculation about possible surprise candidates was rampant during the early part of that week and, although Beaverbrook did his best to find out who had taken up the challenge to Baldwin, he was unable to do so. Finally, the St George's Conservative Association learned on Thursday that Alfred Duff Cooper had volunteered to give up the safe seat which he was nursing to try his luck in London.[22] Naturally Sir James Erskine was furious at the news; his hopes of regaining his old seat faded with the appearance of a much younger man who had the advantage both of a distinguished war record and of having been Financial Secretary under Worthington-Evans in the late Baldwin administration. (Nor could Beaverbrook have been pleased by the choice: he was a close friend of Duff Cooper's wife – a daughter of the Duke of Rutland – and the godfather of the candidate's small son.) Nevertheless, Erskine insisted that he was still a candidate for the nomination and both he and Duff Cooper came to meet the executive committee of the St George's Association.

By this time some of the committee had become exasperated by the proceedings in the constituency. At the meeting which had been called to interview the two candidates for the nomination, one member withdrew before the ballot because he favoured 'an altogether different course of action', while another resigned from the committee after Duff Cooper had received an overwhelming majority of the votes because he felt 'a little out of harmony with the decision of the committee'.[23] Perhaps some members resented the interference from Central Office; indeed, the resolution passed by the Association may have protested too much, for it described the selection thus: 'The Executive Committee most emphatically repudiates the suggestion in some sections of the press that any pressure had been brought to bear upon the Executive Committee, or any names suggested in order to influence its choice.' This did not convince the dissenters within the association and it did not convince Sir James Erskine. He had already made a strong attack on Baldwin's leadership before the committee which

[22] See A. Duff Cooper, *Old Men Forget* (1953) for an account of this move; also *The Times*, 9 Mar 1931, for Baldwin's letter to the chairman of Winchester Conservative Association.
[23] Minutes of the St George's Conservative Association, 5 Mar 1931.

interviewed him, but at a general meeting of the association held on Friday 6 March to adopt Duff Cooper formally, he claimed that if the association had chosen him as its candidate there would have been no opposition at the by-election. Even if Erskine believed this himself, however, it was clearly not believed by the association, which gave a warm reception to Duff Cooper. Thereafter Erskine's support went to Petter.

In his address to the association, Duff Cooper commended Baldwin's handling of the Indian problem but skilfully identified neither India nor Empire Free Trade as the main issue to be decided by the election. Instead he focused attention on the Conservative Party's right to change its leader in its own way and its own time and on the attempt by the Press Lords to dictate to the party's members. This move was a very shrewd one because a campaign based on the actual efficacy of Baldwin's leadership might have been somewhat shaky. By turning the question into one of principle, Cooper had cast Beaverbrook and Rothermere in the role of evil and insolent conspirators whose presence on the political stage was a threat to the integrity of British public life.

As the constituency prepared itself for a campaign in what, as Lady Diana Cooper put it,[24] was to be 'no baby- or butcher-kissing election', Baldwin's personal fortunes began to look up a little. News of the Irwin–Gandhi agreement reached England on the morning of 4 March and this had proved an 'absolute godsend' for the Tory leader. Several senior members of the party scented a change in the mood of the rank and file, and Baldwin's Newton Abbot speech of 6 March was both an attempt to build on the foundation of the good news from India and a vigorous assertion of his determination to retain the leadership. This strategy was not altogether successful and Baldwin's enemies interpreted a part of the speech to mean that future sessions of the Round Table Conference would be held in India. The party's India Committee held a tense, angry meeting and Baldwin mishandled the situation by allowing its hostile resolution to be given to the press. The resolution (which welcomed Baldwin's decision not to allow the Conservative Party to be represented at any future conference in India) was seen as a triumph for the diehards; the only reason why this

24 Lady Diana Cooper, *The Light of Common Day* (1959).

mistake did not injure Baldwin more seriously was that by 11 March the campaign had opened in St George's, and press and public alike became absorbed with the affairs of the constituency.

The campaign: 'Mayfair goes mad'

In her autobiography,[25] Lady Diana Cooper said that the St George's by-election was more reminiscent of an election in one of Disraeli's novels than of any of the contests she had experienced in the twentieth century. The novelty of a contested election and the extent of the coverage given to the event in the national press added to the excitement. Open-air meetings proved ill-suited to the constituency and it soon became clear that the messages of the rival candidates would have to be spread by the traditional house-to-house canvass. This had its amusing side in an area inhabited by large numbers of the aristocracy as well as by some fifty Conservative MPs. Lady Diana recorded that 'after the hurly-burly' of an evening's canvassing, the following would occur: '. . . some greater or lesser house, the Londonderry's or Juliet Duff's or Portia Stanley's would spread an open supper table with hot soup and restoratives for the fighting men and women.' Beaverbrook's office memoranda, on the other hand, are filled with notes such as: 'Please note Sir Harry McGowan will vote for Petter.' The fact that Beaverbrook was a friend of Lady Diana's (she recorded that she was in touch with 'the enemy' throughout the campaign) meant that the pro-Petter press did not spend all its time trying to vilify Duff Cooper, although the *Daily Mail* insisted on referring to the Tory candidate as 'Mickey Mouse'. Nevertheless, there were plenty of opportunities for both sides to fling verbal mud. Rothermere and Beaverbrook were described as an 'insolent plutocracy' by Baldwin, who excelled himself in eloquence during the campaign. The unfortunate Petter was labelled by Duff Cooper as 'the marionette and puppet of the Press' (see cartoon). The Rothermere press tried hard to make capital out of Cooper's attendance at an Independent Labour Party summer school in 1927 and constantly accused him of being a 'political softy' with no

[25] Lady Diana Cooper, *The Light of Common Day* (1959).

[DRAWN BY JOHN REYNOLDS.

Imperial sentiment. The most ludicrous of these assertions had come before the opening of the campaign proper, when Lord Rothermere – apparently ill-versed in the English language – had charged Cooper with a lack of patriotism because he had delivered a lecture in Germany entitled 'An Apology for the British Empire'.

Petter's speeches in the campaign were generally rather weak and his presence at election meetings was usually overshadowed by that of Lord Beaverbrook, who addressed audiences in the constituency every evening before polling day. Sometimes Petter and Beaverbrook would conduct their meetings in separate halls at different ends of St George's and then – at a pre-arranged time – would jump quickly into cars and cross to the other's meeting. The unfortunate chairman who was expected to maintain order while the transfer of speakers was effected would frequently be besieged by Cooper supporters so that Petter or Beaverbrook – when they eventually arrived – would have to retake the platform by force.[26] But where Sir Ernest Petter emphasised India and the need to remove Baldwin, Beaverbrook hammered home his own theme of Empire Free Trade. Even India he managed to present as an economic issue:

> Mr Baldwin announcing his policy at Newton Abbot the other day said that his object is the prohibition of unfair discrimination against British trade. That is not the policy of the Empire Crusader. No, the policy of the Empire Crusader is an advantage in the Indian market for English trade. For India is an economic issue in any case. Give prosperity to India and at once you give a desire for ordered government. With desire for ordered government all this agitation comes to an end. Empire Free Trade will bring prosperity to India as well as to every other part of the British Empire.

It was, of course, difficult to tell whether this was really Beaverbrook's considered opinion of the Indian problem or

[26] Petter's son recalls the fact that Lord Beaverbrook frequently brought in bodyguards from the East End to 'take care' of hecklers, and he remembers that these 'rough-necks' would regularly return after the meetings to 'collect' for their services (letter to the author, 27 Sep 1972).

whether it was simply a way of exploiting the maximum personal advantage from a topic which his allies had raised but which rather bored him. The approach, however, cleverly raised the spectre of further economic distress in Britain and may have been seen as a means of attracting not only the votes of those concerned with the question of unemployment but also of those Westminster electors who had voted Labour in 1929; certainly, Beaverbrook was anxious to catch whatever protest votes were going in 1931 and he made an explicit appeal to non-Conservative voters thus:

> I want to make an appeal to the other parties to support Sir Ernest Petter, too, and he is advocating the only policy before the country that attempts to deal with the evils from which we suffer. The policy of Mosley in many respects resembles the policy of Empire Free Trade. So far as he supports the policy of Empire Free Trade, I say, God bless Mosley.

There was an obviously populist note in Beaverbrook's orations, and this – combined with his hammering of the unemployment issue and his call for a democratisation of the Conservative Party – may have impressed working-class voters. His denial of Baldwin's taunt that he was an 'insolent plutocrat' was hardly designed to appeal to the traditional Tory voters in St George's:

> Mr Baldwin says that I am an insolent plutocrat. I wasn't born a plutocrat anyway. I wasn't born with any silver spoon in my mouth, I was born in humble circumstances, the son of a humble preacher of the Word and the grandson of an agricultural labourer. . . . I have known what it is to work with my hands and I have known what it is to want food. . . .

This was good demagogic stuff; it perhaps did not strike quite the right note in Hanover Square.

By comparison with the colour of Beaverbrook's campaign, the meetings held by Duff Cooper were somewhat dull. Yet his political machine was brought into operation effectively and his agent, L. A. Coombs, was vastly more competent than Clinton, who was organising Petter's campaign. The most memorable words uttered on Duff Cooper's behalf were undoubtedly contained in Baldwin's famous speech at the Queen's Hall two days before the constituency was due to poll. The words were not coined by Baldwin but by his cousin Rudyard Kipling and were hailed by the editor of *The Times* as a triumph.[27] Lord Rothermere had sneered that the Conservative leader could hardly be a fit person to restore the fortunes of the country when he had lost his own personal fortune; infuriated, Baldwin replied:

> The paragraph itself could only have been written by a cad. I have consulted a very high legal authority and I am advised that an action for libel would lie. I shall not move in the matter and for this reason: I should get an apology and heavy damages. The first is of no value, and the second I would not touch with a barge-pole. . . . What the proprietorship of these newspapers is aiming at is power, and power without responsibility – the prerogative of the harlot throughout the ages. . . .

In vain did Beaverbrook protest that Rothermere had stolen the limelight from Petter and from himself; Baldwin had come off best in the oratorical battle, although it was by no means clear that this victory would be reflected in the votes.

The last days of the campaign were thus marked by a great deal of tension and excitement which spread far beyond the boundaries of the constituency. It certainly touched Parliament and, although the Conservative Members were obviously affected most, the by-election had an impact on Labour and Liberal Members too. Tory Members who lived in the division of St George's became directly involved when forty-five of them composed a letter of encouragement to Duff Cooper which was duly published in all the newspapers on 16 March. The only problem about this letter was that not *all* the Tory Members who were voters in St George's had signed it. Some were conveniently out of London,[28] but one – Sir William

---

[27] Baldwin Papers, Dawson to Baldwin, 17 Mar 1931.

[28] See Baldwin Papers, memorandum from Sir Patrick Gower to Sir Geoffrey Fry, 19 Mar 1931. It lists the MPs in St George's who definitely refused to sign a message of support to Duff Cooper. They were Commander Bellairs, N. Colman, Colonel Gretton, Sir Alfred Knox, Sir Basil Peto and R. Purbrick.

Wayland – actually went so far as to send a letter of support to Petter. The letter ran thus: '. . . We are in urgent need of men such as yourself in the House, men with independence of thought, will-power and moral courage, as an antidote to the sloppy sentimentalism and turn-the-other-cheek spirit which is all too prevalent today.' This caused a storm in Wayland's constituency of Canterbury, and both the president (Lord Cushendun) and the chairman of the local Conservative Association (Lord Fitzwalter) publicly condemned its Member's action. But the real surprise came from the Labour benches when the Member for South Derbyshire, Major Graham Pole, wrote to Duff Cooper thus: 'I intend to vote for you as will three others in my household. No one who respects the decencies of public life can approve of the scurrilous Press propaganda against Mr Baldwin, and the return of your opponent would be a calamity from the point of view of clean fighting in politics.' The standards of public decency which Harold Laski had invoked in a personal message to Baldwin before the Tory leader faced the party meeting of October 1930 had thus prompted a Labour Member to vote for the official Conservative, although the *Daily Herald* and the majority of Labour Members maintained the disdainful neutrality which they had shown throughout the campaign. Two Liberals followed Major Pole's example: H. J. Tennant, a former MP and the brother of Lady Oxford and Asquith, announced his support for Duff Cooper, as did Geoffrey Mander, the MP for Wolverhampton East. It seemed to the majority of onlookers that the campaign based on personality assassination had been counter-productive – insofar as the assassinated personality had been Baldwin. Perhaps Sir Ernest Petter's allies realised this – although they could have argued that Baldwin and Duff Cooper had been hurling as much abuse as anyone else – and the last days before polling saw a shift of emphasis to the Indian issue. The *Daily Mail* and *Evening News* had been featuring this issue by printing the slogans 'Gandhi is watching St George's' and 'Put Petter in and you put Gandhi out' in boxes throughout the papers during the election campaign. Beaverbrook was not too happy with this tactic for, although he knew that it was good propaganda and that the majority of the St George's electors read the

Beaverbrook–Rothermere press,[29] he felt that it broke the spirit, if not the letter, of the law governing election expenses.

Yet when polling day actually arrived, *The Times's* prediction that canvassing efficiency would be crucial was largely borne out; and Duff Cooper's organisation was superior to Petter's both in the efficiency of the original canvass and in getting the voters out on the day. Baldwin and his wife voted early in the morning and some 20 per cent of the voters had cast their preferences by midday. Although the rate fell off as the day wore on, the initial mood of excitement was sustained and then at six o'clock there was a great rush to the polls by residents on their way home from work. Odd spectacles could be seen throughout the day and the *Westminster and Pimlico News* waxed truly lyrical at the sight of 'master and man' going into the polls *together* – because the master had arrived in a chauffeur-driven car.

The Petter machine could only be described as erratic. At one point Ward Price became furious because he had just made a tour of the Pimlico area without seeing a single Petter car and had then come upon ten Petter cars standing idle in Chester Square. This was doubly irritating because Duff Cooper's cars had been making house-to-house calls all over the constituency while as yet Clinton had only managed to send for people who had definitely promised to vote for Petter. Ward Price telephoned Beaverbrook thus: 'Send a peremptory order to Clinton to send his cars to Pimlico making house-to-house calls. . . .' It was also imperative that the final canvassing and collecting of the Petter supporters should be done during the middle of the day because otherwise it might be impossible for them to leave their homes and workplaces – especially if they were domestic servants.

An hour before the poll closed, Lord Beaverbrook telephoned Lady Diana Cooper to tell her that on his reckoning Cooper had won. He then gave her a breakdown of how the polling had gone by polling district, and this estimate – as she later admitted[30] – turned out to be remarkably accurate. It is

[29] Newspaper circulation in St George's broke down as follows: *Daily Express*, 11,200; *Daily Mail*, 9,200; *Daily Chronicle*, 6,150; *Daily Herald*, 3,900; *Daily Telegraph*, 2,400; *The Times*, 2,100; *Morning Post*, 1,650 (Beaverbrook Papers).   [30] Lady Diana Cooper, *The Light of Common Day*.

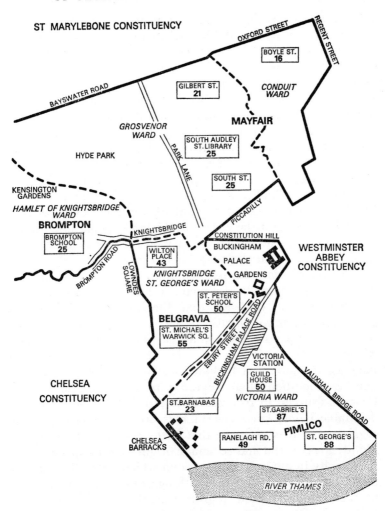

ST MARYLEBONE CONSTITUENCY

OXFORD STREET

REGENT STREET

BOYLE ST.
16

CONDUIT
WARD

BAYSWATER ROAD

GILBERT ST.
21

MAYFAIR

GROSVENOR
WARD

PARK LANE

SOUTH AUDLEY
ST. LIBRARY
25

HYDE PARK

SOUTH ST.
25

KENSINGTON
GARDENS

PICCADILLY

*HAMLET OF KNIGHTSBRIDGE
WARD*

BROMPTON

KNIGHTSBRIDGE

CONSTITUTION HILL

BROMPTON
SCHOOL
25

WILTON
PLACE
43

BUCKINGHAM

**WESTMINSTER
ABBEY
CONSTITUENCY**

BROMPTON ROAD

LOWNDES SQUARE

PALACE

*KNIGHTSBRIDGE
ST. GEORGE'S WARD*

GARDENS

ST. PETER'S
SCHOOL
50

BELGRAVIA

ST. MICHAEL'S
WARWICK SQ.
55

EBURY STREET

BUCKINGHAM PALACE ROAD

VICTORIA
STATION

**CHELSEA
CONSTITUENCY**

GUILD
HOUSE
50

VAUXHALL BRIDGE ROAD

ST. BARNABAS
23

VICTORIA WARD

ST. GABRIEL'S
87

PIMLICO

CHELSEA
BARRACKS

RANELAGH RD.
49

ST. GEORGE'S
88

RIVER THAMES

WESTMINSTER ST GEORGE'S BY-ELECTION
Percentage voting for Petter by polling station
(Beaverbrook's estimates)

difficult to say how Beaverbrook managed to predict the result so perceptively (see map), but when the result was declared it was found that Duff Cooper had won by almost 6,000 votes.

It is impossible to establish where the Petter votes came from with any certainty, but the Beaverbrook document prompts a number of speculations about the basis of the Empire Crusade's support. The constituency, although very wealthy, had a large pocket of poverty in the Pimlico area. In the period 1885–1910, before the Westminster St George's constituency was formed from St George's Hanover Square and Westminster, it was recognised that Pimlico with its prostitutes and immigrants was becoming 'increasingly disreputable', while the area between Victoria Street and the river was distinctly poor.[31] Sir Ernest Petter's son, who helped his father with the canvassing in 1931, records the fact that the 1929 Labour vote came largely from the Pimlico district with its predominantly Italian population of small shopkeepers, barrowmen and labourers.[32] The housing statistics provide evidence that the Victoria ward of the constituency was comparatively overcrowded. It is interesting to note that a measurement of housing pressure in London as a whole reveals that it was worst in three LCC boroughs – St Pancras, Islington and Paddington. Whether or not the poor housing conditions had anything to do with the Empire Crusade's success in Islington East and Paddington South is a debatable point; but Beaverbrook's breakdown of the voting suggests that it is probable that Petter's supporters were of a slightly lower social and economic origin than Cooper's. There is difficulty in analysing information which, in addition to the normal difficulties associated with aggregate data, is impaired by the very low turnout registered at the by-election. Nevertheless, the figures do seem to reveal a distinct pattern. Petter received the overwhelming support of the voters in the poorest districts of the constituency which were towards the river and the Vauxhall Bridge Road. The only significant exception to

[31] See Henry Pelling, *The Social Geography of British Elections, 1885–1910* (1967).

[32] Gordon Petter is, however, of the opinion that his father alienated the Catholic vote in Pimlico by his refusal to support separate schools for the Catholic minority in Westminster (letter to the author, 27 Sep 1972).

the trend in this area is the St Barnabas polling district which was on the doorsteps of Chelsea barracks. Apart from the obvious appeal of Cooper with his war record and his experience in the War Office, the Conservative organisation was sufficiently well organised to bring many service voters and their wives back to London for the poll. Petter – who had difficulty in transporting electors who lived within the constituency – was unlikely to be able to convey them from Aldershot. Belgravia appears to be a transition area with the vote fairly evenly divided. The districts to the north around Mayfair were overwhelmingly pro-Cooper in character. It is important to note that this is the area which gave Erskine his support when, as an Independent with the backing of the Hanover Square Conservative Association and the Anti-Waste League, he successfully challenged the official Conservative candidate in 1921 and 1922. Petter, who had after all been a member of the equally right-wing National Party, might have been expected to enjoy some support from this area if the Empire Crusade appeal had been orthodox and right-wing. But its appeal was populist and Petter accordingly gathered in only some lower-middle- and working-class support together with a proportion of the protest vote which was unlikely to go to Cooper. The upper-middle classes and the aristocracy closed ranks in defence of the established order.

The impact of St George's

Duff Cooper's victory was widely interpreted as Baldwin's triumph. The Tory leader acknowledged his debt to the new Member for St George's by acting as one of his sponsors when he took his seat in the House of Commons. Those standards of public life so dear to all parties had, it seemed, been preserved from the attack mounted by impertinent outsiders who would not play the political game decently; the organ of the Establishment celebrated the result thus: 'St George's has done a good day's work for democracy and for the Press. Democracy must founder without newspapers to give it the facts along with the arguments. . . .' The *News Chronicle* declared in its leader that the influence of Rothermere and Beaverbrook was destroyed: '. . . the St George's election has ended in the decisive defeat of the Wicked Uncles and their unfortunate candidate.'

Those people mainly concerned with the election's implications for Indian policy were even more relieved by the result than those who disliked the growing power of the press barons. Undoubtedly, the use to which the problem of Indian constitutional advance had been put in the campaign was deleterious to British relations with India and could have had far-reaching repercussions, as a letter to the Indian politician Sir Tej Bahadur Sapru shows: 'Thank God the St George's scandal is over! It was a miserable business. India was wantonly dragged in by the reptile press in order to injure Baldwin. Fortunately the attempt did not succeed.'[33]

Beaverbrook was bitterly disappointed by the result in St George's but he thought that he had been forced to fight on the wrong issues. He was sure that the Empire Crusade ought to concentrate on the economic advantages of the policy of Empire Free Trade and ignore problems such as India which would only attract the elderly diehard vote. What Beaverbrook wanted was a programme which would attract votes from all parties. As he wrote shortly afterwards: 'The defeat is due to my own stupidity. It was wrong to fight on India and the leadership of the Conservative Party. The issue might have been the cause and cure of unemployment. On that platform we can turn and win Socialist and Liberal votes.'[34] A. J. P. Taylor implicitly rejects this thesis, but the somewhat fragmentary evidence that exists at least invites an open mind on this issue. Beaverbrook never really got another chance to test the truth of his opinion before the formation of a National Government in August 1931 altered the whole basis of British political life – at least until 1945. Beaverbrook took what he could from the Stornoway Pact and continued to encourage the formation of local Empire Crusade groups in the Home Counties, but his enthusiasm had waned. Although St George's formed its own Empire Crusade group shortly after the by-election, the constituency had declared that the movement would never again be of national significance.

What, then, can be said of St George's in retrospect? Clearly,

[33] Sapru Papers, Polak to Sapru, 23 Mar 1931.
[34] Quoted in Taylor, *Beaverbrook*, p. 305.

it was soon forgotten despite the tremendous build-up it had received in the press prior to polling day. Indeed, the claims made for it at the time look somewhat ludicrous now. To be sure, it *had* killed the Empire Crusade, but whether the voters of St George's ever really grasped the policies at issue is open to doubt; it is much more likely that those who supported Petter in St George's – like those who voted for the Empire Free Trade candidate in Islington and Paddington – were expressing a vague feeling of dissatisfaction with the state of parliamentary politics at the time. And an analysis of this 'protest vote' suggests that Beaverbrook might well have improved his position had he carried on his campaign on the lines which *he* envisaged rather than on those dictated by Rothermere. St George's certainly saved Baldwin from immediate disaster, but it hardly ensured him a tranquil future. India loomed on the horizon as an issue which would have to be handled with as much care as the tariff question; but it is probably fair to say that if Baldwin had been defeated at St George's, there would probably have been no revolt over India simply because it is unlikely that any other leader would have felt so personally committed to a liberal policy as to risk splitting his party over it. As for saving Britain from press dictatorship, the impact of St George's was more apparent than real; all it decided in that respect was that such influence as existed would be exerted from Printing House Square. And that perhaps, in a curious way, points to the real significance of St George's. For above all it was a victory for the Establishment and a victory for the *status quo*. It was incidentally also a victory for the forces of moderation in British public life. British politics might have been totally shattered by the slump and a new kind of party might have emerged from the flux; St George's proved that the conventional party machines and the Establishment were still strong enough to resist attack, and crushed one of the figures who might have made such an attack successfully. Baldwin was able to take a reasonably united party with him into a Coalition Government just five months after the by-election. It is conceivable that if St George's had voted differently, there might have been no National Government, no Government of India Act and no Conservative Party as we know it today.

BIBLIOGRAPHICAL NOTE

The material contained in the Beaverbrook Papers in the Beaverbrook Library, London, is a rich source of information about the Empire Crusade and about its founder. The Baldwin Papers in the University Library, Cambridge, provide details about the effect which the Crusade and its supporters had on the Conservative Party at the time as well as giving an insight into Baldwin's personal view of these events.

Material about the constituency itself is to be found in the Worthington-Evans Papers and in the very full records of the St George's Westminster Constituency Association. The Worthington-Evans Papers have recently been given to the Bodleian Library, Oxford, while the St George's records are now deposited in the Westminster Central Library, London.

For the press account of the by-election and its prelude, I have relied heavily upon the *Westminster and Pimlico Gazette*, *The Times*, the *Daily Express*, the *Daily Mail* and the *Daily Herald*. All newspapers and periodicals dealing with current affairs and British political developments naturally commented upon Baldwin's difficulties and the Empire Free Trade movement; similarly it is possible to find reference to these events in the records of a number of other public figures of the period. The Salisbury Papers at Hatfield House, the Sapru Papers on microfilm in the Centre for South Asian Studies, Cambridge, the Halifax Papers in the India Office Library and the Davidson Papers in the Beaverbrook Library are particularly valuable in this respect and for the background material which they contain.

Note: 1931 to 1939

By JOHN RAMSDEN

In the 1931 general election the new National Government was given a more overwhelming vote of confidence and Labour suffered a more comprehensive defeat than either had thought possible. Labour lost 215 seats and the National Government was returned to power with the support of 521 MPs out of 615. But the result was much less clear than the figures suggest, mainly because the composition of the government itself was to change. During the 1931 general election it included all prominent Liberals except Lloyd George, all prominent Conservatives except Churchill, and a number of ex-Labour leaders. After Snowden retired and MacDonald and Thomas were seen to represent little but themselves, the National Labour element in the government was less impressive than it had been in 1931.[1]

However, the major problem of interpretation is provided by the Liberals; the National Government was originally supported by almost all Liberal MPs and seems to have been supported by most Liberal voters in 1931. Only in about a quarter of the constituencies was there a Liberal candidate in 1931, and these fought the election as three teams rather than as one. Subsequently, the Liberal Nationals ('Simonites') remained in the government, while the other Liberals ('Samuelites' and Lloyd George's personal following) gradually disconnected themselves. It was therefore to be expected that Liberal support for the National Government would be less consistent in by-elections than it had been in 1931, but that it would fall away at different rates in different places. If leading

[1] In the 1931 general election MacDonald spoke of Labour 'betraying' the national interest and Snowden attacked his late colleagues with great bitterness. There is little doubt that this was a great electoral asset to the National Government, as described below.

local Liberals were 'Samuelites', then support might fall away rapidly, but if they were 'Simonites', local Liberals would remain loyal to the government. This sporadic pattern would also reflect the concerns of Liberals with the topical issues of the day, especially where they related directly to Liberal priorities, such as free trade or international co-operation. In 1931 Liberal voters had had to make a second-best choice in order to save the country from economic disaster; it was to be expected that their Liberalism would reassert itself as the determinant of their vote, but as long as the party was in confusion, their reaction would also be confused. The pattern would not be regular, in any geographical or chronological sense, but would reflect the real confusion that traditionally Liberal voters felt in a post-Liberal world. This would not of course preclude the Liberal voters in an individual constituency from moving overwhelmingly against the government if they were convinced that a real Liberal principle was at stake.[2] However, there appears to have been a general tendency for Liberals to move into opposition to the National Government, just as Liberal MPs were doing at Westminster. This can be shown by looking at seats which had had Liberal candidates in the 1929 general election. If 1929 is taken as the base, then the by-elections of 1932–4 can be measured to show whether the withdrawal of Liberal candidates helped either government or opposition. There were 24 such elections in 1932–4, and these show an interesting variation: in contests from which the Liberal withdrew, there was a mean swing to Labour of just 0·1 per cent, but when Liberals put forward a candidate for the by-election, there was a swing to the Conservatives of 1·8 per cent. There was thus an apparent tendency for the withdrawal of Liberal candidates to help Labour in these years. The point can be pressed further by looking at the last six months of 1933, during which the Liberal Party actually moved into opposition at Westminster. The mean swings during that time were: when Liberals withdrew, 5·4 per cent to Labour, and when Liberals stood again, 1·8 per cent to the Conserva-

---

[2] See below, p. 124–6, for a consideration of how Liberal voters reacted at East Fulham. The concept of a block of ex-Liberal voters in the 1930s is discussed in D. E. Butler and D. Stokes, *Political Change in Britain* (1969) pp. 249–74.

tives. The defection of Liberal supporters who had voted solidly for the National Government in 1931 may therefore be the major explanation for the governments' decreasing votes in 1933 and 1934.

Not only had the government done outstandingly well in 1931, but Labour had also done very badly. Most of the gains can be explained by the maximisation of Conservative and Liberal votes in favour of the government, but it is also clear that many Labour voters abstained, for the total Labour vote dropped by 1¾ million. The shock of Labour's sudden disappearance from power and the appearance of Snowden and MacDonald on the hustings attacking their late colleagues provide an adequate explanation for this. But it meant that, unlike the National Government, which had surely polled its maximum possible vote in 1931, Labour had some ground to make up. Time would cool fears that Labour had betrayed the nation in 1931, and time would therefore bring at least some Labour resurgence.

Indeed, some contemporaries expected that the extreme nature of the 1931 result would make government losses inevitable. This in itself suggests an equilibrium view of the party system, whereby any violent lurch would be followed by a compensating reaction. Thus, barely a week after the biggest general election win on record, Baldwin was warning the Conservative Party that great efforts would be needed if they were to retain some of the unlikely gains that they had made. The tone of his address suggested that the size of his victory was more an embarrassment than a cause for rejoicing; he warned his party not to be surprised if seats were lost, and clearly expected that they would be.[3] There was no particular reason why a government with a large majority should lose a large number of by-elections, but this had happened in 1900, 1906, 1918 and 1924.[4] Nor was it only the actual size of the government's majority which gave cause for alarm, but also the way in which the majority had been achieved. By going to the

[3] Conservative Party National Union Minutes at Conservative Central Office, meeting of Executive Committee, 4 Nov 1931.

[4] It also occurred to governments with large majorities in 1931, 1935, 1959 and 1966. The apparent exception is 1945, which is discussed on pp. 191–2 below.

country as a combination of parties which was asking for a 'doctor's mandate', they were hoping to place the National Government securely above the old party battle-cries. On that platform, they had succeeded completely, but their very success made them more than usually vulnerable to the charge that by-elections lost would indicate the loss of popular support. As a National Government, their credibility depended much more on popular backing than a normal party government requires: if it was everyone's government, it was also no one's government, for the normal constraints of party loyalty would not apply. It is against this yardstick that East Fulham and Baldwin's desperate search for a rearmament mandate should be measured.

East Fulham was in fact the fourth seat which Labour gained from the National Government, but the first which could not have been anticipated in the aftermath of 1931. A. L. Rowse later described it as the loss by the government of just one of the 500 seats which they had won in 1931, and therefore a result of no significance at all.[5] But East Fulham was also the loss – by a large margin – of a seat which no Conservative had ever lost before, and in a straight fight with Labour. It was not important for itself, but because of the view that it had been caused by pacifism, and because of the implications which it suggested for other seats. This is an interesting comment on the changed expectations of governments since 1922: the Lloyd George government had regarded any loss as a serious blow, but the National Government woke up to its unpopularity only when it lost a seat which it regarded as rightfully its own. It was a sign that the 'new politics' was establishing itself that the Conservatives could regard some seats as hopeless and others as almost invulnerable. It was when an apparently invulnerable seat was lost at East Fulham that the panic set in. The spectre of 1931-scale rout, in reverse, was raised.[6]

Throughout 1933 and 1934 the National Government lost more seats to Labour and suffered large adverse swings. Plenty of explanations have been suggested: economic troubles and

[5] A. L. Rowse, 'Reflections on Lord Baldwin', in *The End of an Epoch* (1947) p. 86.

[6] The concept of the 'new politics' is described on pp. 19–20 above.

unemployment, housing, the means test, and increasing concern about foreign affairs. Labour's optimism and the Conservatives' despair both grew as Hammersmith North, Upton, Lambeth North, Swindon and West Toxteth all changed hands. Only in mid-1935 did the government begin to recover; at last they justified their existence by producing an economic recovery and at last foreign affairs became an advantage rather than a hindrance to them. Lord Bayford noted on 21 April 1935:

> Till quite lately things have been going badly for the Govt. The peace propaganda undoubtedly did them harm. . . . But the greatest point in the Govt's favour has been Hitler's declaration as to German rearmament. Bobby Monsell told me Hitler made his increased estimates for the Navy quite easy to obtain. I never knew our Central Office people so rattled as they were in February. They looked on no seat as safe.[7]

East Fulham was the only justification for such panic; it was the only traditionally Conservative seat which was lost to Labour in a representative contest throughout the 1930s. Thus, although they had approached the 1931 Parliament with a realistic view of the situation and a belief that losses were likely, the Conservatives ended in a blind panic when their expectations were realised. The Government really did no worse than might have been expected; it lost only 9 of the 48 government seats which fell vacant. However, an additional cause for concern was the small margins by which the other 39 were held. Here too the results were distorted by the government's victory in 1931; for no period of any length did they suffer swings which would have put Labour into power at a general election. Only East Fulham and Liverpool Wavertree of Labour's gains had not been won by Labour in 1929 (when Labour had *not* won a parliamentary majority), and these

[7] J. A. Ramsden (ed.), *The Diaries of Sir Robert Sanders, Lord Bayford* (forthcoming). Bayford had been Deputy Chairman of the Conservative Party during the Coalition Government and had a long-standing involvement in Central Office; Sir Bolton Eyres-Monsell was First Lord of the Admiralty and had previously been Chief Whip. Both of them therefore knew the mood of the party over several years.

were both wildly untypical. In some constituencies the Conservatives did worse than in 1929, but in others, such as Skipton, they did better.

What, then, is the explanation for the government's performance? The most likely hypothesis again concerns the votes of Liberals and others who were not committed to Labour or Conservative. Most of these had voted for the National Government in 1931 or had at least withheld their votes from Labour, but a by-election presented them with a different kind of choice. In 1931 the only issue was whether *in principle* there should be a National Government; at by-elections after 1931 voters could express their dissatisfaction with government policies, without worrying about alternatives. Nor was this attitude confined only to Liberal and uncommitted voters, but was shared equally by Conservatives. Over the issue of India, the right wing of the Conservative Party kept up an unceasing barrage of criticism of the National Government. When they had failed to reverse government policy through the House of Commons or through the party, they somewhat belatedly appealed to the electorate. In February 1935 Randolph Churchill contested Liverpool Wavertree as an Independent Conservative opposed to the government's India policy. By splitting the Conservative vote he let Labour in, and a month later he supported another Independent Conservative at Lambeth Norwood. In November 1935 Churchill was an official Conservative and National Government candidate at the general election, in Liverpool West Toxteth – right next door to the seat which he had handed over to Labour in February. By February 1936 he was a rebel again, standing against Malcolm MacDonald at Ross and Cromarty. It is not entirely fanciful to see Randolph Churchill's antics as symbolic: he was prepared to intervene at by-elections to influence government policy so long as the fate of his party or of the government was not at stake. When a general election was called, he came back into line, and surely many voters must have acted similarly. The losses of East Fulham and Wavertree were keenly felt, but it was less widely reported that the government had won both seats back without difficulty in the 1935 general election. Of the other seats which it had lost to Labour, only Swindon was regained (by 975 votes). It can thus be argued that two distinct trends had emerged: on the one hand, Labour was winning back support which it had lost in 1931, and which it would now expect to retain; on the other hand, the National Government was generating protest votes which would disappear as soon as its survival was in doubt.

The ease with which the government retained power in 1935 seems to have devalued by-elections as political indicators. The government's worst fears had proved to be groundless in 1934–5, so perhaps they were determined not to be led astray again. The government lost more seats during 1935–9 than during its first term of office, but these losses never made the same impact and the mean swing did not reach the same level as in 1934. Once again, the gradual recovery of the economy and the reduction of unemployment provides the best single explanation. However, the same factors applied as before 1935: the government had been re-elected with a quite unspecific programme and so individual by-elections could be treated as referenda on particular aspects of government policy. In the context of the late 1930s, this inevitably meant that foreign affairs became a major issue. Oxford and Bridgwater were not just by-elections which happened to take place soon after the Munich settlement: they were the 'Munich by-elections'.

This period, for the first time, did not consider by-elections in complete isolation. The first opinion polls were being taken and the British Institute of Public Opinion was founded in 1937. Gallup began a regular series of surveys on Britain and Tom Harrisson founded Mass-Observation.[8] These were all different in style and in reliability – Gallup was self-consciously scientific, while Mass-Observation was basically impressionistic – but they all shared the same concern, which was to find out reliably and in detail what the public were thinking. They may have seen by-elections, the traditional indicator of public mood, as more suspect than before, but they were certainly influenced by the increasing use of public opinion as a political force. The League of Nations Union had organised the 'Peace Ballot' in 1934–5 in order to mobilise opinion against re-armament; the public outcry had driven Sir Samuel Hoare from office in 1935 after the Hoare–Laval Pact, and Baldwin

[8] See T. Harrisson and C. Madge (eds.), *Britain, by Mass-Observation* (1939), and Hadley Cantril, *Public Opinion, 1935–1946* (Princeton, 1951).

had made a masterly use of public feeling during the Abdication crisis.[9] If the public and its views were to be so directly consulted, then it was at least desirable that those views should be reported accurately. The crude medium of by-election results therefore became merely a secondary political pointer instead of the only one. Instead of by-elections being used to interpret public opinion, public opinion – as measured in opinion polls – would henceforth be used to interpret by-election results, and even to predict results in advance. It was to be several years and several general elections correctly predicted before opinion polls became predominant, but the trend began in the late 1930s.[10]

Overall, the pattern of results in 1935–9 was not unlike that of 1931–5; Labour gained 13 seats from the government, but only one of these (Greenock) had not been held by Labour before. There were some big swings to Labour, but never big enough to suggest an overall Labour majority.[11] In only 3 of their 13 gains did Labour win by a margin which implied a parliamentary majority, and in no year did the mean swing reach that level. Once again, the government was caused discomfort by the intervention of Independent Conservatives. This time there were no such interventions in seats which could be lost to Labour, but the public was treated to the rare spectacle of unpredictable and possibly close contests in Kinross and West Perthshire, and in Cheltenham. However, foreshadowing the disasters of 1943 or 1944 and recalling the dark days of 1934 were the interventions from Independents of the Left. These were at Combined English Universities in 1937 and then at Oxford City and at Bridgwater in 1938, described in Chapter 6 below.[12]

[9] During the Abdication crisis the mood of MPs changed dramatically over one crucial weekend. Baldwin said: 'I have always believed in the weekend. But how they do it I don't know. I suppose they talk to the stationmaster.' G. M. Young, *Stanley Baldwin* (1952) p. 242.

[10] Gallup began regular surveys in Britain in 1938, but were not the first in the field. A poll conducted by Harrods among its customers in 1924 was surprisingly successful, and magazines had also tried to predict general elections. However, it was only after the failure of the *Literary Digest* in the 1936 presidential election that the need for proper sampling methods was recognised.

[11] D. E. Butler, *The Electoral System in Britain* (1953 ed.) p. 184.

[12] The Universities had a tradition of electing Independents, so it was not until Oxford that much attention was paid to this. The comparison

The common theme of all by-elections in the 1930s is the fact that many electors did not much like what the National Government was doing, although they did not of course all dislike the same things. Conversely, there was never during the inter-war years a majority of electors who favoured a Labour Government, and since that was the only alternative to a National Government in the 1930s, by-elections and general elections showed considerable differences. However, it was only when there were extreme circumstances (East Fulham) or a split Conservative vote (Liverpool Wavertree) that the National Government was in any real danger from Labour. It was only when an official or unofficial man of the Left was able to win *more* votes than a normal Labour candidate could do (Oxford or Bridgwater) that real difficulties arose, but then only at by-elections and not at general elections. That is the background to the by-elections of 1943–5, in which the basic political equilibrium of the 1930s was shattered.

---

with 1934 and 1943–5 is because it was only at those times that the government was threatened by candidates who could poll more than the maximum Labour vote, as in 1938.

5 Interpreting East Fulham

By MARTIN CEADEL

General Election, *1929*		(Electorate 51,066)
Vaughan-Morgan (Con.)	15,130	*(44·4)*
Palmer (Lab.)	13,425	*(39·4)*
Greenwood (Lib.)	5,551	*(16·3)*
Con. majority	1,705	Turnout 66·8%

General Election, *1931*		(Electorate 51,688)
Vaughan-Morgan (Con.)	23,438	*(68·7)*
Maynard (Lab.)	8,917	*(26·1)*
Greenwood (Lib.)	1,788	*(5·2)*
Con. majority	14,521	Turnout 66·1%

By-Election, *25 Oct 1933*		(Electorate 51,642)
Wilmot (Lab.)	17,790	*(57·9)*
Waldron (Con.)	12,950	*(42·1)*
Lab. majority	4,840	Turnout 59·5%

General Election, *1935*		(Electorate 50,682)
Astor (Con.)	18,743	*(51·4)*
Wilmot (Lab.)	17,689	*(48·6)*
Con. majority	1,054	Turnout 71·9%

The East Fulham by-election of 25 October 1933 has aroused
more controversy than any other. Caused by the death in
August 1933 of Sir Kenyon Vaughan-Morgan, the Conservative who had held the seat since 1922, it was won dramatically
two months later by Labour on a turnover of over 19,000 votes
and a swing of 29·1 per cent. But it was not merely as a spec-

tacular electoral upset that the result at East Fulham became controversial. It was cited as an indicator of the popular pacifism which delayed the National Government's rearmament programme, and it therefore became notorious as a political symbol of the locust years – the vital early years of the Hitler regime – during which Baldwin and MacDonald failed to build up adequate national defences. More recently, the by-election has become a matter of dispute among historians who have disagreed over the issues which the result reflected, despite subjecting the campaign at East Fulham to the minutest scrutiny.[1] This account will therefore seek not to retell the details of the campaign, but to answer three questions of interpretation which lie at the heart of the East Fulham controversy. Why did East Fulham become a political myth? What was the decisive issue or issues which determined the result? And what was the contemporary impact of the result?

1. *The political myth*

That East Fulham achieved political notoriety was a demonstration of the speed with which conditions in the 1930s changed, rendering obsolete and ludicrous attitudes and positions which had seemed sensible in the previous context. East Fulham, on 25 October 1933, was the first, most dramatic, and the only actual government loss among six bad by-election results within five weeks. It occurred at a time when the National Government faced major problems both domestically and internationally. The domestic problems were the social effects of the economic crisis: unemployment and cuts in the social services. The international problems arose from the growing threat posed by the nine-month-old Nazi regime to the peace of Europe, for which the success of the World Disarmament Conference that had been sitting at Geneva since February of the previous year was seen to be crucial.

During the three years it took for East Fulham to become the centre of political controversy, the situation changed. There was a measure of economic recovery, but all prospects of

[1] For the historiography of East Fulham, see the Bibliographical Note at the end of the chapter, but I should like here to acknowledge my particular debt to the work of Mr C. T. Stannage and Mr R. Heller.

disarmament faded and an arms race had begun. The most vocal criticisms of government defence and foreign policy were no longer those of militaristic warmongering but of inadequate vigilance and determination. It was while defending the government's rearmament programme in the Commons on 12 November 1936 that Stanley Baldwin invoked East Fulham and thereby ensured it political immortality. In reply to Winston Churchill's criticisms, he explained: 'We started late, and I want to say a word about the years the locusts have eaten.' These were the years 1933–4 when Baldwin, not yet (until June 1935) Prime Minister, had nevertheless been the most powerful man in the government. He went on, in what was to become one of the most notorious speeches of the decade:

> I put before the whole House my own views with an appalling frankness. From 1933, I and my friends were all very worried about what was happening in Europe. You will remember at that time the Disarmament Conference was sitting in Geneva. You will remember at that time there was probably a stronger pacifist feeling running through this country than at any time since the War. I am speaking of 1933 and 1934. You will remember the election at Fulham in the autumn of 1933, when a seat which the National Government held was lost by about 7,000 [sic] votes on no issue but the pacifist. You will remember perhaps that the National Government candidate who made a most guarded reference to the question of defence was mobbed for it.

The accuracy or otherwise of Baldwin's interpretation of the issues at East Fulham, which now interests historians, received less attention than did the implications of what Baldwin went on to say:

> That was the feeling in the country in 1933. My position as the leader of a great party was not altogether a comfortable one. I asked myself what chance was there – when that feeling that was given expression to in Fulham was common thoughout the country – what chance was there within the next year or two of that feeling being so changed that the country would give a mandate for rearmament? Supposing I had gone to the country and said that Germany was re-

arming and that we must rearm, does anybody think that this pacific democracy would have rallied to that cry at that moment? I cannot think of anything that would have made the loss of the election from my point of view more certain.

Four years later, in war-time when circumstances had once more dramatically altered, this unfortunately worded admission came to be quoted as part of the mounting indictment of Baldwin's inadequate leadership. With Churchill as Prime Minister of a Coalition Government unable to prevent the British Expeditionary Force being driven into the sea or the fall of France, ex-appeasers, Conservative anti-appeasers and the Labour Party found unity in a time of national crisis by agreeing to condemn Baldwin for the country's unpreparedness.

The fact of Baldwin's negligence was not discussed, merely the degree of his culpability. In his influential indictment of the National Government written in the immediate aftermath of Dunkirk, 'Cato' (Michael Foot) misdated the East Fulham by-election into 1935 and interpreted Baldwin's remarks about the loss of an election to refer to the 1935 general election.[2] Baldwin therefore stood accused of failing to alert the British people to the need for rearmament as late as November 1935. This error was compounded by Hamilton Fyfe in an article in 1941 which bowdlerised (and misdated) the 12 November 1936 speech so as to put into Baldwin's mouth an admission of having failed to inform the country of German rearmament explicitly in the 1935 election. Fyfe's article had been on 'Leadership and Democracy',[3] and the mistaken reference to 1935 crept even into constitutional textbooks as a stock illustration of when representative government should not defer to the general will.[4]

It was not until 1948 that R. Bassett put the record straight

---

[2] 'Cato', *Guilty Men* (1940) pp. 31, 37. By the end of 1940 the book had run through 27 impressions in which the misdating of East Fulham was corrected but not the implication about the 1935 general election. Foot's co-authors were Frank Owen and Peter Howard, and the publisher was Victor Gollancz.

[3] Hamilton Fyfe, 'Leadership and Democracy', *Nineteenth Century* (May 1941) p. 470.

[4] See W. Ivor Jennings, *The British Constitution* (1941) pp. 216–7.

by pointing out that Baldwin was referring to a hypothetical election in the years 1933–4.[5] On the outcome of such an election Baldwin's judgement had been anticipated less than three weeks previously by Hugh Dalton, who wrote in the *New Statesman*: 'When early in the life of the last Parliament John Wilmot won East Fulham, though his outstanding personal qualities swelled his majority, he proved that a tide was running which, had a General Election come soon after, might easily have carried us to victory.'[6] Yet Baldwin had so phrased his speech as to invite the charge of putting party before country. In the words of his official biographer, G. M. Young: 'Never I suppose in our history has a statesman used a phrase so fatal to his own good name, and at the same time so wholly unnecessary, so incomprehensible. One can think of half a dozen ways of ending that passage, all convincing and all true.'[7] Young's lack of sympathy with his subject has become notorious, but his impressionistic style evoked not a 'guilty' man but an inadequate one. The 'appalling frankness' speech was an incompetent admission rather than an admission of incompetence. Baldwin's cloudy and equivocal phraseology has made it hard to estimate the degree to which he sought a mandate for rearmament in the 1935 general election campaign itself.

Although the recent biography by Middlemas and Barnes has argued that he did explicitly seek such a mandate, earlier critics had argued that the notion of a mandate was irrelevant in a representative democracy. In the debate of 12 November 1936, Winston Churchill had argued that 'The responsibility of Ministers for the public safety is absolute and requires no mandate'. This remark was quoted approvingly in 1941 in A. L. Rowse's essay, 'Reflections on Lord Baldwin', which criticised Baldwin for failing to give public opinion the political leadership which the situation required and the apparently impregnable electoral position of the National Government facilitated. Churchill's remark was also quoted by C. L. Mowat in an article prompted by Young's biography which

---

[5] R. Bassett, 'Telling the Truth to the People', *Cambridge Journal* (Nov-1948) pp. 84–95.

[6] *New Statesman*, 24 Oct 1936, p. 617.

[7] G. M. Young, *Stanley Baldwin* (1952) p. 229.

added very little to Rowse's arguments.[8] Baldwin having died in 1947, East Fulham had exhausted itself as a source of political controversy by the middle of the affluent 1950s.

2. The campaign issues

The facts. The explosion of historical research in the 1960s meant that East Fulham was rediscovered as a source of problems to resolve, in particular the central problem of whether or not East Fulham had been 'lost in a wild flood of pacifism'.[9] Baldwin's view in 1936 that the election had been decided 'on no issue but the pacifist' had been accepted by his supporters and critics alike, but more recently it has been investigated by several historians, and in 1971 two detailed articles devoted entirely to the by-election appeared simultaneously. This historical activity has produced a fundamental division of opinion between those who regard the international situation as decisive, and those who believe that the domestic situation provides the explanation.

On many aspects of the election, however, all accounts are in agreement. For an indication of the political complexion of the constituency, which dated from 1918, the 1929 result was a better guide than the panic election of 1931.[10] Though the Conservatives had always held the seat, they were by 1929 closely challenged by Labour, with the Liberal vote holding the balance of power. Three factors contributed to the by-election result: Conservative abstention, a high turnout of Labour supporters, and a significant number of Liberals voting Labour.

This analysis is supported by the literary evidence, which is

[8] Rowse's article was reprinted in his *The End of An Epoch* (1947) pp. 77–89; C. L. Mowat, 'Baldwin Restored', *Journal of Modern History* (1955) pp. 169–74.

[9] Young, *Stanley Baldwin*, p. 177.

[10] The figures for 1929, 1931 and 1933 are printed at the beginning of the chapter. Comparing 1933 with 1929, the Conservative vote fell by 2,180 (a 2·3 per cent fall in their share of the vote); the Labour vote increased by 4,365 (18·5 per cent); the Liberals, who in 1929 had polled 5,551 votes (16·3 per cent), failed to put up a candidate in 1933. Numbers voting fell by 3,366, but the electorate had increased by only 576 (1·1 per cent) over the four years.

surprisingly clear-cut. All accounts agree that East Fulham is an extreme case of a disastrous candidate with a weak organisation being defeated by an outstanding one with strong support. To start with the Conservatives, their adoption of Alderman W. J. Waldron as candidate had occasioned considerable in-fighting among a local party organisation of acknowledged weakness, and his diehard views on India meant he had only half-hearted support from Central Office. Lacking the personal popularity of his predecessor who had held the seat for the five previous contests, Waldron had nevertheless been Mayor of Fulham six times in the 1920s, but, far from being a source of political strength, it identified him as responsible for imposing wage cuts on the borough council staff in 1931. As a local property-owner he was on the defensive over the housing problem. His campaign fared badly, culminating in the tactical blunder of a 'smear' leaflet about his opponent which completely rebounded.

The Labour candidate, John Wilmot, was, at the age of thirty-eight, nineteen years younger than his opponent but of equal political experience. His organisation was helped by nearby constituencies, including Kennington where he lived. The organiser of the London Labour Party acted as his agent, and the party's national organisation, untroubled by any policy divisions, sent their leader, George Lansbury, plus J. R. Clynes, Hugh Dalton, Herbert Morrison, A. V. Alexander, Arthur Greenwood and others to speak for Wilmot. It was Wilmot who took the initiative in the campaign, branding his opponent as a warmonger, and making a personal investigation of the housing situation in the borough, contrasting his findings with the plans of the Tory council. Waldron's attempt to wrest the initiative from Wilmot had been to 'smear' him with his involvement with a local Shareholders Provident Association, which Waldron claimed was inconsistent with his professed Socialism. But since the association was known to protect the small investor against fraudulent company promoters, it was a source of political strength – not least among middle-class voters – for Wilmot, who made his career in banking and later in business.

This raises the question of the Liberal vote. The Liberal Association had maintained its organisation and contested every previous election except 1924. Although its 5,551 votes in 1929 had slumped to 1,788 in the crisis election of 1931, Wilmot believed Liberalism to be a force worth courting. He advocated free trade and electoral reform, and over the question of India he claimed his opposition to Waldron's diehard stance to be in the best Liberal tradition of Campbell-Bannerman. Waldron's chances of winning Liberal support were slender, since the tide of Liberal opinion was moving away from the National Government. In 1931 the Liberals had 'agreed to differ' on the question of protection, but after the Ottawa Conference the Liberal Ministers had resigned in September 1932, although they continued to sit on the government benches. In response to pressure in the National Liberal Federation they were to cross over, in November 1933, on to the opposition benches, leaving only the Simonite Liberal Nationals in the administration. There was no Simonite organisation in East Fulham, and indeed throughout the campaign Sir John Simon was playing an unhappy role in the international crisis which broke during the campaign. Since the Great War, foreign affairs, and in particular support for the League of Nations, had become one of the two major areas of Liberal interest, and as the economic depression made free trade seem an unrealistic ideal, internationalism became the predominant Liberal preoccupation. Waldron actually attacked the League of Nations, to which most Conservatives were careful to pay lip-service. Therefore it was scarcely a surprise when, having sent a questionnaire to both candidates about their attitudes to matters of interest to Liberals, the Liberal Association announced a week before polling day that 'The replies of the two candidates having been received and considered, the Association, regarding the question of disarmament as of vital importance, recommends all Liberal voters to give Mr Wilmot their support'. The former Liberal candidate, J. H. Greenwood, joined Wilmot on his platforms to speak on disarmament, leaving Wilmot to deal with food prices and housing. The *Times* reporter, basing his calculations on the assumption that the Liberals would divide evenly, underestimated Wilmot's vote which was over 4,000 higher than the best previous Labour vote. A case can thus be made for hypothesising that Liberalism was still a recognisable political entity in Fulham, and that in 1933 it largely supported Wilmot, mostly because of the disarmament question.

Where no opinion polls exist to provide additional evidence, all descriptions and explanations of electoral behaviour must necessarily be hypothetical and approximate. It is here argued that the most plausible such explanation of East Fulham was that Waldron failed to turn out all the Conservative voters, whereas Wilmot succeeded in mobilising the maximum Labour vote. Waldron was a poor candidate in a difficult political situation, whereas Wilmot possessed all the qualities necessary to exploit grievances against the National Government. In addition, Wilmot was able to mobilise a significant majority of Liberals on the disarmament question. In this sense it can be argued that the disarmament issue was decisive.

But when looking for the 'decisive' factor, most historians have sought, not an explanation in terms of influence on a marginal group of floating voters, in this case ex-Liberals, but for an issue which predominantly influenced all voters. In seeking this their methodology has approached that of a literary content analysis of the manifestoes and local press reports, on the implicit assumption that the significance of an issue is related to the number of references to it, with some weighting given to statements made near polling day. In the case of East Fulham this method has produced basic disagreement, and social and foreign policy questions were much discussed in a campaign which took place at a time of economic depression and international crisis. The evidence for each of these two schools of thought must be examined in turn.

Domestic issues. Three days after the election, Neville Chamberlain wrote to his sister Ida:

> Fulham made the PM very miserable but I confess I did not lose a minute's sleep over it. The press put it all down to Housing and lies about War. Both no doubt were factors but I heard yesterday from a friend who had been talking to a speaker (street corner) from Fulham what I had all along suspected, that the real attack was on the means test.[11]

This view is quoted by A. J. P. Taylor, who notes in his volume of the Oxford History that 'later investigation has confirmed

[11] Iain Macleod, *Neville Chamberlain* (1961) p. 177.

this judgement'.[12] But if there was a major social issue articulated during the campaign, it was undoubtedly the overcrowded housing conditions, which Wilmot 'muck-raked' with great effect. Waldron, who was tactically routed on this question, might have pointed out that 17 of London's 28 boroughs were more overcrowded than Fulham, although of course to argue that things were worse elsewhere did not mean that housing could not be an important factor at Fulham, since simultaneous by-elections in other London constituencies *might* have produced even greater anti-government votes.

Inadequate housing plans were a consequence of the government's policy of deflation, and by October 1933 the economic tide had turned, so that rising food prices were becoming a source of discontent. The other important domestic grievance was unemployment, and Waldron was able to point out that the number out of work in Fulham had been reduced since the start of the year from 6,086 to 4,487. London was less troubled than other areas and, within London, Fulham had a good employment record. Thus although an atmosphere of economic gloom persisted, conditions had improved steadily throughout the year, and it is hard to see that social conditions were as dominant in Fulham as they had been at Rotherham in February 1933, where the National Government had lost the seat on a 19·9 per cent swing. Social discontents were too deeply ingrained by the depression years for a Labour candidate to omit to exploit them, and they provided an appropriate stick with which to beat a local alderman and landlord. Nevertheless, by themselves they do not obviously explain why such a dramatic result should have occurred where and when it did.

Foreign issues. The argument that foreign affairs were the decisive issue provides an explanation not only for the National Government's poor by-election performance over the winter of 1933–4, but also for the fact that East Fulham was markedly the worst of those results. The World Disarmament Conference, which had been sitting at Geneva since February 1932 and on which hopes for European peace were seen increasingly to hang, was throughout 1933 in a state of continuous crisis. On 14

[12] A. J. P. Taylor, *English History, 1914–1945* (1965) p. 367.

October 1933, just eleven days before polling at East Fulham, the crisis broke and Germany withdrew from the Conference and from the League of Nations. This walk-out was timed to follow a speech at Geneva by Sir John Simon, the British Foreign Secretary, in which he outlined a new plan for progressive general disarmament down to the level already imposed on Germany by the Treaty of Versailles. Since Germany was already rearming illegally, this plan, agreed by Britain, France, the United States and Italy, was less favourable to Germany than a previous Draft Convention put forward by Britain in March 1933. Germany had already studied the plan before it was formally presented to the Disarmament Conference by Simon, and had decided in advance to withdraw. However, the timing of the German withdrawal looked as if it had been precipitated by the British Foreign Secretary going back on an earlier offer to Germany. This impression was confirmed by a talk by the popular radio commentator on international affairs, Vernon Bartlett, which was broadcast by the BBC on the evening of 14 October. Though Bartlett was five years later the anti-appeasement victor of the Bridgwater by-election, he was initially sympathetic to the international aspirations of the Nazi regime. His talk, which he later admitted was 'a very strong, if indirect, criticism' of the British Foreign Secretary, ended his career as a regular BBC staff broadcaster, though 90 per cent of the thousands of letters he received supported his views. His broadcast had been an early plea for appeasement, implying that Britain and France were the potential threats to peace: 'our behaviour during the next few weeks is going to decide the issue between a real peace and another war. . . . We can swallow a little of our pride and meet the German point of view. It is worth swallowing any amount of pride if peace is at stake; civilisation is more valuable than prestige.'[13] According to this analysis, any rearmament by Britain would be an unhelpful and provocative act.

Germany never returned either to the Disarmament Conference or to the League of Nations. John Wheeler-Bennett's judgement, made the following summer, has stood the test of time: 'October 14th, 1933, may well go down as one of the

[13] Vernon Bartlett, *This Is My Life* (1937) pp. 188–92; *Listener*, 18 Oct 1933, p. 570.

outstanding dates in European history, for on that day the second or Locarno period of post-war history came to an end; what may come forth from the period which then began is still thought of with fear and horror.'[14]

Interpretation. Where the quantity of discussion on any particular issue is not obviously preponderant, mere immersion in the terms of that discussion will not provide the answer as to which issue was decisive. Certain interpretative judgements must be made.

The first such point is methodological. How meaningful is it to expect a by-election result to be explicable in terms of a single issue? Modern work on electoral behaviour has undermined the nineteenth century's rationalist view of elections in terms of the voters listening to the evidence like a jury and delivering a verdict on the merits of the case. Voters vote in accordance with an overall image, compounded of habitual class and party loyalties as well as the issues of the moment. Yet historical by-elections are often still analysed as if they necessarily reflect a single predominant issue. At East Fulham the dichotomy of 'social' and 'foreign' issues, around which the historiography of the by-election has revolved, is a false one. Rather than being alternatives, they were often linked together. Thus, in the 1920s and the depression of the 1930s the 'Clydeside' group of MPs argued that in conditions of social deprivation the worker had nothing to lose by foreign invasion. That money spent on armaments should be reallocated to the social services was a popular justification for disarmament, but an East Fulham heckler asked Waldron: 'What's the use of putting up houses if they are going to be knocked down by bombs?' Marxist analysis, to which the depression years gave an opportunity for unprecedented influence and relevance, provided a common critique of social and international questions. But the predominant linking theme was hostility to the National Government which had betrayed the trust which the nation had placed in it in 1931. Action and reaction being equal and opposite, disillusion was extreme. Wilmot talked of the need to check Fascism in Britain, a line of thought which implied that militarism was the necessary concomitant of the

[14] John W. Wheeler-Bennett, *The Disarmament Deadlock* (1934) p. 181.

National Government's defence of the social and economic *status quo*, and illustrated the extent to which political trust had declined.

The context. In arguing that social and foreign policy questions were not mutually exclusive but different aspects of a widespread distrust of the National Government, the discussion has been widened from the election campaign itself to the general context of ideas and opinion. The importance of looking to the context of ideas to break the interpretative deadlock about the election is the second point that must be emphasised. This will, in a way that mere listing of references cannot, allow one to judge the relative emotional leverage of the various issues. It will be argued here that the impact of the peace question has been underestimated by historians impressed with the quantity of references to social issues. For example, in his article Heller describes as 'colourless' a message from Arthur Henderson urging the electors to vote Labour and avert another arms race. But Henderson, who had the previous month returned to Parliament at the Clay Cross by-election, was, as the President of the Disarmament Conference, at the peak of personal popularity, and Wilmot had commented on the importance of his message in an interview in the *Daily Herald* on 27 October 1933. Heller quotes two other messages, one by Wilmot and one by his wife, on the peace issue, describing the first as 'a studied piece of emotional ambiguity, a repeated invocation of the magic words Peace, League and Covenant', and the second as 'blatantly emotive'. But he fails to draw any conclusions as to why an intelligent, hard-headed and ultimately successful candidate should have resorted to such propaganda unless he believed it to be electorally efficacious. At East Fulham one candidate was branded as a warmonger, and a local paper, the *West London and Fulham Gazette*, wrote on 27 October that 'the masses were scared at the prospect of another European war, or the possibility – however remote – of Hitlerism gaining ground in this country'.

A knowledge of the background of ideas on war is necessary to explain this fear. In his speech to the House on 12 November 1936, Baldwin claimed that Waldron had 'made a most guarded reference to the question of defence'. But in 1933 the whole question of defence was a confused and highly emotive issue. Matters were poised on a knife-edge: if disarmament were not achieved then an arms race would result, for Nazi Germany was bent on securing equality with the victors of the Great War, so that if they did not at once disarm to her level, she would rearm to theirs. And it was an orthodoxy of the inter-war period that arms races led inevitably to war, the horrors of which had been painstakingly emphasised in order to gain support for the Disarmament Conference. On 29 November 1933 John Wilmot told the Commons that Lord Rothermere's *Daily Mail*, which was calling for massive and immediate air rearmament, was 'the principal organ, which represents – so nearly, as a rule – the opinions of the Government'. In such an atmosphere a 'guarded reference' to defence was impossible. Foreign affairs rarely interest voters simply because they rarely impinge on their daily existence. An air war was one drastic way in which foreign affairs could be brought home with a vengeance. The fear of war manifested at East Fulham was an unusual feature for an election campaign. It may therefore go far towards explaining an unusual result.

But how unusual was the East Fulham result when seen in the context of the other by-elections of 1933, and in particular of the 'little general election' of November 1933? 1933 produced several heavy swings against the government, but this was inevitable after the landslide of 1931, and in fact the little general election took place in seats which had swung more than average to the National Government in 1931. This is shown by comparing the 1933 by-election performances with both the 1931 and the 1929 general elections.[15] East Fulham stands out from contemporary by-election results which show a reasonably uniform reaction against 1931, and especially against 1929. It

[15] Average government (i.e. Conservative) share of vote in 1933 compared with 1929 and 1931:

	1929	*1931*
By-elections, Jan–Sep 1933	+6·2	− 15·5*
East Fulham, 25 Oct 1933	− 2·3	− 26·6
By-elections, Nov 1933	+6·2	− 22·9

* Excluding East Fife and Altrincham, where there were no contests in 1931.

must be pointed out, however, that in an age that was innocent of the concept of 'swing' for comparing electoral performances, it was above all when a seat changed hands that contemporaries were impressed. This helps to explain why a 26·9 per cent swing at Putney in November 1934, which the National Government survived, attracted little attention.

The 1933 by-elections showed that, although the slump was still a cause for concern, the peace issue replaced it as the Labour Party's trump card. The peace question was a less 'objective' or predictable determinant of electoral behaviour than were economic conditions, since a crisis atmosphere depended on the vagaries of the international situation and on the ability of the candidate to exploit them. The first 'peace' by-election had been at Clay Cross on 1 September 1933, when, however, Arthur Henderson's official position as President of the Disarmament Conference prevented him from attacking the government. There were no such inhibitions at East Fulham, where the German withdrawal from the Conference and from the League, and the contrasting talents and views of the candidates, provided additional emotional fuel. The peace question continued to play a considerable role in the five by-elections of November 1933, as Dr Kyba has shown. John Wilmot visited Kilmarnock to speak for the Revd James Barr, who as MP for Motherwell from 1924 to 1931 had supported unilateral disarmament motions in Parliament and was later to be a sponsor of the Peace Pledge Union. At Skipton the Labour candidate claimed to be a pacifist. At Rusholme, Rutland and Harborough the Labour candidates all talked emotively of the horror of the next war, and claimed that Labour was the only peace party.

But even if it is conceded that the interesting factor about East Fulham was the crisis atmosphere about the 'peace' question, was it therefore, as Baldwin claimed, a 'pacifist' by-election? Both Heller and Stannage agree that, however important were the questions of disarmament, the future of the League of Nations, the foreign policy of the National Government and fear of war, these did not amount to pacifism. But although we can now see a distinction between these questions and a statement of pacifism, this distinction was hard to recognise in 1933.

The problem is partly semantic. The word 'pacifism' changed its meaning during the inter-war period. When first coined in the first decade of the century it meant simply being in favour of peace and arbitration rather than of militarism. With the development of anti-war feeling in the late 1920s to the point where almost no one would admit to being a militarist, the word became too vague to be helpful since we were 'all pacifists now'. The peace movement no longer needed to change people's attitude to war; what was required was to harness anti-war feeling into an effective method of war prevention. There were several alternative methods advocated by different sections of the peace movement. One of these, the technique of non-resistance and personal refusal to bear arms, which was historically associated with the Quakers, was described as 'pacifism'. This particular meaning has taken over from the general meaning as the primary one, but in 1933 there was no primary sense. Instead there was linguistic confusion which reflected intellectual confusion.

The peace movement tended to view non-resistance, support for the League of Nations and revolutionary pacifism as complementary rather than conflicting alternatives, since all could be reconciled with support for the Disarmament Conference. But in January 1933 Hitler came to power, and the spectacular deterioration in the international situation in 1933 threatened the Disarmament Conference and brought the first European war scare since 1918. This produced two effects on the public mind. The first was an emotional reflex whereby the idea of expressing total opposition to militarism was confused with that of adopting a totally opposite position, pacifism. The most famous expression of this reaction was the Oxford Union's resolution 'That this House will in no circumstances fight for its King and Country', passed on 9 February 1933. But if this emotional response added to the confusion surrounding pacifism, it served also to stimulate discussion of war prevention at which the differences within the peace movement began to be clarified. This process can be seen at the National Peace Congress held at Oxford in July 1933.

But clarification itself produced confusing divisions. Although the Labour Party exploited the peace question, it was more seriously divided than the Conservative Party by the dispute between isolationists and those believing in the need for British commitments. On the Right, isolationism is well known for Lord Beaverbrook's campaign against the Locarno treaties, for which he claimed East Fulham to be a triumph. On the Left, Sir Stafford Cripps opposed Henderson's policy of support for the League of Nations by advocating a general strike against any attempt by the British Government to go to war, even in support of the League of Nations Covenant. This split dominated both the League of Nations Union's annual meeting at Edinburgh in June 1933 and the Labour Party Conference at Hastings in October 1933. At Edinburgh a compromise was adopted, but at Hastings confusion triumphed. A resolution was passed 'to take no part in war', as well as a composite resolution calling, among other things, for the creation of an International Police Force, which was the most extreme demand of the League's supporters.

Linguistic confusion persisted even after the intellectual problem had been resolved. Thus Lord Allen of Hurtwood (formerly Clifford Allen, who had been imprisoned as a conscientious objector in the Great War) and Sir Norman Angell both insisted they were still 'pacifists' even after they had abandoned their absolutist aversion to military sanctions. Baldwin also still used the word in its wider sense. Speaking in the Commons on 29 November 1933 on air defence, he reminded the opposition speakers, who had included John Wilmot, that 'the most ardent pacificists, using the word in its best sense, are among the soldiers and sailors and airmen of our country who took part in the last war and who know what the next war will be like'. ('Pacificist' was an early – and technically more correct – variant of 'pacifist', which became less common during the 1930s.) Wilmot himself had served in the Great War, and soon developed into an orthodox supporter of collective security. Yet as late as 14 March 1935 he could tell the Commons: 'I do not quite know what is meant by a pacifist, but if it means a person who desires more than anything else to keep his countrymen from the horrors of war, then I plead guilty to being a pacifist.' Confusion about the word was such that in 1933 few contemporaries would have made a distinction between the 'peace' question and the 'pacifist' question.

3. *The contemporary impact*

The contemporary impact of a by-election depends of course not on what actually happened, but on what was believed to have happened, and on what lessons it was believed could be learned from what happened.

For the national press the peace issue was the most noteworthy feature of East Fulham and the by-elections which followed. *The Times* had predicted a good Labour result on the basis of Wilmot's peace propaganda. The *New Statesman* concluded that 'Mr Wilmot's campaign was very largely fought on the peace issue', which thereafter became the basis of the Kilmarnock and Skipton elections.[16] The *Spectator* stated a similar view more judiciously: 'At Fulham, as everywhere, local and particular issues no doubt had their place, as well as general issues like housing, but it is clear that the question on which beyond all others votes turned was disarmament. It was on that, certainly, that the Liberal vote, such as it was, went to the Labour candidate.'[17]

But it was for the National Government to decide whether the election offered any lessons for governmental policy. Beyond Neville Chamberlain's letter to his sister, which has already been quoted, there appears to be no contemporary evidence for East Fulham being more than an understandable political disappointment for Baldwin. Indeed, the assertion that it was a traumatic shock rests largely on a personal anecdote related by G. M. Young: 'And it seemed to me that the shock had broken Baldwin's nerve. "It was a nightmare," he once said, speaking, for the only time, of the past with passion.'[18] A. L. Rowse has quoted an admission made to him by Baldwin during the Second World War that 'Of course, at that time I was holding down a job which I was physically incapable of'.[19] It may therefore be that Baldwin's state of health rendered him peculiarly vulnerable to upsets. An

[16] *New Statesman*, 11 Nov 1933, p. 575.

[17] *Spectator*, 27 Oct 1933, p. 562.

[18] Young, *Stanley Baldwin*, p. 177. J. C. C. Davidson has written that East Fulham 'stunned' Baldwin, but his draft memoirs, written thirty years later, were probably influenced by subsequent accounts. Robert Rhodes James, *Memoirs of a Conservative* (1969) pp. 397–8.

[19] A. L. Rowse, *All Souls and Appeasement* (1961) p. 55.

alternative explanation is that in his declining years the reputation for honesty which Baldwin cultivated as part of his political style developed into a 'frankness' even more 'appalling' than that of 1936.

There is no evidence for East Fulham directly affecting the rearmament programme, since at the time there was no programme to be affected. The Hankey Committee did not report until February 1934, and there was no agreement about defence priorities. But nevertheless, discussions of defence all took place in the clear knowledge that rearmament was politically unpopular, especially if it meant building bombers and equipping an Expeditionary Force. However, the conclusion that rearmament should be kept to a minimum was dictated equally by diplomatic and economic considerations.

The effect of East Fulham and the by-elections which followed was to make the government conscious of the need to explain its foreign policy to the public as skilfully as possible. Stannage has shown that the government believed it had been misrepresented over the German walk-out from the Disarmament Conference. Simon wanted a White Paper to be published, and when Gilbert Murray expressed sympathy Simon telegraphed back that he would welcome a letter to *The Times* showing the government to have the support of the Chairman of the League of Nations Union.[20] The Conservative Party commissioned a report on East Fulham from Arthur Baker of *The Times*, who believed Wilmot's peace propaganda to have been decisive. Whether or not Baldwin saw this report, his speeches attempted to expose the opposition's tactics:

> What an unedifying spectacle we have been witnessing during the last two or three weeks. What an outburst of scaremongering, largely because of Germany's withdrawal and largely because there were half-a-dozen by-elections taking place. . . . I am the last person to mind attacks, but attacks on the Government to try to make people believe that the Government is not in earnest in its desire for peace have no other effect than to weaken our counsels in the world. . . .[21]

[20] Murray Papers, Sir John Simon to Gilbert Murray, telegram, 9 Nov 1933.

[21] Speech to the annual conference of the Scottish Unionist Association, Edinburgh, 17 Nov 1933; see *The Times*, 18 Nov 1933.

After the announcement of the rearmament programme in July 1934, the government once again found it was being branded as a warmonger, most successfully by Dr Edith Summerskill at Putney in November 1934, where the swing against the government nearly equalled that of East Fulham, although the seat did not change hands. Since the strategic situation changed more quickly than did the entrenched hostility to armaments, defence remained a politically delicate issue. Only in the Abyssinian crisis of 1935, when the Labour Party committed itself to military force in support of collective security, did Baldwin manage to find the recipe that sugared the pill of rearmament. But he still made the distinction between a programme of repairing gaps in national defence and the still unthinkable policy of 'great armaments'. This distinction accounts for the ambiguity over whether Baldwin obtained a mandate for rearmament in the 1935 general election.

Baldwin did not believe public opinion could be hurried in a democracy, and accepted, somewhat fatalistically, a two-year time-lag behind the dictatorships. But his reluctance to guide public opinion more energetically was also due to the fact that his own mind was not made up. In particular, he seems to have simultaneously accepted and shied away from the need to build an air force strong enough to deter Germany. His famous speech of 10 November 1932, which had warned that 'the bomber will always get through', was ceaselessly quoted both by pacifists and rearmers as vindication of their viewpoints. By November 1936 the rearmers were in the ascendancy. When Baldwin referred to East Fulham he was citing it, not as a specific event, but as an example of the prevailing attitude which, it was implied, acted as an external constraint on government action. It was ironic that, in playing down his own doubts about rearmament, Baldwin laid himself open to the far graver charges of political cowardice and lack of statesmanship.

Conclusion

The historiography of East Fulham is a case study in the limitations of historical explanation. Since in the last analysis the mind of no one voter will ever be known, all explanations of collective behaviour can at best be simplistic hypotheses. With this in mind, certain statements must be offered tentatively about East Fulham. It became a political myth because events moved so rapidly in the 1930s as to make former attitudes and policies soon seem disastrously misconceived, a factor which was exacerbated by Baldwin's injudicious phraseology in his speech of 12 November 1936. As for the campaign, it can be argued that a poor Tory candidate failed to mobilise the full support of a divided party, whereas an outstanding Labour candidate brought out his own support and attracted a considerable amount of Liberal support, explicitly on the issue of disarmament. To believe necessarily in the decisiveness of a single factor can lead to over-simplification, and to expect to find one among campaign literature, which tries to spread the vote-catching net as widely as possible, is unlikely to succeed except in unusually simple cases. East Fulham was not such a simple case, and can only be interpreted in its context. On that basis, it is here argued that although social questions were widely discussed, it was the peace question which had the greatest emotional impact. The 'peace' question covers all fears of war and discussion of the international situation, and was dominated by the suspicion that the National Government had prejudiced the peace of Europe by provoking a German withdrawal from Geneva. The contemporary impact of East Fulham depended on what the result was believed to show. Most contemporary comment agreed with John Wilmot's description of the by-election in his maiden speech to the Commons on 13 November 1933 'as a symptom of what is a general feeling, a passionate and insistent desire for peace, not merely a nebulous desire for peace, but a demand that that desire should be translated into some practical disarmament accomplishment'. Baldwin quoted East Fulham not as an event with immediate consequences but as a symbol of a widespread popular attitude to armaments, which he himself shared. His successor as Prime Minister, Neville Chamberlain, provides another example of the consequences of sharing the peace-loving aspirations of public opinion.

BIBLIOGRAPHICAL NOTE

The evidence for the campaign can be found in detail in the following articles: C. T. Stannage, 'The East Fulham By-Election, 25 October 1933', *Historical Journal*, XIV 1 (1971) 165–200; R. Heller, 'East Fulham Revisited', *Journal of Contemporary History*, VI 3 (1971) 172–96.

Other accounts include A. J. P. Taylor, *The Trouble Makers* (1957) p. 186; J. P. Kyba, 'British Attitudes toward Disarmament and Rearmament, 1932–1935', Ph.D. thesis (London, 1967) pp. 318–19; K. Middlemas and J. Barnes, *Baldwin* (1969) pp. 744–6 (which all assert the primacy of the peace question); A. J. P. Taylor, *English History, 1914–1945* (1965) pp. 367, 387; A. Marwick, *Britain in the Century of Total War* (1968) p. 251 (which both argue that social issues were more important).

All quotations from parliamentary speeches are taken from *Hansard*. The Baldwin Papers contain nothing on East Fulham, and no political papers survive for John Wilmot (created Baron Wilmot of Selmeston in 1960, died 1964). I am indebted to his widow, Lady Wilmot, for discussing with me the election and her husband's career. The discussion of the context of ideas and opinion on the peace question is derived from the author's own forthcoming work on pacifism and the public mind in Britain in the inter-war period.

6. Oxford and Bridgwater

By IAIN McLEAN

Oxford

General Election, 1935   (Electorate 38,557)

Bourne (Con.)	16,306	*(62·8)*
Gordon Walker (Lab.)	9,661	*(37·2)*
Con. majority	6,645	Turnout 67·3%

By-Election, 27 Oct 1938   (Electorate 36,929)

Hogg (Con.)	15,797	*(56·1)*
Lindsay (Ind. Prog.)	12,363	*(43·9)*
Con. majority	3,434	Turnout 76·3%

General Election, 1945   (Electorate 45,775)

Hogg (Con.)	14,314	*(45·3)*
Pakenham (Lab.)	11,451	*(36·2)*
Norman (Lib.)	5,860	*(18·5)*
Con. majority	2,863	Turnout 69·1%

Bridgwater

General Election, 1935   (Electorate 43,367)

Croom-Johnson (Con.)	17,939	*(56·9)*
Blake (Lib.)	7,370	*(23·4)*
Loveys (Lab.)	6,240	*(19·8)*
Con. majority	10,569	Turnout 72·7%

By-Election, 17 Nov 1938   (Electorate 44,653)

Bartlett (Ind. Prog.)	19,540	*(53·2)*
Heathcoat Amery (Con.)	17,208	*(46·8)*
Ind. Prog. majority	2,332	Turnout 82·3%

General Election, 1945 (Electorate 53,896)

Bartlett (Ind. Prog.)	17,937	(*45·8*)
Wills (Con.)	15,625	(*39·9*)
Corkhill (Lab.)	5,613	(*14·3*)
Ind. Prog. majority	2,312	Turnout 72·7%

The Oxford and Bridgwater by-elections pose problems of interpretation in many ways similar to those at East Fulham five years earlier. The British electorate is notoriously uninterested in, and uninformed about, foreign policy issues; yet here are three by-elections which, in the eyes of the candidates and of most commentators, were won and lost on foreign policy. The results were almost universally regarded as the voters' verdicts on the foreign policy issues of the day. Baldwin thought that East Fulham had been fought and lost 'on no issue but the pacifist', and that the voters' verdict made it impossible to present the country with a rearmament programme. In October and November 1938 Oxford and Bridgwater were taken to be the voters' commentary on Munich, though there was some dispute as to what the voters were saying.

When Chamberlain returned to Britain with the Munich proposals, on 30 September 1938, an unusually large number of by-elections were imminent. Of the eight contests between Munich and the end of 1938, Oxford (27 October) and Bridgwater (17 November) have attracted special attention as tests of Chamberlain's popularity, because in each case the conventional opposition parties withdrew in favour of a non-party, anti-Munich candidate.

The main problem in interpreting Oxford and Bridgwater is the same as for East Fulham: can we confirm or rebut the hypotheses about public opinion offered by contemporary politicians and journalists and quarrelled over by historians? As this chapter will largely be about 'public opinion', it seems fitting to mention at the outset some of the traps for the unwary involved in the study of opinion, especially when this involves election results and 'swing'.

'Swing' is not simply a matter of the net transfer of votes from one party to another between two elections. It involves all manner of other movements, for example: to and from abstention; into and out of the constituency; on to and off the electoral roll by comings of age and deaths. So it is not possible to infer anything about individuals, or even groups of individuals such as 'the Liberal vote', from aggregate election statistics. Indeed, it only makes matters worse to speak, as commentators often do, about the behaviour of 'the Liberal vote', 'the women's vote' and so on, as revealed in election statistics. Not only can we not tell whether blocks of voters moved in a certain way, but we have no right to assume that such blocks exist in any size. By the late 1930s the social bases of the traditional Liberal vote were rapidly crumbling. If 10 per cent of the electorate voted Liberal in each of two successive elections, there is no reason to infer from the statistics that even one individual voted Liberal both times. There is always a danger of ascribing to the electorate more coherent patterns of partisanship than it in fact displays.

It is both the strength and the weakness of the measure 'swing' that it attempts to collapse all the movements of electoral opinion into one. It is the only yardstick yet devised for comparing different elections, and it will be used in this way in this chapter. But its effectiveness diminishes rapidly as the number of parties rises above two. And unfortunately, even in a straight fight there is a third alternative, or 'party', available, namely abstention. Therefore we cannot assume that swing tells us anything about the proportion of the electorate which has switched from one party to the other. To avoid being hoist with my own petard whenever I mention 'swing' in this chapter, let me state that I regard it as simply a measure of the change in party A's share of the electorate relative to party B's (and therefore I have related it, in this chapter, to the total electorate, not only to those who voted). It makes no assumptions as to how this change has come about. All the figures of swing used in this chapter assume that there are only two parties: the National Government and the Opposition. Seats where both Liberals and Labour were strong in 1938 have been omitted from all comparisons.

Another problem of interpretation arises from the common assumption by the political élite that it knows how ordinary electors think. This view is still prevalent today; it was almost universal in the 1930s. It strongly coloured the relationship between press and politicians. Around the time of Munich, Chamberlain even regarded Geoffrey Dawson as a guide to the state of public opinion. Dawson wrote on 28 September 1938:

> My leader [the first leader in *The Times* the previous day] produced a good deal of attention and approval. One sentence in it suggesting that public opinion was ahead of the Government in seeing the urgency and importance of a settlement with Berlin caused the PM to ask me to come and see him . . . so that he might tell me what he at any rate had been trying to do.[1]

Duff Cooper, who resigned as First Lord of the Admiralty over Munich, also had a narrow view of what constituted public opinion. He noted that 'Many would have expected that women would have been more ready than men to accept the spurious peace at its face value. . . . But it was not so.'[2] His justification for this categorical view was that he knew twelve married couples who were divided over Munich, and in each case the husband was pro-Chamberlain and the wife was against. Life would be much simpler if we could accept that the views of Duff Cooper's friends accurately mirrored those of the mass electorate; but there is no reason whatever why they should.

These remarks may appear depressingly negative and destructive. But it is vital that we should realise the immense difficulties in the way of anyone who tries to assess public opinion in times before there were tools to measure it – and that we should suspect the credentials of anyone who professes to do so. It is better to come to cautious conclusions that can be justified than to bold ones that cannot. And the outlook is not entirely bleak. Some statements can be made from aggregate election statistics, and the by-elections of 1938 and 1939 as a whole provide a series about which some useful observations can be made. Oxford in 1938 saw the first constituency opinion poll ever taken in Britain. And Mass-Observation, which had recently been founded by an anthropologist, Tom Harrisson,

[1] Dawson's diary, as quoted in F. R. Gannon, *The British Press and Germany, 1936–39* (Oxford, 1971) p. 73.
[2] A. Duff Cooper, *Old Men Forget* (1953) p. 251.

was taking a keen interest in political affairs and accumulating reams of information about public opinion. Neither of these bodies of data is based on what would now be regarded as reliable sampling methods, but we can be sure that they give us a better picture of public opinion than that handed down by a tiny élite of politicians and journalists. Before looking at their figures, however, we ought to study the history of the two campaigns.

In August 1938 Captain R. C. Bourne, the Conservative MP for Oxford, had died. In 1935 he had had a majority of 25·6 per cent of the votes cast in a straight fight with Labour. The pre-war Oxford constituency did not include the Cowley motor works and their attendant working-class housing, so that it was a less hopeful prospect for Labour than might be thought from a look at the city today. The Conservatives' chances at the by-election appeared to observers to be enhanced by the likelihood of a three-cornered fight. The Liberals' prospective candidate had withdrawn in June, but in September they invited a recent graduate, Ivor Davies, to take his place. Davies was already prospective candidate for Aberdeen Central, and his only connection with Oxford was that he had presided at a Liberal students' conference there earlier that year. The Labour Party readopted Patrick Gordon Walker, who had fought in 1935. The Conservatives chose Quintin Hogg, a young Fellow of All Souls whose father, Lord Hailsham, was Lord President of the Council and an ex-Lord Chancellor.

On 13 September, long before the Munich crisis had reached its peak, Davies offered to stand down on condition that the Labour candidate did likewise and a non-party anti-Conservative should be put up. This was, by Davies's own subsequent admission, a 'gimmick', but it set in motion a chain of unexpected consequences. It produced turmoil in the Labour camp because of its suggestion of a Popular Front. The heat which the question of candidatures was to arouse in the following month can be understood only in the light of Labour feelings about Popular Fronts. The Popular Front was a Communist doctrine, so to the orthodox it was heresy, and any prominent Labour supporter who favoured it was made the victim of an Albigensian crusade. The most famous victim, of course, was Stafford Cripps, who was expelled from the party in January 1939.

There were some bona fide reasons for suspecting the Communists' enthusiasm for Popular Fronts. It was nothing but the result of a violent lurch in Comintern policy in 1934, which had been obediently followed by the leaders of all the surviving Western Communist parties. The operation of Popular Fronts in France and Spain had been unhappy. In France the Popular Front administration of 1936 had quickly collapsed into dissension, and in Spain the Communists spent more energy in annihilating the rest of the Left than in fighting Franco.

Nevertheless, the British Labour Party was probably too insular to pay much attention to these events; and in any case the truth of what was happening in Spain was not widely known, partly through the refusal of Gollancz to publish Orwell's *Homage to Catalonia* and of the *New Statesman* to print his articles from Spain. Native anti-Communism is enough to explain the Pavlovian reaction of Labour's National Executive Committee (NEC) to any Popular Front talk.

The Oxford Constituency Labour Party was already deeply suspect. In June the National Agent fired a shot across its bows: 'It has been reported to us that the Oxford CLP is associated with a movement in the city consisting of Communists and Liberals, and we shall be glad if you will let us know if this is accurate or not.' On hearing the party confess that the rumour was true, Transport House gave it fourteen days to leave the Oxford Co-ordinating Committee for Peace and Democracy, on pain of disaffiliation. The party did so unwillingly: 'at the same time the Secretary was asked to inform Transport House of the discouraging effect on workers in the party of the attitude of the NEC'.[3] Not all the local Labour Party was opposed to the line Transport House was taking. One of those who strongly supported it was the prospective candidate, Patrick Gordon Walker. Although himself a left-winger at this time, he was driven by his unwillingness to give up a chance of winning the seat into the arms of Transport House and the local right-wing, anti-Communist faction.

As the foreign affairs situation worsened during September,

[3] Minutes of Oxford Constituency Labour Party.

Davies's 'gimmick' – by this time backed by the willingness of Gilbert Murray to run as an Independent anti-Government candidate – was taken up in two independent initiatives by two left-wing academics and Labour councillors, R. H. S. Crossman and Frank Pakenham (now Lord Longford). Their favoured candidate was A. D. Lindsay, the Master of Balliol. Lindsay was a Scottish philosopher, whose recent term as Vice-Chancellor of the University had strengthened his reputation for combining high moral principles with consummate skill in political in-fighting. In the by-election, however, the former quality predominated. Lindsay weighed his passionate opposition to Munich against his desire for a quiet life after his term of office, and decided to stand if Liberals and Labour would both withdraw. A new appeal for them to do so was made on 10 October by Roy Harrod, the economist. ('Oxford . . . is the home of compromise and sweet reasonableness', he wrote, ignoring a more famous reputation.) This initiative was welcomed by most of the Liberals and a large part of the Labour Party, but it stiffened the attitude of Gordon Walker and Transport House. On 11 October a meeting of the elections sub-committee of the NEC forbade Gordon Walker from standing down, a decision he accepted with gratitude.

The dominant, pro-withdrawal faction of the local party, however, was not prepared to accept this as final, and appealed to Transport House on the grounds that the circumstances were unique and quite different from the usual 'Popular Front' situation; and that Lindsay, if elected, would not fight the seat again at a subsequent general election. After three days' hard bargaining, Transport House eventually relented and announced that it would 'leave a definite decision in the hands of the local Labour Party'. This body finally decided by a large majority to withdraw Gordon Walker's candidature.

The Liberals were less well disposed to Lindsay, who was a long-standing Labour Party member – especially when he threatened to stand even if only Labour and not the Liberals withdrew. The party spent some £200 or £300 on their campaign, and when they eventually met on 17 October to consider whether to withdraw, this expenditure seemed to be a fatal obstacle. It was only when a Labour councillor of substantial private means offered to pay this bill that the way was finally cleared for Lindsay's candidature, as an 'Independent Progressive'. It was greeted enthusiastically by Davies, and extremely coolly by Gordon Walker, whose offer of help to Lindsay was prefaced: 'I am convinced that Labour has a policy wide, popular, and constructive enough to rally the country behind it. The Oxford City party has decided otherwise. I am not standing down. The local Labour Party is withdrawing the Labour candidate.'

The campaign was short but highly unusual. The *Oxford Mail* thought that 'All the spirit of old-time electioneering campaigns was recalled and spectators began to recall the scenes in 1922 when Frank Gray won the constituency for Liberalism'.[4] The University was passionately stirred by the issues, the city somewhat less so. *Picture Post* noted that:

> An interesting feature of the by-election was the intense interest taken by undergraduates, who had no votes, and the comparative apathy of the townsmen, who had. University men crowded to Dr Lindsay's meetings, although many of the older dons disapproved of his candidature. . . .
>
> Although Proctors, and even candidates, opposed too much activity by them, Oxford undergraduettes took a lively part on both sides.[5]

'A vote for Hogg is a vote for Hitler' proclaimed loudspeaker vans on Lindsay's behalf, though without his authority. (This slogan was reputedly devised by the linguistic philosopher J. L. Austin – 'the only proposition of Austin's I ever managed to understand', A. J. P. Taylor recently confessed.) This, *The Times* noted, 'caused resentment on the Conservative side'. Letters, manifestoes and counter-manifestoes from dons and public figures proliferated in the *Oxford Mail* and spread into *The Times*. A pro-Hogg group of dons was worried that 'Mr Lindsay's nomination may contrive to obscure the central issue. For it is almost inevitable that a part of the votes he

[4] For the rumbustious electioneering of Frank Gray, Liberal MP for Oxford from 1922 until his unseating on petition in 1924, see C. Fenby, *The Other Oxford* (1970).

[5] *Picture Post*, 5 Nov 1938; reproduced in T. Hopkinson (ed.), *Picture Post, 1938–50* (1970) pp. 24–30.

secures will have been cast as a tribute to his Vice-Chancellor-ship.'[6] Lord Nuffield wrote in to deny a rumour that he was supporting Lindsay: '. . . my political opinions favour no individual party, as I am convinced that a continuation of a National Government is our best assurance of the furtherance of the successful legislation and statesmanship which we have enjoyed since its inception.' Sir William Beveridge, Master of University College, wrote to Lindsay stressing his scholarly neutrality as an economist, but adding: 'what you said in your election address was jolly good'.

The candidates spoke of almost nothing except foreign affairs, Hogg going as far as to observe: 'I believe that Mr Chamberlain has shown himself a greater expert on foreign policy, by what he did at Munich, than anyone in the last twenty years.' Hogg's public support came basically from National Government supporters, including National Labour men such as Kenneth Lindsay, the Labour candidate for Oxford in 1924, and Lord Sanderson, a former principal of Ruskin College. There were some signs of the support for appeasement by organised Nonconformity – what A. L. Rowse once rudely called 'political Nonconformity in its deliquescence, without its conscience' – in that one pro-Hogg manifesto was signed by H. A. L. Fisher, Dr A. E. W. Hazell (Principal of Jesus College) and Dr L. P. Jacks (of Manchester College).

Lindsay's support was extraordinarily diverse. On the Conservative side it included Churchill, Eden, Duff Cooper, Harold Macmillan and Edward Heath. Macmillan was the only Conservative MP actually to go to Oxford to speak for Lindsay, although, according to Oliver Harvey, Eden felt 'tempted' to intervene. Some Labour leaders, including Dalton, were hoping for a massive anti-Munich revolt among the Conservatives, which might have led the NEC to reconsider its attitude towards Popular Fronts. But the Munich rebels were too diverse to form a homogeneous group. Many of them were liberals who were sharply divided from Churchill because of his reactionary views on India.

The bulk of Lindsay's public supporters were Liberal, Labour or non-party figures. Here again was confusion, because within the Labour camp those most keen on Lindsay's

[6] *The Times*, 20 Oct 1938.

candidature were not those closest to his own views but those most remote: the Communists and fellow-travellers. Because of the Popular Front imbroglio, there was a gap in Lindsay's support which ought to have been filled by right-wing Labour supporters. But they were unenthusiastic, as was Gordon Walker, who appeared on Lindsay's platforms only at the very end of the campaign. The extreme heterogeneity of Lindsay's support is aptly reflected in the report of a speech by the chairman of the City Labour Party, one of the leading local Popular Fronters. He assured his audience that Lindsay understood the working class, 'and that the reason the working class is in the position it is today is because of the rotten system under which we live. We know there are many Conservatives in Oxford, like Mr Churchill and Mr Duff Cooper, who are not at all satisfied with the way things are going on.' The startling juxtaposition of Winston Churchill and the cause of the international proletariat shows clearly how diverse were the springs of Lindsay's support.

The result was declared on the night of 27 October; the figures appear in the table at the head of this chapter. An attempt will be made later to assess its significance.

In the three weeks following the Oxford by-election, four others took place. Three were more or less conventional party contests, at Dartford, Walsall and Doncaster, where the swings[7] against the National Government were respectively 2·9, 0·4 and 2·6 per cent. The fourth was in the predominantly rural Bridgwater division of Somerset. This election again has attracted attention because the Labour and Liberal parties supported an anti-Munich Independent.

On 10 October 1938 it was announced that the Conservative MP for Bridgwater had been appointed a High Court judge. This came as a complete surprise to local politicians, including Conservative ones, so that no party had any opportunity to make advance preparations for the necessary by-election. Within ten days, however, the local Conservative Executive had drawn up a short-list of two potential candidates, which was presented to the party's Central Council at a meeting in Bridgwater. That body adopted, almost unanimously, Patrick

[7] Based on the electorate, not the total of voters, as explained above.

Heathcoat Amory, a member of a well-known Devon landed family, who expressed his pleased surprise at having been offered 'such a good constituency as this' at only twenty-six. Choosing an opposition candidate was less straightforward. Sir Richard Acland, Liberal MP for Barnstaple (later to be a founder of the war-time Common Wealth Party and later again a Labour MP), had for some time been campaigning on behalf of a Popular Front. One of his supporters, a local vicar, suggested approaching a war-time colleague of his, Vernon Bartlett. Bartlett was a professional communicator. He had been a foreign correspondent for *The Times* and the *News Chronicle*, was well known as a writer and broadcaster, and had been Secretary of the League of Nations Union. On being asked to stand, he complained that he knew nothing about party politics and less about agriculture. The complaints were swept aside: the fact that his grandfather had been a parson in the constituency for fifty-seven years, his supporters assured him, would be enough to secure for him the affections of Bridgwater.

The Labour Party was split in the same way as at Oxford, but the prospects seemed better for the Popular Fronters. Relatively, Labour was much less important at Bridgwater (the Liberals had come second in 1935 and Labour had got only 19·8 per cent of the vote) and the local party was much poorer, not having well-connected Socialist dons to fall back upon. Accordingly, Transport House voted 'not to encourage a contest' at the by-election. A Labour candidate would receive no support from the party's by-election fund, to which the Bridgwater party had not paid its due contribution.

Besides, Oxford had driven a wedge into Transport House's anti-Popular Front campaign. If there were valid reasons for letting the Oxford Labour Party support Lindsay, then they should operate to let the Bridgwater party support Bartlett, who was patently no more a Communist dupe than Lindsay. So when, on 18 October, the Secretary of the Labour Party told Bartlett that Transport House would 'strongly oppose' an Independent Progressive in Bridgwater, the threat had no more content than the famous warning of the *Skibbereen Eagle* that it had its eye on the Kaiser. By refusing for financial reasons to support a Labour candidate, the party had lost its only means of leverage on Bartlett and his supporters. Having been already endorsed by the Liberals, Bartlett received the official endorsement of the local Labour Party on 5 November.

The fame of the Bridgwater election has been mostly posthumous. While in progress it excited no especial attention – certainly much less than Oxford. A galaxy of anti-Munich speakers came down to help Bartlett, but their effect on their audiences, and even their presence, went totally unrecorded in the local press – in sharp contrast with both Oxford, and Kinross and West Perthshire, which polled in December.[8] The absence of this information makes it even more difficult than elsewhere to assess the impact made on the constituency by foreign affairs. After the election Bartlett told acquaintances that he was surprised how much interest there was in foreign affairs. But he also said on occasion that he owed his victory to Tom Harrisson, of Mass-Observation, who insisted that he should speak about agriculture to his audiences, however ignorant he felt about it. At the annual dinner of the Bridgwater Chrysanthemum Society, 'Mr Vernon Bartlett said chrysanthemums were yet another subject about which he did not know as much as he ought to do (laughter)'.

The confusion in popular attitudes to Munich was the same in Bridgwater as elsewhere. Immediately after Munich, the Vicar of Bridgwater said in a thanksgiving service: 'We owe a debt of gratitude to our Prime Minister which can never be repaid. . . . Death was robbed of its spoil by his faith, his perseverance, his prayers. The news was too good to be true.' When the campaign was under way, a Mrs Daisy Pryce-Michell entreated the women of Bridgwater: 'So, my friends, . . . we must send Mr Amory to Parliament to help Mr Chamberlain in his great effort for peace. If only I was not too delicate, I would gladly come and see some of you to help dispel any doubts you may have in your minds. God bless you all, and

[8] Bridgwater was principally served by a Conservative weekly, the *Bridgwater Mercury*; Oxford by an independent daily evening paper, the *Oxford Mail*. Since there are few reports from Bridgwater in other papers circulating in the area, it is clear that this is not a case of a local paper suppressing news because of its political bias. In the national press, also, Bridgwater got much less coverage than Oxford – perhaps because it was further from London and no leading communicators of the day had spent three years of their youth there.

give His blessing of peace.' Unquestionably, however, many electors were beginning to have doubts. At one of Bartlett's meetings, an Amory supporter claimed that Chamberlain 'went to Munich like a British bulldog'. To which a voice from the back retorted: 'Next time why doan't 'ee send a retriever, so 'er bring us back summat?' In the local press, pro- and anti-Munich letters were about as numerous.

Bartlett's own attitudes were characteristic of the liberal intellectual of the time. In the early 1930s he had been one of those who condemned the Versailles Treaty, and explained (if not excused) Nazi Germany by reference to its iniquity. Indeed, one of his broadcast talks, attacking the British Foreign Secretary for being unduly harsh on Germany at the Disarmament Conference in 1933, had led to the end of his regular contract with the BBC around the time of East Fulham (see above, p. 128). In a book on Nazi Germany published in 1933 he made several statements which have worn rather badly:

> . . . The Government now propose to get rid of the concentration camps without much delay.
>
> This drilling of youth, these provocative speeches near the frontiers, these boring brass bands on the radio – they are obviously all political blunders, but they are not made because Germany wants war![9]

Remnants of the liberal 'let's be fair to Germany' attitude still persisted in 1938. The candidates were often asked at meetings about their attitudes to German colonial claims, and Bartlett replied: 'Remembering that these colonies up to twenty years ago belonged to Germany we should be prepared to make sacrifices ourselves . . . [but] in any concessions granted to Germany there must be safeguards that she did not treat her colonies as she had treated the Jews.' None the less, the bulk of his campaign was devoted to attacking Chamberlain's 'weak and vacillating foreign policy', while Amory announced that he stood 'entirely behind the Prime Minister's policy of rearmament on the one hand and conciliation on the other hand'. Polling was on 17 November; the result was announced the following afternoon.

[9] C. V. O. Bartlett, *Nazi Germany Explained* (1933) pp. 243, 267.

As at Oxford, turnout had risen sharply – this time by 9·6 per cent – and there was a much greater swing than at Oxford against the government (7·6 per cent compared with 3·9 per cent). Bartlett was to retain his seat against opposition from both main parties in 1945, but in 1950, when he resigned, his successor as Independent candidate came last.

What can the Munich by-elections tell us about public opinion at the time? Contemporaries were agreed in seeing Bridgwater as a triumph for the opponents of Munich. Feelings about Oxford were more mixed. Conservatives naturally saw the result as a vindication of Chamberlain: 'It is not my victory. It is Mr Chamberlain's', as Quintin Hogg said after the announcement of the result. Those on the other side have tended to take the view expressed by Lindsay and recently endorsed by his daughter:[10] namely that Oxford started the anti-Chamberlain bandwagon, Bridgwater gave it a push and the Norway debate of May 1940 saw it home. This has been contrasted in a recent article[11] with the view that public opinion stayed with Chamberlain until Hitler occupied Prague in March 1939, and then deserted him. I shall attempt to examine these views in the light of what evidence we have.

As mentioned earlier, Oxford in 1938 was the scene of a pioneer opinion poll. Its methods were crude and its main defect was a serious under-representation of prosperous electors – 'not because of an intentional boycott, but usually because the maidservants answering the canvasser's ring could not supply the information for the members of the household'.[12] But with all its faults it is a precious document – the only systematic evidence from any of the Munich by-elections of what electors thought, as opposed to what journalists and politicians thought they thought. Respondents' voting intentions in 1938 were compared with their reported votes in 1935, with the results shown in Table 6.1.

Unfortunately, the reports of the poll give no information

---

[10] D. Scott, *A. D. Lindsay* (Oxford, 1971) p. 254.
[11] R. Eatwell, 'Munich, Public Opinion and the Popular Front', *Journal of Contemporary History*, VI 4 (1971) esp. p. 139.
[12] S. F. Rae, 'The Oxford By-election: A Study in the Straw-Vote Method', *Political Quarterly*, X 2 (1939) 268–79. The quotation is from p. 277.

TABLE 6.1

Oxford: Reported Vote 1935 by Voting Intention 1938

	Hogg 1938	Lindsay 1938
	%	%
Bourne 1935	70	16
Gordon Walker 1935	5	50
Didn't vote 1935	25	34
	100 (n =96*)	100 (n =88*)

* Note that these figures are close to the actual proportions voting for the two candidates – which increases confidence in the survey.

about those who said they would abstain at the by-election. The information in Table 6.1 is therefore incomplete, as is that in Table 6.2, which inverts the above results to show how those who reported voting for each candidate in 1935 said they would vote in the by-election. These figures suggest that the Hogg

TABLE 6.2

Oxford: Voting Intention 1938 by Reported Vote 1935

	Bourne 1935	Gordon Walker 1935	Didn't vote 1935
	%	%	%
Hogg 1938	83	10	38
Lindsay 1938	17	90	62
	100 (n =81)	100 (n =49)	100 (n =64)

vote was substantially the traditional Conservative vote, and that the largest component of the Lindsay vote was the traditional Labour vote. It was thought at the time that Lindsay might not capture it, for several reasons. There was the reluctance of Gordon Walker and one section of the Labour Party to help him, or do any canvassing for him. There was the fear that working-class women might (*pace* Duff Cooper) be drawn into approving of Chamberlain as the man of peace. (In the survey, working-class women split 27:23 in favour of Lindsay and working-class men 28:16 – but we do not know whether the women were proportionately less 'conservative' in 1935.)

It was also thought that Lindsay might suffer because of his remoteness from the working-class electorate, his hasty campaign and his diffidence as a candidate. As Tom Harrisson rather acidly observed, '. . . his donnish advisers took it for granted that everyone in the town knew him as well as they did. They were wrong. Over half the Oxford electorate didn't know Lindsay from Adam.'[13] The chairman of the Liberal Association described Lindsay as 'magnificent but inaudible'. One of his students observed that he found it a 'harrowing experience' to have to go shaking hands with shop girls at a department store. (Since Lindsay was an active WEA organiser, it was presumably embarrassment, not dislike of the lower classes, that induced this feeling.) Ivor Davies described him as 'the worst Parliamentary candidate I have ever encountered'. The pollsters in 1938 failed to record the previous vote of potential abstainers, so that we cannot make any guess at what proportion of the 1935 Labour vote went to abstention. Given the sharp rise in turnout, however, it is unlikely that it was very great.

The organiser of the survey thought that the high proportion of the Lindsay vote which came from previous non-voters indicated 'a considerable body of Liberal support for Lindsay, which was withheld in the case of the Labour candidate in 1935'. It is difficult to be sure. A large proportion of the 1935 non-voters turned up by the survey must be not abstainers, but those either too young to vote in 1935 or not then living in the constituency. In the absence of a Liberal candidate in Oxford since 1929 one cannot tell how large the Liberal vote would have been, given the continued decline of the party throughout the 1930s.

The survey's most interesting finding is in the comparison of voting intention with newspaper taken (Table 6.3). These figures show a correlation between the political opinions of a paper and the voting intentions of its readers, and also between social class, as measured by paper taken, and voting intention. The figures are unlikely to be reliable enough to be worth analysing in such a way as to separate out these two correlations. But one column demands close attention. The readers of The Times split two to one in favour of Lindsay. Not only was part of the social élite deserting the candidate favoured by most of the upper classes, but it was a part which read the paper more than any other identified with appeasement – the

[13] In Picture Post, 5 Nov 1938.

TABLE 6.3

Oxford: Voting Intention by Newspaper Taken

	Daily Mail %	Daily Telegraph %	Daily Express %	Oxford Mail %
Hogg	80	80	60	50
Lindsay	20	20	40	50
	100	100	100	100

	Daily Mirror %	Times %	News Chronicle %	Daily Herald %
Hogg	38	33	25	16
Lindsay	62	67	75	84
	100	100	100	100

paper which, as we have seen, took it upon itself to tell Chamberlain on 27 September that public opinion was in favour of a settlement with Berlin. This finding seems neatly to confirm that the Lindsay vote was basically a working-class Labour vote, plus a tiny élite (probably consisting mostly of dons) who supported Lindsay either because of his University reputation or because they shared his concern over Munich. People of this sort had, of course, made most of the running in the Lindsay campaign. Indeed, it was they (together with the working-class Popular Fronters in the Labour Party) who had been responsible for Lindsay's candidature in the first place. Their assumptions about public opinion were shared by some of their opponents – for instance, the group of dons already quoted who wrote to *The Times* to complain that Lindsay might get an unfairly high share of the vote because of his reputation as Vice-Chancellor. But in fact the working-class electorate from which came most of Lindsay's support was quite unaffected by his standing in the University. Distinguished dons who spoke at meetings in east Oxford about 'The Master' in reverent tones were met with total bewilderment.

It is both easier and more difficult to talk about the meaning of the Bridgwater result: easier because it seems to be more clear-cut, but more difficult because we do not have a contemporary opinion poll to hand. The swing of 7·6 per cent against the National Government was one of the highest – though not the highest – between Munich and the outbreak of war. The electorate may have been closer than at Oxford to sharing the candidates' concern for foreign policy. Soon after the election Oliver Harvey recorded: 'Vernon Bartlett told me about his election and how all the country people are passionately interested in foreign affairs and frankly bored by the agricultural part of his speeches.'[14] On this point the evidence is conflicting; but there are certainly grounds for saying that Bridgwater is a rare case in British electoral history of a by-election whose unusual result can be traced to a foreign policy issue.

But Oxford and Bridgwater are not the only by-elections of their period. In all, 19 by-elections were held in 1938 and 17 between January and August 1939. A meaningful figure for the swing against the government can be derived from 31 of these 36.[15] The by-elections may be divided into four periods, with one gap during which there were no contests.

1. January to July 1938: pre-Munich, 8 elections.
2. October to December 1938: in the shadow of Munich, 7 elections.
3. January to March 1939: post-Munich, pre-occupation of the rump of Czechoslovakia, 4 elections.
4. March to August 1939: from the occupation of Czechoslovakia to the outbreak of war: 12 elections.

Two main interpretations of the results of this group of elections have been offered. One is that of, for instance, Robert Rhodes James:

[Oxford] . . . may be seen as evidence that revulsion against Munich had not yet assumed substantial proportions. Bridgwater . . . was an encouragement, but it was soon checked when the Duchess of Atholl was defeated. These indications of popular feeling . . . demonstrated that the post-Munich situation was still on balance to the Government's advantage. . . .

[14] J. Harvey (ed.), *The Diplomatic Diaries of Oliver Harvey* (1970) p. 234.
[15] For a note on the exceptions, including Kinross and West Perthshire (the Duchess of Atholl's seat), see below, Appendix I, p. 163.

The real turning point did not come until the occupation of the rest of Czechoslovakia in March 1939.[16]

The other, already mentioned, is that of two recent commentators on Oxford, D. Scott and R. Eatwell: namely that Oxford began a trend against the government which grew steadily, or at least continuously, until the fall of Chamberlain in May 1940.

Neither hypothesis, unfortunately, has been tested systematically against the evidence from by-elections. Even as crude a measure as 'swing', with all its defects, shows that the truth is too complex to fit either. The swings against the government in the four groups of elections are as shown in Table 6.4.

TABLE 6.4

By-Elections 1938–9: Mean Swing (Based on Electorate)
against National Government, and Standard Deviations

	Swing %	Standard deviation %
1. Pre-Munich	2·6	2·8
2. Munich	4·1	4·6
3. Post-Munich	3·8	4·4
4. Post-Prague	3·3	4·9

There is little comfort for either school of thought in these figures. The elections which took place after March 1939 – when appeasement was finally pronounced dead – actually show a lower swing than those which occurred in the Oxford and Bridgwater period. Certainly, there was a consistent trend against the government. The notion that it would have won an overwhelming victory in an October 1939 general election, to which Robert Rhodes James seems to give a qualified endorsement, receives no support from these figures. Only one election in the series shows a swing the other way (the Caerphilly result in July 1939, which yielded a bizarre swing of 6·7 per cent to the Conservatives). The other 30 at least all swing in the same direction. But there is no observable pattern, and little consistency within the four groups corresponding to the changing pattern of foreign affairs (as is shown by the high figures for standard deviations about the mean swings). Few

[16] Robert Rhodes James, *Churchill: A Study in Failure* (1970) p. 340.

ways of categorising the elections can impose any pattern on the results. Take, for instance, the five highest swings:

Bridgwater	17 Nov 1938	7·6%
Lewisham West	24 Nov 1938	5·2%
Ripon	23 Feb 1939	7·5%
Westminster Abbey	17 May 1939	8·2%
Hythe	20 July 1939	6·9%

These are all safe Conservative seats, but they have nothing else in common. They are certainly not the seats most affected by foreign policy discussions – except for Bridgwater.

The series of elections shows no correlation between changes of turnout and swing: high and low swings are distributed randomly among elections with large and small changes in turnout. However, one observation can be made which distinguishes Oxford and Bridgwater from other elections. At 27 of the 31, turnout dropped by amounts ranging from 0·6 per cent to 22·7 per cent. At two it rose by under 1 per cent. But at Oxford it went up by 9 per cent, and at Bridgwater by 9·6 per cent.

This is the best confirmation of the traditional view that popular concern about foreign policy led to increased interest in these elections. But this did not on its own produce unusually large swings. A plausible way of interpreting this is to suppose that heightened interest in foreign affairs brought out marginal supporters of *both* sides – pro-Chamberlain as well as anti-. A vivid picture of the state of public opinion during the crisis is provided by Mass-Observation, some of whose early reports were collected in a Penguin Special called simply *Britain*, published in January 1939. This neglected source shows up the intensity, the confusion and the sheer changeability of opinion during the crisis. The percentage figures given are not based on reliable quota or random samples, but they were taken in working-class areas and certainly give a better measure of public opinion than do élite perceptions of it. Mass-Observation reported a succession of remarkable shifts in public opinion. Chamberlain's stock stood high on 15 September, after he had announced his first visit to Hitler over Czechoslovakia: 70 per cent of those asked thought his visit would help peace. Revelation of the Godesberg terms, however, provoked a sharp reaction against him on 21 and 22 September, with a striking difference between men and women (see Table 6·5). 350 answers to the question 'What do you think about Czechoslovakia?' were divided into four categories: Indignant (Czechs unfairly treated), No War (maybe unfair, but it avoids war), Pro-Chamberlain, and Don't Know. The slump in

TABLE 6.5

Views on Czechoslovakia, 22 September 1938: Mass-Observation Sample

	Men %	Women %	All %
Indignant	67	22	40
No War	2	16	10
Pro-Chamberlain	14	27	22
Don't Know	17	35	28

pro-Chamberlain opinion was followed by a second peak after his announcement on 28 September of his proposed Munich visit. On the 29th a London sample produced the results shown in Table 6·6. The volume from which these figures are

TABLE 6.6

Popularity of Chamberlain, 29 September 1938: Mass-Observation Sample

	Men %	Women %	All %
Pro	46	59	54
Anti	20	4	10
Mixed feelings	16	7	10
Don't know	16	30	26

taken went to press before any post-Munich opinion figures became available, but there is no reason to doubt its assertion that 'at the moment of writing [November], antis are tending rapidly to build up again, while among men . . . this build-up is more than among women'.

These figures suggest several points. They leave no room for doubt that women were in fact more pro-Chamberlain than men. They show very wide fluctuations of opinion over a very short time, perhaps partly engendered by the contrary pressures of fairness to the Czechs and desire for peace. Chamberlain was overwhelmingly popular on 30 September. But the Munich terms were in many ways worse than the Godesberg ones which had made such an unfavourable impression on the public only a week earlier. So the hysterical relief of 30 September lasted days rather than weeks, and by the time of Oxford and Bridgwater confusion had set in again. People were still stirred by foreign affairs. But it was difficult for the ordinary elector to assess claim and counter-claim: 'Chamberlain got us peace'; 'Chamberlain gave Hitler all he wanted'. At Oxford and Bridgwater, with their Independent Progressive candidates, the confusion produced a rise in turnout. Elsewhere, sheer bewilderment may have driven supporters of both parties to abstain.

There is also an alternative explanation. Many commentators have assumed, without examining the evidence, that popular discontent with Chamberlain's foreign policy rose steadily from October 1938 onwards. This is not borne out by the by-election results, which show no correlation between the government's popularity and successive events abroad which cast doubt on the wisdom of appeasement. But, arguably, 'public opinion' was neither for nor against Chamberlain, except when dramatic events were in the offing. Most people, most of the time, had no views at all about foreign policy; foreign affairs played little or no part in their assessment of leading politicians. To look for a relationship between international events and the government's popularity may be to overestimate not only the electors' interest in foreign affairs but also the sophistication of their attitudes. Mass-Observation data, this time unpublished, provides a useful corrective. The surveys of attitudes conducted at Oxford and Bridgwater have unfortunately been lost; but one survives for Kinross and West Perthshire (21 December 1938), the other by-election to have been fought by the candidates specifically on foreign affairs. But the electors thought otherwise. 65 per cent of those asked thought home affairs more important than foreign, 15 per cent thought foreign affairs more important, and the remaining 20 per cent did not know. Pro- and anti-Chamberlain views were related to personalities, not abstractions:

Woman, 50: 'Oh, the Duchess [of Atholl] is a fine woman – she is an' all. Ye know she will get in easily.

> I dinna know much about politics but I do
> know that if the Duchess says Mr Chamberlain
> is wrong he canna be right.'

Woman, 55: 'I've always been for the Duchess, but you
can't do better than what Mr Chamberlain did,
an old man – he went to Germany – why they
might have killed him.'

The Mass-Observation organisers had concluded about an
earlier election (Fulham West in April 1938): 'No wide
understanding about what is happening abroad. When
concerned with foreign affairs it is almost always from a
personal point of view: it will affect the family, take away a
son, send up prices, let in foreigners, etc. Remarkable absence
of clear-cut attitudes to the foreign position.' This impression
of the nature of the 'belief-systems' of the electorate has been
confirmed by modern studies of a more rigorous kind.[17] For
this reason alone, stereotypes of public opinion around the
time of Munich would need to be queried. We have already
discussed two hypotheses about public opinion: that a groundswell of anti-Chamberlain feeling built up from Oxford to
May 1940, and that the nation supported its Premier until,
but not beyond, March 1939. Neither is supported by the
evidence, any more than the contemporary press view, that
Chamberlain would have won an October general election
with a massive majority.[18] The truth seems to be that for the
most part electors were uninterested in foreign affairs, but that
when they were interested they were confused and bewildered
with no idea where to turn. Beyond this, grandiose generalisa-
tions about the changing mood of the British public ought to be
left to the Churchills, the Catos and the old newsreels. Commentators would be wise to take heed of a warning written
within two months of Munich:

> The month of September, 1938, will provide the historian of
> the future . . . with a supremely illuminating insight into

[17] See especially G. A. Almond and S. Verba, *The Civic Culture* (Princeton,
1963); P. Converse, 'The Nature of Belief Systems in Mass Publics', in D.
Apter (ed.), *Ideology and Discontent* (New York, 1964).
[18] The Gallup Poll figures for voting intention in February 1939 were:
Government, 50%; Opposition, 44%; Don't Know, 6%.

sense and statesmanship and the *status quo*. But if, as has been the custom in the past, the historian accepts as statements of fact the numerous published assertions as to what the public of England are thinking about it all, he will, as so often before, be a typically lousy historian'.[19]

APPENDIX I: BY-ELECTIONS OMITTED IN THE COMPILATION OF TABLE 6·4

They are: Pontypridd and West Derbyshire (no contest in 1935), Combined Scottish Universities (no contest at the by-election), Colne Valley (where the strength of three parties, Conservative, Labour and Liberal, makes 'swing' worthless), and Kinross and West Perthshire. In this seat the Duchess of Atholl, elected as a Conservative in 1935, resigned in 1938 as a protest against the government's foreign policy and stood again as an Independent. In a straight fight with a Conservative, which took place on a day of heavy snow, 21 December 1938, she lost by 1,313 (5·8 per cent). We cannot derive a useful 'swing' figure from a pair of contests when the same person is the government candidate in the first and the anti-government candidate in the second; so it has had to be omitted, in spite of its inherent interest and foreign policy overtones.

APPENDIX II: A NOTE ON SOURCES

For Oxford

I. Davies, 'How Hogg Won Oxford', *New Outlook* (Oct 1963).

R. Eatwell, 'Munich, Public Opinion and the Popular Front', *Journal of Contemporary History*, VI 4 (1971).

S. F. Rae, 'The Oxford Bye-Election: A Study in the Straw-Vote Method', *Political Quarterly*, X 2 (1939).

——, 'The Concept of Public Opinion and its Measurement', Ph.D. thesis (London, 1939).

D. Scott, *A. D. Lindsay* (Oxford, 1971).

For Bridgwater

C. V. O. Bartlett, *And Now, Tomorrow* (1960).

R. Eatwell, art. cit.

For public opinion generally

T. Harrisson and C. Madge (eds.), *Britain, by Mass-Observation* (1939).

Old newspapers, both national and local, are necessarily a staple for any article such as this. To save footnotes, quotations from the *Oxford Mail* and the *Bridgwater Mercury* have not been individually identified.

Useful source material can also be found in the Local History Collection, Oxford Central Public Library, and in the Mass-Observation Archives in

[19] T. Harrisson and C. Madge (eds.), *Britain, by Mass-Observation* (1939) p. 103.

Sussex University Library. I am most grateful to Tom Harrisson, Director of the Mass-Observation Archives, for giving me permission to see them and to quote from them. I am also very grateful to Alan Knight for lending me his unpublished essay on the Oxford by-election, and to those participants who answered my inquiries.

7. By-Elections of the Second World War

By PAUL ADDISON

The by-elections of 1939–45 were so unlike normal by-elections that at first it is hard to make sense of them. There were no contests between the three main parties. At the outbreak of the war, under the Chamberlain government, the Chief Whips of the Liberal, Labour and Conservative parties concluded an electoral truce whereby, when a seat fell vacant, the party which had held it previously would nominate a candidate, while the other two parties agreed not to do so. The agreement was to last for the duration of the war, or until one of the signatories withdrew. The purpose of the arrangement was to preserve a measure of national unity by confining party differences to the House of Commons. When all three parties joined the Churchill Coalition in May 1940, the truce acquired a deeper significance, as an essential precondition of unity within the government. Hence, although the rank and file of the Labour Party at times grew very restless with an arrangement which protected a Conservative majority of over 200, the truce was never seriously in question. Of the 141 seats which fell vacant during the war, 66 were filled unopposed, by the nominee of the incumbent party. In the remaining 75 seats a contest was forced by Independents and minor party candidates. A new party, Common Wealth, was formed in 1942 as a direct result of the vacuum created by the truce, and won three by-elections against government candidates.

The 104 citizens who came forward to fight by-elections were, naturally, a mixed bunch. Most have their interest as individuals, but too much concentration upon particular personalities can obscure their general significance. Broadly speaking, three types of candidate were dominant during three different phases of the war. Of the 22 who stood between September 1939 and the King's Norton by-election of May

1941, 15 were anti-war candidates of one kind or another, defying prevailing opinion. The arrival of the colourful carpetbagger, Noel Pemberton Billing, at the Hornsey by-election, marked a new departure. He was the first of a series of candidates who tried to tap the mainstream of underlying discontent with war-time conditions, and the growing record of military failure. Four such Independents defeated government candidates in the first six months of 1942. The candidates of this phase were very much the products of a particularly frustrating phase of the war, and yet they have a broad relevance. War brought about a radical social climate at home, and this entailed for many a disillusion with pre-war Conservatism. Apart from this factor, it was inevitable that the grumbles engendered by war-time conditions should be directed first and foremost against the Conservatives, since they were the dominant power in the House and the government. The candidates of 1941–2 therefore displayed a vague radical anti-Toryism, preparing the way for the more positively opposed candidates of 1943–5.

The publication of the Beveridge Report in December 1942, with its promise of a New Deal for all, coinciding with the turn of the military tide towards victory, marked the beginning of a new phase. There was a strong trend back towards normal party strife, and the majority of challengers to the electoral truce in 1943–5 stood for recognisably Liberal or Socialist programmes. There was, then, an underlying logic to the long procession of candidates who followed in the footsteps of Pemberton Billing. After allowing for several exceptions, they can be described as harbingers of the Labour assault on the Conservative Party in the general election of 1945. The whole weight of their offensive, as Table 7·1 below indicates, was borne by the Conservative-held seats. This was partly because the majority of seats falling vacant were Conservative; primarily because the home front was characterised by a growing anti-Tory movement, while Conservatives themselves, enjoying their great majority in the House, and confident that Churchill would bring them a sweeping victory at the post-war general election, had no incentive for 'rocking the boat'. Even when Labour seats were contested, later in the war, it was never by spokesmen for unofficial Conservatism.

TABLE 7·1

Contests and Unopposed Returns in Conservative and Labour Seats,
May 1941 to April 1945

	Labour		Conservative	
	Vacant	Contested	Vacant	Contested
1941	6	0	16	8
1942	13	2	12	11
1943	2	1	21	18
1944	4	3	7	6
1945	2	2	3	3

In analysing the behaviour of voters, we are again faced with the extreme abnormalities of war-time. Until the Motherwell by-election of April 1945, all by-elections were conducted according to the electoral register of March 1939, thus ignoring the rising crop of young voters, and the great movements of population necessitated by the war. A constituency in a great industrial area would be denuded not only of conscripts to the services, but of women and old people evacuated away from the risk of bombing, and key workers directed to different parts of the country. An electorate might, therefore, be considerably distorted in its social composition. The victor of the Wallasey by-election, George Reakes, thought that one reason for his success was that, of the original population of 100,000 in 1939, 40,000, most of them from among the more well-to-do, had left in order to escape from an area of very high bombing.[1] Such shifts in population also make it difficult to estimate the level of turnout in most by-elections, and hence the level of interest aroused by the campaigns. Estimates were sometimes made of the live register, as opposed to the theoretical register of 1939. If we can rely upon such estimates for half a dozen of the by-elections of 1943–5, the effective electorate represented between 52 per cent and 78 per cent of its strength on paper. This may enable the exceptionally low turnout figures for war-time by-elections to be put in perspective. 30 of the 75 contests resulted in a nominal turnout of over 40 per cent. In constituencies with one-third of the electorate absent, a common enough situation, this would imply effective turnouts of 60 per cent and over. Electioneering itself had to be carried on despite considerable handicaps, notably the absence of cars

[1] G. L. Reakes, *Man of the Mersey* (1956) p. 78.

to take voters to the polling booth. In rural areas, farmers' hay wagons and pony traps were pressed into service – a slight feudal advantage accruing to the Conservatives. The candidates were allowed a ration of 200 gallons of petrol each for personal transport, and often ran out in the more rambling constituencies.

One of the major distorting factors which complicate analysis was the strong moral sanction which the government and its candidates sought to bring to bear against the interlopers. After May 1940 every by-election bore a double aspect. On the one hand it was a matter of deciding which alternative the voter preferred. On the other it was a question of whether the voter, as a supporter of the government and adherent of one of the three parties which had signed the truce, should obey the advice given by all the party leaders, and vote for the government candidate regardless of his party label. Patriotic duty seemed to interfere with normal choice. At the Eddisbury by-election of April 1943 the government candidate made use of the slogan 'Hitler is watching Eddisbury'. The same month the government candidate at Daventry, Reginald Manningham-Buller, told one of his audiences: 'Three countries will be pleased if I am defeated – Germany, Italy and Japan.'[2] After losing four by-elections to Independents in the first half of 1942, the party leaders banded together and issued a joint message, signed by Churchill, Ernest Brown (the National Liberal leader), Attlee and Sinclair, to electors at subsequent by-elections. The text, apart from the name of the constituency, served for the rest of the war and read as follows:

> The verdict recorded by a single constituency is flashed round the world as though it were the voice of Britain that had spoken, and Barsetshire will realise that it has the responsibility at this moment of indicating to the United Nations, and to neutral countries, that we are united among ourselves in our unflinching determination to organise our total resources for victory.

Churchill usually sent an additional personal message to Conservative and allied candidates, commending their virtues.

[2] Mass-Observation Archive, University of Sussex, Mass-Observation file report No. 1669N (Eddisbury) and No. 1669M (Daventry).

'Let the electors ask themselves', he wrote to the candidate at Chelmsford in April 1945, 'what possible good it would do to the country to return to Parliament in these present times a member of a disintegrating political fragment such as the Common Wealth Party.'[3] Yet the electors returned the Common Wealth candidate. It may well be that this heavy hand jogging the voter's arm lost as much support as it gained. Perhaps the most outstanding fact about the war-time by-elections is that, despite the official line, the government lost nine contests in the period 1942–5, or eleven if the exceptional cases of Belfast West and the Combined Scottish Universities are taken into account. An opinion poll taken in April 1942 produced a notable majority in favour of by-elections being contested.[4] Whatever Coalition propaganda made out, voters knew that an expression of dissent implied no disunity about the will to victory, nor would it affect the course of the war. 'To labour that point', wrote the *East Anglian Daily Times*, 'would be to insult the intelligence and the patriotism of a people who know quite clearly that without victory all their high hopes for the eventual peace are simply chimerical.'[5] It is very likely indeed that one of the functions of by-elections, as Attlee argued in private, was 'the attraction to people, who have to submit to many Government regulations, of being able to act contrary to the wish of the Government with impunity. The more the Government expresses its support of a particular candidate, the greater is the attraction.'[6] Another very obvious problem in analysing voting behaviour is the difficulty of comparing results when the Independent candidates were of such variable quality and appeal. Only by comparing a large number of results can we expect that variables will tend to cancel each other out. For example, in the eight seats which the Conservatives defended after and including Hornsey, in 1941, their share of the poll increased on average by 5.6 per cent. The first half of 1942 was by contrast a phase of almost undiluted military disaster. Over the ten by-elections up to and

[3] *The Times*, 20 Apr 1945.

[4] Hadley Cantril, *Public Opinion, 1935–1946* (Princeton, 1951) p. 195.

[5] *East Anglian Daily Times*, 22 Feb 1944.

[6] Attlee Papers, University College, Oxford, box 7, note by Attlee on the electoral truce, for circulation to the Labour Party NEC, Feb 1944.

including Salisbury in July 1942, the Conservatives suffered an average loss of 6·9 per cent. As these figures indicate, even at this point, when in theory party politics lay submerged by the urgencies of war, by-election results tended to fluctuate around the norm of the pre-war Conservative percentage of the vote, with the war-time opposition candidate(s) picking up a share related to the pre-war Labour and/or Liberal vote. Several of the results from 1943–5, as will be argued, provide good evidence of a swing to Labour. But Tom Harrisson of Mass-Observation was almost alone in deducing that Labour would win the general election at the end of the war: contemporaries paid considerable attention to by-elections, and members of the government worried about adverse results, but hardly anyone seemed to understand what was happening.

Throughout the war there was no more depressing period than the opening nine months – the 'phoney war'. The Chamberlain government watched apprehensively for signs of anti-war feeling. Three British Union of Fascists candidates each failed to secure more than 3 per cent of the vote, and the Communists, who adopted an anti-war line after the Russo-German partition of Poland, fared little better. Only the ILP, providing an outlet for frustrated Labour voters at Stretford in December 1939 and Renfrewshire East in May 1940, appeared to evoke any response for peace. Lord Beaverbrook, who was also against the war at this time, toyed with the idea of financing ILP candidates.[7] It was difficult for local Labour caucuses to abandon the fight against the friends of Chamberlain, and at Glasgow Pollok in April 1940 the divisional party broke the rules, put up its own candidate and was disaffiliated. Had the 'phoney war' been prolonged, the truce would almost certainly have provoked a general revolt in the Labour Party. But on 10 May Churchill became Prime Minister, and the peril of the moment effaced party feeling.

It had always been a temptation for a party caucus in a safe seat to put up its own candidate without paying very much attention to the opinion of the rank and file. The electoral truce apparently made safe seats safer still, and there were two striking examples in war-time of a rank-and-file rebellion against a Conservative association. At Newcastle North in

[7] A. J. P. Taylor, *Beaverbrook* (1972) pp. 404–6.

1935 the Conservative majority was 17,990. In May 1940 the local association adopted H. Grattan-Doyle, the son of the retiring Member, as its candidate by a vote of 239 to 5. At the invitation of dissatisfied Conservatives, a rival candidate was nominated: Sir Cuthbert Headlam, a leading figure in the region, and experienced former MP. To the great annoyance of the electorate, these two candidates, supported by rival associations, campaigned against each other while the BEF struggled to escape from Dunkirk.[8] Headlam won a resounding victory. Brighton was still more certainly Conservative, a two-Member constituency where the majority in 1935 was 41,626. The local association adopted Flight-Lieutenant William Teeling as their candidate at the by-election of February 1944. Teeling had travelled the world as a writer and worker in the Roman Catholic cause, but he was almost unknown in Brighton. With a few minutes to go before nominations closed, a rival appeared: Bruce Dutton Briant, a well-known local barrister of undoubted Conservative loyalty. The Mayor of Brighton was his brother, and the Mayor of Hove signed his nomination papers. Briant alleged that the local party, in collusion with the party chiefs in London, had fixed up a rush election in order to get Teeling in without opposition. There seems to have been strong resentment in the local business community against the choice of an outsider. The hotel and boarding industry needed to be set on its feet again, and Briant belonged firmly in the town oligarchy whose interests were at stake. The local party arranged for Churchill to send down a thunderbolt, a letter condemning Briant's candidature as an 'attempted swindle'. This proved to be a *faux pas*, and after an outburst of local resentment Churchill sent another and more reasoned letter.[9] Briant, with 46 per cent of the poll, came close to upsetting Teeling.

These two contests were, however, only side-shows by comparison with the main theme of war-time by-elections, the radical assault on Conservative seats. Hardly anyone could have been more unsuitable as the pioneer of this development than Noel Pemberton Billing. One of the wild young men of

[8] Mass-Observation file, Report No. 195.
[9] On Brighton, see *Sussex Daily News*, 27 Jan–3 Feb 1944; Mass-Observation file report No. 2020.

aviation before 1914, Billing was a lone survivor of the jingoism of the Great War. A similar electoral truce had operated in the years 1914–18 and Billing had been the first Independent to defy it successfully, at the East Hertfordshire by-election of March 1916. He had stood as the champion of air power, and later in the war emerged as the hero of a libel case in which he alleged that the Germans possessed a black book containing the names of 47,000 perverts in high places in Britain. In the Second World War he stood for the defeat of Germany by bombing alone, and the defence of Britain by equally spaced upward-pointing lights which would confuse the enemy and enable the RAF's fighters to see the bombers against a background of light. For post-war policy, he argued that general elections should be replaced by the multiplication of by-elections, and an additional assembly of trades and professions be set beside the Houses of Parliament. There should also be a Woman's Parliament, 'to deal with domestic matters'. Billing fought four by-elections in the second half of 1941, and made quite an impression with his forceful speechmaking and yellow Rolls-Royce.[10] He was soon joined on the campaign trail by another diverting figure, Reg Hipwell, the founder and editor of the forces' newspaper *Reveille*, a vehicle for the grumbles of the ordinary soldier, and a never-failing source of pin-up girls. Hipwell announced at Scarborough in September 1941 that he was fighting for a 3s.-a-day minimum for servicemen, with £2 weekly for wives, 8s. 6d. for each child and an increase of at least 20 per cent in old-age pensions. He accused the president of the divisional Conservative Association of leaving Dunkirk ten days before the men under his command, and argued that although the Conservative candidate claimed to be unfit for service because he had only one leg, Douglas Bader had none and had still served his country. Hipwell's style was entirely uninhibited. He admired, he claimed, many of the planks in the Conservative platform, yet felt he also stood for the best that the Labour and Liberal parties had to offer. An observer for Mass-Observation thought it unlikely that Hipwell had ever read anything on economics or politics. 'For Democracy not Vested Interest' was one of his slogans, but he confided after his defeat: 'I only came up here for a holiday – something

[10] Mass-Observation file report No. 725.

to make a change.'[11] Hipwell not only fought four by-elections himself, the last at Hartlepools in June 1943, but put up his *Reveille* assistant Winifred Henney at Harrow in December 1941, and acted as W. J. Brown's agent for his conquest of Rugby in April 1942. Both Billing and Hipwell were, in their different ways, irresponsible candidates. But they chalked up respectable polls, and *The Times* noted their emergence as an encouraging sign of a desire to ginger up the war effort.[12]

The first Independent to defeat a government candidate was Denis Kendall, who won Grantham in March 1942 with 50·8 per cent of the poll. The background was one of crisis in the war effort. In Russia the Red Army was barely holding its own, and a clamour was beginning in Britain for a Second Front. The Japanese had overrun the Far East, sinking the *Prince of Wales* and the *Repulse* on 10 December, and capturing Singapore on 15 February. The press and the House were obsessed by real or imagined deficiencies in war production, and Churchill had reshuffled the government, bringing Sir Stafford Cripps into the War Cabinet. Cripps, who had just returned from eighteen months as Ambassador to Russia, appeared to be the long-awaited dispassionate brain who would introduce efficiency into all branches of the war effort. Kendall was Grantham's Cripps, as one of his leaflets boasted: 'Denis Kendall is another Stafford Cripps. Independent yet Churchillian.' A Yorkshireman who had made good in the United States, Kendall was the manager of a local engineering firm. He paid high wages and provided his workers with such additional welfare benefits as dances on Saturday night and services on Sunday morning – at which he read the lesson. He saw himself as a 'production man' who would go to Parliament 'not to learn politics but to teach members what production meant to the Country and the Empire'. Formerly a member of the local Labour Party, he had approached the Conservatives for nomination at the by-election, one reflection of a get-ahead approach which also included the demand that inefficient firms should be taken over by the government, and cost-plus – the system whereby government contractors were guaranteed a margin of profit above their estimate of cost – be abolished.

[11] *Scarborough Evening News*, 10 and 23 Sep 1941; Mass-Observation file report No. 902.   [12] *The Times*, 29 Sep 1941.

His opponent, Sir Arthur Longmore, had recently been retired by Churchill from the command of the RAF in the Near East. Although the RAF was a great force in local society, it was also a divisive one, while Kendall could play the card of local man versus outsider. The local Communist Party, following the new line laid down since Hitler's invasion of Russia in 1941, produced a special pamphlet calling on the electorate to show their solidarity with the Red Army by voting for the government candidate. The local Labour Party decided, after much heart-searching, to lie low, and had to restrain their prospective candidate and other party workers from aiding Kendall.[13]

At Grantham the Conservative share of the vote fell by 8·9 per cent compared with 1935. At Rugby, W. J. Brown, a perfect stranger to the constituency, reduced it by 13·3 per cent. Rugby had been the seat of the former Conservative Chief Whip and Secretary for War, David Margesson, and was thought to be entirely safe. The Conservative candidate, Sir Claude Holbrook, had been chairman for fifteen years of the local association. He not only declared that the electors of the division were against the holding of an election, but on the eve of poll wrote an article for the local press on 'Why I Won'. Brown had been a Labour MP in 1929–31, broke away to join Mosley's short-lived New Party, and subsequently fought bitterly against all the party machines. He was best known as the General Secretary of the major white-collar union, the Civil Service Clerical Association, which he had founded. His politics revolved around the idea of the general will as understood by W. J. Brown and thwarted by the party caucuses. In detail his programme ran as follows: '(1) Total efficiency in total war effort; (2) reconstitution of the Government on a non-party basis; (3) breaking through the contradictions in production, the Civil Service, politics and propaganda, which hinder the war effort; (4) maintenance of the freedom of the public Press and of public criticism against the growing tendency of the Government towards suppression; (5) democratisation of the Army; (6) real equality of sacrifice.'

[13] For Kendall, see *Picture Post*, 18 Apr 1942; for the Labour position, *The Times*, 23–24 Mar 1942; and, in general, Mass-Observation boxed material on Grantham, and the *Lincolnshire Echo*. I am very grateful to Dr Owen Hartley for explaining the local political background to me.

The local Labour Party was split over Brown's candidature, while the National Council of Labour passed a resolution condemning him as a disruptive individual, not a fit and proper person to represent the working classes. At the last minute Brown came out in favour of the Second Front; and although Margesson himself warned voters that Hitler would gloat if Brown got in, Brown got in.[14]

The circumstances at Wallasey, where George Reakes defeated the government candidate at the by-election of April 1942, were again different. This time both the main candidates were local men. The Conservative, Alderman Pennington, had served on the town council since 1924; Reakes, who was formerly Labour, since 1922. A third candidate, the wealthy shipowner Major Leonard Cripps, the right-wing brother of Sir Stafford, issued one of the most unexceptionable manifestoes of the war. He declared that he stood for victory, the support of competent Ministers such as Churchill and Cripps, the impartial examination of complaints and criticism, 'facing up to our mistakes' and avoiding 'hiding our heads in the sand'. Cripps received help from Liberal and Conservative quarters, but Reakes got none from Labour, unlike Brown and Kendall. During the Chamberlain period he had drifted away from the local Labour Party by championing conscription and rearmament, and praising the Munich agreement. 'The outstanding feature of the by-election at Wallasey', said the *Times* special correspondent, 'is the extent to which the Left has worked for the return of the National Government candidate. . . .' Pennington and Reakes were old friends and, but for the intervention of Cripps, the contest would have been thoroughly cosy. According to the veteran Liberal campaigner Ivor Davies, Reakes was 'the local personification of the little man. Reakes had about him a wholesome humanity and real simplicity that made him impossible to dislike.'[15] He was good at canvassing in a saloon bar, and 'bore a remarkable resemblance to Arthur Askey'.[16] Reakes stood at the request of a

[14] For Brown's past and his account of the by-election, see his autobiography, *So Far* . . . (1943); for his programme, *Birmingham Post*, 14 Apr 1942; in general, *The Times* 18–30 Apr 1942, and Mass-Observation's boxed material on Rugby.   [15] Ivor Davies, *Trial by Ballot* (1950) p. 155.
[16] Donald Johnson, *Bars and Barricades* (1952) pp. 240–2.

group of local Conservatives who feared that an outside candidate would be foisted on the constituency. Once Pennington had been chosen, Reakes was left with little to say, apart from the fact that his own candidacy gave the electors a chance to vote against the party politicians. Nevertheless, the Conservative share of the vote fell by 35·7 per cent. Reakes attributed his triumph partly to the migration of Conservative voters from the constituency, partly to the stresses and strains of war, but above all to the revulsion against the appeasers, a curious argument from Wallasey's most notable man of Munich.[17]

The most common explanation of these results was popular frustration with the discouraging progress of the war, and Tom Driberg's victory at Maldon on 25 June was inevitably linked with the loss of Tobruk on 21 June, a frighteningly unexpected defeat. Driberg himself maintains that Tobruk was not decisive. Unlike the other Independents of 1942, he was consciously and openly on the Left, although not a member of the Labour Party. He was already well known as the author of the 'William Hickey' gossip column in the *Daily Express*, and continued to write it for a year after his election. It was Tom Hopkinson, the editor of *Picture Post*, who suggested to Driberg that he stand. Hopkinson belonged to a gathering of leftish public figures known as the 1941 Committee, which had devised in May 1942 a 'Nine-Point Declaration' as a platform for future by-election candidates. Driberg adopted the Nine Points as the basis of his campaign. Slightly abbreviated, these comprised:

(1) *Greater equality* of work, payment, sacrifice and opportunity; (2) *Transfer to Common Ownership* of services, industries, and companies in which managerial inefficiency or the profit motive is harming the war effort; (3) *Reform of the Government Supply Organisations*; (4) *Establishment of effective Works Councils*; (5) *Elimination of Red-Tape in the Civil Service*; (6) *Maximum freedom of expression*; (7) *British initiative in planning an Offensive Grand Strategy*; (8) *Repudiation of any policy of Vengeance*; (9) *Preliminary Post-war plans* for the provision of

[17] For Reakes and Wallasey, see Reakes, *Man of the Mersey*, pp. 72–83; *Wallasey News*, 4, 11, 18, 25 Apr 1942; *The Times*, 8, 24, 25, 29 Apr 1942.

full and free education, employment and a civilised standard of living for everyone.[18]

Could the electors of Maldon have told the difference between Driberg's programme and Kendall's? Since they both concentrated on efficiency in the war effort, and described themselves as Independents, it must be doubtful. Nevertheless, Driberg's campaign had considerable significance behind the scenes. From the Left's point of view, Kendall, Brown and Reakes were rootless minor demagogues, stealing the by-election game from true progressives. The Nine-Point programme was designed to drive out irresponsible candidates.

Driberg's most important supporter at Maldon was the Revd Jack Boggis, the secretary of the Braintree Labour Party, who organised his campaign committee. But this was by no means confined to Labour supporters. The Conservative candidate, Reuben Hunt, was an elderly and uninspiring farmer who made little effort and the Independent Agricultural candidate remained obscure. Tom Wintringham, J. B. Priestley and Vernon Bartlett all spoke for Driberg. His luckiest break, he believed, was being the only candidate to appear for the opening of a new Anglo-Soviet bookshop in Braintree. On polling day the Conservative share of the vote was down 22 per cent on 1935.[19]

The election of four Independents could be interpreted as simply a patriotic response to bad war news, as part of a wider drift away from all party politics or, as Driberg saw his own success in retrospect, as part of the swing to the Left. All three explanations are compatible. Just as the Liberal Party declined in popularity during the Great War, as it became the chief scapegoat for everything that went wrong, so Dunkirk and the defeats of 1941–2 struck a blow at Conservative support. In the spring of 1942 Mass-Observation conducted a poll in three separate parts of the country in which people were asked who they thought would win the next general election. About half

[18] Angus Calder, 'The Common Wealth Party, 1942–1945', Ph.D. thesis (Sussex, 1967) part I, pp. 90–1.
[19] For Driberg and Maldon, see Tom Driberg, *The Best of Both Worlds* (1953) pp. 181–5; Mass-Observation boxed material on Maldon; and Calder, op. cit., pp. 93–6.

would express no opinion – understandably since there was no discussion whatever of the subject in the press or on the radio at that time. In the London area 12 per cent expected a Conservative and 27 per cent a Labour win; in the Midlands, 14 per cent a Conservative and 33 per cent a Labour win; in the North, 17 per cent a Conservative win, 26 per cent a Labour win.[20] These figures suggest that Conservatism was in far worse trouble then than in 1945, and the by-elections rather confirm this. Throughout the war, until April 1945, the out-of-date register, by excluding the growing number of new and certainly more left-wing voters, contained a built-in pro-Conservative bias. Despite this, the Conservative at Maldon did much better in the general election of 1945 than at the war-time by-election. But it is doubtful whether the swing away from the Conservatives meant a swing to Labour at this point. As late as the spring of 1943 Mass-Observation, commenting on the steady leftward trend of opinion during the war, also defined it as a trend away from *all* parties: 'This growing mass of politically leaderless people have no group in which to embody their aspirations and no clear idea as to how their hopes can be fulfilled.'[21] Obviously, however, the most likely implication of a leftward trend was a swing to Labour. The left-wing candidates of 1943–5 succeeded in providing a perfect half-way house between vague discontent with the *status quo* and a positive commitment to Labour.

The crystallisation of pro-Labour feeling may be dated from the publication of the Beveridge Report in December 1942. Although commissioned by the government, this great landmark was in effect a one-man political manifesto, carefully publicised in advance. Beveridge had been asked to work out a plan for co-ordinating the various schemes of social insurance. He not only proposed a comprehensive social insurance plan for all, but ranged far beyond his original brief with demands for 'a comprehensive policy of social progress' to include a national health service and the maintenance of employment. The Report created profound popular interest and approval, but the government, like the Conservative Party and the

[20] Tom Harrisson, 'Who'll Win?', *Political Quarterly*, xv (1944) 27.

[21] Mass-Observation, 'Social Security and Parliament', *Political Quarterly*, xiv (1943) 246.

leaders of industry, treated it with reserve.[22] In the debate of 16–18 February 1943 Ministers accepted most of the Report in principle, as the basis for working out their own proposals. But 97 Labour MPs rebelled and voted for an amendment demanding its implementation at the earliest possible moment. In effect, Labour had broken with the Conservatives on a major issue. In March an opinion poll registered 47 per cent of people dissatisfied with the government's response to Beveridge, as against 29 per cent who were satisfied.[23] It was not until September 1944 that the government's own social security plan was announced, and in the interval progressive politicians rode the Beveridge boom with the cry of 'Beveridge in full and at once'. Churchill had stressed that victory must come first; but victory was already in sight, and people's thoughts inevitably turned towards post-war life. Propagandists had often raised their hopes since 1940, but there was a strong collective memory of Lloyd George's promise of 'a land fit for heroes to live in', and the subsequent years of mass unemployment.[24] The Left warned that Toryism would put the clock back to 1939, and cited Churchill's involvement with the relics of Vichy France and Fascist Italy, Darlan and Badoglio. What kind of future would the troops come home to? Here was a climate of doubt in which Common Wealth and other progressive candidates could flourish.

Common Wealth was founded on 26 June 1942 by the merger of two organisations, the Forward March and the 1941 Committee. Forward March was the creation of the MP for Barnstaple, Sir Richard Acland, a member of an old-established Liberal family comparable with the Foots or the Trevelyans. He had been converted in 1936 to Socialism, and in 1940 to Christianity. His book *Unser Kampf*, published in March 1940, called for the conversion of the war into a moral crusade; redemption and victory could be achieved only by the abandonment of private property, the root of all selfish behaviour. There must be a great change of heart leading to

[22] For an excellent survey of reactions to the Report, see Arthur Marwick, *Britain in the Century of Total War* (1968) pp. 300–14.

[23] Cantril, *Public Opinion, 1935–1946*, p. 361.

[24] This is one of the points stressed in Mass-Observation's study of attitudes towards reconstruction, *Journey Home* (1944).

the establishment of common ownership. Acland wanted to found a mass movement; the 1941 Committee, by contrast, was a loose association of highly placed professional people whose main concern was the efficient conduct of the war. It arose out of a famous series of broadcasts given by the novelist J. B. Priestley after Dunkirk, with Edward Hulton, the owner of *Picture Post*, as its chief patron. The 1941 Committee was ready to accept Acland's demand for common ownership, at least for the sake of an efficient war effort, but most of its members shrank from the idea of establishing a mass political movement, and almost all the personnel of the 1941 Committee abandoned Common Wealth within a matter of weeks.

As a movement, Common Wealth therefore bore the dominant impress of Acland's own personality.[25] Its appeal was almost exclusively to the suburban middle class, and especially the professional employee. It attracted idealists who before the war might have worked for the League of Nations Union, but were put off the Labour Party by its cautious machine politics and rough-and-tumble atmosphere. The professional ethic and the ideal of service, rather than class interest, were the basis of its appeal, devolution ('Vital Democracy') as against the growth of state planning: managers and workers were to own factories and co-operate in running them. The moral flavour of Common Wealth is caught in the slogan of its candidate at Newark in June 1943, Flight-Lieutenant Moran: 'Human Fellowship not Inhuman Competition; Service to the Community not Self Interest; The Claims of Life not The Claims of Property.'[26] Typically, Common Wealth candidates were sincere young men who genuinely believed in a kinder and better world.

Acland and the majority of keen rank-and-file members imagined they were heading for a millennium in which the

[25] My comments on Common Wealth derive, except where otherwise indicated, from Angus Calder's thesis, already cited. This not only provides a definitive study of the movement, but includes an important analysis of war-time by-elections (see part II, pp. 175–89). I have also consulted, by permission of the Secretary of Common Wealth, the minutes of the National Committee and Working Committee. I am also grateful to Sir Richard Acland for allowing me to examine his papers concerned with Common Wealth.

[26] Calder, op. cit., p. 166.

existing and corrupt old Labour Party would be transformed or displaced. But this was not the only view. One of the most prominent figures in the party was Tom Wintringham, the former commander of the British battalion of the International Brigade in the Spanish Civil War. Although detached from the Communist Party, Wintringham remained a Marxist and believed that Common Wealth's role was to be found within a Popular Front of left-wing parties. A still more realistic view of Common Wealth was taken by R. W. Mackay, who entered the party in 1943 and gradually gave it a viable central, regional and electoral organisation. Mackay was a solicitor from Australia who had come to Britain and become a Labour Party stalwart. Apart from Labour, his chief causes were federal union and proportional representation. Like many people on the Left, Mackay was very alarmed that Labour, having entered the Coalition, would be persuaded by Churchill to arrange another 'coupon' election at the end of the war. The only way to prevent this, he argued, was to establish an effective opposition party in the country, 'carrying on electoral organisation against the Coalition or Tory Government in preparation for the General Election when it comes'.[27]

By September 1944 Common Wealth possessed 321 branches with 12,049 members. 68 prospective candidates had been listed in March. Ironically, the movement depended heavily for its finances upon its two rich men – Acland himself, and Alan P. Good, an industrialist and survivor of the 1941 Committee. In 1943 they contributed almost £17,000 of the party's total income of £20,000.[28] As the end of the war drew closer, Acland was obliged to recognise the limits of what Common Wealth could achieve. In the autumn of 1944 Common Wealth applied for affiliation to the Labour Party and was brusquely rejected. It fell back on the strategy of contesting seats where there was no Labour candidate, or where there was some special argument for putting up a candidate. In the end it fielded only 23 candidates in 1945, only one of whom, Wing-Commander Ernest Millington at Chelmsford, was elected. From the historical standpoint

[27] R. W. Mackay, *Coupon or Free?* (1943) p. 21.
[28] National Committee Minutes, 2–3 Sep 1944; 11–12 Mar 1944; Common Wealth Conference Report, 1944, p. 30.

Common Wealth was a tiny tributary through which Acland himself, Millington, Desmond Donnelly, Elaine Burton, Raymond Blackburn and George Wigg passed eventually into the ranks of the Labour Party in the House, and a few thousand voters were added to its mass support in the country.

There were several by-elections between 1943 and 1945 at which there was clearly one Independent candidate of a Socialist or Labour character, a reasonable substitute from the elector's viewpoint for an official Labour candidate. The ILP succeeded in fulfilling this role with two of its nominees in the last months of the war, and if we include them with Common Wealth and Independent Labour candidates, we have 14 seats where a swing to highly unofficial Labour may usefully be calculated (see Table 7.2).

TABLE 7.2

Swings to Labour Substitutes, 1943–5, and to Labour, 1945

	Constituency	Candidate	By-Election	1945
11 Feb 1943	Midlothian and North Peebles	Common Wealth	+11·0	+11·8
12 Feb 1943	King's Lynn	Ind. Labour	+3·6	+12·2
16 Feb 1943	Portsmouth North	Common Wealth	+6·9	+18·4
18 Feb 1943	Bristol Central	Ind. Labour	−4·5	+16·5
23 Feb 1943	Watford	Common Wealth	+11·5	+17·0
20 Apr 1943	Daventry	Common Wealth	+7·5	+12·0
9 June 1943	Birmingham Aston	Common Wealth	−6·7	+30·7
15 Oct 1943	Peterborough	Ind. Labour	+4·2	+5·9
7 Jan 1944	Skipton	Common Wealth	+6·7	+3·6
17 Feb 1944	West Derbyshire[a]	Ind. Labour	+16·2	+8·3
8 July 1944	Manchester Rusholme	Common Wealth	+11·0	+16·6
20 Sep 1944	Bilston	ILP	+0·3	+19·2
26 Apr 1945	Chelmsford[b]	Common Wealth	+28·3	+22·6
17 May 1945	Newport	ILP	+4·6	+12·0

[a] Compared with the 1938 by-election, the Conservative being unopposed in 1935.
[b] Millington stood as Common Wealth in the general election.

Given the restricted character of the war-time register, most of these results co-ordinate well with British Institute of Public Opinion findings on voting intention at the next general election, which showed Labour leads varying between 7 per cent and 18 per cent at times between June 1943 and June 1945.

Studies in two particular constituencies, as well as overall constituency membership figures for the Labour Party, show that grass-roots organisation was beginning to recover in 1942–1943.[29] The 'Independent Labour' candidates were another sign of this. Although the local Labour parties involved issued official statements declaring their support of the electoral truce, they were ready to break it on the quiet. Thus, Fred Wise at King's Lynn, a prospective Labour candidate jumping the gun, announced that he was still a member of the Labour Party, fighting on 'a good Socialist policy'. He wanted the Beveridge Report to be implemented quickly, while Sir Thomas Cook, MP, supporting the Conservative candidate, thought it was 'early days yet to pass judgement upon such a scheme covering so many aspects'.[30] At Bristol Central, Jennie Lee announced that she was standing at the invitation of local Liberal, Labour and church leaders. The Borough Labour Party, reluctantly obeying Transport House and accepting the truce, expelled an alderman and six councillors for supporting her. 'I stand', she said, 'for every word, letter and comma in the Beveridge Report.' Her opponent Lady Apsley, in an article setting out her credo, would say nothing about the Beveridge Report except that social security could not come about without being earned.[31] The prospective Labour candidate for Peterborough, Sam Bennett, aided by Common Wealth, the ILP and local Labour workers, included freedom for India, total acceptance of the Beveridge Report and increased service pay among his campaign points. For once the Conservative nominee, Lord Suirdale, came out in favour of unbalanced budgets to create employment, and full support of Beveridge.[32] Of all these unofficial Labour fights, the most successful was the minor but choice political classic at West Derbyshire. This seat and its neighbourhood had been a family heirloom of the

[29] Frank Bealey et al., *Constituency Politics* (1965) pp. 91–2; A. H. Birch, *Small-Town Politics* (Oxford, 1959) p. 61.

[30] *Norfolk News and Weekly Press*, 23 Jan, 6 Feb 1943; *Norfolk Chronicle*, 12 Feb 1943.

[31] *Bristol Evening Post*, 18 Jan, 8, 15, 16 Feb 1943.

[32] Common Wealth Working Committee Minutes, 30 Sep 1943; *Peterborough Standard*, 24 Sep, 8 Oct 1944.

Cavendishes from the time of Good Queen Bess. Since the boundaries of West Derbyshire were drawn in 1885 it had passed out of the family's hands on only two occasions, when the Liberal C. F. White won it in 1918 and 1922. On 24 January 1944 the Duke of Devonshire told the local association that his brother-in-law, Lieutenant-Colonel Henry Hunloke, MP for the constituency, was retiring. The Duke's heir, Lord Hartington, was happily at that moment on leave and waiting outside the door. He was immediately adopted as the candidate, and two days later another of the Duke's brothers-in-law, the Government Chief Whip James Stuart, arranged for the moving of the writ in the House. This blue-blooded impudence met its match when Charlie White, the son of the Liberal MP of 1918–23, replied by standing as an Independent Labour candidate. Prior to this event, there had been a marked feud between Common Wealth and the Kendall–Brown–Reakes group, polarised at Newark in June 1943 with the adoption of rival candidates and a resultant slanging match during the campaign. Now a common front was achieved. Common Wealth sent in a team of six organisers, while Kendall, Reakes, Clement Davies and T. L. Horabin all spoke for White. Even the Communist Party renounced the truce and worked for his return. Among their other uses, by-elections were a source of light relief from grimmer affairs, and the comic aspects of West Derbyshire were played up by reporters, who were delighted when Lord Hartington said he was under the impression that the coal-mines had already been nationalised.[33] One of the stranger features of his defeat was the uniquely depressed Conservative share of the vote for this period of the war: in 1945 the Conservative did considerably better – instead of even worse, as in most constituencies.

Three Common Wealth candidates won supposedly safe government seats in the last years of the war: Warrant Officer John Loverseed took Eddisbury in April 1943; Hugh Lawson, Skipton in January 1944; and Wing-Commander Ernest Millington, Chelmsford in April 1945. Loverseed, a former pilot for the Spanish Republic who had fought in the Battle of Britain, was a strong candidate who 'captured the imagination

---

[33] See the account of the contest in Angus Calder, *The People's War* (1969) pp. 552–4. See also *Daily Mail*, 8 Feb 1944.

of the working classes and the young people and made a real stir and personal success'.[34] There was unusually strong local interest in the contest, despite the far-flung nature of the constituency. The government candidate, Thomas Peacock, laboured under an important disadvantage. The seat had been Liberal in 1929 and unopposed National Liberal since 1931; but Peacock, while standing as National Liberal, was known to be a Conservative. The Liberal label still counted, and Loverseed played on the issue by adopting a thoroughly Liberal stance with no hint of 'common ownership'. This was a wise tactic in a seat which had never been contested by Labour. Labour feeling in the area was, however, growing – farm wages were a major issue – and this must be part of the explanation of Common Wealth's success. For Liberals of the Sinclair variety, opposed to the National Liberals, there was an Independent Liberal candidate. Since a Sinclair Liberal retained a similar share of the poll in 1945, it looks as though Common Wealth was not benefiting from that quarter. The answer must lie in a defection by National Liberals who returned to the fold in 1945 – no doubt encouraged by the fact that Loverseed was by then standing as Labour – with the appearance of a true National Liberal candidate, Sir John Barlow. Eddisbury, then, does not fit into the pattern of swings to Labour: it voted Barlow in with a landslide majority in the general election.

Skipton was again an unusual constituency. On the normal swing between 1935 and 1945 it should have gone Labour at the post-war general election. But the swing away from the Conservatives seems to have gone instead to the Liberals, keeping Labour in second place. Common Wealth's victory in 1944 bore many hallmarks of Labour parenthood: the local Labour Party was persuaded by Lawson to back him, on the understanding that he would if necessary stand down for a true Labour candidate at the general election, and Tom Wintringham's wife Kitty wrote of the result: 'The hard core of the vote for Lawson came from Labour, the industrial workers of the wool industry.'[35] By this time Mackay had

[34] Mass-Observation file report No. 1669N. My account of the contest is based on this report.
[35] *Common Wealth Review* (Mar 1944) p. 8.

geared up Common Wealth's electoral machine to a fine pitch, and apart from full-time organisers, about 200 youthful volunteers arrived in the constituency to canvass, many of them schoolteachers making use of the Christmas holiday.[36] Lawson was determined to take his stand for the whole bible of Acland-ism and nothing less; yet he seems to have picked up a few votes from farmers disgruntled with farm prices and ploughing-up policy.[37] Although Common Wealth won narrowly, there was comfort for the Left in the fact that Alderman Joe Toole of Manchester had stood as Independent Labour and split the vote. Why Skipton failed to follow through in 1945 is a puzzling question.

Chelmsford was the first English constituency fought on the up-to-date register. Millington was again a strong candidate, the commander of a famous heavy bomber squadron who allowed his political views to remain strangely vague during the campaign. His victory was simply a product of the Labour tide – although the intervention of a Liberal at the general election again damped down the Common Wealth rather than the Conservative vote.

Some of the younger Liberals of the war years, like their successors in the late 1950s, believed in the possibility of a fundamental Liberal breakthrough. 'The possibility was inherent in the situation of breaking the power of the caucus in British political life for ever', Ivor Davies argues.[38] The Radical Action group founded by Donald Johnson in 1941 reflected a desire to ginger up the party leadership and led on to his own attempt to fight Chippenham as an Independent Liberal in August 1943, and Honor Balfour's stand at Darwen in December 1943. With precious little help from anyone, they achieved 49·4 per cent and 49·8 per cent of the poll respectively. Encouraged by these portents, Mrs Corbett Ashby put up at Bury St Edmunds in February 1944, and at last Liberals from outside the constituency rushed into the fray. Despite the

[36] *Manchester Guardian*, 10 Jan 1944.

[37] Appendix on the Skipton by-election in Calder, op.cit. *Sunday Express*, 9 Jan 1944.

[38] Davies, *Trial by Ballot*, p. 164 and *passim* on the Liberal candidates. See also the account of Chippenham by Donald Johnson in *Bars and Barricades*, pp. 229–48.

backing of a local United Progressive Front of Liberal, Labour and Communist activists, and help from Common Wealth, she was not as successful.[39] Nor were any of these results meaningful for the future of Liberalism. All three of the seats were undergoing the transition from a Conservative–Liberal to a Conservative–Labour dichotomy: the war-time Independents were gathering a brief bloom of Lib.–Lab. co-operation in the seclusion of the electoral truce.

No by-election candidate, save perhaps the anti-war elements of 1940–1, ever publicly called for Churchill to be replaced as war leader. It is plain from every by-election that the very idea was unthinkable. The strongest line ever taken against him occurred, predictably, in May 1942 at the Chichester by-election, when Flight-Lieutenant Gerald Kidd, a protégé of Hipwell, made rude comments about the sinking of the *Prince of Wales* and called on Churchill to give up the post of Minister of Defence.[40] Equally, none of the by-election contestants of the more radical type supported Churchill as leader of the Conservative Party. By the last phase of the war, 1943–5, this had become a cardinal point in by-elections. Kay Allsop, Common Wealth's campaign organiser, noted the feeling at West Derbyshire:

> . . . speakers in support of White would make references to Churchill's war record and the debt owed him by the people of this country. Great and enthusiastic applause always greeted this. Then they would go on to say that despite his services to the nation no man, Churchill nor any other, had the right to dictate to the people of this country how they should use their vote. Invariably this brought louder applause.[41]

This distinction between Churchill the war leader and Churchill the party politician ran deep; as a post-war leader Churchill was not wanted. This was one of the reasons which Tom Harrisson of Mass-Observation gave, in a remarkable article in the autumn of 1943, for predicting a Labour victory at the

[39] For Bury, see *New Statesman*, 26 Feb 1944; *Tribune*, 10 Mar 1944.
[40] Mass-Observation boxed material on Chichester.
[41] Kay Allsop, in *Common Wealth Review* (Mar 1944) p. 9.

general election. Commenting on the poor Conservative performance at by-elections, he wrote:

> It is hardly necessary to underline such results. No machine, no big names, no helpful register, no suitable 'political atmosphere', wartime difficulties, the current weight of *status quo* leaders, plus the much used argument of wartime disunity, can only just stem the success of independent, almost 'private' candidates, often of a quality lower than we expect after the war. Consider the difference with a nation-wide drive, a popular policy, backed by popular national figures, in an atmosphere of sanctioned rivalry.[42]

The assumption that Churchill had only to descend from Olympus and scatter the Left with a whiff of electoral grapeshot was almost universal. In March 1943, in a broadcast on postwar reconstruction, Churchill invited Labour to continue in coalition with the Conservatives after the war to carry out his 'Four-Year Plan' – a plan of which little was ever heard again. The Labour leaders were so incapable of believing they could ever beat him at the polls that they responded warmly. Dalton, Bevin and Morrison all raised the idea of a revised form of 'coupon' election at which the parties composing the Coalition would oppose each other in the constituencies, but go to the country pledged to continue in alliance after the general election, the Coalition reforming according to the new ratio of seats in the House. In September 1943 Hugh Dalton was telling the editor of the *New Statesman*, Kingsley Martin, that it would be 'total lunacy' for Labour to fight an election against Churchill while the laurels of victory were still fresh on his brow.[43] It was probably the rank and file of the party who determined the Labour leaders to go it alone.

The Labour Ministers were perhaps as displeased as Churchill himself by the defeat of government candidates, which gave the embarrassing impression abroad that people in Britain were fed up with their leaders, or even with the war effort. Lord Haw-Haw commented upon the striking results at

[42] Harrisson, 'Who'll Win?'.

[43] The diary of Hugh Dalton, 6 Sep 1943. For the coupon idea, see the diary for 22 Mar and 16 Sep 1943, and Hickleton Papers, diary of Lord Halifax, 18 Aug 1943.

Brighton and Skipton.[44] The government Whips cranked up their own by-election machine: 10 Conservative MPs spoke for Lady Apsley at Bristol Central in February 1943, while 25 were booked for Bury St Edmunds in February 1944.[45] The defeat of the government candidate at Skipton irritated Churchill considerably, and on 1 February 1944 the Cabinet revoked the pre-war rule preventing Cabinet Ministers from speaking at by-elections.[46] By this date there were signs of unease in all three parties, perhaps a sense that the party system itself was being eroded. Lady Violet Bonham Carter of the Liberals, Lord Hinchingbrooke of the Conservative Reform Committee, and Herbert Morrison (in private) for Labour, aired the possibility of a return to normal party warfare in the constituencies, without prejudice to the Coalition. But, as Attlee pointed out, party competition below would inevitably draw in the party leaders and disrupt the Cabinet; the idea faded away.[47]

War-time by-elections served many purposes. The basic one was to replace 141 generally aged MPs by younger representatives, many of them acting servicemen. As Driberg suggests, the Independents by contesting Conservative seats at least gave the local caucus the incentive to select an able candidate. From the voters' point of view, contested by-elections were an opportunity to express a variety of frustrations. Chief of these was the absence of a candidate of the voter's party. Thus Conservatives were able to vote Scottish Nationalist rather than Labour at Motherwell in April 1945, giving Dr R. D. McIntyre enough extra votes to become the first Scottish Nationalist MP. No doubt the sheer frustration of enduring the war also expressed itself at the polls. But, as has been argued, 'mere' protest of this kind easily shaded into an anti-Tory disposition. For hard-pressed Cabinet Ministers, operating an almost totalitarian system for the emergency, the high adverse votes were a tiresome but useful reminder that they were supposed to be democratic politicians. The press rubbed

[44] *Reynolds News*, 5 Apr 1944.
[45] *Bristol Evening Post*, 28 Jan 1943; *Yorkshire Post*, 28 Feb 1944.
[46] PRO, PREM 4-64/2.
[47] *Observer*, 27 Feb 1944; *News Chronicle*, 12 Jan 1944; Attlee Papers, Morrison to Attlee, 9 Mar 1944, and Attlee to Bevin, 1 Mar 1944.

into them the kind of lesson it thought should be drawn. *The Times*, fairly typically, interpreted the Eddisbury result as 'a call, which cannot safely be neglected, for prompt and un-equivocal measures to give effect to the great programme of social reform which has been embodied in a series of reports to the Government'.[48]

Historically, the by-elections provide valuable evidence of the role of the war in initiating a new leftward swing. David Butler has demonstrated, in an analysis of the by-elections of 1935–9, that there had been 'no very appreciable change in party support' since 1932.[49] Why did few people understand the new trend after 1940? 'No Tory agent need yet be seriously alarmed', said the *Observer* after West Derbyshire. 'It is cer-tainly true', added the *Economist*, 'that there are no signs of any enthusiasm for Labour.'[50] 'Chips' Channon was relieved to hear from the editor of *The Times* in September 1944 that there was no serious swing to the Left: '. . . so much for the foolish prophecy of that very nice ass Harold Macmillan who goes about saying that the Conservatives will be lucky to retain a hundred seats at the election.'[51]

The failure to sense Labour's growing majority was a measure of the lack of communication between the world of Westminster, with its fixed assumptions, and the mood of the public. Mass-Observation sought to enlighten the situation, and the polls conducted by the British Institute of Public Opinion predicted a Labour victory on six occasions after June 1943. But the study of voting behaviour was only just beginning, and the professional pundits of the day ignored its conclusions.

[48] *The Times*, 9 Apr 1943.
[49] David Butler, 'Trends in British By-Elections', *Journal of Politics*, XI 2 (1949) 396–407.
[50] *Observer*, 12 Mar 1944; *Economist*, 4 Mar 1944.
[51] Robert Rhodes James (ed.), *Chips: The Diaries of Sir Henry Channon* (1967) p. 393.

Note: 1945 to 1960

By CHRIS COOK

The massive Labour victory in the 1945 general election produced a changeover of seats comparable only to the National Government victory of 1931. Labour emerged from 1945 with a net gain of 199 seats, compared with a net loss of 215 in 1931; the Conservatives finished with a net loss of 161 seats in 1945, having had a net gain of 202 in 1931.

Considering this tremendous switch of seats and votes, it is quite astonishing that so few constituencies changed hands at by-elections between 1945 and 1950. In the whole lifetime of the two Attlee governments, only the following constituencies changed hands:

Constituency	Date	Change
1. Combined English Universities	13–18 Mar 1946	Con. gain from Ind.
2. Down	6 June 1946	Unionist gain from Ind. Unionist.
3. Combined Scottish Universities	22–27 Nov 1946	Con. gain from Ind.
4. Glasgow Camlachie	28 Jan 1948	Con. gain of seat won by ILP candidate in 1945, who had subsequently accepted the Labour whip.

In no case had the Conservatives either gained a seat from Labour (except for the Camlachie result, in which the Labour–ILP feud makes comparisons impossible) or indeed had Labour gained a Conservative seat. For the record, the Liberals neither gained nor lost a seat, nor indeed did they look remotely like doing anything in particular. Between 1945 and 1950 Liberals fought only 14 of the 52 by-elections. Indeed, only in by-elections in the City of London and in Bermondsey Rotherhithe could they obtain over 20 per cent of the poll. Elsewhere, they forfeited 9 deposits from 14 candidatures.

Labour's ability to retain the seats won in the landslide victory of 1945 was nothing short of remarkable. Indeed, in the first few by-elections after 1945 there was a brief honeymoon period in which such seats as Smethwick (1 October 1945) and Ashton-under-Lyne (2 October 1945) actually swung to the government. Even in early 1946 there were swings to Labour at Preston (31 January), South Ayrshire (7 February) and Glasgow Cathcart (12 February).

A very different result occurred, however, at Bexley on 22 July 1946. At a by-election in which turnout fell from 76·7 per cent to 62·6 per cent, the voting, compared with 1945, was:

	1945			*1946*	
Lab.	24,686	*(56·9)*	Lab.	19,759	*(52·5)*
Con.	12,923	*(29·8)*	Con.	17,908	*(47·5)*
Lib.	5,750	*(13·3)*			

Even assuming that the bulk of the Liberal vote had moved to the Conservative, the fall in Labour's share of the total vote was an indicator that the political climate was turning cooler for the government. The growing economic difficulties of the Attlee administration produced a series of heavy swings to the Conservatives during 1947: 10·2 per cent at Liverpool Edge Hill (11 September), 8·5 per cent at Islington West (25 September) and 8·8 per cent at Epsom (4 December).

Apart from a few exceptional very heavy pro-Conservative swings during 1948, such as Glasgow Gorbals (17·0 per cent) and Edmonton (16·2 per cent), the by-elections during 1948 and 1949 settled down to show fairly consistent swings of between 4 per cent and 6 per cent away from Labour: in the last 12 by-elections of 1948–9, 6 of the contests showed a swing within these limits. There was relatively little in these by-elections to indicate the extent to which the Conservatives would recover lost ground in the general election of 1950.

After the 1950 election, although Labour retained all 8 seats it was called on to defend, in no case was there a swing in its favour. Nor did the climate get better for Labour; rather, it deteriorated considerably. From the autumn of 1950 (beginning with a 3·7 per cent swing against Labour in a by-election on 28 September at Leicester North-East), a fairly continuous swing to the Conservatives appeared, although swings were much higher in Conservative-held safe seats, as the following figures indicate:

No. of by-elections in Con.-held seats: 6.   Swing: 7·01%.
No. of by-elections in Lab.-held seats: 8.   Swing: 2·45%.

Unfortunately for analysis on these lines, no marginal-held seats really occurred after the Glasgow Scotstoun election of October 1950. It is thus hard to estimate the effect of Labour's divisions and resignations in by-election terms prior to the 1951 election.

The Conservative victory in the 1951 general election ushered in a period of remarkable electoral stability. Indeed, in the 45 contested by-elections up to the 1955 general election, only one seat changed hands – a Conservative gain from Labour in the highly marginal Sunderland South seat on 13 May 1953. Even more remarkable was the number of constituencies which, without changing hands, showed a quite definite swing to the Conservatives. Examples of this swing to a government in power at a mid-term by-election occurred at Canterbury (12 February 1953), Birmingham Edgbaston (2 July 1953), Ilford North (3 February 1954), Haltemprice (11 February 1954), Bournemouth West (18 February 1954) and Sutton and Cheam (4 November 1954). Even in early 1955 there was a swing to the government in four of the six contested by-elections; ironically, in view of events seven years later, the government's best result was at Orpington (20 January 1955).

It is true that, in the more safely Labour-held territory, there were swings against the government, but even here only two constituencies – Dundee East in July 1952 and Shoreditch and Finsbury in October 1954 – registered swings above 4 per cent. No doubt, as is argued later in this volume (see p. 328), the improving economic climate was one important factor at work. None the less, the achievement of the Churchill administration was quite remarkable.

Almost as remarkable – although for distinctly different reasons – was the Liberal performance. During these years the fortunes and morale of the party hit a new rock bottom. In the 45 contested by-elections, only eight Liberals were brought forward. Mercifully for the party, no Liberal seats fell vacant. Seven of the eight Liberal standard-bearers lost their deposit: indeed, only one of the seven achieved 10 per cent of the poll. However, in all this darkness there appeared one beacon. In a by-election in Inverness in December 1954 a Liberal who had not even contested the seat in 1951 took 36 per cent of the poll, sweeping Labour into third place. Admittedly, turnout was very low (down from 69·3 per cent to 49·2 per cent), but the by-election heralded, a decade in advance, the breakthrough the Scottish Liberals were to make in the Highlands in 1964 and 1966. Apart from 16 per cent of the poll for a Plaid Cymru candidate at Aberdare in October 1954, none of the other smaller parties achieved any success between 1951 and 1955.

After the return of the Conservatives again in 1955, the party did not enjoy a honeymoon comparable to the period after 1951. Partly, of course, the Suez affair served to disrupt the political scene, but equally the economy proved very soon to be a weapon that could increasingly be used against the government. In fact, however, the first feature of the by-election returns after 1955 was a series of impressive Liberal results. At Torquay on 15 December 1955 a Liberal took 23·8 per cent of the poll. At Hereford on 14 February 1956 the party took 36·4 per cent and on the same day achieved 21·6 per cent at Gainsborough.

Partly because the luck of the by-election draw gave the Liberals no likely territory to contest, this first semblance of a revival petered out during 1956: indeed, the party suffered its worst-ever humiliation when, at Carmarthen, Lady Megan Lloyd George won the by-election in February 1957 for Labour.

Long before this, however, the main feature of the by-elections during and after the summer of 1956 was a growing disenchantment with the Conservatives. At Tonbridge on 7 June 1956 there was a swing of 8·4 per cent to Labour. After the Suez episode, the by-election caused in the Melton division by the resignation of Anthony Nutting saw a 7·6 per cent swing.

Curiously, despite continuing fairly heavy swings against the

Conservatives in 1957 – reaching 12·2 per cent at Warwick and Leamington on 7 March 1957 (Eden's old constituency) – only one Conservative seat was lost to Labour, the marginal Lewisham North. Meanwhile the Liberals had begun to achieve some impressive results during 1957, taking over 20 per cent of the poll at Edinburgh South (29 May), North Dorset (36·1 per cent of the poll on 27 June), Gloucester (12 September) and Ipswich (24 October).

Early in 1958 the Conservatives began the year with three consecutive and sensational by-election losses. Of these contests, Rochdale was perhaps the most extraordinary. In a straight fight in 1955 the Conservatives polled 51·5 per cent of the vote. For the by-election the Liberals waged a spirited campaign with Ludovic Kennedy, a well-known TV personality, as their candidate. The result was:

	1955			*Feb 1958*	
Con.	26,518	*(51·5)*	Lab.	22,133	*(44·7)*
Lab.	24,928	*(48·5)*	Lib.	17,603	*(35·5)*
			Con.	9,827	*(19·8)*

The result was a humiliation for the Conservatives and a near-triumph for the Liberals – their final triumph coming on 26 October 1972 when a fortuitous by-election at Rochdale produced a Liberal gain (see below, pp. 269–70).

After Rochdale, the Conservatives suffered a further rebuff when, on 13 March, the Kelvingrove division of Glasgow was lost to Labour on a swing of 8·6 per cent.

Two weeks later the Liberals achieved the by-election breakthrough that had eluded them for a generation when they won Torrington from the Conservatives. Without detracting from Mark Bonham-Carter's individual triumph, the by-election was not quite the dawn of the promised land that many Liberals imagined. The seat had been held by George Lambert, sitting as a Conservative and National Liberal. No independent Liberal had fought in 1955, and clearly much of the traditional Liberal vote in this constituency had either abstained (turnout rose by 11·4 per cent to 80·6 per cent in the by-election) or found a temporary home in the Conservative ranks. As it was, the Liberals gained Torrington by the narrow margin of 658 votes – only to lose the seat again in 1959.

Torrington failed to inspire any similar Liberal break-through, although the party polled some impressive performances in a variety of residential and agricultural seats: 24·5 per cent at Weston-super-Mare and 27·5 per cent in Argyll (both on 12 June 1958), 24·3 per cent in East Aberdeenshire (20 November 1958), 24·2 per cent at Southend West (29 January 1959) and 25·7 per cent in Galloway (9 April 1959).

With the exception of these safe Conservative seats in which signs of a Liberal inroad were evident, the most significant feature of the by-elections was the marked lack of Labour success after the spring and early summer of 1958. As 1959 progressed, by-elections in such seats as South-West Norfolk (25 March 1959), Penistone (11 June 1959) and Whitehaven (18 June 1959) showed virtually no move from Conservative to Labour. Even without the summer sun and the even more comforting warmth of Macmillan's affluence, the Labour Party was in a weak position to face a general election.

For the whole period from 1945 to 1959 the degree of political stability witnessed in these by-elections cannot be overemphasised. During these fourteen years only a handful of seats changed hands. The full statistics are set out below:

By-Elections, 1945–59

Total no. of by-elections:	168
No. of contested by-elections:	163
No. of Conservative candidates:	163
No. of Labour candidates:	157
No. of Liberal candidates:	42

Seats Changing Hands at By-Elections, 1945–59*

13–18 Mar 1946	Combined English Univs.	Con. gain from Ind.
22–27 Nov 1946	Combined Scottish Univs.	Con. gain from Ind.
28 Jan 1948	Glasgow Camlachie	Con. gain from ILP
13 May 1953	Sunderland South	Con. gain from Lab.
14 Feb 1957	Lewisham North	Lab. gain from Con.
28 Feb 1957	Carmarthen	Lab. gain from Lib.
12 Feb 1958	Rochdale	Lab. gain from Con.
13 Mar 1958	Glasgow Kelvingrove	Lab. gain from Con.
27 Mar 1958	Torrington	Lib. gain from Con.

* This list excludes, because of their peculiar nature, the by-elections in Down (6 June 1946), Mid-Ulster (8 May 1956), Liverpool Garston (5 Dec 1957) and Ealing South (12 June 1958). In both these last-named seats, Conservatives won seats in which the outgoing MPs had become Independent Conservatives.

The triumph of Macmillan in October 1959, and the third successive defeat at the polls of the Labour Party, was a watershed in British politics. The internal dissensions that were unleashed within the Labour ranks, and the subsequent Liberal revival that culminated in the summer of 1962, led to a markedly more turbulent period of by-election history than had occurred since war-time days.

Ironically, in the first by-election after 1959 a very small swing to the Conservatives was sufficient for the party to capture the highly marginal Brighouse and Spenborough seat from Labour.

After this initial contest, however, the lesson of the by-elections became unmistakably apparent: a Liberal revival, quite unlike anything seen since the late 1920s, was under way. The causes and course of the road that led to Orpington deserve a separate study.

8. Orpington and the 'Liberal Revival'

By KEN YOUNG

General Election, 1959		(Electorate, 51,872)
Sumner (Con.)	24,303	(*56·6*)
Hart (Lab.)	9,543	(*22·2*)
Galloway (Lib.)	9,092	(*21·2*)
Con. majority	14,760	Turnout 82·8%

By-Election, 14 Mar 1962		(Electorate, 53,779)
Lubbock (Lib.)	22,846	(*52·9*)
Goldman (Con.)	14,991	(*34·7*)
Jinkinson (Lab.)	5,350	(*12·4*)
Lib. majority	7,855	Turnout 80·3%

General Election, 1964		(Electorate, 54,846)
Lubbock (Lib.)	22,637	(*48·4*)
McWhirter (Con.)	19,565	(*41·8*)
Merriton (Lab.)	4,609	(*9·8*)
Lib. majority	3,072	Turnout 85·4%

The road to Orpington

For more than fifty years following the landslide victory of 1906, the Liberal Party suffered a slow, steady, seemingly inexorable decline in its parliamentary representation. By the 1955 general election there seemed a possibility that the party might disappear from British politics altogether (see Table 8.)1; yet the decline was arrested, and the party in the post-Suez era was about to experience a change in its fortunes significant enough to create the illusion of a 'revival'.

TABLE 8.1

The Liberal Vote in Post-War General Elections

	Candidates	Percentage votes cast	Deposits lost	No. of MPs
1945	305	9·0	76	12
1950	475	9·1	319	9
1951	109	2·5	66	6
1955	110	2·7	60	6

In February 1958 came the best result to date: 35·5 per cent of the poll and a good second place at Rochdale. The expected breakthrough came just one month later, at Torrington in Devon.

Increased party activity followed this success: the Liberals fought 19 of the 52 by-elections in the 1955–9 Parliament, and entered the 1959 general election with a new confidence. This time 216 seats were fought, and the Liberal share of the poll more than doubled. North Devon was won, and Torrington lost; but having fought almost twice the number of constituencies, the number of lost deposits was less than in 1955, and more Liberals finished second than at any time since 1945. The Liberal Party, it seemed, was seriously in national politics once more. The stage was set for a revival of Liberalism, aided by the internecine conflicts which racked the Labour Party in the years following the 1959 election.

While the party's by-election record continued to improve, equally significant results were to be seen in the local elections. In 1959 the Liberal Party was represented in local government by only 475 councillors and aldermen. The 1960 municipal elections increased this to 641. In 1961 came a great increase to 1,065, a figure which included a number of important gains in the county councils. 1962 saw a further great increase to 1,603. Most of these gains were made in the south of England, and predominantly in the Home Counties; relative success in the suburbs and poor performance in the cities seemed to be the pattern.

The importance of the local election campaigns were clearly recognised by the party, as an essential base from which to build up the party's parliamentary strength. In Mark Bonham-Carter's words, 'it is easier to change people's voting habits at local elections than at by-elections, and at by-elections than at general elections'.[1] The party decided that the way to Westminster lay necessarily through town and county hall, and in 1960 appointed Pratap Chitnis to head a new local government department at Liberal HQ. The successes which followed, however, were not due simply to the increased interest of the party leadership and organisation; the key to local success lay in the local community where, tactically, 'Liberals were quicker to seize upon and exploit local dissatisfactions than were the other two parties'.[2]

Nowhere was this more true than in Orpington UDC, a suburb in the south-east corner of Greater London, where the Liberal Party was building up an organisation for the local elections which would eventually pay startling dividends in the parliamentary by-election of 1962. In 1955 the Orpington Liberal Association had decided to form ward committees and fight the local elections. During the following year the Conservative-controlled council decided to seek borough status for the UDC, a policy which in Orpington, as in other places, brought a 'ratepayer' reaction based on the supposition that municipal status would necessarily entail higher rates. The Liberals campaigned on this issue, and on that of opposition to the Conservative council's proposals to means-test council tenants; substantial numbers of votes were won on the latter issue in wards with a high proportion of municipal housing, and Liberal candidates came second in four of the five Conservative-held seats contested. 1957 began with party membership at the low level of under 200, but with a clear ambition to become a major political force in the district. Accordingly, the 1957 elections were fought on the slogan of 'Labour Can't Win', and the election literature presented the Liberal Party as the second party of the district. Membership trebled during the next twelve months, as the party continued to campaign on such skilfully chosen local issues as the council's failure to plan for more multiple stores to serve the district's rapidly growing population.

In 1959 the party won two council seats, a significant achievement in a year when the Conservatives did rather well

[1] Quoted in Alan Watkins, *The Liberal Dilemma* (1966).
[2] Ibid., p. 109.

in local elections throughout the country. Although the Conservative vote increased, a Liberal candidate won the Biggin Hill ward – at his fourth attempt – with a majority of 113, while another Liberal won the Goddington South ward.

The party's advance at the local elections continued in 1960. The St Mary Cray ward was won from the sitting Labour councillor with a majority of 384. A subsequent win in a local council by-election gave the Liberals 7 members on the UDC. In 1961 further gains were made on the UDC, Liberals winning a majority of the votes cast (see Table 8.2) to bring their representation up to 12 on the 33-member council, and a county council by-election in September 1961 gave the Liberals their first seat on the Kent County Council.

TABLE 8.2

Orpington UDC Election Results, 1956–61: Votes Cast

	1956	1957	1958	1959	1960	1961
Conservative	9,903	9,509	9,763	11,828	8,882	11,009
Liberal	2,443	2,460	3,584	6,716	8,046	11,771
Labour	5,123	6,297	5,348	2,580	1,570	1,725

In the autumn of 1961 the resignation was announced of the sitting Conservative MP, Donald Sumner, upon his appointment as a County Court judge. The Liberals were ready for the by-election, although, despite their local election successes and the excellent fettle of their election machinery, there was little ground for expectation that the seat could be won. The percentages of votes cast for the parties at parliamentary elections since 1950 were as shown in Table 8.3.

TABLE 8.3

Orpington Constituency Parliamentary Election Results, 1950–9

	1950	1951	1955 (by-election)	1955 (general election)	1959
Conservative	56·7	No Liberal	No Liberal	59·9	56·6
Labour	32·8	stood	stood	27·6	22·2
Liberal	10·5			12·6	21·2

Jack Galloway, the Liberal candidate, was an experienced and popular man who had nursed the seat since before the general election, when he had achieved a close third place to Labour. But Liberal headquarters, alive to the possibility and importance of a good result at Orpington, no longer felt him to be a suitable candidate for the by-election. He had brought to their notice a change in his personal circumstances which, if it became public, could mean political disaster. Liberal Whip Donald Wade pressed Galloway to withdraw, which he declined to do. Further pressure from other members of the Liberal Parliamentary Party and the officers of the local association only stiffened Galloway's resolve to fight. A general meeting was called, at which the officers appealed to the party membership to withdraw their support, alluding to, but never revealing, the information in their possession. This failed; the local party was split, and the majority backed the candidate. But two months and several meetings later Galloway reluctantly stood down, sensing that the tide of opinion, fed by suspicion and rumour, was turning against him.

Expecting a writ for the by-election to be moved at any time, the Liberals moved quickly. An emergency meeting of the executive officers sought the advice of Donald Wade, who insisted that they adopt a local man; the choice fell upon Eric Lubbock, a local councillor and an engineer. It did not seem at the time to be a particularly momentous decision. In Eric Lubbock's words: 'My political experience was very limited, but as the most we could expect was a good second, nobody thought it mattered. My employers, after a perfunctory look at the 1959 voting figures, with the Liberals at the bottom of the poll, generously agreed to let me have three week's paid leave for the campaign.'[3] Shortly after this November meeting, the Conservative Association adopted Peter Goldman as their candidate, and the Labour Party Alan Jinkinson. Goldman was an intelligent and able Conservative researcher, a close associate of party chairman Iain Macleod; he had previously fought West Ham South, an East End seat, and was widely regarded as being of Cabinet calibre. Jinkinson, the youngest of the candidates at twenty-seven, was a NALGO employee.

The writ was not moved in the few weeks following the resignation of Donald Sumner. Rather, the government preferred to wait until the new electoral register was ready in

[3] Eric Lubbock, MP, 'My First Campaign', BBC Radio 4, 3 Apr 1970.

February. At first sight the effect of this decision was to hamper the Labour Party, for the problems of tracing voters who have changed their address and of organising the postal votes is generally handled more capably in the Conservative Party. But, in so far as this put a premium upon organisation, it happened to benefit the highly efficient Liberal machine even more. Paradoxically, the party split over Galloway's candidature also resulted in improved Liberal organisation in the wards. The heightened emotions and sharpened rivalries engendered by the affair intensified the efforts of the party workers, so pro- and anti-Galloway factions each determined to outshine the other in ward organisation and canvassing effort. In addition, delay in moving the writ fostered a local resentment which was skilfully exploited by the Liberal Party, who collected 3,500 signatures on a petition deploring the 'disfranchisement' of the Orpington constituents. This was delivered to the House of Commons with appropriate publicity by Jeremy Thorpe and Eric Lubbock.

Press interest in the campaign was considerable. The *Daily Mail* gave particularly full coverage, and was the only national daily to see the potential significance of Orpington. On 14 December the *Mail* asked:

> Will the word Orpington be engraved on the coffin of the Macmillan government? At the moment the outer London dormitory constituency is only a very small cloud on the horizon – and most politicians have scarcely considered that it could become the name of a famous disaster. . . . There is a distinct possibility that Lubbock might beat Goldman – in which case the word Orpington would become the beacon to set the Liberals alight all over Britain. . . .

The *Mail* followed up this speculation six weeks later with evidence that their prescience had been soundly based: the Conservatives were shown by the latest NOP poll to have a slender 1·1 per cent lead over Lubbock, with the Labour candidate trailing a very poor third. 'The pending by-election', prophesied the *Mail* on 26 January, 'could provide the Liberals with their most spectacular victory for years. And the Tories with their most damaging defeat.'

Eric Lubbock's campaign was certainly going well, seeming

consistently to hit the right note. Identification with the candidate was the cornerstone of the Liberal appeal, and the campaign literature put heavy stress upon his young family, with whom he was photographed in several appealing domestic poses. It stressed his professional standing as an engineer, and added, for good measure, that he was heir to the Avebury peerage. It also bore the effective message that, having established 12 Liberal councillors upon the UDC, the electors of Orpington should now cap this with the election of a Liberal MP. Eric Lubbock's meetings centred upon the kind of grievance likely to strike a chord among the relatively hard-pressed owner-occupiers, as was the case with his call for consumer representation upon the newly created NEDC.

By 1 February the *Daily Mirror* was prepared to concede that 'Orpington is, according to every report, far from the good Tory constituency it was'. *The Times*, however, unwilling to stoop to vulgar speculation, assured its readers on 23 February that Peter Goldman was 'confidently astride a thumping majority [and] is planning a first-class ride to Westminster'.

Mr Goldman's plans, however, seemed increasingly likely to go awry. He was fairly widely regarded as an outsider, foisted upon a constituency which had a long tradition of localist Members. His executive committee had short-listed from 99 applicants, and had been forced to add two local candidates to the short-list in order to placate the strong localist sentiment within the association. Significantly, on 25 February, James Margach in the *Sunday Times* discussed 'the twilight of the carpetbaggers', adding that they were 'at a discount these days'. Peter Goldman, however, continued to run a rather aloof campaign, not canvassing in person as Eric Lubbock did, but touring in his campaign caravan while knockers-up spread the news that the candidate was available to hold court.

With a curiously mistaken view of political tactics, the Conservatives concentrated the full force of their campaign upon the Liberal Party. The local Conservative magazine proclaimed that 'the forthcoming by-election will be a test of the Government and the strength of the local Liberals'. The campaign literature claimed that 'the political opposition in the Division is now almost entirely Liberal', a claim which was largely self-fulfilling, and served to concentrate attention upon Lubbock as the main contender for the seat. In these circumstances the Labour campaign assumed decreasing relevance, and reports of Labour activists supporting the Liberal cause as the best means of blocking Mr Goldman were rife. The final stages of the campaign were clarified by the withdrawal of two Independent candidates, Francis Pym, who clearly withdrew in the Liberal interest, and Harry Onslow-Clarke, representing the British Radical Party, who withdrew for family reasons ten days before the poll. National political figures were prominent at campaign meetings, George Brown and Bessie Braddock appearing on Alan Jinkinson's behalf, and Iain Macleod and Enoch Powell supporting their fellow Tory intellectual. But Jo Grimond's meetings pulled the largest crowds, and Eric Lubbock was also backed up on the doorsteps by Jeremy Thorpe, Donald Wade, Frank Byers and Mark Bonham-Carter. On polling day itself Mr Grimond toured the constituency, ensconced in the boot of a vast white Chevrolet.

Lubbock's only moment of real political danger came when both Peter Goldman and the Gaitskellite Alan Jinkinson attacked him for displaying overt sympathies with CND; at the height of the bewildering period of accusation and ambiguous denial the three candidates were scheduled to take part in a television discussion. Liberal Party headquarters, anxious about charges of irresponsible unilateralism, advised Eric Lubbock to withdraw; this he did, presenting both opponents with the opportunity to put the worst possible construction upon his reticence. They were quick to do so, and further implicit criticism came from academics David Butler and Robert McKenzie who, in a joint letter to *The Times*, urged amendment of the Representation of the People Act to prevent a single candidate vetoing broadcast discussions.

Canvass returns for both the leading contenders were promising, and in the final week it seemed that the result would be decided by differential turnout. But in the last two days of the campaign the opinion polls showed that a remarkably large proportion of voters had yet to decide how to cast their vote. Conservative agent Brian Wilcox declared that 'on anything above a 65 per cent poll we are home and dry' and directed his efforts to organising a high turnout. The Liberal returns also suggested that a high poll would aid them, as promises of support, although a fallible guide, indicated sufficient potential supporters to win the seat. On 13 March, the day before Orpington polled, the electors of Blackpool North had their opportunity to pronounce upon the performance of the Macmillan government. The result, in a seat vacated by Sir Toby Low on his elevation to the peerage as Lord Aldington, was better than the Liberals expected, the Conservative majority being cut from nearly 16,000 to 973. The Liberal candidate increased his share of the vote from 20·6 per cent to 35·3 per cent. The NOP poll, published the previous day in the *Daily Mail*, had slightly underestimated Liberal strength, while being otherwise highly accurate; the result suggested that a last-minute effort by the Blackpool Liberals, encouraged by the NOP prediction, had brought them close to victory.

This phenomenon, coupled with the large proportion of uncommitted voters in Orpington, meant that the eve-of-poll survey there by NOP was to be crucial. It clearly showed a probable Liberal win, and Lubbock's enterprising agent, Pratap Chitnis, secured several thousand copies. He used these for free distribution to the homecoming commuters at Orpington's Southern Region station on polling day and flooded the normally Labour-voting council estates with copies. When polling ended at 9 p.m. Chitnis was optimistic. Everything he saw and heard, he announced, told him that the Liberals would win, 'although my commonsense tells me we cannot'. The result, when announced by the returning officer, was sensational, Eric Lubbock's own exact figures being drowned in the exultant roar from the many Liberals who, on one pretext or another, had contrived to be present at the count.

The Liberal majority was 7,855. In the television studio, Jo Grimond registered honest bewilderment: 'My God . . . an incredible result' was his spontaneous reaction. Equally bewildered was Peter Goldman, unable to believe that he had been so resoundingly defeated. Eric Lubbock, chaired by his supporters, drank exultantly from a convenient bottle and toasted, with understandable hyperbole, 'the next Liberal government'.

Why Orpington elected Lubbock

The Orpington result was universally regarded as being of quite unprecedented significance. Lessons were drawn, correctly or incorrectly, from the result and had a definite impact on the shape of British politics during the next few years. Localism, the changing social structure, the effect of published opinion polls, the unpopularity of the Macmillan government, anti-Semitism and the collapse of Labour in Orpington were variously cited as 'causes' of Peter Goldman's defeat. Unusual among by-elections, Orpington was also closely analysed after the event by social surveys carried out on behalf of both the Conservative and Liberal headquarters. With the benefit of the Liberals' survey, it is possible to go beyond speculation and offer some reliable data on the behaviour of the Orpington electorate.

'The two candidates', remarked the authors of the Liberal post-election survey, 'were antithetical to a remarkable degree.' Mr Goldman was not favourably regarded, except by a minority of Conservative voters, who stressed his ability and his professionalism. He was widely seen as over-confident and remote, with an 'unfortunate' manner. That he was not a local man was deeply resented, but more so among Conservatives who nevertheless voted for him than among those who defected to the Liberals. More important was his lack of identifiability; few electors thought him 'one of us'. Jewish by birth, Peter Goldman was to some degree a victim of anti-Semitic sentiments, although their exact effect is hard to gauge; certainly, consciousness of his Jewishness was the leading feature of Conservative voters' perceptions of the contest. Having previously fought an East London seat without success, he was often regarded as 'from the East End' and, by association, 'not a gentleman'. Little more than one-fifth of all electors rated him a 'good' or 'very good' candidate.

Eric Lubbock, on the other hand, was almost universally popular. He was regarded as likeable and sincere. Well known locally, both by family association, residence and his activities on the UDC, he was with his young family (and children at the local school) an easy candidate with whom to identify. He had a great deal running in his favour: although regarded by a very large majority of electors as 'one of us', he also picked up votes from the deferential, who appreciated his connection with the peerage, and he thus paradoxically benefited from displaced Conservatism. A curious aura of hope surrounded Mr Lubbock and his party; voter approval was consistently couched in terms of what it was *hoped* Eric Lubbock and the Liberal Party would achieve. He was, it seems, given the benefit of every doubt, while these benefits were equally consistently denied to Goldman. The only count against him was his seeming lack of a strong personality. But, significantly, 70 per cent of *all* electors rated him a 'good' or 'very good' candidate.

The party images were by no means as dichotomous as those of the candidates. Both the Labour and Conservative parties had clearly distinct images, expressed usually in terms of social class and socialist/capitalist stereotypes. But Orpington voters found it difficult to describe what the Liberal Party meant to them. The predominant impression was of a party of youth, distinct from the other two parties on an age rather than a class continuum, an impression doubtless heightened by the saturation of the constituency by young activists during the campaign itself. Lacking a class image, the Liberals were seen as 'the middle way', a party both of all classes and of none. Such vagueness and novelty could only be given form in terms of expressed hopes of the party's future; by and large, voters projected on to the party their own particular favoured policy proposals as being measures which, it was hoped, Mr Lubbock and his parliamentary colleagues would promote. Recognition of these factors, as we shall see, had an important impact upon the party's subsequent electoral strategy.

Disappointment and disillusion with the Conservative Government was naturally a factor in influencing voting behaviour, particularly among voters normally supporting the Conservative Party. Specific objections were made to the pay pause, rising prices and high and inequitable taxes. Discontent is always fairly readily apparent where it exists, and the election was widely read as a judgement on the Macmillan government. But perhaps the most curious fact about the Orpington voter is that this discontent was by no means commensurate with the turnover of votes. Of the Liberal voters who, it might be expected, were judging the government harshly, a relatively modest 46 per cent thought the government was doing 'a bad job'. More than one-fifth of Liberal voters approved the government's performance, while a further third were unable to offer either a positive or a negative verdict. The Orpington voters, it seems, simply thought it 'time for a change'.

The Liberal victory might not have been possible without the collapse of the Labour campaign and the defection of Labour supporters to the Liberal camp. Lubbock's victory was based, it has been estimated, upon a numerically high transference of voters from the middle classes from Conservative to Liberal, and upon a numerically smaller but proportionately very high support from working-class electors, who deserted the other parties to support Lubbock. Of the 24,000-odd electors who voted for Donald Sumner at the general election, an estimated 7,500 switched to Eric Lubbock in 1962. Of the 9,000 Labour voters at the general election, some 3,500 deserted their party for the Liberals. The Labour loyalist rump that remained was overwhelmingly a middle-class intelligentsia; it was the working-class Labour voters who supported Lubbock, partly out of dissatisfaction with their own party, but largely, it seems, because Labour was seen as having no chance of winning. It was Labour rather than the Liberals who were on this occasion the victims of the third-party squeeze.

Finally, it is clear that the local elections had provided a *passage* for electors to transfer their allegiance from the Conservatives to the Liberal Party. In politics, electoral success is vital; the last result largely shapes electoral perception of the next. The Liberals had shown they could win the by-election by polling in the 1961 UDC elections more votes in total than the Conservatives. Mark Bonham-Carter's dictum was borne out by the Orpington experience, for there was a close correspondence between Liberal voting in the by-election and at previous UDC elections; in the words of the Liberal survey: '. . . the Council elections may have been a stepping-stone into the Liberal camp for some voters who were not, therefore, voting Liberal for the first time in 1962.'

In the aftermath of the by-election it became apparent that Orpington was no Torrington. Liberal support was firmly founded and looked like enduring; Orpington Conservatives warned Central Office that they did not expect to recover the seat at the next general election. The Liberal survey lent this prediction support: asked about their future voting intentions, 50 per cent of all voters declared themselves for Lubbock; only 2 per cent of those who had voted Liberal vowed to return to the Conservatives This support was irrespective of the recognition that the Conservative Party was likely to win a majority of seats nationally; again in the words of the survey: 'Few people now regret voting as they did, and few intend to go back to their former parties at the next general election. The Liberal position seems reasonably secure The majority thought the Liberals would win next time in Orpington . . . .'

To summarise the foregoing, the factors which led to a Liberal win of astonishing proportions in Orpington can be readily enumerated. The Liberal survey lists them as follows:

1. Lubbock was more attractive than Goldman.
2. The Liberal image was reasonably attractive.
3. The government was under heavy general attack.
4. It was thought that the Liberals could win.
5. It was thought that Labour could not win.
6. Liberal organisation was efficient.

These are not exhaustive, but were probably the most important factors. But while some – the relative attractiveness of the two candidates, for instance – are easily understood, others require further explanation. The Liberal Party was in a position to capture the seat because of its remarkable local strength; but why *was* the Liberal Party so strong in Orpington?

The source of the Liberal strength

The answer which comes most immediately to mind is that given by Donald Newby, one-time chairman of the Orpington Liberals, that Orpington benefited from the dedication and determination of a small band of Liberal activists, whose aim was eventually to overturn the massive Conservative majority. But such an explanation is inadequate. Committed Liberals exist in many constituencies, and the ambition is a common enough one, if rarely achieved. It raises the further question of how the Orpington Liberals were able to succeed, and why no further seats, vulnerable on Orpington form, fell to the Liberals in the months which followed.

Other, more sophisticated explanations were offered, which had more apparent plausibility if lacking in predictive power. Foremost among these was the view of Orpington as the home of a new social group, the young professional middle-class, aspirant, upwardly mobile, committed to neither major party nor to class stereotypes. Soon after the Orpington result, Philip Goodhart, Tory MP for neighbouring Beckenham, ascribed the loss of Orpington to the tensions of social mobility which had itself arisen from Conservative social policy: 'now the extent and the growth of this social mobility can be seen for the first time', lamented his letter to the *Daily Telegraph* of 23 March. The *Spectator*, on the same day, ran a leader on social mobility and 'the new men', and posed the question: 'Is the new middle-class radical in its temper?' Mark Abrams's famous survey carried out in the aftermath of Orpington in suburban constituencies in north-west and south-east London, and in the suburbs of Manchester, found the most striking feature of 'the new Liberals' to be their classlessness;[4] an unusually large proportion refused the interviewers' questions about self-assigned class. Thus, Orpington was to be explained in terms of a concentration of the new men (and their new wives) in a commuter suburb to which they were attracted. The weakness of the 'new men' theory is that other constituencies could easily be identified in which the socio-economic profile closely resembled that of Orpington, and yet which failed to give the Liberals an Orpington-type result.

A further tentative explanation may now, however, be offered, using an analysis derived not from political sociology but from social ecology. The first point to be made is that stereotypes of suburbia are highly misleading, for suburbs vary along a continuum from the dormitory to the industrial; Douglass, Berger, Duncan, Beyer and Schnore are just a few of the sociologists who have stressed the variety of suburban form. Similarly, the family structures of suburbs vary widely; Mowrer in particular has distinguished the 'commuter suburb' from other types in terms of its younger population, shorter length of residence and larger family. Dobriner has identified

[4] Mark Abrams, 'Who are the New Liberals?', *Observer*, 1 July 1962.

the attitudinal differences between the established residents ('locals') and the newcomers ('cosmopolitans'), while Elias and Scotson have shown how, under certain circumstances, acute tensions between 'the established' and 'the outsiders' can arise.

Consider, then, the position of Orpington: not an established residential suburb, like neighbouring Bromley or Beckenham, but a new, growing suburb within the outer metropolitan/rural fringe metropolitan ring. Orpington UDC contained more Green Belt land than any other of the areas soon to be included within Greater London; and yet the northern end of the district contained a considerable amount of modern industry, producing in the main consumer durables, and housing its workers in the pre-war overspill estates built by the London County Council. Very little indeed of Orpington matches the description given it by the *Daily Mirror* as 'the home of the well-to-do stockbroker, the higher grade civil servant, the "comfortable" business man . . .'. Orpington's distinctiveness lay in its substantial and continuing rate of suburban 'colonisation'. This is readily apparent from a comparison of the intercensal growth figures for the district and its neighbours: between 1931 and 1951 Orpington grew more rapidly than any other part of suburban Kent, with the exception of Chislehurst–Sidcup (an area with which Orpington Liberals were later to claim a special identification). Orpington's growth rate during those two decades was 4·59 per cent per annum. After 1951 it was the outer metropolitan ring, beyond the Green Belt, which grew more rapidly than Greater London as a whole; yet in the politically crucial decade 1951–61 Orpington's rate of growth was still considerably higher (at 2·39 per cent per annum) than any of its suburban neighbours, and indeed higher than any other district in Kent with the exception of Strood, in the depths of the rural county. In numerical terms, Orpington's population grew by almost 17,000 during the 1950s from 63,364 to 80,293. The anti-Conservative element of Liberal success was predominantly in the rapidly growing areas of the district, as the figures in Table 8.4 show.

How is this correspondence between the Liberal vote and population growth to be explained? The suggestion put forward here is that the politics of Orpington were largely the

TABLE 8.4

Some Originally Conservative-Held Wards in Orpington

High-growth wards	1951 pop.	1961 pop.	Political history
Goddington North	4,692	7,844	Lib. win 1961
Goddington South	5,164	7,709	Lib. win 1959
Green Street Green	6,987	8,247	Lib. win 1961
Knoll	4,894	6,052	Lib. win 1962
Crofton South	5,963	10,404	Lib. win 1962
Stable wards			
Petts Wood	6,779	6,880	remained Conservative
Farnborough	4,125	4,828	remained Conservative

politics of the established versus the newcomer. Certainly, the kind of issues used by the Liberals to mobilise their vote – lack of provision of shopping facilities to serve the rapid population growth, for example – suggest a conscious preoccupation with the newcomer and his family's problems. The Conservatives, in Newby's view, 'were the local establishment. . . . They were obviously insensitive to the aspirations of their rapidly expanding population and failed to keep abreast of its social needs.' Similar situations have been described by Wyn Grant as a *local regime conflict*; the polity in which this occurs is often the rapidly expanding area which provides a venue for a conflict between the established, long-resident ruling group and the recent arrivals. Grant has shown that 'local regime conflicts' are often fought between an established political party and a non-partisan or 'ratepayer' group, and both he and Professor Vile have drawn attention to the peculiar case of the purely 'local' political party. Such an interpretation suggests that the challenge to the local establishment in Orpington might well have taken the form of a 'ratepayer' movement, had not the small band of resident Liberals been ready and able to channel dissent in a more avowedly political direction.

It is clear, therefore, that 'Orpington man', as a synonym for a suburban classless Liberalism, arose from a misunderstanding of the variety and complexity of suburban life-styles. Orpington was no archetypal prosperous middle-aged established suburb, but an area of growth, conflict and change. The political sub-culture of Orpington comprised a more unusual pattern of attitudes than has been realised. But without the Orpington myth, the history of the three major political parties might have been very different. It is to the impact of Orpington on the Conservative, Labour and Liberal parties that we must now turn.

The impact of Orpington

Orpington, *The Times* pronounced on 15 March, was 'the most severe blow the Conservatives have suffered since they returned to office in 1951'. The day following the by-election, senior Ministers were due to address a meeting of the Central Council of the Conservative Party in London. Unexpectedly, the Prime Minister himself turned up to steady the members' nerves. Iain Macleod had already been dismissive, describing Orpington as a second Torrington; when Mr Macmillan rose to placate his troubled followers he conceded that Orpington was 'a disappointment, even a shock', but:

> What has happened is that Conservative voters have abstained, or voted Liberal as a by-election protest against some things they don't like, some things they don't understand, and some things where perhaps they are not patient enough to look to the end. I do not blame them. I am sorry about it but I understand it. I suppose the lesson to us is that if it is due to lack of knowledge and understanding, I and my colleagues . . . who have the task of explanation must set about it with new endeavour. . . .[5]

The new endeavour was, however, tempered with prudence; the *Sunday Express* on 18 March revealed that a new creation of life peers was to be delayed to avoid any unnecessary by-elections in even the safest seats.

The tensions in the Cabinet were clearly mounting, and the party rank and file were restless. In the following three months other by-election results, at Middlesbrough West, Stockton-on-Tees, Derby North, Montgomeryshire and West Derbyshire, all showed Conservative stock to be at its lowest. Then, on 12 July, came Leicester North-East, where the Conservative ran third to the Liberal candidate. On the following day the Prime Minister announced the reconstruction

[5] *The Times*, 16 Mar 1962.

of his Cabinet, dispensing with the services of seven of its members, including the Chancellor, Selwyn Lloyd, to whose 'pay pause' so much of the Conservative unpopularity was ascribed. None of these events is directly attributable to Orpington, and yet Eric Lubbock's victory was the most threatening of the spate of by-election results which boded ill for the Conservative Party. One particular policy response that has been attributed to Orpington, not least by Mr Lubbock himself in a radio broadcast, was the abolition of the 'Schedule A' property tax, announced in the budget speech of 8 April. 'Schedule A' had been thought to be a significant issue at the by-election; but it is certain that its abolition had been long planned and owed nothing to Peter Goldman's defeat. At a lower level within the party, the carpetbagger's stock fell even further; Michael Rush reports that in the aftermath of Orpington neighbouring Conservative associations were aware that failure to adopt a locally known candidate was a great political risk.[6]

Just as reformers within the Conservative Party grew concerned at their failure to attract 'the new men,' so also did the middle-class progressive elements within the Labour Party. There is no doubt that Orpington, and recognition of the new forces it seemed to herald, greatly strengthened Labour's liberal wing; although the *Daily Worker* could explain Labour's failure at Orpington in terms of the failure of Jinkinson to proclaim a Socialist message, the contrary conclusion was more widely drawn. Orpington ideally illustrated the Crosland and Abrams thesis: that traditional social divisions were being eroded, and that Labour must adapt to these fundamental changes in society. As Woodrow Wyatt warned his constituency Labour Party in a speech a few days after the by-election: 'There is a new social group emerging. It is young. It is white collar. It is skilled. It is ambitious to advance socially and economically. It will decide the next election. It does not want the Tories but it does not want a cloth cap Labour Party either.'[7] The message was repeated in the leading revisionist journal, *Socialist Commentary*. In an article contributed to the May issue, college lecturer Geoffrey Rhodes warned

[6] Michael Rush, *The Selection of Parliamentary Candidates* (1969) pp. 105–6.
[7] *Observer*, 18 Mar 1962.

that 'the Labour Party must take account of this new factor in British politics or be ultimately replaced as the principal opposition party. . . . time will not be on the side of a party which plods along as though no major social changes have taken place since the 1930s.'

Socialist Commentary continued to promote this interpretation of the Liberal success and the failure of the Labour Party to make a political breakthrough at a time when the government's popularity was low. Despite the gradual fall-off in support for the Liberal Party which occurred in the midsummer of 1962, the August issue of *Socialist Commentary* carried a leader devoted to the subject of Liberal support. This dealt mainly with the findings of Mark Abrams's survey in the London and Manchester suburbs, which had appeared in the *Observer* on 1 July. Unless Labour adapted to the patterns of social change, it warned, and ceased 'to think in class terms where these have become irrelevant . . . there will be no stopping the Liberals' advance'. But with the election of Harold Wilson to the party leadership following the death of Hugh Gaitskell, and his adoption of a technocratic appeal, exemplified in his Scarborough speech on science, Labour Left and Labour Right united behind a revisionist programme. Wilson himself, with an oblique reference to Orpington, declared his aim to be 'acceptability in the suburbs'. The message, it seemed, had been read aright, and heeded.

Owing perhaps to their predisposition to believe that the tide of social change was flowing in their favour, many in the Liberal Party accepted the 'new men' interpretation of Orpington. But, as Alan Watkins has written: 'The Liberals claimed both too little and too much; too little in the sense that Mr Lubbock's support already had a broader base than the rising middle class; too much, in the sense that there was no sign of a repeat performance in any other Home Counties constituency.'[8]

It was a serious error. The major parties, each with a solid bedrock of class-based support, could compete for the uncommitted vote of the young professional middle class in the knowledge that whichever party succeeded in winning it could have a majority at the next general election. But the

[8] Watkins, *The Liberal Dilemma*, p. 120.

Liberal Party, even if successful in its aim to monopolise the support of this group, was unlikely to win a single parliamentary seat on *that support alone*. As John Vincent wrote some years later:

> The Liberals have been obsessed for ten years with the belief that they, like the Congregational Church, have a vocation to serve the 'new' middle class. This is market research gone mad. It has got them precisely nowhere. . . . The Liberals set their cap at the London commuter and ended up with the Ross and Cromarty crofter. . . . They tried to win by spotlighting a particular social group. They should have spotlighted place.[9]

In order to win parliamentary seats, it is necessary to attract majority or very substantial minority support in a number of specific constituencies. The 'new men' on whom the Liberal revival was to be based were fairly evenly distributed throughout the country, with a strong bias towards the affluent South-east. Their support, if gained, could provide the Liberal Party with a respectable vote in a large number of areas, but nowhere would it be sufficient to elect a Liberal MP. And in October 1964 this social group gave their vote largely to a Wilsonian Labour Party.

The significance of Orpington in the fatal misdirection of Liberal electoral strategy which followed should not be underestimated. The survey carried out for the LPO was more than just an analysis of the factors leading to Lubbock's triumph. It was also read for the formula which would produce more Orpingtons elsewhere. The party's most vulnerable point, the survey showed, was its vague image, which had contributed little of positive value at Orpington. In the words of the survey report:

> While people may have quite clear beliefs about the party (for example that young people support it) they find it difficult to put into words just what the party stands for, when they can easily describe the others in terms of class and socialist/capitalist stereotypes. *It seems likely that doubt about the party would diminish if it could be associated explicitly*

[9] John Vincent, 'What Kind of Third Party?', *New Society*, 26 Jan 1967.

with young people, their problems and approach – a feature of this
approach being rejection of class. . . . [My emphasis.]

The problem of the Liberal image is of course a perennial one.
The solution offered, however, turned out to be no solution at
all. Perhaps it was a mistake to seek a positive image. Orpington, after all, had been won despite its absence, and the
'image' never reflected the substance of Liberal support. The
Liberal publicity campaign in the following general election
was schizophrenic, combining Celtic fringe and West Country
appeals to local and agricultural interests, with a national
television campaign to win the support of 'the new man'. It
was the former that brought such results as were achieved.

Was there a Liberal revival?

The success at Orpington 'gave an enormous but dangerous
fillip to Liberal plans and activities. Electorally, everything
thereafter seemed a disappointment,'[10] That this was so is
attributable in some degree to the press, who predicted further
unrealisable 'Orpingtons' in the subsequent by-elections.
Middlesbrough West in June 1962 was breathlessly awaited,
with the press billing a repeat Liberal triumph. But the local
candidate polled only a respectable 25·8 per cent of the votes –
a good result, comparable with Tiverton, Moss Side, Bolton
East or Carshalton but, given the inflated expectations, a
disappointment. And although the seemingly 'marginal' seat
of Montgomeryshire was held comfortably in May, the Liberals
failed to win West Derbyshire, Chippenham or Colne Valley,
all seats which they could reasonably have expected to capture.
From March 1963 electoral decline set in, and the deteriorat-
ing by-election results (average vote 17 per cent, as against
28 per cent in 1962) were matched by the inexorable decline in Liberal support as indicated by the opinion polls (see
graph).

Orpington was, of course, merely one event, though an
important one, in the period of the Liberal 'revival'. Although
the downturn in publicly expressed support for the party came

[10] D. E. Butler and A. King, *The British General Election of 1964* (1965)
pp. 101–2.

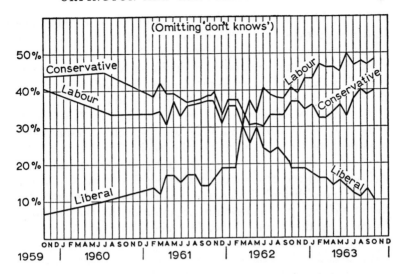

within two months of Orpington (and after the sensational NOP poll which indicated hypothetical majority support for the Liberal Party), the steady improvement in the more immediate aspects of the party's well-being continued for some time. Most notable were the growth in membership, income and full-time agents (see Table 8.5).

TABLE 8.5

Liberal Party Membership, Finance and Full-Time Agents

	1959	*1964*
Paper membership	150,000	300,000
Annual income	£24,000	£70,000
Full-time agents	32	60

Less tangibly, the party enjoyed the heady period when for a while it was 'smart' to profess a Liberal allegiance, and especially 'smart' to do so in normally unpolitical circles. Moreover, the party seemed to have monopolised the political commitment of the young. This illusion is largely attributable to the social visibility of an articulate young élite and the blurring of the distinction between the activist and the ordinary voter. Liberal Party activists were overwhelmingly young; but the young voters were not overwhelmingly Liberal. The number of Young Liberal branches rose from around 150 to some 500 in the years 1959–63. It claimed, in that latter year, to be the fastest-growing youth organisation in the country. And as Abrams and Little remarked, 'a significantly high proportion of Young Liberals came from white collar and professional families with a tradition of civic or political activity'.[11]

The influx of activist youth into the party was, however, a transient phenomenon. So long as by-election results and opinion polls were encouraging, the 'revival' was largely self-confirming. But in late 1962 and 1963 support began once again to coalesce around the major political parties. Liberal support now dwindled, and the Young Liberals became the fastest-*declining* political youth organisation in the country. From 1964 the Young Liberals suffered an annual rate of decline in the order of 20 per cent per annum, as compared with rates for the Young Socialists and Young Conservatives of 5 per cent and 2·5 per cent respectively. More important than the ingress and egress of activists was the failure of the Liberals to make any inroads into the political commitment of the younger voter. The young, as Abrams and Little in a separate study discovered, were neither more radical nor more conservative – nor indeed more Liberal – than their elders. They pointed out that 'the young do not give the Liberals more support than other age groups. This reflects a direct failure of a major campaign by the Liberal party in 1962–3 to identify itself with the interests of the young. . . .'[12]

Given, then, the decline of popular support after Orpington, and the failure to secure the support of the special 'target' groups of voters, the general election, when it came, was no revivalist occasion, although the results were an improvement on 1959, as Table 8.6 shows.

The gains – and especially the untabulated second places – do perhaps illustrate the one long-term consequence of Orpington: that the Liberal Party was once again taken seriously as a national political institution. On 16 March 1962 the *Daily Mirror* had announced that it would henceforth present the

[11] P. Abrams and A. Little, 'The Young Activist in British Politics', *British Journal of Sociology* (Dec 1965) p. 325.

[12] P. Abrams and A. Little, 'The Young Voter in British Politics', *British Journal of Sociology* (June 1965) p. 99.

TABLE 8.6

Liberal Performance in 1959 and 1946 General Elections

	Candidates	MPs elected	Deposits forfeited	Total votes	% of UK total
1959	216	6	55	1,640,760	5·9
1964	365	9	52	3,099,283	11·2

Liberal viewpoint to its readers 'as a public service'. The Liberals were news, and in the words of the party's then Director of Research, 'almost every national newspaper has given the Liberals space to answer the Tory charge that Liberals have no constructive programme. The result has been a crystallisation of Liberal policy in terms of the problems of today.'[13] But the concomitant of this was that every Liberal candidate had now to face the opposition of both major parties, all existing electoral arrangements being abrogated. From then on, the Liberal Party was fighting for survival; its credit had expired.

LIST OF SOURCES

B. M. Berger, 'The Myth of Suburbia', *Journal of Social Issues*, no. 1 (1961) pp. 38–49.
Glenn Beyer, *Housing and Society* (New York, 1965).
J. Bonham, R. H. Pear, H. T. Cowie, articles in *Political Quarterly* (July–Sep 1962).
Alan Brier, 'A Study of Liberal Party Constituency Activity in the Mid-1960s', Ph.D. dissertation (Exeter, 1967).
Census 1961, England and Wales, County Reports: Kent (1963).
D. Chapman, *The Home and Social Status* (1955).
Chris Cook, 'The Liberal and Nationalist Revival', in C. P. Cook and D. McKie (eds.), *Decade of Disillusion* (1972).
J. T. Coppock, 'Dormitory Settlements around London', in J. T. Coppock and H. T. Prince (eds.), *Greater London* (1964).
W. M. Dobriner, 'Local and Cosmopolitan as Contemporary Suburban Character Types', in Dobriner (ed.), *The Suburban Community* (New York, 1958).
Roy Douglas, *The History of the Liberal Party, 1895–1970* (1971).
H. P. Douglass, *The Suburban Trend* (New York, 1925).
Otis Duncan and Albert Reiss, *The Social Characteristics of Urban and Rural Communities* (New York, 1956).

[13] H. Cowie, 'Liberalism's New Deal', *Political Quarterly* (July–Sep 1962) p. 255.

N. Elias and J. L. Scotson, *The Established and the Outsiders* (1965).

Wyn Grant, '"Local" Parties in British Local Politics: A Framework for Empirical Analysis', *Political Studies* (June 1971) pp. 201–12.

J. H. Johnson, 'The Suburban Expansion of Housing in London, 1918–39', in Coppock and Prince (eds.), *Greater London* (1964).

Ernest Mowrer, 'The Family in Suburbia', in Dobriner (ed.), *The Suburban Community* (New York, 1958).

Donald Newby, 'The Orpington Story', *New Outlook* (Mar 1963) pp. 3–18, 27–42.

'The Orpington By-Election: Report on a Survey by the Political Research Unit, Liberal Party Organisation'.

Jorgen Rasmussen, *The Liberal Party: A Study of Retrenchment and Revival* (1965).

G. Rhodes, 'Labour and the Young Professionals', *Socialist Commentary* (May 1962) pp. 12–4.

Leo Schnore, 'The Functions of Metropolitan Suburbs', *American Journal of Sociology* (Mar 1956).

——, 'Urban Form: The Case of the Metropolitan Community', in Werner Z. Hirsch (ed.), *Urban Form and Life* (New York, 1963).

Socialist Commentary, leading article (Aug 1962).

Michael Steed, reply to Vincent (see above, p. 217, n. 9), *New Society*, 3 Feb 1967.

M. J. C. Vile and F. Whitemore, paper read to joint meeting of Political Studies Association and Political Sociology Group of the British Sociological Association, Birmingham, Jan 1972.

Various issues of *The Times, Guardian, Daily Mail, Daily Express, Daily Mirror, Spectator, New Statesman, Daily Telegraph, Evening Standard, Daily Herald, Economist, Daily Sketch, Sunday Express, Sunday Times, Observer.*

Party election literature.

Interviews with participants.

9. By-Elections of the Wilson Government

BY DAVID McKIE

Until 1966, it had for many years been a rare exception for a seat to change hands in a by-election. The Labour Governments of 1945–51 lost only one seat. The Conservatives survived over five years after their return to power without any casualties, and actually picked up a seat from Labour in May 1953 – the first time since 1924 that the government had captured a seat from the opposition at a by-election. In the whole of their thirteen years the Conservatives lost only 10 seats – 8 to Labour, 2 to the Liberals.

The astonishing thing about the by-elections of the 1966 Parliament was that, far from being an exception, the loss of seats by the government became for a time the almost invariable rule. In one ten-month period alone, September 1967 to June 1968, Labour lost almost as many seats as the Conservatives had in their thirteen years. Of the two others they defended in that period, one was saved by a mere 1·4 per cent of the total vote. By the time they lost office in June 1970 they had shed 16 seats out of the 31 they defended in just under six years of office – more than in their whole previous parliamentary history (15 were lost between 1900 and 1964). Swings which had once seemed disastrous now came as a relative relief. No government in thirty years had experienced anything remotely like it.

The first shock for Labour, almost unheralded, and for over a year unmatched by any other by-election result, had come early in the 1964 Parliament, at Leyton. It was a self-inflicted wound. Patrick Gordon Walker, Harold Wilson's choice for Foreign Secretary, had been defeated in the 1964 general election at Smethwick, a seat he had held since 1945, after a contest in which the race issue had been heavily against him. Wilson was determined to have him in the Commons, all the more so because of the circumstances of his defeat. So Transport

House began to look around for a suitable seat within reach both of Whitehall and of Gordon Walker's Hampstead home. After a while their eyes lit on Leyton.

Reginald Sorensen had first been elected for Leyton West in 1929. He lost the seat in 1931, regained it in 1935 and transferred to the new Leyton constituency in 1950. He had left school at fourteen to become an errand boy, trained at theological college and become minister of the Free Christian Church in neighbouring Walthamstow. He was a man of many good causes, especially those devoted to peace and to the Indian sub-continent. Unfortunately for him, he was also seventy-three years old.

When it was first put to him that he might move conveniently aside and enable Gordon Walker to occupy Leyton, he was, by all accounts, shocked and horrified. 'Heavens above! God forbid!' he is said to have exclaimed. He was opposed to peerages on principle. But pressure was applied, and Sorensen duly resigned his seat to go to the Lords.

Leyton is one of those suburbs of London which once used to regard itself as a self-contained township but is now sinking more or less resignedly into metropolitan anonymity. Holmes and Sutcliffe made a record opening stand of 555 there for Yorkshire, in the days when Leyton was not London but Essex. Mainly, it is street upon street of turn-of-the-century terraces, a place which expanded fast when the railways came and has seen comparatively little building since. At the time of the by-election, some 45 per cent of homes were owner-occupied;[1] about 40 per cent were privately rented; only some 13 per cent were council-owned. Nearly 30 per cent of the electorate were aged sixty or over.

The campaign was a bleak affair. The weather was not cruel, as it might have been for a January election, only cheerless. And cheerlessness was the hallmark of the campaign. Gordon Walker's arrival in the constituency was marked by the setting up of a mini-Foreign Office at Leyton Town Hall where he could transact vital business. Leyton, said some enthusiasts, was on the map as it had hardly been since Holmes's and Sutcliffe's day. At Labour headquarters too there were hurried

[1] *Census 1966: United Kingdom General and Parliamentary Constituency Tables* (1969).

rearrangements. The agent, Peter Kelly, was edged out to make way for the local regional organiser, Wilfred Young. That made two local casualties of Gordon Walker's arrival. Gordon Walker campaigned from the back of a furniture van, haranguing half-empty street corners. The general atmosphere was lugubrious: Labour began to be worried that its candidate was 'not getting across'.

Some of those around him protested that the candidate was not the cheerless figure that people took him for. He himself blamed the press: 'The papers', he said after the contest, 'didn't print one picture of me smiling'.

But in truth there was little to smile about. Reporters who trudged the Leyton streets soon formed the impression that the Labour vote would slump heavily. The removal of Reginald Sorensen was clearly resented, both by party members and by constituents with no particular affiliations. The voters of Leyton were being exploited to suit the private purposes of Harold Wilson and his government. The same resentment had been clear in the St Marylebone by-election of December 1963; it was also reported from Nuneaton, which polled on the same day as Leyton, where another long-serving Member was being turned out to make way for the Minister of Technology designate, Frank Cousins.

And Gordon Walker had the mark of a loser: Smethwick hung round his neck. Smethwick Conservatives dropped a plan to send a canvassing party to Leyton to work against him, but the Conservatives reminded the electorate time and again of how and why Gordon Walker had had to come to Leyton. He had, said Iain Macleod, been 'a casual and inefficient MP.'[2]

The immigration issue had unseated him at Smethwick; there were those determined to use it against him here as well. Colin Jordan, leader of the National Socialist movement, moved in on Leyton. He invaded an early press conference.

---

[2] For a similar opinion, see Lord Wigg, *George Wigg* (1972). For a contrary view, see A. W. Singham, in D. E. Butler and A. King, *The British General Election of 1964* (1956) pp. 363–4. Gordon Walker may also have been accident-prone. When NOP were carrying out an inquest on their inaccurate poll in Leyton, one elderly lady told them she had decided not to vote Labour after learning at the last minute who their candidate was. 'It was that Lucky Gordon Walker', she explained, 'that was in the Christine Keeler case.'

Then two Labour meetings, one addressed by Denis Healey, the other by George Brown, were interrupted by demonstrations involving Jordan and his associates.[3] There had been no history of racial disturbance in Leyton. There was, at the 1966 census, a coloured population of some 3,000; as one voter told a reporter: 'There are quite a lot of dark people round here. There didn't seem a lot of animosity. We heard nothing about it at the General Election. We never had fighting and that sort of thing before. We've always been a very peaceful borough, up to now.'

The Conservative candidate was Ronald Buxton, a civil engineer and a local employer who campaigned in a curious ginger overcoat. He called for tougher immigration controls, but denounced allegations that his canvassers were using the race issue on the doorstep.

On the face of it, Labour should not have been in trouble at Leyton. The opinion polls were favourable: Gallup put them 9 points ahead in December, with 48 per cent satisfied with the government's record – though the January lead fell to $3\frac{1}{2}$ per cent. The electorate seemed unenthusiastic: there was grumbling about prices, particularly, it seemed, among pensioners. But a National Opinion Poll taken shortly before polling day suggested that everything would be all right on the night: it predicted an increased Labour majority, thus giving the party all the more reason to discount the warnings of sympathetic reporters as mere pessimism. They were not to know that NOP had here produced the most inaccurate reading in its history.

On 21 January, Gordon Walker lost the seat by 205 votes. Even the Conservatives had not expected it. 'I didn't think we would do it', Buxton admitted as he set off for an impromptu celebration at which he played 'Land of Hope and Glory' on the piano before a cheering audience of 400.

The swing at Leyton was 8·7 per cent. Not, perhaps, very spectacular compared with some of those the Conservatives had

[3] This meeting also produced a memorable piece of heckling. After the clashes on immigration were over, Reginald Sorensen was explaining to the audience that, although they might be surprised to see him going to the Lords, the peerage and democracy were not incompatible. After all, we had just been celebrating the anniversary of the birth of British democracy, which we owed to Simon de Monfort, who was a baron. Voice from the back: 'And *he* was a bloody immigrant, too.'

suffered in the late days of Harold Macmillan. But coming so soon after Labour's general election victory, and at a time when, despite unpleasant economic measures, they had still seemed to have a solid backing of public support, it was a major political sensation.

Yet at least there were special circumstances to explain it: the eviction of Sorensen, the failure of Leyton to take Gordon Walker to its heart. And subsequent by-elections produced nothing to match it. There were seats where the Labour vote slumped, but these were places where it didn't really matter anyway; and it was widely noted that the beneficiaries seemed to be the Liberals. Much speculation broke out as to whether the voters were constructing a series of informal 'radical alliances', supporting whichever of the leftward parties was challenging the Conservatives.

The emergence of this pattern gave the Liberals an excellent chance at Roxburgh, Selkirk and Peebles, which polled in March. This was a ripe slice of luck for the Liberals. There were only two seats (North Cornwall and Chippenham) where they had run the Conservatives closer at the previous year's election. It had been a Liberal seat from 1950 to 1951. Their candidate, David Steel, was young, energetic, fluent and familiar from frequent television appearances. He had made a very considerable hit as candidate in the 1964 election. And he had a ready-made issue. The Borders, he said were falling into neglect. Successive governments had ignored them, had stood by while the whole area fell into decline. It was difficult to find poverty and squalor in Roxburgh, which is a well-heeled, mellow and very beautiful constituency. But it was a great deal easier to expose a very real fear among its people of what the future might hold for them. It was soon clear that the Liberals had built up a very considerable momentum, all the more impressive for the fumbling performance of their main opponents. The Conservatives had chosen Robert McEwen, a lawyer, who suffered a double disadvantage: he was a laird, and he was also a Catholic – a marked misfortune for a man involved in Border politics. There was never any sign that he would overcome these difficulties. The Liberals turned out in force at his meetings and made question time a purgatory for him. 'I am doing well everywhere', Steel told a reporter in mid-campaign, 'but especially where McEwen has spoken.'

Steel needed a swing of only 2 per cent to land the seat, and as the enthusiasm mounted it became clear he was likely to get it. 'His reception at some of the knitting and cloth mills', wrote Peter Preston in the *Guardian*, 'was more like a pop idol than a politician.' In the last few days of the campaign, Labour workers were urging on the doorsteps: 'If you can't vote for our man, make sure you vote for Steel.' On 24 March, Roxburgh sent Steel to Westminster with a 4,607 majority on a swing from Conservative to Liberal of 7·3 per cent. It wasn't another Orpington, but it certainly helped put the party back on the political map.

Meanwhile Labour was still picking its way along the tightrope of its tiny majority. The crisis created by the death of a Conservative Speaker had been successfully navigated by steering a Liberal, Roderic Bowen, into the office of Deputy Speaker, thus leaving the government's voting power unimpaired. But it was a nerve-racking business. Apart from the maverick activities of Woodrow Wyatt and Desmond Donnelly on the party's Right, there was always the fear of death or accident creating a difficult by-election. The Labour Member for Falmouth (majority 6·9 per cent) was known to be in very poor health. But the seat which eventually came on to the market was more precarious still. Henry Solomons, who died on 7 November 1965, had taken Hull North off the Conservatives at the 1964 general election by a mere 1,181 votes (2·5 per cent). Gallup was still putting Labour well ahead of the Conservatives (by 6½ points in December 1965). But after Leyton, one couldn't feel entirely reassured by that.

The Conservatives moved in on Hull with every sign of confidence. Newspaper dispatches from the battleground were virtually unanimous in reporting that they were setting a cracking pace. Their candidate, Toby Jessel, adopted the practice of campaigning on the trot and occasionally at the gallop, rushing from house to house, hands outstretched, with a troupe of presentable young women panting along behind him. Labour's chances of holding the seat were also complicated by the arrival of Richard Gott, until then a leader-writer on the *Guardian*, who wanted to restore Labour to a more aggressively radical position and who was particularly opposed to the government's acquiescence in America's involvement in Vietnam. Bearded, eloquent, capable of turning the simplest press conference into a high-powered seminar, Gott fascinated the reporters who covered Hull North and ate up the column inches even in newspapers which normally found his position repugnant. Labour's candidate, Kevin McNamara, seemed in danger of becoming the forgotten man. 'The most self-effacing candidate I have ever met', declared the man from the *Financial Times* disapprovingly.

The bookmakers rated the Conservatives at evens. *The Times* and the *Telegraph* predicted a Conservative victory; the *Guardian* thought McNamara's difficulties were 'well nigh insuperable'. And yet, in reality, McNamara was building himself a strong position. Though not Hull-born, he lived and worked in the constituency. He was much more in keeping with the provincial sobriety of the place than were Jessel and his acolytes, invading the quiet of the terraced streets with the confident well-polished accents of the posher London suburbs. And while the *Guardian* might declare in a headline on 19 January: 'Mr Gott a highly important factor at Hull North', there was no evidence that the ordinary voters of Hull North attached any significance to him at all.

And so it was that, amid the satisfying crunching sound of pundits eating their words, Labour were able to celebrate a notable victory. The Liberal vote – a respectable 15·9 per cent in 1964 – collapsed, as so often happens in a situation where a seat may change hands; Richard Gott collected just 253 votes; and Kevin McNamara earned himself a double claim to space in the record books. It was the biggest pro-government swing in a by-election since Ilford North in February 1954, nearly twelve years before. And it was the sign Harold Wilson needed that the time was right to call the general election for which everyone had been waiting almost since the moment he first entered Downing Street.

One of the less remarked features of Harold Wilson's electoral triumph in 1966 was the advance made by the Scottish Nationalists. Their average vote increased from 10·7 to 14·3 per cent, and in one region, around the Forth and Tay, they fought every seat and did not lose a single deposit.[4] In West Lothian they took more than 35 per cent of the vote, and in three other constituencies their vote topped 20 per cent. In Wales, results were disappointing for the Nationalists. On average their vote dropped by 0·1 per cent. In Caernarvon, their strongest seat in 1964, they managed to improve their position by only 0·3 per cent (to 21·7 per cent). In Merioneth their vote fell from 16·8 per cent in 1964 to 11·4 per cent. In general, there was little to celebrate. But there was one exception to this pattern, and it was to outweigh in significance everything else which happened to the Nationalists in 1966. That exception was Carmarthen.

Carmarthen is the largest constituency in Wales: there are 820 square miles of it. It is mainly farming country, but there is mining in the Gwendraeth and Amman valleys. The 1966 census found 26·6 per cent of the working population in farming and 11·7 per cent in mining. In 1966 the county had 4,497 registered milk producers, double the total in any other Welsh county.

It had a highly individual political history: Liberal from 1923 to 1929; Labour until 1931; then Liberal again until 1935; Labour from 1935 to 1945; then regained and held by the Liberals until the death of Sir Rhys Hopkin Morris in November 1956. The Labour candidate in the subsequent by-election was Megan Lloyd George, who had herself been a Liberal MP (for Anglesey) for twenty-two years up to 1951. She had joined Labour in 1955. Her selection in 1957 helped convert a Liberal majority of 3,333 (6·8 per cent) into a Labour majority of 3,069 (6·1 per cent). In each case, no Conservative stood; Plaid Cymru took 7·8 per cent in 1955 and 11·5 per cent in the by-election.

In 1966 Lady Megan had her biggest majority yet: 9,233, or 20·1 per cent, over the Liberals. But she was by now a very sick woman, and took no part in the campaign, which was fought on her behalf by a Pontypridd solicitor, Gwilym Prys Davies. She sent an enthusiastic message to her adoption meeting, but was never able to enter the constituency during the campaign, and died six weeks later on 14 May.

[4] Michael Steed, in D. E. Butler and A. King, *The British General Election of 1966* (1966) p. 290.

It was immediately recognised that the chemistry of Carmarthen might produce a very striking contest indeed. On the face of it, there was a chance here for the Liberals to add a thirteenth seat to the twelve they had already collected at the general election. They had, after all, been runners-up in every election since they lost the seat; and assuming (as they confidently did) that Lady Megan had prospered on the votes of liberals drawn to her by her political past and family background, they could now cheerfully expect to pick up the reversion.

But it was not, in fact, the Liberals who now became the centre of attention. The candidate whose performance in the 1966 general election had done so much to light up the general Nationalist gloom was Gwynfor Evans, president of the party since 1945 and far and away its most commanding personality. Born in Barry, in Glamorgan, he had established his local credentials by long residence in the county; he lived at Llangadog, where he ran a market garden and was a deacon and Sunday-school teacher. He was now in his eighteenth year on the county council.

His vote in 1966–7,416 (16·1 per cent) – was the second-best in Wales, and a steady advance on the 5·2 per cent of 1959 and the 11·7 per cent of 1964. He was in 1966 still a long way behind the Liberal and a full 14,000 votes behind Lady Megan. But this by-election was undoubtedly as good an opportunity as any that could have come his party's way.

Labour chose Prys Davies, Lady Megan's lieutenant, to fight the by-election. Though not a local man (he came a from Merioneth), he had strong constituency associations; his firm were legal advisers to the NUM, which was thought to be a useful recommendation for him in the mining areas. He had, too, a Nationalist past. Like Elystan Morgan, who had won Cardigan for Labour in 1966, he was a former member of the Blaid;[5] he had even belonged for a time to the more extreme Welsh Republican Party. The Liberals retained Hywel Davies, their candidate in the general election; the Conservatives also ran their general election candidate, Simon Day.

Both Labour and Liberal began by maintaining that it was

[5] Nationalist usage is Plaid Cymru, but 'the Blaid'.

a two-horse race, and they were the two horses. But whatever they might say publicly, they could hardly mistake the fact that Gwynfor Evans was making the running. He had assembled a fine collection of local fears and grievances and he hammered away at them with vigour and enthusiasm. His meetings were packed (though opponents liked to point out that many of his most devoted supporters were too young to vote for him) and he returned time and again to the same theme: you must choose, he declared, between Wilson and Wales. Are you really grateful to Labour, he demanded, for closing mines and closing railways; for the lack of industry in Carmarthenshire, for the appalling inadequate roads; for depopulation, for unemployment? If you vote Labour at this election, won't people inevitably assume that you are? If you really want to make your vote count in this election, Gwynfor Evans told the people of Carmarthen, vote for a man of independent mind, endowed with freedom to act in your interests, rather than a statistical component in a Westminster majority.

All this was designed to put Labour on the defensive; and events played into Evans's hands. The selective employment tax, introduced in Callaghan's post-election budget, was particularly unwelcome in a constituency of this kind. And it didn't help when Callaghan, anxious to offset the damage the issue was doing to Labour, told a local farmer that he was tired of this kind of complaint from farmers who 'spend as much on an afternoon at Ascot as they would on SET'. Farmers in Carmarthenshire do not customarily spend much time at Ascot, or much money either.

The closure of the Carmarthen–Aberystwyth railway line was a perfect symbolic issue for the Nationalists. It had been decreed from London, against the interests of the community; it worsened the communications of the county, which were already universally bemoaned; and Labour could be blamed for it. There had been promises at the previous election that they would keep it open; but in an adjournment debate in the Commons on 20 June, a junior Transport Minister, John Morris (another Welshman – he was MP for Aberavon), had to tell Elystan Morgan that he had no power to order its reopening. In fact, as Labour repeatedly emphasised, the loss of the line had resulted from a decision taken in September 1964 when the

Conservatives were in power. But such factual niceties tend to be overlooked in election campaigns.

And, while Labour were still comfortably ahead in the opinion polls, they were clearly running into deep political trouble. The headlines cried gloom and doom day after day. The mounting financial crisis which was to result in the July measures was already looming unmistakably: the balance-of-payments deficit of £38 million in May had widened in June to £49 million.

The seamen were on strike from 16 May to 2 July. The Minister of Labour, Ray Gunter, warned on 9 June that Britain was facing 'the most serious industrial crisis for more than a generation'. Wilson's outburst against 'tightly knit, politically-motivated men' during that strike may not have impressed the staunch trade unionists in the mining areas; Frank Cousins's resignation, symbolising union disillusion with the government, was thought by some in the constituency to have damaged Labour too.

The Liberals declared that they were the true radicals, that the Nationalists were so busy inventing grievances that they had no time to deal with real ones. Labour said Evans was 'parochial'. Parochial? He picked up the taunt and paraded it like a flag. 'In the present by-election', reported Adam Hopkins and Peter Tinniswood in the *Western Mail* on 12 July, 'the government is not on trial as the government of Britain, but as the government of Carmarthen and nowhere else.'

And, as the government of Carmarthen, it got a resounding vote of no confidence with Gwynfor Evans's victory on 14 July. (Characteristically, voters making their way to the polls in the afternoon and early evening passed newspaper posters heralding a rise in Bank Rate to 7 per cent.) Evans had laid claim to 15,000 votes; he passed his target with more than a thousand to spare. His vote was well over double the general election figure, and he had clearly done serious damage to all his rivals. Labour had suffered most grievously; but even Conservatives seemed to have come over, leaving Simon Day with fewer than 3,000 votes.

Though the other parties did their best to minimise it, it was difficult to challenge the Blaid's contention that this was a historic result; and there were those among the Labour ranks

who privately agreed that it was 'only a beginning'. 'Throughout Great Britain', reported the *Carmarthen Journal* proudly,
'his history-making win put news of the increased bank rate and
stringent financial measurers into second place.' There were
wild emotional scenes at the count – a good deal too wild and
emotional for some observers, who were later to compare them
with the excesses of one-party states, with Nazi rallies.

Gwynfor Evans's progress to Parliament became a series of
jubilant demonstrations and triumphant parades. He was the
first Nationalist to sit at the House since the Scot, Dr R. D.
McIntyre, who represented Motherwell for a few weeks at
the end of the 1945 Parliament. What, he was asked, could one
man hope to achieve, among 630 at Westminster? 'Keir Hardie',
he replied, 'was the only one in Parliament at one time.' Fourteen coachloads of supporters came up to see him take his seat;
a millionaire rancher flew in specially from Bogota. And a
porter who was submerged in the celebrations when the new
MP arrived at Paddington was later reported as saying: 'There
has been nothing like it since the Beatles were here.'

For eight months Labour escaped further by-elections. Then
on 9 March 1967 they fought three. One was Nuneaton, now
vacated by Frank Cousins, a seat subjected for the second time
to the need to stage an election because of the internal needs of
the Labour Party, and therefore likely to be dejected and
apathetic – but not on anyone's card a likely loss. The other
two were more serious: Rhondda West and the Pollok division
of Glasgow. In both, all normal rules ceased to apply: Labour
was once more facing the challenge of the now rampant
Nationalists.

Rhondda West was a constituency in decline. People were
leaving the valley at an estimated rate of 800 a year. Nationalists calculated that some 400 houses were standing empty.
Three pits had closed in the last year. (The 1966 census put
the percentage of the work-force engaged in mining at 27·9.)
Housing conditions were bad, and had not been notably
improved either by three years of Labour government or by
decades of Labour control in local politics. Only 38 per cent
of houses had inside lavatories, a situation made all the more
unsatisfying by the contrast with that easy, civilised and cos-

seted life which people in South-east England could be assumed to have, if only from that projection of metropolitan living standards which comes over on commercial television. But the one over-riding and inescapable preoccupation of people in the Rhondda in the early months of 1967 was unemployment, which stood at more than 9 per cent and showed every sign of being chronic. It was twice the average for Wales, and four times the average for Britain as a whole.

It was a situation made for the Nationalists. Not that this was an area of Nationalist strength in the way that Carmarthen had been: Nationalism had never flourished in urban areas as it had in the outlying areas with their isolated lives and strong cultural traditions. And yet if the Nationalists had been able to choose an urban constituency to fight, this would have been high on their list. The Blaid had once been stronger here than in most of Wales: in 1955 they had taken 15·3 per cent of the vote and in 1959, 17 per cent. In 1964 their vote had slumped to 10·2 per cent, and in 1966 to 8·7 per cent (still enough, in the politics of this part of Wales, to put them into second place in that election). But disappointing though that figure was, it was still second only to Merthyr in the urban seats.

The Nationalist candidate of 1966, Victor Davies, had remained active in Rhondda politics and was readopted now. Labour chose the secretary of its local party, Alec Jones, a teacher, who had grown up in the area, moved away to London and then returned.

Jones wanted to widen the campaign, but found it virtually impossible. 'You kept on coming up against unemployment. It was like a wall', he recalled later. When he tried to discuss the other issues, to raise foreign policy, Vietnam, he met near-incomprehension. It was not that people in the Rhondda considered these things intrinsically unimportant; it was simply that they saw them as irrelevant to the present political discussion. Unemployment in these valleys is 9 per cent, they said; the situation has been worsening for years. What has your party done about it? And what will it do to rescue these valleys from disaster?

The second question was easier to answer than the first. There was Labour's new regional strategy, the setting-up of an economic planning machinery, the incentives for industry to come to deprived areas: a relative wealth of measures which were now on the way. But what was there to show for Labour's administration, here and now, in the Rhondda valley in the winter of 1967? There was much in the air, practically nothing on the ground. Gwynfor Evans, who had been using Parliamentary Questions to milk the official information services, displayed his discoveries triumphantly on a Rhondda platform. The total number of men given new jobs in advance factories in 1965 and 1966, he told them, was 140. The total number of men in new jobs in state-owned in industries in Wales since 1964 was 226.

Alec Jones called for the government to set up and operate new industry in the Rhondda. And at Tonypandy on 20 February the Secretary for Wales George Thomas was able to foreshadow a new and tangible improvement in the lives of people in the Rhondda: the government, he revealed, were about to publish their plans for leasehold reform. It was a crucial issue in the Rhondda. Only some 8 per cent lived in council housing, 17 per cent in privately rented properties. Some 72 per cent were owner-occupiers, many of them leaseholders.

This was useful, but by no means enough to offset the difficulties under which Labour were working. There had been a dispute over the selection of the candidate, with Jones opposed by his own party chairman and a miner nominee failing, in what had been traditionally a miners' seat, even to get on the short-list. It was not the signal for massive rebellions in the party, for refusals to join in the campaign; but it didn't help.

Labour brought in their regional organiser, J. Emrys Jones, to run the campaign, as they had at Carmarthen. His ideas, though conventional in British politics, were not in keeping with the peculiar inbred traditions of the Rhondda. There must, he said, be a canvass. 'A canvass?' exclaimed an astonished local loyalist. 'We *never* canvass in Treherbert.' Since the lowest majority since 1950 had been 55 per cent, in 1959, they had never really needed to.

The headlines were as bad as they had been in Carmarthen. Bank Rate was down, which helped; the wage freeze was over, but celebrations were muted by the knowledge that it had been replaced by a period of severe restraint. 'Tighten your belts' was an injunction which sounded peculiarly inappropriate in the circumstances of the Rhondda valley. The party at Westminster was again in fierce dispute over the government's attitude to Vietnam, and over defence: good Welsh radicals observed the government's replies to its rebels, heard that Harold Wilson had threatened to take away their 'licences', and were not encouraged.

Even so, it wasn't until the Sunday before polling day that Labour began even to consider the possibility of defeat. At that time such an upset seemed a good deal more unlikely than it was to do a year or two later. And the canvass returns were encouraging: no signs of mass abstention there; Nationalist claims that Labour voters were coming over thick and fast could be dismissed as propaganda, or inexperience, or just euphoria.

Yet the crowds were large, and the posters were everywhere. The Nationalists staged a motorcade with 700 cars, then an eve-of-poll meeting at Treorchy at which Davies and Gwynfor Evans drew a crowd of 1,250. The poll, it was clear from the start, would be enormous: they had had an 80·3 per cent turnout at the general election, but this contest topped even that.

The Nationalists failed; but they had cut the Labour majority in one of the most cast-iron of all Labour seats to a desperately marginal 2,306 (9·1 per cent). The increase in the Nationalist vote was far greater even than in Carmarthen. Again there were riotous scenes of celebration: Alec Jones, drowned by barrackers, described them as 'the worst manifestation of Rhondda politics in many years, and a threat to democracy'. But the immediate threat was to the Labour Party Carmarthen could be, and indeed was, dismissed as rural, isolated, untypical. Rhondda was a bedrock of the Labour movement; the Nationalists' base had been feeble compared with Carmarthen. And yet they had very nearly captured Rhondda West too.

Simultaneously, the Scottish Nationalists struck their own blow at Pollok. The Scots, as the 1966 election results indicated, had been far ahead of the Welsh in electoral terms. They had not yet had a Carmarthen. But as early as November 1961 they had polled 18·7 per cent of the vote in a by-election at Glasgow Bridgeton; in the West Lothian by-election of June 1962, fighting a seat not previously contested, they had taken second place with 26·2 per cent of the vote. Here was their first chance to show that they could match, or more than match, any damage the Welsh had done to Harold Wilson.

Pollok had once been a Conservative stronghold. But then the Labour-controlled Glasgow council began, as Labour councils do, to build large council estates in the midst of Tory territory. The 1966 census showed that 55·7 per cent of homes in the constituency were council tenancies. It was clear that there was much disaffection on the estates about the record of Labour government. The unemployment rate in Glasgow stood at 4·3 per cent – far below that in the Rhondda, but still twice the national average. There was general awareness of the threat to the economy of south-west Scotland in the decline of traditional industries. The Labour Party in Glasgow, too, had fallen on bad days: the party was much criticised and much suspected; it had, it was said, spent too long in office without the necessary challenge to its reign.

Labour imported Dick Douglas, a thirty-five-year-old economics lecturer from Dundee who had formerly lived in the city. Will Marshall, Scottish Secretary of the Labour Party, took charge of the campaign. He had unmatched experience as a political campaigner, and a *Financial Times* reporter described the organisation he set up as 'superb'. But he was unwary in his predictions. The Nationalists meant nothing. They would not even keep their deposit. It was designed to minimise their threat; but the threat was too real to be minimised in that way, and such tactics at such times have a way of being counter-productive.

The Conservatives, hurriedly dispensing with the candidate who had fought the seat for them in 1966, brought in Esmond Wright, Professor of Modern History at Glasgow University and a familiar and accomplished Scottish television celebrity (though in fact he was not a Scot: he was born and schooled in England). Assured and knowledgeable, he was described in the *Economist* as 'the best individual Tory candidate recruited in this decade'.

The Nationalist was George Leslie, a leading figure in SNP politics in the city and a veterinary surgeon. They staged a lively and eventful campaign on the model which the party was then evolving, featuring much singing of Scottish songs, both topical and traditional, and a showbiz flavour exemplified by the endorsement of their candidate by the screen James Bond, Sean Connery. The headlines were, as we have seen with the Rhondda, almost uniformly bad. Labour managed to produce sweeteners in Scotland as in Wales: a government boost for the shipyards in the Industrial Bill in February, approval for a container-ship terminal at Greenock on the eve of the poll. But the government was also at this time embroiled in a number of pay disputes with Scottish industry. In particular, Scottish local government workers had been refused a pay rise already granted to their counterparts in England. 'Another Scottish pay rise frozen' said a headline on 18 February: it was exactly what Dick Douglas didn't need in his struggle to hold on to Pollok.

In the event it was Esmond Wright who went to Westminster, but the Nationalists who could fairly claim to have put him there. The Labour vote fell by 9,000, the Conservative vote by only 5,000, which meant the Conservative was in. The Nationalist, fresh to the constituency, took 28·2 per cent of the vote. The Liberals suffered worst of all, taking only 1·9 per cent. The turnout, at 75·7 per cent, was almost up to general election level. The Nationalists might not be justified in saying, after this result, that every seat in Scotland was in their grasp. But they could fairly claim that there were now very many seats where they could completely disrupt the established pattern, and could virtually dictate the result, even if they were not elected themselves.

Most of all, the Pollok result, attained in one of Scotland's major cities, established their credibility as a political force. Success tends to breed success in electoral politics, as failure tends to breed failure. The bandwagon was rolling. It rolled still more powerfully in the municipal elections in May. Anxiously, the party awaited another chance to show its paces. And in September 1967, when Tom Fraser, who had been dropped by Wilson as Minister of Transport at Christmas 1965, took the post of Chairman of the North of Scotland Hydro-Electric Board, it came.

The Hamilton division of Lanarkshire must, even after Pollok, have seemed a reasonable risk to Labour. It was the ninth safest seat in Scotland; Fraser's 1966 majority had been

16,576 (42·4 per cent). The Nationalist track record was unimpressive: 6·2 per cent of the vote in 1959 and no candidate since. They had done well in the county areas at the municipal elections but not in the burgh.

But once again the Labour campaign immediately ran into difficulties. There was a bitterly contested selection: among those rejected was the chairman of the local party. The choice fell on a miner, Alex Wilson, from Forth; now fifty, he had worked in the pits from the age of fourteen.

It seemed to some a backward-looking choice. This had once been a mining constituency. Fraser had been a miner; so had his predecessor, Duncan Graham. But Hamilton was changing. Only 4·5 per cent of the work-force were now employed in the pits. There was a new breed of bright, ambitious middle-class voter in the constituency who would not be attracted by this appeal to tradition. The Nationalist candidate, on the other hand, a vivacious, original and infectiously enthusiastic woman lawyer of thirty-seven, Winifred Ewing, looked tailor-made for them.

Labour intended to install an outside agent; but this was resisted, and the part-time agent for Hamilton, Alex Reid, remained in charge. There was disaffection in the local party, particularly over the rejection of the local chairman, and this was reflected in an unwillingness to turn out for the cause. The Labour organisation was well-meaning but weak and thin on the ground. The *Hamilton Advertiser*, which kept up a lively and disrespectful commentary on events (and was, in general, a good deal more informative than local newspapers usually are at election times), was scathing about Labour's performance – the selection, the organisation, the tactics, the intentions. 'Has anyone seen Alex Wilson – apart from the party faithful?' it asked at one point. Some had, and reported that there was more to him than the electorate had so far been able to recognise. But he made little impact. Later, in an article in the *New Statesmen*, Iain Ogilvie, one of Labour's frustrated supporters, wrote:

Compared to the Scottish National Party's lively machine and with-it campaign Labour's election strategy and lack of organisation were pitiful. The technological revolution was light years away from Hamilton's weary committee rooms where well-meaning ladies prepared mountains of food and gallons of tea for election workers who never came. . . . Against the all-things-to-all-men ball of fire, Mrs Ewing, he [Wilson] was a non-starter.

Mrs Ewing, by contrast, seemed dazzling. She was basically Left in politics (which could not by any means be said for her party as a whole); she was witty and inventive; she had a good eye for publicity. The campaign was full of the crowd-pleasing gimmickry which became the hallmark of Nationalist politics. Pollok (Hamilton is only 11 miles from Glasgow) had been the dress rehearsal: this was the real thing. The repertoire of songs had been expanded: 'The Nationalists', said the *Glasgow Herald*, in its rather stuffy way, 'have a wide variety of folk songs whose banal lyrics nonetheless bring a measure of approval in the supermarket and launderette.'

Labour were now trailing the Conservatives on the polls (Gallup gave the Conservatives a 5-point lead in October, widening to 6 per cent in November) and trouble was raining in on the government thick and fast. The platform had suffered defeats at conference; unemployment remained extremely serious (though at least, by polling in November, Labour avoided the peak period of winter unemployment). There were crisis situations in the docks and in the railways. And reading the signs one could only assume that things were going to get worse. Partly because of the dock strike, the trade deficit for October reached £162 million. Bank Rate was pushed up on 19 October. The wage freeze was over but delaying power over wage increases had been retained. Everywhere people were grumbling about the endless climb of prices in the shops.

All this was exactly the diet on which Nationalism fed. There were even signs that religious differences were working in their favour. The available statistical evidence suggests that Catholics stayed more faithful to Labour in the troubles of the 1966–70 Parliament than did Protestants.[6] Certainly, in Hamilton, there was believed to be an 'Orange vote', and the signs were that Mrs Ewing was collecting it.

[6] Iain McLean, *The Rise and Fall of the Scottish National Party*, offprinted from *Political Studies* (Oxford, 1970).

People said that hers would be a protest vote. That didn't worry the Nationalists at all. A letter to the *Glasgow Herald* on 14 September made their point:

> It was correct to say the SNP were collecting a large protest vote . . . they are protesting against 22 years of unbroken Tory and Labour misgovernment of Scotland since the end of the war. Protesting that, after these 22 years, their wages, employment prospects, housing conditions and general living standards are still inferior to England's and to independent European countries of similar size and resources to Scotland. . . .

The Shetlands, it was reported at this time, were talking of seceding from Britain, even of seeking the overlordship of the Danes.

It was difficult for Labour to reply. Scotland's problems, wrote the Secretary of State, William Ross, to the Scottish TUC in September, were deep-seated. They required wide-ranging structural changes which could not be accomplished quickly. Which was true, but not much help to Alex Wilson in Hamilton.

The failures of the government, more than desire for Scottish independence, explain Hamilton, as they do all the Nationalist shocks of the period. An Opinion Research Centre poll carried out for the ITV programme *This Week* found that 28 per cent rated Labour's record as the big issue; 21 per cent said it was Home Rule. The breakdown by party allegiance as they voted in the by-election was as shown in Table 9.1. The poll

TABLE 9.1

Main Issues Identified

	Dissatisfaction	Home Rule	Other reasons (including 'don't know')	Total
Voted Nationalist	33	28	39	100
Voted Labour	20	11	69	100
Voted Conservative	42	10	48	100

also confirmed that support for the Nationalists was highest among the 21–34 age group (Labour's most faithful supporters were the over-55s).

And so, on the night of 2 November 1967, Hamilton passed into the hands of the Scottish Nationalists in a result which set the experts searching vainly for precedents. Here was a seat, not even contested eighteen months before, in which 46 per cent of voters, 33·9 per cent of the total electorate, had turned out for Mrs Ewing. The only recent parallel was Torrington, won by the Liberals at a by-election in 1958 although not even contested in the previous general election. But as a blow to government morale and to the security of a great party, Torrington was never in the Hamilton class. Off went Mrs Ewing for a celebration party at the Zambesi Hotel. 'No Scottish MP', she declared triumphantly, 'is safe . . . except me.'

Opinions differed about how long the phenomenon would last; but it was difficult to dispute that after Hamilton, as the government staggered on from crisis to crisis (the parity of the pound survived Hamilton by only sixteen days) and Labour's support on the polls sank to a mere 30 per cent, the Nationalists were now a serious and potentially a decisive political force. Nor were they merely conducting a kind of spoiling operation on other people's votes. They were mobilising previous non-voters too.[7] Their supporters did not predominantly want to see Scotland independent; there was undoubtedly force in the view that many who advocated a complete cut-off from England might have changed their views very sharply had that ever become a real political possibility. But they wanted to register the fact that Scotland and Wales, after electing Labour Governments for years, only to be frustrated by the Conservative English,[8] were gravely dissatisfied with the Labour Government which was now directing their fortunes from far-away London. They wanted to be free of centralised direction, because they could see no great advantages from it, and very much to complain about.[9]

Membership was booming. In 1963 the Party had 40 branches; it was to grow to 486 by 1969. There was a steady

[7] Ibid., p. 364. See also James Kellas, in D. E. Butler and M. Pinto-Duschinsky, *The British General Election of 1970* (1971).

[8] Wales has elected a majority of Labour MPs in every election since 1945. Scotland elected Labour majorities in all but 1951 and 1955. In 1951 Labour and Conservative had 35 Members each and there was one Liberal.

[9] McLean, *Rise and Fall of the SNP*, p. 363.

advance in municipal politics, most significantly in the largest city, Glasgow. Here again, they were recruiting not only dissidents from other parties but also those who had not voted before.

In the municipal elections of 1968 the party took 35·8 per cent of the vote in Glasgow, compared with 34·8 per cent for the Progressives and Conservatives and 25·5 per cent for Labour With 13 seats, they held the balance of power on the city council. Their share of the three-party vote in Scotland, according to calculations by Iain McLean,[10] reached 34·1 per cent, against 33·0 per cent for Labour and 32·9 per cent for right-wing parties.

The party had become more than a political force; it was a social force as well. Scottish Nationalism did not have the inner core of cultural tradition which was to be found in Wales, but it did contribute to the pattern of people's lives and to the enhancing of their feelings of Scottishness. 'The rafters in the Stag Hotel, Lochgilphead,' reported the *Highland Nationalist*, the party's paper in Argyll, 'rang to the music of Fraser Mac-Glynn and his band whose foot-tapping beat was enjoyed by over 200 dancers. . . . There can be no doubt that in this area at any rate the SNP are always ahead in providing the kind of function that the dancing public want.'

It was always difficult to discover precisely what the party represented. Labour called them Tartan Tories; and although some leading figures, notably Mrs Ewing, unmistakably belonged to the Left, there were others who just as unmistakably did not. Nationalists could be found, for instance, working in the campaign to 'Save the Argylls'. Although party policy on main issues was delineated in official publications, there were areas where one was told, though in rather more grandiose terms, to wait and see. 'This', said one official, asked about the party's attitude to capital punishment, 'is a matter for the Scottish people to decide.'

All three main parties were thrown by the Nationalists' success. The Liberals disputed: collaboration – or outright opposition? Some Liberals, including the former leader, Jo Grimond, urged that the two parties should seek common ground. ('Grimond', said one jaundiced critic, 'wants to be the

---

[10] See table, ibid., p. 362.

first Scottish Prime Minister.') Others, like George Mackie, former MP for Caithness and chairman of the Scottish Liberals, stood out against it. It was, in any case, blatantly clear that the Nationalists did not wish to co-operate. Why should they? In the summer of 1968 it looked as though they might do it on their own.

The Conservatives too were driven to conclude that policy changes might be needed. The result was Edward Heath's proposal in March 1968 for an elected Scottish Assembly. A committee was set up to discuss how this might be organised: as a guarantee to those Scottish Conservatives who thought it a somewhat hare-brained scheme, even an undignified surrender, the chairmanship was entrusted to Sir Alec Douglas-Home. Labour alone remained immobile: indeed, the official line seemed actually to be hardening against greater self-determination for Scotland. William Ross, the Scottish Secretary, took to calling the SNP 'the Scottish Narks' Party'. He was not, he declared after Hamilton, worried by 'this phoney party'. 'This is not politics,' he said, 'this is emotion. When it comes to a General Election, reason will take over.'

Others disagreed. There were those like John Mackintosh, the Labour MP for Berwick and East Lothian and a former Professor of Politics at Strathclyde, who thought that greater devolution was not just a realistic electoral strategy but a desirable political end in itself.[11] Others, while not prepared to crusade for devolution, thought Labour had some lessons to learn: Mrs Ewing's vivacity and talent, said James Jack, Secretary of the Scottish TUC, were 'not without significance' for the Labour Party. But in general, amid much grumbling among some of their younger comrades about their antique view of life, the Scottish Labour establishment stood firm.

Certainly, it still remained possible, even now that Carmarthen, Pollok and Rhondda West had been capped by Hamilton, to regard it all as a Poujadiste wave which, if treated with appropriate disdain, would eventually go away. There was no such consolation over the ground which was now being lost to the Conservatives. Judged against Nationalist successes, the damage the Conservatives had been doing to Labour in by-elections was unspectacular. But judged by the normal

11 J. P. Mackintosh, *The Devolution of Power* (1968).

standards of seats lost and swings between the parties, it was very serious indeed.

In April 1967 Labour had lost control of the Greater London Council in a landslide, hanging on to only 18 of the 100 seats. In May they had the worst set of municipal election results since the war. The polls, which until April had been favourable, now turned sharply against them; though Labour recovered ground in midsummer, the Conservative lead lengthened in the autumn. Six weeks before Hamilton, Labour had defended two seats in by-elections, Cambridge and Walthamstow West. There was never much hope of holding Cambridge: it had been won in 1966 by only 991 votes and would go back to the Conservatives on a swing of 1·1 per cent. It was, as it turned out, the most marginal seat to be defended by Labour during the 1966–70 Parliament. But Walthamstow West should have been a different story. This had been Attlee's old seat. Even in the best Tory years it had never been remotely in danger: the 1966 majority had been 8,725 (36·4 per cent). True, the place was changing: new council flats were now decorating the Walthamstow skyscape. True, there had been spectacular swings against Labour in the local elections. But history showed that governments did not, except in the most extraordinary circumstances, lose constituencies like this one.

But, in fact, both seats were lost. The apathy was deeper at Walthamstow than at Cambridge; the distress over prices was sharper and more sustained. The swing against the government in Walthamstow was 18·4 per cent, nearly 5 points higher than anything the Conservatives had suffered in the worst of the Macmillan years – and their worst, Stratford, was the by-election which resulted from the Profumo affair. It comfortably beat the previous post-1945 record – the 17·0 per cent swing to Labour in the Gorbals division of Glasgow in 1948.

At Cambridge the turnout fell, compared with the general election, by 14·2 per cent and the swing to the Conservatives was 8·6 per cent. At Walthamstow the drop in turnout was 17 per cent and the swing 18·4 per cent. So apathy did go some way to explain it; but there was more to it than that. Most unusually, the Liberals, third at Walthamstow with 14·1 per cent at the general election, substantially improved their position in a contest in which a seat was changing hands, taking 22·9 per cent of the vote at the by-election. (Some drew the conclusion that former Labour supporters might have behaved on the assumption, which in normal circumstances would have been entirely justified, that the seat was not at risk.) Still more significantly, the Conservatives, for the first time in this Parliament, recruited a larger proportion of the total electorate than they had at the general election. The turnout had dropped by nearly one-fifth; but even so, the Conservative vote was numerically up on 1966. This result reflected more than abstention: it meant that 1966 Labour votes were crossing over in significant numbers to other parties.

Gallup analysed the result in the *Daily Telegraph* on 4 October. Of the 1966 Labour vote, they suggested, 41 per cent had stayed faithful to Labour; 10 per cent had gone to the Liberals; 5 per cent had switched right across to the Conservatives; and 2 per cent had voted for the two Independents, one of whom was for free trade and against the Common Market while the other built his campaign exclusively around free radio. (The two Independents in fact polled a total of more than 600 votes; the free-trader's haul of 63 was one more than the final Conservative majority.)

For the rest, 7 per cent had left the register and 35 per cent had stayed at home. Although Gallup's analysis concluded that most of this abstention was deliberate, it found that at least 600 Labour voters might have failed to turn out as a direct result of inadequate organisation, having received no kind of notification from the party. The biggest Labour losses had occurred in the poorest homes and among women, who had been especially attracted to the extremely able woman Liberal, Mrs Margaret Wingfield.

After Walthamstow it was clear that Manchester Gorton and Leicester South-West, which polled on the same day as Hamilton, were going to be hard to hold. Gorton, which became vacant on the death of Konni Zilliacus, its Labour MP since 1955, would be lost on a swing of 10·1 per cent. The Leicester seat, vacated by Herbert Bowden, the Commonwealth Secretary, who was leaving politics to become chairman of the ITA after twenty-two years as an MP, would change hands on a swing of 8·7 per cent.

In Leicester, where municipal elections had signalled massive disaffection on the vast council estates which contained some 44 per cent of all homes in the constituency, Labour drifted towards disaster. But in Gorton Labour was putting up a very solid fight. Gorton is a dour, self-respecting Manchester suburb: by no means affluent, but a cut above the living conditions of a division like Exchange. More than half its households were owner-occupied. The Labour candidate was Kenneth Marks, a headmaster in nearby Blackley, a cheerful, rubicund, common-sense man who seemed just right for the constituency. The Conservative, whose selection had caused much excitement, was Winston Churchill, grandson of the former Prime Minister. There were three others in the field: John Creasey, a novelist who had set up his own All Party Alliance and lost deposits at Nuneaton and Brierley Hill; Terry Lacey, one of the key figures in the Young Liberal 'Red Guard' movement, and a candidate with some of the attractions of the ill-fated Richard Gott; and a Communist, Vic Eddisford.

From the start there were doubts about whether Churchill's selection had been the right one. 'Churchill is green in rough-and-tumble politics' wrote Joseph Minogue, of the *Guardian*, who has known Gorton all his life. 'He has matured considerably during the campaign, but Gorton is the wrong kind of seat for him. . . .' Churchill was twenty-seven, without previous experience, and out of character with the constituency: compared with Marks, his selection seemed almost to have about it a certain un-Gortonian levity.

The issues were unremittingly the economic ones; it was difficult for anyone, candidate, agent or voter, to get his mind away from them for long in the circumstances of late 1967. The electorate was generally reported to be apathetic. Yet in fact, unlike any of the other English contests so far, this one had actually managed to get the voters involved. The turnout was 72·4 per cent – only 0·2 per cent short of the general election figure.

That was what saved Gorton for Labour: they got out the vote. It was easy to say afterwards, comparing the 9·4 per cent swing at Gorton with the 16·5 per cent which put the Conservatives in at Leicester, that the choice of Churchill had cost the

Conservatives the seat. Yet in fact the Conservatives increased their numerical vote. They pulled out over 3 per cent more of the total electorate than they had at the general election, against a decrease of 0·9 per cent at Leicester. The big difference between the two seats was the Labour performance. Churchill's choice perhaps strengthened the appeal of Marks; there was also a belief that Zilliacus had never polled his full weight because of his foreign-sounding name. (Presumably those susceptible to such considerations knew enough about his Labour successor not to spell his name with a final 'x'.) At any rate, Labour had come out of the night of 2 November 1967 with one bit of much-needed comfort to clutch to themselves.

So, at the end of just over nineteen months of Labour government, the by-election scoreboard looked like Table 9.2.

TABLE 9.2

By-Elections, July 1966–November 1967

	Defended	Attacked	Held	Lost	Gained	Lost deposit	Change
Labour	9	2	3	6	–	–	–6
Conservative	2	9	2	–	4	2	+4
Liberal	–	9	–	–	–	4	–
Nationalist	–	4	–	–	2	–	+2

This was far worse than anyone in the Labour Party could have expected, and worse than could have been deduced from the testimony, itself by no means comforting, of the opinion polls. But a pattern was emerging: party workers reluctant to work, disillusioned not only by the government's economic record but also in many cases by its behaviour over defence and Vietnam; and voters who saw no reason to turn out for a party which in their view had brought down upon them a cruel collection of miseries.

It was a demonstration of protest on a scale unparalleled in thirty years: that was the almost universal interpretation. Yet it was also in a sense reflection of the pace at which Labour had gained ground in two successive elections. Certainly, in 1966 there had been many voters, some up till then unwavering Conservative supporters, who wanted to see Labour win, and for two main reasons: first, the belief in Harold Wilson as the most astute and competent of political operators then on the stage; second, the feeling that Labour had not really been given a chance in a mere eighteen months of office to show what they could do.[12] In 1966, therefore, Labour had polled well above its natural constituency. Clearly, the allegiance of many of the voters who had come over to it then was likely now – nineteen months, a dozen crises and one devaluation later – to be frail.[13] Gorton, with its demonstration that on a poll of general election size the swing could be held down, was therefore especially precious. It was natural to grab at such a comforting thought; yet to anyone who had observed a campaign like that at Leicester South-West, it seemed at the time a bit unreal.

Devaluation, the veto on British entry into Europe, the painful convolutions within the party over South African arms and Harold Wilson's leadership, prescription charges, the end of free milk in secondary schools, cuts in housing programmes, deferment of the raising of the school-leaving age: the winter months of 1967–8 were punctuated by a stream of enforced decisions all damaging to the government's standing in the country and especially bitter for the Labour faithful to swallow. Many could not swallow them at all.

Three crucial by-elections were arranged for 28 March 1968: at Dudley (where George Wigg had left politics to become Chairman of the Horserace Betting Levy Board), Acton and the Meriden division of Warwickshire, where the Labour incumbents had died. (A third West Midlands seat, solidly Conservative Warwick and Leamington, was to poll the same day.) Meriden would be lost on a swing of 3·7 per cent, Acton on a swing of 7·7 per cent. Dudley could be lost on a swing of 9·1 per cent, though Wilson was said to have had firm assurances that it could be held before he let Wigg go. But after the punishment they had taken in the last two years, would the party faithful be ready to turn out to defend them? And could anything be done to halt the public flight from Labour which had quickened since devaluation, so that, according to Gallup

[12] See the analysis in D. E. Butler and D. Stokes, *Political Change in Britain* (1969) pp. 436–7.
[13] See Anthony King, 'Why All Governments Lose By-Elections', *New Society*, 21 Mar 1968.

in February, only 23 per cent of the electorate would now support them in a general election, giving the Conservatives a a lead of 19½ points?

Dudley was a curious double-yolked constituency: it comprised the borough of Dudley (an island of Worcestershire marooned in a sea of Staffordshire) to the north, and the borough of Stourbridge five miles to the south. To get from one part to the other, one had to drive through the Brierley Hill constituency – which gave time to reflect on the way that Brierley Hill had swung 7·6 per cent to the Conservatives back in April 1967 when Gallup was putting the Conservatives only 6 points ahead. George Wigg had represented Dudley since 1943, and he had a reputation for fighting constituency battles which few MPs could match.[14] As at Leicester, there were vast council estates (44 per cent of households were council tenancies) which had been giving Labour a hard time in municipal elections. Unemployment – 3·3 per cent in Dudley, 2·2 per cent in Stourbridge – had reached levels to which the prosperous West Midlands were not accustomed; factories were going on to short-time; everywhere there was the bitterness of disappointed expectations.

The Conservatives mounted one of the biggest organisational operations they had ever attempted. It was headed by Jack Galloway, their West Midlands organiser, and widely regarded as one of the shrewdest judges of a by-election in the business. Help flooded in from all over the West Midlands, and beyond. Campaign headquarters buzzed merrily all day long with carefully plotted activity. Galloway was determined to take Dudley. People reporting to help out in Warwick found themselves dispatched there. Even Meriden was left, relatively, to its own devices: Galloway reckoned it was bound to change hands, and backed his judgement accordingly.

The candidate, Don Williams, was a chartered accountant, well to the right of the party: not a local man (he came from Malvern) but not out of place in a town like Dudley. Labour selected, not a local candidate as might have been expected, especially in view of George Wigg's extra-party appeal, but John Gilbert, an accountant and economist who had fought

[14] Some examples of his pertinacity are given in Lord Goodman's introduction to Wigg's autobiography.

Ludlow in 1966 and who had assiduous support from within Transport House. The strategy in the Labour camp was to stress the continuity between George Wigg and Gilbert: 'I'm John Gilbert', the candidate would announce himself on the doorstep, 'I'm the man in George's place.' But unfortunately he did not look or sound the part. Assured, urbane and speaking in the accents of South Kensington, where he lived, rather than of the West Midlands, he was obviously hard placed to deliver a line like that and sound convincing.

The campaign opened with a series of crises and disasters, and continued that way to the end. The local regional organiser, who was to have run the campaign, was ill. Gilbert arrived in Dudley to find almost nothing, and nobody, on the ground. Urgent messages were sent to Transport House; an emissary was dispatched to inspect the situation and immediately reported that it was as bad as Gilbert was saying. Len Sims, assistant National Agent, was put on a train with little more than a toothbrush to accompany him and told to stay as long as necessary. He took charge of the campaign from then on.

Although Gilbert was courteously treated on the doorstep, there were clearly several issues working against him. One was race. Dudley's coloured community – about 2·2 per cent of the population – was modest by West Midlands standards, and despite a frightening outburst of racial violence in 1962 the town had mostly been peaceful. But Dudley is only six miles from Wolverhampton. It reads the Wolverhampton papers. Many go there to work. Enoch Powell's Birmingham speech was still a month ahead, but what was said in that speech was already commonplace in the political discussion of that part of the Midlands. (In any case, the lines of what he was to say at Birmingham were powerfully foreshadowed in a speech at Walsall in February, little noticed by the national press but naturally rather better publicised in the West Midlands.) In January and February, the threat of coloured invasion, so-called, had been dramatically advertised by the plight of the Kenya Asians: day after day the voters of Dudley had seen on their TV screens pictures of the congregations at Nairobi airport, of immigrants thronging into Heathrow. James Callaghan's rush Bill to keep them out went through the House at the end of February. Gilbert advocated strict control (though for white immigrants as well as black). But it was clear that the issue was damaging Labour. On three occasions, Gilbert's appearance in a local pub was the signal for shouts of abuse directed at his and his party's allegedly pro-immigrant associations. The only other issue which produced quite the same virulence among voters – judged by the writer's own experience of many hours on Dudley doorsteps – was the level of social benefits. Everyone, it seemed, knew that most of these fell into the hands of scroungers; everyone knew a family round the corner, down the road, where family allowances were always spent on beer and bingo.

Thirteen days before the election there was George Brown's resignation: embarrassing to any party in a by-election, infuriating for party workers slogging away in an unpopular cause only to read in their newspapers about such antics, such divisions, such personal jealousies, uncontrolled and unconcealed, at the top. (Brown was due to speak at a weekend meeting in Dudley: for hours, no one was able to discover whether he would still be coming or not). And on top of it all came Roy Jenkins's budget of 19 March, the most savage in peace-time history. Over £900 million was to be taken out of the economy. Cigarettes, spirits (though not, as punch-drunk party workers somehow remembered to bring out, beer), petrol and purchase tax were all affected. Worst of all, the road fund licence went up to £25. That hit people in Dudley two ways. It damaged the motor industry, to which many owed their employment; and it directly affected them as motorists. The 1966 census had shown that 47·2 per cent of households in Dudley ran cars; 28·7 per cent of those in employment used them to get to work. (Meriden, which takes in suburbs of both Birmingham and Coventry, including the homes of many car workers, was even more vulnerable: car ownership there was 60·4 per cent, with 35·6 per cent using cars to get to work.)

Almost until the end, the Labour camp, for all their tribulations, thought they might make it. (Galloway was in little doubt: he was making accurate predictions well ahead of polling day.) The final blows came from the opinion polls. The first, in the *Birmingham Evening Mail*, with its forecast of a swing topping 20 per cent, could be waved away with the comment that no poll was infallible. The second, by NOP next morning, telling the same tale, could not. Gilbert greeted his press conference that morning with the words: 'Welcome to the wake.'

The swing was 21·2 per cent: not since the mid-1930s had there been a comparable swing from the government to its principal opponents. The swings at Meriden and Acton were smaller – 18·5 per cent and 15·1 per cent respectively – but they were still far more than was needed to turn Labour out. The humiliation of this night topped even that of Hamilton.

The most damning feature of the Dudley result was the size of the Conservative vote. Labour held only half its general election vote, which was bad enough, but still relatively better than its performance at Walthamstow or Leicester. But the Conservative vote was 20 per cent above the 1966 figure – by far the biggest increase in any by-election so far. In Meriden, too, the Conservative vote was up on the general election; even in Acton, where the electorate was down, it fell only just short of the 1966 level. There was a dangerous comparison here with 1962–3, when the Conservatives were defending seats won in 1959, when they had a Commons majority of 99. (The Labour majority in 1966 was 97.) Despite the severe setbacks which the Conservatives suffered in those years, it was not until the Stratford by-election in August 1963 that Labour succeeded in pulling out a higher numerical vote than they had done in the general election. The implication of Dudley, therefore, was this: here was a result which, unlike those before it, looked at least as much pro-Conservative as anti-Labour. It confirmed what one had found in traditional Labour areas like the Priory Estate: some of the former faithful had become so disillusioned with the government, especially for its economic failures (and the West Midlands tends to think about life in terms of economic success perhaps more than any other region in the country), that abstention was no longer enough.

Six weeks later Labour took only 450 seats in the municipal elections: only 21 per cent, according to Gallup in May, would vote for them if there were a general election; the Conservative lead was a record 24 per cent. (Even in 1963 the Conservatives had never lagged by more than 15½ points.) National Governments, administration by businessmen, were in the air; in the *Mirror*, Cecil King announced that 'enough was enough'. It looked as though Labour had reached rock bottom. But, with the economic problem far from beaten, where did they have to go, except further down?

Yet in fact Dudley can be seen in retrospect as the worst moment for Labour in all its tribulations. Two more seats were lost in June – Oldham West, on a swing of 17·7 per cent, and Nelson and Colne on a swing of 11·4 per cent; but at Bassetlaw in October, a seat which had looked in perilous danger (it was vulnerable on a swing of 11·6 per cent) was held by 740 votes (1·7 per cent).

The swing between Conservative and Labour, on a straight two-party calculation, in all by-elections between October 1967 and March 1968 (but omitting Hamilton because of the Nationalist intervention) was 17 per cent. In the series of contests between June and December 1968 (omitting Caerphilly, again because of the Nationalist complication) it rose to 20·9 per cent. What was more, the Conservative vote, on the Dudley pattern, was pushing well above general election level: 20 per cent up at Oldham, 19 per cent at Brightside, 20 per cent at Bassetlaw, and even 3 per cent up in New Forest, where the issue was never remotely at stake. Yet nothing had quite the same painfully symbolic significance as Dudley. And, encouragingly for Labour, Bassetlaw and Nelson parallelled Gorton. On turnout not far short of general election level, the swing was satisfyingly down.

The message from Caerphilly, too, had a certain bleak, though entirely negative, comfort. The Nationalist threat, sixteen months after Rhondda West, had certainly not receded. On the other hand, it had not actually got worse.

This again was dangerously vulnerable territory. It was an old mining stronghold – 32·8 per cent, according to the 1966 census, were still employed in mining, a higher proportion than in Rhondda West. And if mining was now a declining force, it still remained a deep psychological influence on the place. The worst mining disaster in British pit history had taken place here, at Senghenydd. But recently there had been closures, and two more were even now threatened. In the north of the constituency, in the mining town of Bargoed, which reflected the true nature of the seat much better than comfortable Caerphilly itself, unemployment stood at 10 per cent. Shops in the main street stood empty, with no prospects of being filled.

The Nationalist candidate, Phil Williams, a radio astronomer with a Cambridge double first, was young, fervent and deeply radical: 'the sort of young man', said a visiting Labour MP 'whom we ought to be recruiting as a candidate'. Originally a member of the Labour Party, he had been increasingly impressed by the argument for devolution and had left it for the Blaid. Labour had again suffered a disputed selection. The miners' nominee got left off the short-list, and Transport House had to issue instructions that he be put on to it. The eventual choice was Fred Evans, a fifty-four-year-old miner's son and headmaster of a local grammar school. It was typical of the inbred nature of the campaign, and of the age differential between Labour and Nationalists, that Williams had been educated at Fred Evans's school.

Williams and the crowd of eager young people around him made the whole Labour campaign look elderly, out of date. The audiences at Labour meetings tended to be older people; there was much talk about those who had forgotten, or never known, the politics of the depression. Yet the selection also had its advantages. Evans was very well known and respected. There was a wealth of solidarity, of experience, of rootedness, about him: 'His mother', said his campaign literature, 'was Nurse Evans, of Henry Street, Bargoed, a much loved personality in the Upper Rhymney Valley.'

Both camps had learned from the Rhondda. The Nationalists had a wider range of issues, which Williams exploited with very considerable flair. Unemployment was still central to the campaign; but in Caerphilly, unlike Rhondda, it was not exclusive.

Labour, as at Rhondda, brought in J. Emrys Jones to run the campaign; again, he introduced electoral machinery which Caerphilly, with its long history of unchallenged Labour dominance, had not known before. But there was more scepticism than there had been in the Rhondda campaign. Once again, posters delivered to Labour homes failed to appear in the window, or appeared only to be soon taken down. Once more, Nationalist posters went up in the windows of houses marked down by canvassers as Labour. The excuse was the same as in the Rhondda: 'It's for the kids.' This time Labour was less ready to believe it. The promises on the doorstep, too, which seemed as reassuring as they had done in the Rhondda, were treated with considerable suspicion. One night two Labour canvassers, reaching the top of a street in the village of Penybryn, saw two Nationalists coming along behind them. They waited at the corner, and when the Nationalists caught up with them, persuaded them to compare notes. The promises to both parties were identical.

The Blaid had been stronger here than in the Rhondda. They had polled 11 per cent of the vote in 1964 and again in 1966. Now, on 18 July 1968, they cut the Labour majority from 21,148 votes (59·7 per cent) over the Conservatives in the 1966 election to 1,874 votes (5·2 per cent), pushing the Conservatives into third place and costing them their deposit.[15] The proportion of the total electorate voting Plaid Cymru had been pushed up by 22 per cent – a bigger achievement than at Carmarthen, though just short of Rhondda West.

At the end of 1968 the by-election scoreboard looked like Table 9-3.[16]

TABLE 9.3

By-Elections, July 1966–November 1968

	Defended	Attacked	Held	Lost	Gained	Lost deposit	Change
Labour	17	6	6	11	–	1	– 11
Conservative	6	17	6	–	9	3	+9
Liberal	–	18	–	–	–	9	–
Nationalist	–	5	–	–	2	–	+2

[15] David McKie, 'Two-way Politics', *Guardian*, 20 July 1968.
[16] It was argued at the time that Labour had been unlucky in that a high number of by-elections had occurred during the 1966 Parliament and that an unfortunate number of these had been in marginal constituencies.

Comparison with the 1959 Parliament, when the Conservatives had a majority comparable with Labour's in 1966, gives some support to this contention.

The 1959 Conservative Government defended 35 seats in 60 months. The average majority at risk was 23·6 per cent. The 1966 Labour Government defended 26 seats in 51 months; the average majority at risk was 26.1 per cent. But far more of the Conservative by-elections were voluntary, that is, caused by avoidable resignations or the acceptance of peerages. Discounting those by-elections which appear to have been avoidable, the figures are less favourable to Labour. Labour had 20 involuntary elections

The opinion polls had shown a Labour recovery in the autumn, a recovery which the Bassetlaw result confirmed. But soon the signs of renewed economic crisis were unmistakable. On 22 November petrol, spirits and purchase tax were hit again as Roy Jenkins took emergency action to halt the slide which had begun with the pressure on the French franc. By Christmas the Conservatives had a 20-point lead over Labour on Gallup.

The Conservative establishment, though, were more cautious about their prospects than some of their supporters. Their own private polls were instructively filling out the published evidence. 'These analyses', says Robert Rhodes James,[17] 'confirmed what many politicians and political observers had felt in their bones for some time – and which the work of political scientists had also demonstrated – that the days of the large "bloc" vote, with the small floating element that decided elections, were definitely over.' The new volatility in the electorate, now working in their favour, could work the other way.

One party had fallen short of the heady achievements which the smaller battalions had been notching up in Wales and Scotland. The Liberals had failed to turn Labour's unpopularity to their own account in the way they had done with the Conservative misfortunes of the early 1960s. In Carmarthen, on paper one of their most promising seats, they had, as we have seen, been gazumped by the Nationalists. In Honiton, West Derbyshire, South Kensington, New Forest, Weston-super-mare and Chichester they had pushed Labour out of second place, but had still finished streets behind the Conservatives.

But they had also had humiliations: 5·9 per cent of the poll at Gorton; 3·6 per cent at Caerphilly; 1·9 per cent at Pollok. The one real achievement was still the greatly increased vote in a marginal situation at Walthamstow West.

But, as had happened before with the Liberals, both at Orpington and Roxburgh, a sudden stroke of luck put them back on the map. Birmingham Ladywood did not have the immediate statistical desirability of the two predecessors. It

---

in 51 months with an average majority of 26·6 per cent at risk. The Conservatives, in 60 months, had only 13, with an average majority at risk of 28·0 per cent.

[17] Robert Rhodes James, *Ambitions and Realities* (1972) pp. 124–30.

was far from being the most marginal Labour-over-Liberal seat: the Labour majority in 1966 had been 35·2 per cent. But the Liberal candidate in Ladywood, Wallace Lawler, had recently led the Liberals into a succession of impressive local election successes. His own intensive campaigns on behalf of his local government constituents – in particular, his campaign drawing attention to the danger of old people dying of cold – had thrust him into the public consciousness. A lot of Liberals distrusted him. He was attacked for his attitude on race, but critics were unable to prove their charges against him. It was said that he was not a Liberal, but a Lawlerite: a populist successfully practising under a Liberal label. Lawler seemed unworried by such charges. He stood, he said, by his record. And in any case, what interested him was hard practicalities rather than highfalutin idealism.

The Ladywood constituency contained much of his local government base. It was a constituency in decline: the electorate had fallen from 46,000 after redistribution in 1955 to 25,000 at the 1966 general election and 18,095 now. The construction men were everywhere, tearing down the old slums, running up new flats. At the 1966 census, 87 per cent of households had been council tenancies.

Though it was up to Labour to move the writ, since a Labour MP had died, the Labour Party in Birmingham seemed strangely unready when it came. A call that day to the head of the party organisation in the city, Dick Knowles, produced the information that he had gone to Leeds for the weekend and they were doing their best to get in touch with him. The Conservatives, as the by-election approached, dropped the candidate they had already chosen on the reported grounds that he was 'not abrasive enough' and then chose in his place a sixty-five-year-old local GP. The Liberals, patching up feuds which had recently split the party in the city, threw a united weight behind Lawler, under the direction of Pratap Chitnis, then head of Liberal Party Organisation, who had been Eric Lubbock's agent when he captured Orpington.

They carried all before them. Doubts about whether the bandwagon was really rolling the way Liberal enthusiasts claimed must have been dispelled by a remarkable picture of a block of council flats in which Wallace Lawler's name was spelt out, letter by letter, in descending windows. His 2,713-vote (28·8 per cent) victory over Labour's Mrs Doris Fisher on a swing from Labour to Liberal of 32 per cent was a triumph for all those in the party who had claimed that hard slogging at local issues was the way in which the party could fight itself back into a strength not entirely dependent on the Celtic fringes – though their satisfaction was not to last long: Lawler lost the seat at the 1970 general election on an 18·6 per cent swing back to Labour.

The loss of Ladywood, on 26 June 1969, was the last of the great Labour disasters. By autumn the trend on the polls was dramatically improved; Gallup put the Conservative lead at 12½ points in August, 9½ in September, then 2 per cent in November. On 30 October five Labour seats were defended: Islington North and Paddington North, in London, both greatly reduced in numbers since 1966; Newcastle-under-Lyme, in Staffordshire; Glasgow Gorbals, the safest seat in Scotland; and Swindon, where Francis Noel-Baker had finally resigned after months of anxious speculation. The result was both a relief and a disappointment. Only Swindon fell – helped on its way by the success of Christopher Layton, fighting on a radical ticket, moving in hard on the Labour vote, and taking 15·3 per cent of the total vote in a seat the Liberal Party had not fought since 1950. A Communist and a far-left Independent also polled a total of 964 votes, twice the margin by which Labour lost the seat. But the three other English seats were held, and the Nationalist challenge was beaten off in the Gorbals. (Even so, the Nationalists polled 25 per cent of the vote and took second place, which would have been sensational progress up to the time of Pollok.) And the swings, though not in the 1968 class, were still too big for comfort: 9·2 per cent at Islington, 11·4 per cent at Paddington, 10·7 per cent at Newcastle, 12·9 per cent at Swindon. No echo here of the message of the polls that the gap between the main parties had now been closed.

In December, Labour lost Wellingborough on a swing of 9·7 per cent and were on the wrong end of a 14·3 per cent swing at Louth, though this was probably inflated by bad weather. The swing against them dropped to 8·6 per cent at Bridgwater on 12 March – the first by-election in which eighteen-year-olds were able to vote. But it was not until South Ayrshire, on 19 March, that the party really had something to celebrate. The swing against them was assessed on normal calculations at 3 per cent. But even this probably exaggerated the extent of the damage. On a two-party calculation, there was a swing to Labour of 0·6 per cent.

Moreover, this had happened despite the presence of a Nationalist candidate with strong local associations. He polled 20·4 per cent of the vote: again, a fair achievement by pre-Pollok standards, but not enough to suggest that the now widely celebrated decline of the Nationalist parties had been effectively checked.

The slide had been very marked in local elections. The SNP vote in municipal elections fell from 30·1 per cent in 1968 to 22·0 per cent in 1969 and was to slump still further in the elections fought seven weeks after South Ayrshire. The SNP won 13 wards in Glasgow in 1968, one in 1969 and none at all in 1970.

To some extent, the party's very success in local government may have helped to explain its decline. It had lost its political virginity: having been voted into office, SNP councillors had been forced to establish their positions, had taken unpopular decisions, had failed to produce the goods in the semi-miraculous fashion which some supporters had been expecting. In Wales, where the party is less involved in local politics, the decline in Nationalist fortunes was less sharp.

Those who at the height of the Nationalist tide had given the advice 'stand firm' were now waiting about with hopeful faces expecting to be congratulated. Yet the Nationalists had left their mark. They had certainly left it on the Liberals, with whom they continued to dispute, at the 1970 general election, a lot of common territory. They had moved the Conservative Party down the devolution road; Sir Alec's committee had developed the Heath proposal for a Scottish Assembly and it was approved by the Scottish Conservative conference in May 1970. In December 1968 Labour had made its own bow to Nationalist success in setting up the Crowther Commission on the Constitution, which had a dual advantage: its creation showed that the aspirations of people in the regions were not overlooked; and it would not report until after the general election.

Largely, though, Labour soldiered on because they could do little else. The only cure for economic grievances was a dramatic upturn in the economy; and while better balance-of-payments figures were very welcome, no one supposed that they could in themselves set people dancing in the streets of Hamilton or Bargoed. There was still no sight of an end to high unemployment.

Some said Labour's fault was that it was not receptive, denied the rank and file the participation they coveted. 'There has got to be a real dialogue', said Anthony Wedgwood Benn in mid-1968, 'so that we can listen to what people are trying to say to us and not just appear to be shouting at them all the time.' But in fact, of course, only the totally deaf could have been in any doubt about what people were saying at Oldham and Sheffield Brightside, Nelson and Caerphilly. Labour knew very well what people wanted of them: the difficulty was that they knew no way of providing it.

There was always a cynical note in Labour's dismissal of Nationalist politics. 'They'll come to their senses when we get to a general election', it was said, as if the views people expressed three years out of four could be taken as an aberration, and the only criticism which deserved attention was that which might eventually turn you out of power. Had Labour won the 1970 election, this complacency would have been rewarded, would have become a sanctified part of conventional political wisdom: the significance of by-elections as a force for administering shocks to unpopular governments would have been diminished. But on 18 June 1970 the nation reserved its right to behave unpredictably at general elections as well as in between them.

The explanations of that sudden lurch into big-dipper politics which marked the by-elections of 1966–70 have yet to be fully established. But it will be surprising if the immediate impressions which they made on the uncommitted observer are eventually discredited. There was, it seemed, a new volatility in the electorate; a new willingness to abandon traditional patterns of voting – or, among the younger voters, a greater disposition to regard such traditions as irrelevant; a new readiness to cross, as so many people did on the council estates of Dudley and Leicester and elsewhere, from one's normal allegiance to that directly opposed to it; there was, too, at a time when none of the established parties had much to boast about, an unusually strong advantage in fielding a candidate who, like Kenneth Marks at Gorton, seemed in sympathy with the spirit of the people whom he aspired to represent.

There was, in this series of by-elections, a certain element of unchannelled emotion, a compound of disappointment, frustration, even despair; and on this score, Labour could fairly argue that its worst punishments were out of any real proportion to its crimes. But there was also, one suspects, something else: a mood of rampant pragmatism unusual in British politics. Harold Wilson, as the prophet of political pragmatism, should be the last to complain of that.

10. Lincoln: The Background to Taverne's Triumph

By JOHN RAMSDEN and RICHARD JAY

General Election, 1970		(Electorate 53,243)
Taverne (Lab.)	20,090	*(51·0)*
Alexander (Con.)	15,340	*(39·0)*
Blades (Ind.)	3,937	*(10·0)*
Lab. majority	4,750	Turnout 74·5%

By-Election, 1 Mar 1973		(Electorate 51,199)
Taverne (Dem. Lab.)	21,967	*(58·2)*
Dilks (Lab.)	8,776	*(23·3)*
Guinness (Con.)	6,616	*(17·5)*
Simmerson (Ind. Con.)	198	*(0·5)*
Waller (Ind.)	100	*(0·3)*
Justice (Ind.)	81	*(0·2)*
Dem. Lab. majority	13,191	Turnout 72·6%

On 6 October 1972 Dick Taverne resigned his seat as Labour MP for Lincoln[1] and on 1 March 1973 he was triumphantly returned to Parliament with an overwhelming majority. His re-election was on the platform of the newly formed Lincoln Democratic Labour Association and was opposed by the full weight of both Conservative and Labour party machines. It was the first victory by any Independent candidate in post-war by-elections, and was perhaps the greatest *personal* election victory in British political history. Taverne's resignation had been the result of a long-standing dispute with the Lincoln Labour Party, and so the election campaign seemed to involve

---

[1] The announcement of resignation was on 6 October, but Taverne was not formally appointed to the Manor of Northstead until the following week.

both the issue of Labour's future role as a party, and the entirely separate question of the independence of a Member of Parliament. For this reason, the Lincoln by-election was widely seen as more than a freak local contest, from which no lessons could be drawn. Along with other by-elections in the winter of 1972–3, Lincoln was used by a section of the press to demonstrate the desirability – even the inevitability – of a fundamental realignment in the two-party system.

The national background

The background to the by-elections of the winter of 1972–3 was more concerned with the opposition than with the government. In one sense this was hardly surprising, for four of the six contests were in Labour-held seats, but in terms of what is expected from modern by-elections it does require some explanations. Right from the day of his unexpected election victory of 1970, Edward Heath began to put into practice his declared intention of giving the nation less government, and less-publicised government too. Although, by the middle of 1972, the government had gone back on a great deal of its declared policy of non-intervention in the spheres of industry and economic management, it was keeping to its intentions in the general political sphere. The 'low profile' which the government tried to present in Ulster was typical of the style which it adopted in the whole area of domestic politics: strikes came and went without the government either trying to escalate conflict or trying to avoid it. At the same time, Cabinet meetings, which had been 'as leaky as an old sieve' under Harold Wilson, were replaced behind the normal veil of secrecy by Edward Heath. In these circumstances, the harsh spotlight of television and press was turned onto the Labour Party almost as much in opposition as it had been in power. No news may be good news, but it makes bad newspapers.

There was also plenty happening in the Labour Party which could be reported, especially as the party's Common Market split began to deepen during 1971. However, Labour's position must be seen in the context of the government's legislative record in its first two years. Labour regarded the Industrial Relations Act (1971) and the Housing Finance Act (1972) as deeply divisive measures which could only make social and economic problems worse. It was paradoxical that just when many believed that the Labour Government of 1964–70 had been too concerned with compromise and consensus, so the new Conservative Government seemed to have abandoned that consensus for a 'lurch to the right'. It was against this background that the split over the Common Market became so deep; supporting 'entry on the Tory terms' became much less acceptable in a party which was more virulently anti-Conservative than it had been for a generation. On the vote on the issue of principle, Labour was outmanœuvred by the Conservative decision to allow a free vote on their side of the House, and 69 Labour MPs defied the party whip to vote for Europe. This only delayed the real problem for both parties: by February 1972, in the midst of a protracted and bitter strike by the miners, the government's very existence seemed to hang in the balance. On the crucial vote on the Second Reading of the European Communities Bill, the survival of the 'divisive' and 'socially irresponsible' government was only assured by the votes of five Liberals and the abstention of four Labour MPs. Furthermore, during the long Committee stage of the Bill, Labour pro-Marketeers let it be known that they would provide whatever votes were necessary to ensure the passage of the Bill without major amendments. By this time the number of identifiable Labour pro-Marketeers had fallen, and the group that remained were almost exclusively on the right of the party. To those on the left, the chance to get rid of the Conservative Government seemed to be the only question, but to those on the right, consistency on issues like the Common Market was of equal importance. This ambiguity of approach derived essentially from Labour's Common Market policy of 1967 to 1970. There was never a full policy commitment to anything more than negotiations, but the party's official spokesmen described their intentions in terms which suggested much more. Harold Wilson had prepared the way for negotiations by lining up a team of convinced Europeanists in all the important positions: George Brown, Michael Stewart, George Thomson, Lord Chalfont (at the Foreign Office), Roy Jenkins, Harold Lever and Dick Taverne (at the Treasury) were all genuinely convinced pro-Marketeers, but they were not representative of the party. As the party's policy towards Europe hardened in 1971, this group (increasingly referred to as the 'Jenkinsites') felt betrayed. As the issue became increasingly one of Left and Centre against Right, each group felt that the others had shifted their ground on Europe. The issue came to a head when several 'Jenkinsites' resigned from the front bench with Jenkins, in protest against the party's new commitment to a referendum on the European issue. (One of the resignations which attracted least attention at the time was that of Dick Taverne.) Thus, by May 1972, there appeared to be an opposition within the Opposition: not only were several ex-Ministers now on the back-benches of their own volition, but some of those who remained (Shirley Williams, Roy Hattersley, and Harold Lever when he came back to the front bench in the autumn) were openly discontented with the party's policy on Europe.[2]

However, all this was far from the fundamental split in the Labour movement which sections of the press were reporting. It was in vain that Roy Jenkins launched a series of wide-ranging speeches on social issues, calling for a reappraisal of the party's attitudes: this attempt to re-emphasise the unity of the Labour Party as a party of radical reform was simply dubbed by the press as an open challenge to the leadership. Jenkins's speeches were more interesting, though, in the style of party which they envisaged, with a greater emphasis on constructive reform and less concentration on Tory-bashing. This was the more important for by this time, in the summer and autumn of 1972, the Conservatives had adopted a more interventionist industrial policy and an incomes policy. If Labour were to recapture the 'middle ground' in British politics, it would presumably have to fight for it. Unfortunately for Jenkins and his supporters, they would not be fully trusted in their own party as long as the Common Market question divided them from the majority of their colleagues. And the Common Market question seemed to drag on and on. The party conference of October 1972 virtually committed the party to all-out opposition by naming essential terms for entry which were wholly unrealistic, and by insisting that in the meantime

[2] Uwe Kitzinger, *Diplomacy and Persuasion* (1973) esp. pp. 276–330, 371–406, gives a much fuller account of Labour's divisions over Europe.

Labour should take no part in Community institutions. This policy took something of a knock when George Thomson accepted nomination by the government as a European Commissioner, but when the enlarged European Parliament met in January 1973 no Labour Members were present. It was for this reason that Europe remained an open wound in the Labour Party, despite the desire of all groups in the party to avoid a confrontation.

It is in this context that the intervention of *The Times* must be assessed: like much of the press, it had shown a great deal of sympathy for the Jenkinsites ever since 1970, but during 1972 it began to argue for a new party of the moderate Left. This line was systematically pushed through editorials, through the column written by Bernard Levin, and through news coverage. *The Times* was not alone in urging the cause of moderation when both parties seemed bent on confrontation, but *The Times* was by far the most outspoken. The reasons as stated were basically threefold, leading to a conclusion that only a new party would meet all the requirements: it was said that the Labour Party was an irreconcilable contradiction between social reform and Marxist dogma; it was said that both major parties were being dominated by their extremists; finally, it was said that the electorate was visibly disillusioned with the existing parties and was looking for something new. The first two points had of course been made before and were anyway matters on which opinions differed widely; it was the final argument, public opinion, that was used most heavily.

Elections and polls during the Conservative Government had presented a confusing picture. The government lost the Bromsgrove by-election (27 May 1971) on a swing of 10·1 per cent; in local elections, government candidates were routed in 1971 and 1972; in opinion polls, the government was constantly behind. But despite all this, the government's performance was much better than might have been expected: although over a million people were unemployed, and although inflation was rampant, the Labour lead in the opinion polls in 1972 was only a steady 7 to 10 per cent. Although Bromsgrove had been lost, Macclesfield and Kingston-upon-Thames were held, and Arundel and Shoreham actually showed a swing to the Conservatives. All this was small beer compared with the huge swings of 1962–3 and 1967–8, and to the large government opinion-poll deficits of those years. Conservative leaders had plenty of time left in which to choose a good moment for a general election, and had much less ground to make up than previous governments which had almost secured re-election. Nor did minor parties improve their positions until the autumn of 1972, when the Liberals began to rise steadily in the opinion polls.

The case for a new centre party was put most explicitly in a full news-spread and editorial, printed in *The Times* on 30 September 1972. This was interestingly timed to coincide with the gathering of delegates at Blackpool for the Labour Party Conference, and came just a week before Taverne's resignation from Parliament. The story included a major opinion poll, specially commissioned, which showed that a centre party of the Liberals and Labour 'moderates' would command the support of almost half the electorate. A strongly worded editorial disposed of all the arguments about the practical difficulty of actually forming such a party, but did not mention the most important difficulty of all – the fact that Labour moderates had no intention of joining any new party. The poll itself was widely quoted and discussed, with comments from politicians of all parties. Henceforth any Liberal revival could be construed as implicitly strengthening the case for and the chances of a centre party. Only the loyalty of Labour pro-Marketeers presented an immovable stumbling-block, and for this reason 'the Lincoln affair' was especially significant. Not only was the by-election at Lincoln a good chance to test the strength of 'centre opinion', but Dick Taverne was the only Labour moderate who was available to act as standard-bearer. Even his commitment was much less than total, for, as he later told Terry Coleman of the *Guardian*: 'If there was such a party, it would have overwhelming support. But it's very difficult to see how it's going to be created.'

Only three by-elections took place in the autumn of 1972: at Rochdale, at Uxbridge and at Sutton and Cheam. All took place after Taverne's resignation, and since the Liberals made two gains, one from each major party, there seemed to be further confirmation of public disillusion. Further examination demonstrates a less clear-cut picture. At Rochdale the Liberals were extremely fortunate in the location of the by-election, for this had been their most improved constituency in 1970. A very strong local Liberal candidate, Cyril Smith, had pushed the Conservatives into third place, and a by-election gave him a perfect opportunity to squeeze the Conservative vote and beat Labour. Smith duly won the seat in exactly that way, which lent credence to a number of theories: an increased Liberal vote could be seen as evidence of 'centre opinion', but equally it could be argued that Conservatives who voted for Smith to oust Labour were still operating within the logic of the two-party system. The two subsequent contests took place on the same day, but with little press enthusiasm for the revival which the Liberals were claiming. Having been caught out by the evaporation of the Liberal revivals of the 1960s, the press were clearly not going to be caught out again. As *The Times* remarked: 'The Liberals have not had a bad press; apart from *The Times* they have had hardly any press at all.' There was indeed more press comment on the weight of Cyril Smith (over 20 stone) than on the implications of his victory. The result of all this was that probably nobody but the Liberals themselves believed that they could win Sutton and Cheam.

The government could have avoided the contest at Sutton, since it was caused by the appointment of the Conservative MP, Sir Richard Sharples, as Governor of Bermuda, and they assumed their inevitable victory right up to polling day. Meanwhile the Liberals imported supporters from all over the country, and planned to 'do an Orpington'. They systematically exploited the frustrations of middle-class voters who were baffled by the government's apparent reversals of policy and by their failure to stop inflation. It was said widely at the time, and demonstrated afterwards by an opinion poll in the *Sunday Times*, that many Conservative voted Liberal simply to give their government a jolt. At the same time the Liberals could round up Labour voters with the argument that here was a once-in-a-lifetime chance to oust the Conservatives. Added to all this was a highly efficient exploitation by the Liberals of local grievances – hailed by Liberals as a 'new breakthrough in community politics' and described derisively by non-Liberals as 'the politics of the parish pump'. On 7 December the Liberal candidate, Graham Tope, easily won the seat from the

Conservatives on a swing beside which even Orpington looked tame.

However, the impact of Sutton and Cheam was considerably lessened by the result at Uxbridge which declared a few minutes later. The Conservatives had held this highly marginal seat, and the Liberal candidate had lost his deposit. Politicians and pundits who had been eating words at a high speed after the declaration at Sutton were now able to declare that it was Uxbridge that was the really significant result. Taken together, the two results provided evidence for every theory and for none: Liberals and Labour had each lost a deposit but the Conservatives had lost a safe seat, and no discussions of candidates and organisation could obscure the basic contradiction. In fact, the same contradiction occurred on 1 March, when both Conservatives and Labour did relatively better in the 'marginal seat' of Dundee East than in the two 'safe' ones. In that sense, the by-elections of December 1972 were inconclusive. As the next round of contests, at Lincoln, Dundee and Chester-le-Street, approached, there was no firm evidence from which to predict their outcome.

The local background

The conflict in Lincoln which resulted in Taverne's resignation and the subsequent by-election reflected Labour Party divisions at the national level. Taverne's decision to join the group of 69 Labour MPs who voted for the Government's Common Market proposals on 28 October 1972 became the key issue in a classic battle between left and right wings in the party. Leaders of the anti-Taverne group in Lincoln consistently argued that they were simply acting upon the right of local parties to exercise some control over the representatives for whom they had worked to send to Westminster, and at the beginning of the fight Taverne himself was content with a simple restatement of Burkean arguments for the independence of MPs. But behind this lay more fundamental divisions over what Taverne called 'different views of Socialism'.

Since the war Lincoln had consistently elected MPs of a moderate Social Democratic style – the local mayor, George Deer, in 1945 and Geoffrey de Freitas after 1950. In 1961, at the height of Hugh Gaitskell's conflict with the Labour Left, Taverne, a leading member of the Campaign for Democratic Socialism, gained the nomination when de Freitas was appointed High Commissioner to Ghana, and won the subsequent by-election with an increased majority. Gaitskellites were the most influential section in the Lincoln Labour Party at this time, and they had used their majority to restrict the short-listed candidates in 1961 to those who shared their point of view. A group, led by Leo Beckett, later to become chairman of the Lincoln Labour Party, had responded by storming out of the nomination committee, declaring that the three candidates were 'all of a kind. . . . They were all right-wing.' The balance in the party very soon shifted in the opposite direction, such that both Taverne and Pat Mulligan, party agent after 1964, could later agree that, from the beginning, there had been latent tension between the Member and his party. 'I was a Gaitskellite MP with a left-wing management committee' was Taverne's comment; Mulligan's, that 'the Lincoln Labour Party has always been to the left and Dick Taverne has always been to the right'. Mulligan himself held a political position close to that of the *Tribune* group in the Labour Party, though he worked closely with Taverne until 1970. The Left also held many other key positions in Lincoln Labour politics at the time of the split. Leo Beckett was party chairman. Ralph Wadsworth, a former chairman and a close ally of Beckett, became leader of the council when, in 1971, Labour regained control after the disastrous local elections of 1967. Left-wingers were prominent as chairmen of council committees. The engineering industry was the mainstay, both of Lincoln's economy and of its Labour Party, and in the 1960s a number of mergers and takeovers had transformed its character and given rise to considerable redundancy. Local branches of the Amalgamated Union of Engineering Workers, once noted for their moderation, increased in militancy. Chief representative of this move was Don Gossop, in 1972 district secretary of the AUEW, a vice-chairman of Lincoln Labour Party and chairman of the council's Industrial Committee, who was responsible in that year for providing Ernie Roberts of the AUEW with a platform on which to advocate his proposal for a political coalition of 'Catholics, Labour and Communist parties'.

The divisions between Taverne and his party centred around different issues at different times. In the early 1960s unilateralism and Clause 4 held the centre of the arena. The Common Market did not materialise as a major question until much later. Taverne in 1962 had committed himself to a strong pro-European position, although with a caveat about possible terms of entry. And though the local party in 1962 and 1965 passed resolutions against entry, this had not led to any serious disagreement even as late as the 1970 election. Other issues had. In 1968, when Taverne was at the Treasury, Beckett had demanded that he resign in protest against the imposition of prescription charges. Beckett's group were also annoyed at Taverne's decision to give firm support to the Labour Government's industrial relations legislation. This issue grew into a major row in January 1971 when Taverne threatened to denounce Gossop and the other left-wingers from the platform of a meeting in Lincoln if they put a resolution calling for strike action against the Conservatives' Industrial Relations Bill. The 'different views of Socialism' held by each side became clear during the by-election campaign of 1973. Taverne declared himself in favour of the 'control' of free competition but against nationalisation, while he referred to the government's incomes freeze as a 'good Socialist incomes policy'; his opponents spoke out against the Industrial Relations Act and the freeze, and supported nationalisation proposals.

Personal differences had accentuated political disagreement. It became clear in the by-election that Taverne's party workers were largely drawn from the young, the more elderly and the middle-class professional people living 'up the hill' in Lincoln; the average, middle-aged, working-class member stayed with Beckett's group in the Labour Party. To these, Taverne's intellectualism and sophisticated charm, matured at Charterhouse, Balliol and the Bar, had less appeal. 'The problem Dick Taverne has', Leo Beckett once said, 'is that he lives on a different plane from what we do, and when you get people like myself who are nothing more or less than a foundry worker, we speak different languages, we live different lives. He seems to find it very difficult when he arrives and is in our company to be at ease.' The Common Market issue accentuated this sense of class separation. Taverne seemed much more ready to consult with Lincoln industrialists and conform to their pro-European views, than to consider the opinions of trade unionists in the city, frightened by possible price rises and worried that 'rationalisation' would endanger even more jobs in a city already characterised by one of the highest unemployment levels in the East Midlands.

Until mid-1971 the divergences were not allowed to get out of hand. Taverne continued to enjoy the support of most of his party, and Beckett's group do not seem to have considered it worthwhile to engage in a stand-up fight. 'We have leaned over backwards over the years to help him', said Beckett in October 1972, '– and there *have* been moves against him.' But the possibility which emerged, given divisions within the Conservative Party, of bringing down the government on the Common Market issue brought matters to a head. On 5 July 1971 the General Management Committee of the Lincoln Labour Party met, 65 members attending, to discuss resolutions to be sent to the October party conference. Six resolutions were considered, two of them referring to the Common Market. One, supported by the Executive Committee, called for unity in the PLP over the issue, and for a general election before the signing of the Treaty of Rome. This was rejected in favour of a much more forceful motion, eventually approved unanimously, which instructed 'its delegates to the annual conference, or any other conference called to discuss the issue, to vote against entry, and calls upon each Labour MP to do likewise'. This effectively threw the gauntlet down before Taverne, who had recently spoken at Lincoln in favour of the Market and defended on a radio programme the Labour Committee for Europe's decision to advertise its case in the national press. Pat Mulligan called the GMC motion an instruction to Taverne to 'respect the wishes' of his local party, and it was clearly intended as a direct challenge to Taverne's independent view on the issue.

The position of Taverne's opponents was strengthened by the anti-Market tenor of the party conference in October, where Ian Mikardo, conference chairman, pointed out that local parties were entitled to eject MPs who refused to follow party policy, and Harold Wilson declared that MPs who came into conflict with their organisations would receive no assistance from the national leadership. Beckett, leader of Lincoln's delegation to the conference, commented to the Lincoln press that he hoped for a 'vote of no-confidence against Mr Taverne if he votes in the Tory lobby'. Although he was looking for some solution which would 'let Mr Taverne off the hook', Taverne 'does not seem to want to get off the hook'. In mid-October the PLP voted 140 to 111 against a free vote on the issue of principle on 28 October, and Taverne's position deteriorated. In order to press their point of view, the anti-Market members of the Lincoln party held an open ballot in the city's main street on Friday and Saturday 22–23 October, asking electors to vote for or against the terms of entry. The vote was 1,031 for and 1,961 against, with 11 spoilt ballots. In spite of the increasing local opposition to his views, Taverne voted for the principle of accepting the negotiated terms on 28 October.

His determination to vote against the party whip was increased by an important event. On 25 October, ATV's *World in Action* broadcast a programme on what was rapidly being recognised as 'the Lincoln affair', in which Taverne was confronted by supporters and critics in his party. The discussion degenerated rapidly into what can only be called a slanging match, from which Beckett and Gossop in particular emerged with badly scarred reputations. An atmosphere was created antagonistic to any form of compromise at the GMC meeting on 1 November, when opponents of Taverne put down a motion of censure, and requested a selection committee to be appointed for another candidate at the next election. Mutual recrimination excluded serious discussion of the motion at this meeting, and a further special meeting was called for 16 November. This time, by 54 votes to 50, with 5 abstentions, a censure motion, expressing 'lack of confidence in the City Member to reflect the political views and aspirations of the members at large', was passed.

Taverne was saved by the new Labour Party rules of 1970. In accordance with these, a further meeting of the GMC had to be called to make the final decision. In the meantime, moderates on the Executive Committee, supported by a petition in favour of Taverne with 5,000 names attached, managed to pass a motion advising that action upon the GMC vote should be shelved (24 November). At the GMC on 6 December, a vote on the initial censure motion produced a stalemate of 45–45; the motion was thrown out, and the Executive Committee's resolution approved.

A hiatus now ensued on the issue until 8 May 1972. But the wave of support which had come to Taverne after the television broadcast, and which had ensured his survival in December, had ebbed somewhat. Two further important events occurred in the meantime. Elections from the wards to the GMC early in 1972 had given the exceptionally well-organised anti-Taverne group considerable additional support. At the annual meeting on 6 March, Peter Archer, treasurer to the Labour group on the council and a moderate, challenged Beckett for chairmanship of the party and was defeated by a 3:1 majority; he then lost his place as vice-chairman to Wadsworth. Elections for seven other vacancies on the Executive Committee resulted in a strengthening of the anti-Taverne group. With the 'no-action' resolution still in force, and the council elections due in early May, action was delayed. It was the imminence of these elections which also postponed conflict after the second major event. On 12 April the PLP decided to demand a referendum on the Common Market, and Taverne, following Roy Jenkins, resigned from the position as front-bench spokesman on financial affairs to which he had recently been reappointed. Anti-Marketeers in Lincoln saw this as the ultimate act in Taverne's apparent determination to flout party unity: 'We have never had to take out the knives', one of his opponents was reported as saying. 'Mr Taverne has them all in his own pocket.' Whoever had possession was induced to keep them hidden until 8 May by an agreement between the two sides.

At the GMC meeting on that day, Taverne explained the reasons for his resignation. The meeting was stormy and the explanations apparently unconvincing. It was decided that the Executive Committee should recommend some course of action to a further meeting of the GMC, and on 15 May the GMC agreed that at a further meeting on 19 June a vote would be taken on a censure motion similar to that of the previous November.

The increasingly bitter exchanges between the two sides were accentuated by the consequences of the borough elections.

Since Labour regained control of the council in 1971, there had been a variety of complaints, from Conservatives, community associations and even from within the Labour group, about high-handed and autocratic means which were being employed by some leading members of the council in the conduct of business. Such charges are, of course, the stuff of local politics. But it does appear that the efficiency with which Grafton House (the name of Labour's headquarters, and increasingly applied as a label for the anti-Taverne group) had conducted its election campaigns was rapidly transferred to the conduct of council business.[3] This efficiency was now turned against Taverne supporters. On 10 May three councillors – Tom Ward, Fred Allen and Clodagh Wilkinson – were removed from their positions as chairmen and vice-chairmen of a number of committees. Pat Mulligan declared this to be a 'normal reshuffle' after the election; but since no reasons were given for the 'reshuffle', it was widely assumed that it was no accident that each was a firm supporter of Taverne. When those councillors who had voiced their views to the press were subsequently censured by a Labour group meeting, the opinion that a witch-hunt was in progress gained force.

From Taverne's point of view, the 'sacking of the chairmen' was a godsend. If the television broadcast of October had provided him with the air of legitimacy he needed to fight his party, this intrusion of a national political question into local politics brought forward a small army of workers, appalled at what appeared the vindictiveness of Grafton House.

Both sides prepared for the GMC meeting of 19 June. Richard Jay was asked to conduct a poll of local opinion on

[3] In January 1972 Councillor Walter Donald had the party whip withdrawn for non-attendance at council meetings. He claimed that this was because he had attempted to make an attack on Councillors George Elsey and Laurie Vaisey, two vehement opponents of Taverne; 'They wanted me out before I got them out', was Donald's defence, although even pro-Taverne figures thought it a somewhat spurious one. But Peter Archer's comment on the incident – 'Since taking control we have been exercising a tight grip on attendance at meetings' – shows how eager the party officers were to keep firm control of the political life of the city. The *Lincolnshire Echo* noted the manner in which council business was being conducted on 12 January 1972, when it made a number of ironic comments on the fact that Councillor Wadsworth had achieved his hat-trick of finishing council meetings by 8 p.m.

the question, and the results, published on 15 June, appeared to show widespread support for Taverne and the stand he had taken.[4] Grafton House in turn brought forward a motion to the meeting of the East Midlands Regional Council of the party on 17 June, deploring the party's inability to censure the 69 pro-Market MPs. The vote of 192 to 153 in favour strengthened its position considerably. Taverne's defences here had been weakened by the recent move of Jim Cattermole from his position as area organiser to become secretary to the Labour Committee for Europe.

At the GMC meeting on Monday 19 June, a heated debate took place. Opponents of Taverne claimed that they had the right to ask an MP to stand down when he had lost the confidence of his local party workers; Taverne argued that he was entitled to vote on an important issue of principle, even if this involved voting against his party, and that Richard Jay's poll had shown his electorate to be behind him on this. His arguments were not accepted. A very large turnout produced a majority of 75–50 in favour of requiring Taverne to stand down before the next general election. 'Regrettably', was Pat Mulligan's comment, 'Dick chose to fight us to the death.'

Taverne had expected to find himself in a minority, and had already made plans to resign and fight a by-election on the issue. But he decided to delay this when he received information about the conduct of a number of ward meetings. Taverne argued – and his interpretation has been supported by many Labour Party members – that the purpose of the party rule allowing a delay between GMC meetings before a final vote is taken on an MP's future is to allow ward meetings to discuss the question and inform their delegates on the GMC of their conclusions. He further claimed that in the Lincoln case this purpose was deliberately frustrated: in some wards, officers who were opposed to Taverne failed to call meetings; in others, meetings were held without the information being passed to his supporters. On these grounds, Taverne determined to appeal to the National Executive Committee.

Two committees of the NEC in July upheld his complaint. A special sub-committee, and the Organisation Committee,

---

[4] Results of this, and of all other polls taken in Lincoln, are given in Appendix I, p. 312.

recommended to the full NEC that the GMC decision be disallowed on the grounds that 'irregularities' had taken place, and that the failure of the Lincoln party to have adequate consultations with ward committees constituted a breach of 'natural justice'. On the full NEC, however, the decision was reversed. Only Shirley Williams appears to have made a strong case in favour of Taverne; the few other members who had any leanings towards a 'Jenkinsite' position were probably aware that they were isolated enough in the party without fighting on this particular issue. Barbara Castle reverted to what had been the major argument of those opposed to Taverne in Lincoln – that the 'conscience clause' of the party would have protected Taverne had he decided to abstain on 28 October 1971, but that his vote against the party whip allowed him no legitimate defence. The major weakness of Taverne's appeal was, however, brought out by the NEC chairman, Anthony Wedgwood Benn. He noted that the party rules did not explicitly prescribe that the 'waiting period' between GMC meetings should be used to consult ward committees, and that Taverne's claim that 'irregularities' had occurred was thus irrelevant. Natural justice should give way to the party constitution.

Throughout the autumn the national press carried rumours that Taverne would make a final appeal against his GMC and the NEC decision to the party conference in October. It was also rumoured that Roy Jenkins and others of his followers were desperately attempting to dissuade Taverne from his intended course of action – that of resigning his seat and forcing a by-election. The first would clearly, in the increasing anti-Market mood of the party, have been futile; and on 6 October, the final day of the conference, Taverne announced his decision to resign and to fight a by-election as an independent Democratic Labour candidate. In his press statement he declared that it was not simply the Common Market which separated him from his party. He attacked it on a wider front. He denounced the 'sham democracy' of the Labour Party, which allowed 'autocratic caucuses' to rule the consciences of MPs,[5] and he condemned its pursuit of 'slovenly politics, the

[5] Michael Foot took up this challenge with the claim that it was 'almost Stalinite' to deny effective power to local parties (*The Times*, 19 Jan 1973).

politics of tactics, manoeuvres, compromise and double-talk which means all things to all men, but in reality means nothing'. The issue was no longer Taverne against Grafton House, but Taverne against the party.

Why did he decide to fight the Labour Party? His own answer was that 'my choice was of fading or fighting. I am not the fading type. If I do not get in, I will at least go out with a bang rather than a whimper.' But there were four other alternatives open to him.

One was possibly not relevant after 19 June, but certainly was earlier. Taverne after all was the only one of the 69 MPs who voted against the whip in October 1971, and the only front-bench spokesman who resigned in April, to be voted out by his local association. The others, although encountering problems in their constituencies, managed to ride the storm. Part of the reason was clearly the ideological gap between himself and his party officers: they saw in the Common Market issue an opportunity to obtain an MP who more faithfully reflected their opinions. Indeed, Taverne supporters constantly claimed that the party officers intended the replacement to come from among their own numbers. Their special position in the local party also made it easier for them to build up support in the GMC. But also important was Taverne's refusal to compromise. Had he felt himself able at some time to give assurances to the party about future 'good behaviour' (as, for instance, the Conservative rebel MP, Richard Body of nearby Boston, was able to do), his opponents might well have found it difficult to mobilise a majority. But Taverne was already on bad terms with his officers to the point that it was difficult for them to meet in other than a strained atmosphere. And he insisted on standing full square behind two principles: that entry into the Common Market should not be opposed, and certainly not be used as a means of defeating the government; and that the local party had no right to exercise control over his adopted position in the Commons. The only product of this situation could be an all-out fight. (Anthony Crosland's statement that 'if Dick Taverne had been a bit more understanding, he would still be Labour MP for Lincoln' is not the whole truth, but contains at least a grain of it.)

A second possibility was offered by Taverne's Lincoln opponents. Although he had been asked to stand down for the next election, he would automatically have earned the right to a place on the short-list during the selection of a replacement, and might have found himself readopted. Given the events of the previous two years, this claim was, to say the least, ingenuous.

A third was to look for an alternative constituency. As Chester-le-Street showed, there were constituencies in which pro-Market Labour candidates could find themselves adopted.[6] But Taverne might well have been justified in believing that, in the existing mood of the party, the national leadership would have exercised all its influence to prevent the readoption of the one defector of whom an example had been made. 'We must find some way to execute Dick Taverne', Taverne once quoted James Callaghan as saying.

A fourth possibility was to travel the route laid down by George Thomson, among other Labour pro-Marketeers, and take some permanent post in the EEC. The Lincoln press was at one stage carefully informed that Taverne had twice been offered £12,000 jobs in the Market – once as late as January 1973 – and had rejected them. Taverne, however, seems to have been determined to stick to his political career, though at one stage he admitted that, even if he later managed to reunite with the Labour Party, he could not expect to hold ministerial office again.

His reasons for this intransigence were similar to those which Desmond Donnelly had put forward a few years earlier. The Labour Party was losing credibility in the country by compromises and reversals on important issues of principle – Taverne particularly pointed to what he saw as changes of policy on Europe and industrial relations; further, it was losing support, and failing to tackle important national questions, by its adherence to an outmoded view of Socialism. But Taverne, unlike Donnelly, does not appear at first to have considered himself as the forerunner of a new, middle-of-the-road Social Democratic party. Despite the attempts of the

[6] But even Giles Radice's adoption in Chester-le-Street, backed by the local party establishment, occasioned considerable bitterness in the party (*New Statesman*, 23 Feb 1973).

editor of *The Times* in September and October 1972 to associate
him with such a new party, Taverne insisted that his hope was
to rejoin Labour. His intention in resigning in October was not
to blaze a trail for a centre party, but, by making a demonstration, to point out to the Labour Party that the swing to the left
which had occurred after 1970 was both irresponsible and
unpopular. And the fact that he delayed the timing of his
resignation until the end of the party conference was interpreted
by many commentators as an attempt to achieve maximum
impact for this point of view in the wake of the various compromises which had been reached to present some sort of party
unity to the public.

The timing of the by-election

Taverne's resignation was formally announced on 6 October,
although – in common with other moments in the campaign –
The Times had carried news of his decision some days before it
was officially announced. Speculation began at once, for it was
thought likely that the timing of the election would materially
alter the result. Moreover, since Taverne was still a Labour
MP when he resigned his seat, it fell to the official Labour
Party to decide the date of the by-election. This must have
presented a difficult problem for Transport House, and for
Bob Mellish, the Labour Chief Whip on whom the responsibility rested. If the by-election were to be delayed, then
perhaps Taverne's campaign would run out of steam and his
local popularity might well evaporate. However, delay would
also make possible a further consolidation of Taverne's local
strength, so that when the election was finally held, it would
present more rather than fewer problems for Labour. The
decision taken was to select a new candidate without undue
urgency, and thus to run the risk of delay. One real influence in
the direction of delay must have been the Lincoln Labour
Party's own internal divisions: only one ward committee had
defected to Taverne as a unit, but individuals had defected
from almost every ward and union branch. There would
be little point in rushing into an election to catch Taverne unprepared if Grafton House were to be equally unready.

   On 9 November, Joe Ghose, secretary of Taverne's Lincoln

Democratic Labour Association, was quoted as saying that they had not yet set up any local machinery. The enthusiasm for setting up a grass-roots organisation was already available to Taverne, as was the manpower; he was perhaps fortunate that Labour gave him time. During the delay, Fleet Street and the local press did a great deal to keep Taverne in the news. It was naturally good copy to portray Taverne as a lone fighter against the faceless men in the machines, and this impression was heightened by the fact that Taverne's frequent challenges were met only with silence from his rivals. All the national papers made periodic references to the coming election, as in the *Sunday Express*'s 'Why is Harold Wilson afraid of me? By Dick Taverne', but *The Times* outshone them all in its devotion to the cause. On 5 December, on the main domestic news page, there was a long report of an address by Taverne to the Smaller Businesses Association in Newcastle-upon-Tyne. By this stage it appeared that Taverne had 'only to sneeze to merit six column-inches in *The Times*', and each time the story of his Lincoln battle was sympathetically retold. So extreme was the partisanship of *The Times* that a number of Labour politicians began to reply directly to the line that it took: Anthony Wedgwood Benn had talked rather wildly of 'Press versus People' in his closing speech at the party conference, and had apparently incited printers to intervene directly against such abuses of editorial power.[7] Harold Wilson contented himself with a remark that Labour did not usually take notice of editors who were failed Conservative candidates, and others drew attention to the friendship of Taverne and William Rees-Mogg from school and university days.[8] It is unusual for politicians to react so directly, especially to the content of unsigned editorials, but it is equally unusual for unsigned editorials to be so partisan. The coverage of Taverne by the local press was less surprising, for after all it was a continuing story of great importance in Lincoln. In any case, the Lincoln press gave free publicity to Taverne only because the other parties refused to compete with him in making news.

[7] This 'interpretation' of his speech was later denied by Wedgwood Benn and rapidly disowned by his colleagues.

[8] As a result of the intervention of *The Times*, one commentator dubbed Taverne's views as 'British Labour Party (Moggist-Levinist)'.

The Lincoln Labour Party chose John Dilks as its new candidate on 18 November and the Conservatives chose Jonathan Guinness the next week, but it was by then almost too late to hold an election in 1972. There was a brief flurry of interest in late November, when the Liberals considered moving the writ themselves, and thus putting the entire question of timing to the test. The risks of such an experiment would have been considerable, for a writ, once moved and defeated, cannot be moved again until the next parliamentary session. For whatever reason, the Liberals did not carry out their threat, and Lincoln was thus spared the risk of a further year without an MP.

Once only since 1959 have by-elections been held in January, and that was when Labour needed seats for two Ministers in 1965. The reason for this, apart from the unpredictable weather, is the fact that a new electoral register comes into force in mid-February; it is said to be undemocratic to hold an election a mere few weeks before a newer register can be used. It is also the case that an old register gives an advantage to Conservative organisation through their collection of postal votes. Labour announced quite early that the Lincoln election, and the others due, would be as soon as convenient under the new register. Grafton House reported to Transport House that the turnover of voters was unusually large, about 16 per cent of the total, and this may have been one reason for further delay. In the meantime, comment after Uxbridge and Sutton and Cheam had concentrated again on the Labour Party rather than the government. This was mainly due to the statements of Lord George-Brown and others about the situation in the party, but when Crosland, Edward Short and Wilson all replied, it only heightened the impression that all was not exactly going well with Labour. If all this could happen when Labour failed to gain a marginal seat at Uxbridge, what might happen if Labour was to lose a seat? Gloomy forebodings continued even after Wilson began his much-praised series of 'new-look' national speeches in January. The *Daily Mirror* wrote of 'The Second Coming of Harold Wilson', but the *Sunday Express* reminded its readers that 'if Lincoln, Dundee and Chester-le-Street go the wrong way, Mr Wilson knows he can stop dreaming of a job at No. 10. He will need all his energy to keep the one he has got.' On 18 January 1973 occurred the tenth anniversary of Hugh Gaitskell's death, which was naturally the occasion for speeches by those who regarded themselves as Gaitskell's political heirs. At a memorial dinner, Roy Jenkins heaped praise on the memory of Gaitskell and implicitly on all those who sought to follow up his ideas, while Dick Taverne was among those listening. Jenkins wrote about Gaitskell in *The Times* in the same week, and again his comments pointed inescapable morals for the present time: was the Labour Party to be 'a broad-based responsible party of power, or a much narrower inward-looking group, compensating for its own defeats by the virulence with which it blamed others for having brought them about'? Richard Crossman commented bluntly that 'some of the praise heaped on his [Gaitskell's] grave last week was surely not unconnected with the struggle for leadership'. All in all, it appeared that Taverne was not the only politician talking of a continuing struggle in the Labour Party.

Briefly, after the Sutton and Cheam result was known, the Liberals seem to have considered going back on their commitment to help Taverne, and indeed the parliamentary party had still to ratify the local Liberals' decision not to contest the seat. A hysterical article by Bernard Levin ('Our Watchword, No Enemy in the Centre') was a day too late because the Liberals had already decided to stand by their earlier decision. The decision involved more than short-term election tactics, for if any new party were to emerge through Taverne's campaign, then the Liberals would have to decide whether to join it. In agreeing to back Taverne, they made explicit their support for a new alignment of parties.[9] On 21 January, David Steel, Liberal Chief Whip, said 'that he would welcome the formation of a new left-centre party comprising Liberals and Social Democrats of the Labour Party. He said on the Tyne-Tees programme *Challenge* that not very much divided Liberals from, say, Mr Roy Jenkins or Mr Dick Taverne.' Nor was

[9] In fact, Liberal support for Taverne counted for very little, for although the local Liberals decided not to oppose him, they also decided not to support him officially. The backing of national figures like Jeremy Thorpe and David Steel was of little help as long as they remained so distant from the fray.

David Steel the only one who, by bracketing 'say Jenkins and Taverne', sought to obscure the relationship between Taverne and the Labour Party.[10]

Press speculation about the timing of the election revived as an announcement approached, but an unusually large number of false stories circulated. Labour was said to be committed to 22 February or 1 March if only to get the elections over before the budget on 6 March. The writs for all three pending by-elections were finally moved on 9 February, with polling to be on 1 March. Lincoln would therefore be without an MP for twenty weeks in all, by no means an unusually long vacancy.[11] It is difficult to escape the conclusion that it was only the contentious nature of the Lincoln vacancy that occasioned so much comment on its length.

The Democratic Labour Association and Taverne's campaign

Two local polls conducted in 1972 showed that Taverne could count upon considerable sympathy in the constituency for his battle against 'Grafton House'. Most political commentators, however, accustomed to the regular disappearance of Independents in post-war British politics, viewed Taverne's ability to translate this sympathy into votes with scepticism. In the 1970 general election, S. O. Davies, ejected Labour MP for Merthyr, had successfully stood against the candidate of his local party; but Davies's age, long tenure of the seat and local roots were seen as creating exceptional circumstances for which there was no parallel in Lincoln. Perhaps greater attention should have been paid to the poll conducted in the city immediately after Taverne's resignation, testing, not sympathy for Taverne's plight, but voting intentions: 49 per cent of respondents declared for Taverne, 14 per cent for official Labour, 16 per cent Conservative, 2 per cent others and 19 per cent undecided. But even this could be discounted, for, as both Labour and Conservative parties hoped, there was sufficient time before polling day for Taverne's campaign to

[10] *The Times*, 22 Jan 1973.

[11] In 1971, for example, the average by-election vacancy was 16½ weeks, but three of the ten vacancies were as long as Lincoln or longer. There was no special comment on any of these.

run out of steam. All would depend on two things: how far Taverne could convince the electorate that he, and he alone, was the issue in the election; and how successfully he could capture the sort of protest vote which has invariably shifted from the two major parties in mid-term elections over the past fifteen years. Almost certainly he could expect a large amount of support from traditionally Labour voters; his chief worry was that the Conservatives would hold firm and squeeze in their candidate on the split Labour vote. The 1970 election had shown how close was the margin between the two parties. Labour won by 4,750 votes, but 3,937 went to Gilbert Blades, a local councillor who had resigned the Conservative whip a few years earlier. It was a moot point whether Blades's supporters were defecting Conservatives, or those genuinely voting for an independent stand. Taverne might take heart from the latter, but not the former.

His most immediate problem after resignation was organisation. Grafton House had been, as one commentator put it, 'grinding out' majorities since 1945 with what was recognised as one of the most efficient party machines in the country. The Conservatives too were by no means weak in what they had always considered a potentially winnable seat, and officials at the annual meeting in 1972 had made a point of noting increased activity and expansion over the previous twelve months. Taverne had little with which to combat these two organisations. Although many Labour officials had regretted the manner of Taverne's ejection, there had been no major split at the leadership level of the local party. Two councillors – Fred Allen and Clodagh Wilkinson – resigned the whip to fight for Taverne, and one ward organisation out of ten went over to him.[12] Taverne claimed immediately after his resignation that he had a group of a hundred people to help him fight the election, and certainly his first meeting, which filled a large hall and left over a hundred people outside to be addressed from the balcony, showed that there were many potential

[12] Although Taverne supporters were not officially ejected from the party, most ward committees passed resolutions soon after Taverne's resignation condemning his action, and thus making it difficult for the two sides to work together. Some Taverneites also found themselves deprived of their positions on ward committees.

activists. Most of the hundred were former Labour workers, although members of the GMC were far fewer than the 50 who had voted for Taverne on 19 June. His support from Labour activists was certainly infinitesimal compared with the 2,000 membership which had been claimed for the Lincoln Labour Party. Numbers in the Democratic Labour Party were made up from a variety of sources. Many young people, who had not formerly participated in politics, were drawn into the campaign for Taverne, and a few local Liberals and Conservatives lent their support. Taverne's agent, Tony Elkington, claimed at one stage that 'the Lincoln Young Conservatives are reputed to be the best organised in the area; the trouble is, twenty-five of them are working for me'. Local Conservatives, however, asserted that the numbers were far fewer, and even these had been on the fringes of the YCs, although when the Conservative agent determined upon his choice of a secretary for the campaign, he was somewhat disconcerted to discover that she had already agreed to work for Taverne. Taverne's officials were also a mixed group. His agent, Elkington, was new to the business of organising a campaign. Of the three trustees appointed in February 1973, one was Fred Allen, a second Ken Rawding, a former chairman and treasurer of Lincoln Labour Party, and the third Joe Ghose, a local businessman who had no previous party affiliations.

But Taverne benefited from a number of events in the autumn of 1972. On 23 October, despite the protestations of Peter Hain and the Young Liberals, officials at Nottingham decided not to run a Liberal candidate in the election, a decision confirmed subsequently by the parliamentary party. Both Taverne and Jeremy Thorpe's assistant denied a charge levelled by local Labour officials and the Labour candidate that the Liberals were backing Taverne, but he certainly received unofficial assistance. Patrick Furnell, who had acquired 6,519 votes for the Liberals in the 1964 election – most of which appear to have gone to Labour in 1966 – wrote to the local Lincoln paper on 2 February 1973 advising Liberals to vote for Taverne; and Elkington claimed that he had had to use the Liberal Party to acquire stationery, canvass cards and the like for the campaign.

Taverne benefited also from the choice of candidates made

by his two major rivals in November 1972. Both might have been well advised to select candidates whose style and position on the political spectrum approximated closely to his: certainly, it would have made less plausible Taverne's claim that he was fighting against the 'extremism' into which the two major political parties had recently fallen. Instead the Labour Party selected John Dilks, leader of Derby council, from a short-list of six, and the Conservatives Jonathan Guinness, chairman of the right-wing Monday Club, in preference to Desmond Fennell, a local-born barrister, and Robert Jackson, a journalist from All Souls College, Oxford. Dilks was of working-class origins, a Co-operative executive, and his reputation was that of a left-winger and a tough and forceful politician. Taverne's supporters were not slow to point out that Grafton House appeared to have selected a man in their own image, and the charge that he was simply a 'tool' of the machine was not gainsaid by Dilks's performance. Certainly, his political qualities were not such that they could counterbalance the style and panache which Taverne threw into his own campaign. His sole adventure was when, in an early speech, he referred to Taverne as having benefited from his party organisation for many years and then suddenly feeling 'that, because the dominant partner in the relationship should begin to question him, he should squeal like a political virgin due to be ravished by the machine'; derision from Taverne supporters prevented a repetition of the experiment.

The choice of Guinness at least protected the Conservatives in part from Reginald Simmerson, a Powellite standing on an anti-Common Market platform as a Democratic Conservative candidate – though the Common Market was one of the few issues on which Guinness bent the knee before official party policy. His nomination was not well received in all quarters. The chairman of the YCs had only a few weeks previously declared that it would need a moderate to do well against Taverne, and in the *Spectator* for 3 February 1973 appeared the report that local Conservatives 'don't intend to do much for Mr Jonathan Guinness because they don't want this tiresome right-winger in the House: and they reckon that a weak Tory effort would help Dick Taverne, thus rubbing Harold Wilson's nose in the mud'. This almost certainly exaggerates local

Conservative disloyalty, although many were friendly towards Taverne.[13] Though in January 1973 the local party chairman lamented the absence of even nominal committees in many city wards and the YC chairman noted the rundown in his organisation's activities over the previous twelve months, there do not appear to have been any major attempts at sabotage or great numbers of defectors. The appointment of Eric Ward, an experienced hand in by-election fights, as agent, guaranteed the seriousness of the contest, and Ward's major problem was much more Guinness's exuberance than his helpers' non-co-operation. Guinness appears to have early determined upon a paradoxical form of 'me-tooism': if the people of Lincoln were intent on an individualist for their MP, Taverne's individualism would pale into insignificance beside his own.

When Taverne resigned his seat, he claimed that there were five issues on which he would be fighting the by-election: the right of an MP to follow his conscience without subsequent punishment; the neglect of Lincoln's problems by the Conservative Government – particularly its refusal to grant development status to the city and its omission of a by-pass for Lincoln from its strategic roads plan for 1980; whether Lincoln Labour Party should be run by a caucus or by consultation; the need for moderation in industry; and the Labour Party's refusal to send representatives to the European Parliament, and its avowed intention of renegotiating the terms of entry on regaining power. This somewhat esoteric amalgam of issues became more clearly defined as the campaign developed, although defined loosely enough for Taverne to take advantage of most of the problems which appeared to be taxing the electorate.

The Common Market issue very soon lost salience. Depite desperate attempts by Dilks, Simmerson and the Majority Rule candidate, Malcolm Waller, to beat Guinness and Taverne with the European stick, both pro-Marketeers were

[13] He was received with acclaim by a dinner consisting largely of local Conservative-voting businessmen soon after his resignation, and one Tory organiser in October 1972 suggested that the party should withdraw and leave Taverne to fight the Labour candidate alone. Neither the Conservatives (with the possibility of splitting Labour votes), nor Taverne (aware of the danger of being elected on what might be claimed to be solely Conservative votes) had any desire that this should happen.

quite justified in blandly stating in mid-February that this was simply not an issue. Dilks also played heavily upon price rises likely to result from entry and the imposition of VAT, but Taverne countered with the idea that VAT could be positively beneficial if food items were taxed at a negative rate. 'Europe on the cheap' constituted quite an effective means of defence.

With Taverne's initial priority to win voters from the Labour Party, it was important for him to stress the 'injustice' which he had suffered at the hands of Grafton House, and blackening its name became a key feature of the campaign. The charge of vindictiveness which had been levelled after the television programme in October 1971 was supported by a number of other minor incidents. Even before Taverne resigned, he had been denied use of his surgery in Grafton House, and the hasty decision one day of some of his opponents to put out on the street a bicycle Taverne had recently acquired to promote the conservation cause resulted in plaintive headlines of the style ' "They even threw out my bicycle", says Dick Taverne'.[14] At the end of 1972 Labour supporters of Taverne attempted to renew their membership of the party, to be told that this could not be done for the time being. As was soon pointed out in the press, this effectively excluded the oldest-serving member of the Lincoln Labour Party, Jack Goodman.

The left-wing character of Grafton House also received attention. There appeared in the *Lincolnshire Chronicle* on 16 February what the *Evening Standard* called 'Lincoln's Zinoviev Letter', in which Llew Davies, a former chairman of Lincoln Trades Council, wrote that Don Gossop was on record as supporting Communist candidates in AUEW elections against candidates who were Labour Party members. Supporting opponents of one's party, it was suggested, was not simply the prerogative of the Taverneites, but of their opponents also. Although the *Chronicle* made great play with the issue, it was not widely reported in the national press, and Taverne was clearly somewhat embarrassed at his press conference by charges that a 'Reds under the bed' (Gossop's phrase) campaign was being launched, although he did attempt to counter-attack with the statement that 'after all these men are Commies'.

---

[14] It eventually transpired that the charge of incompetence could be added to that of vindictiveness: it was the wrong bicycle.

The 'parish pump' issues which Taverne had mentioned in October – unemployment and traffic congestion – were used in criticism of the Conservative Government and candidate, but they were also employed against his former party colleagues. In spite of his declaration that the by-election had nothing to do with local political issues, he (and Guinness) criticised the council's Industrial Committee for not being sufficiently active in dealing with the unemployment problem. This was mildly unfair, since the committee had at that time arranged for Anthony Wedgwood Benn to lead a deputation to Whitehall on the problem – an event, as Guinness pointed out, probably not unconnected with the imminent by-election. Taverne also claimed that Grafton House supporters on the council had not been fulfilling their responsibilities on council-house repairs, and he criticised the controversial proposals for an inner ring-road and for other development projects in the city which had emanated from council planners. The spectre of Grafton House was to be seen behind all that was ill done in Lincoln.

These local issues, though interesting skirmishes on the flanks of the campaign, were not the central issues which Taverne sought to put across. The real issues, he claimed time and time again, were the rights of MPs and the integrity of politicians. And his own refusal to give way on a major issue of principle, despite the assaults of his party and his local 'caucus', was generalised into a view of the national political scene as a whole. The two major parties, he claimed, insisted on making promises they could not keep, and rejecting policies to which they had previously subscribed; the people were losing confidence in their political leaders, and the whole basis of the democratic system of politics was being brought into danger. The interesting spectacle was to be seen of a skilled and experienced politician expressing views which may be heard in any pub late of an evening, that 'the fact is that nobody believes a bloody word that any politician says any more'.

Taverne's style, as well as his platform, dominated the campaign. In January he had told reporters that he was intent on leading a presidential-style campaign, and that, once re-elected, he would gather around him a presidential-style team of skilled experts to advise him on national policies. He made the very best of the bad job that no established political figure dared to support him, by drawing attention to the fact that his was a lone campaign against the powers that be. His only support came from Mervyn Stockwood, Bishop of Southwark, and the astringent *Times* columnist, Bernard Levin, at a meeting, however, which attracted a far greater audience than that which was addressed by any of the major politicians who spoke for Taverne's competitors.[15] Guinness, apt as ever, satirised Taverne's style as that of a 'pinchbeck Kennedy with his Camelot of plastic gnomes'; but it is hard to deny its effectiveness in ensuring that Taverne was *the* issue in the election.

Given the origins of the crisis, Taverne could expect to carry many Labour voters with him. And his position on such issues as industrial relations – he criticised his own union, the General and Municipal Workers, at one stage for the gas strike which was in progress during the election – would appeal to many Conservatives. Yet the charge might plausibly be made that a vote for Taverne was a vote for simply another Labour candidate. In part to meet this difficulty, Taverne, who had originally stressed that his main aim was to rejoin the Labour Party, began to toy with the 'third force' ideas of the editor of *The Times*. In mid-February he told reporters that he thought his anticipated success in Lincoln might be the 'catalyst' to the formation of a new centrist, Social Democratic-style grouping in politics; from being a moderate in the Labour Party, he moved to the position of a moderate between Labour and Conservative extremism.[16] The Gallup Poll of 22 February (if accurate: see Appendix I), which showed him with a small lead over Labour and a larger one over the Conservatives, helped his position. 'A vote for Guinness is a vote for Grafton House' was the way he called upon Conservatives to help him defeat his former party.

Taverne's big problem had always been organisation. Though his small cadre of helpers had had three months to

---

[15] 'Mr Levin declared uncompromisingly that the whole future weight and character of British politics depended on Lincoln's voters. The section that was in the audience took its new responsibility calmly.' *The Times*, 15 Feb 1973.

[16] A position which, within a fortnight of the election result, he had, with Roy Jenkins, formally rejected.

complete the basic tasks in preparation for the election – starting a headquarters,[17] arranging canvass cards, addressing envelopes, etc. – the canvass itself posed major problems of uncertainty: it was impossible to forecast how many workers might materialise to help during the final weeks, and there could be no clear idea of where in the city Taverne voters might be most likely to be found. Tony Elkington hit upon an interesting solution to these difficulties. He decided to abandon the idea of ward committees, and consequently the concept of building the canvass around wards and polling districts. Instead, artificial units – 'canvass areas' – were constructed, built more centrally around polling stations and the geographical location of firm Taverne supporters. Canvass cards were, in general, issued directly to helpers from the headquarters, to be returned directly to Elkington who then translated information received from canvass areas into information about polling districts for the day of the election. There was no institutional link between the agent and the party helper and, although it imposed an enormous burden on Elkington, it did allow him to direct the canvass into areas which seemed most important, quickly and with a minumum of contact with intermediaries.

Canvassing on this sort of basis was intended as the work of the first week after the writ was issued. Unfortunately, after the large meeting which began the campaign, there was hardly anyone to put it into effect. Supporters of Taverne simply failed to materialise, and during the first week of campaigning there hardly existed a Democratic Labour organisation. But support soon picked up, and during the second week Elkington could put into operation the next part of his plan. A brightly painted yellow van was used as a mobile headquarters, which moved gradually through the city, attended by groups of workers, in a bloc canvass. In the final week, pockets which had been missed previously were filled in. Elkington's thesis was that this system allowed maximum flexibility, and certainly it constituted a singularly effective means of solving prob-

[17] Taverne's headquarters, presidentially entitled 'Taverne House', was a decrepit billiards hall, rented for £4 a week, and converted within a couple of months of Taverne's resignation for a cost of £300. It was situated 150 yards from Grafton House.

lems created by the conditions of uncertainty mentioned earlier.

Taverne does not appear to have lacked financial support – though the extent of Labour and Conservative campaigns suggests also that neither of the two major parties were sparing in their outlay on the election. Much of Taverne's money came from local contributors, and Taverne also claimed that many Labour MPs made secret contributions. There were rumours that a small number of large contributors had made funds available, although who these might be was either unknown or unspecified.

The progress of the campaign

The Lincoln campaign was fought out against a backdrop of continuing crisis, but in such a way that national events could not directly affect the result. The economic and industrial troubles of the past few years continued and intensified during the February of 1973. During the first week of the campaign the main political news in the press was about the twin possibilities of general strike or general election, only to be disappointed by the combined sanity of the government and the TUC. However, industrial troubles went on, especially on the railways and in the gas industry, so that by the week of 1 March there were more people on strike than at any time since 1926. None of this produced much impact in Lincoln: Dilks gave qualified support to the strikers, but Guinness did not condemn them completely, and Taverne occupied a middle position which was not fully developed. More controversial was the government's 'counter-inflation' policy, Phase II of which was before Parliament in February. Labour regarded this as fundamentally unfair – they said that it controlled wages but not prices – and many Conservatives were troubled by the abandonment of the earlier policy of non-intervention. It has been shown that many Conservatives had abandoned their party at Sutton because they disliked its 'U-turn' on the issue of incomes policy, but the most general ground for opposition to it must have been that it did not appear to be working; Labour's claims of 'unfairness' and Conservative criticisms of 'interventionism' would surely have been muted if the policy had succeeded in restraining prices. By the end of February it had clearly not done so. Moreover, the debate over incomes policies gave Taverne an excellent platform from which to state his integrity and to demonstrate the bankruptcy of both major parties. Both Conservative and Labour appeared to control wages when in power while denouncing wage control in opposition. Taverne stated the need for a 'fair' policy on wages and prices, and thus again claimed the central position.

Both Conservative and Labour parties had planned their campaigns in the hope that the delay in holding the election would have reduced Taverne's importance. Their intention was variously to 'let him get it all off his chest' and to 'let him bore people sick with his conscience'. Once this had happened, the major parties could open their campaigns in the time-honoured fashion and fight on the old issues: Taverne would be 'ravished' by better-organised political machines. It was consistent with this approach that they should lie very low during the autumn, and that they should fight their campaigns entirely on national issues. Guinness talked about Taverne very little, and Dilks at one time refused even to mention his name, while both of them denied that Taverne was ever mentioned on the doorsteps; if he was ignored, he might go away. Journalists who arrived from London, with their stories about Taverne's gallant fight already half written on the train from King's Cross, found a very different battle being waged in Lincoln. At Conservative and Labour press conferences they found no hint of the Taverne v. anti-Taverne fight which they had expected to see. Both Labour and Conservatives proclaimed that there were two entirely different campaigns going on: one – in the pubs of Fleet Street and the mind of the editor of *The Times* – in which Taverne figured prominently, and one – in Lincoln – in which Taverne figured not at all. A visitor to Lincoln had no way of knowing which of these campaigns was the real one, or which was involving the electors. It is not difficult to see with the benefit of hindsight that Labour and Conservatives *had* to see it this way, if only to keep up their morale, but few recognised that at the time. However, it is worth pointing out that the major parties could have pursued an alternative strategy, although only by a conscious decision at the outset. They could have chosen to fight Taverne on his home ground, 'mixing it' with him on issues like his record as an MP, his integrity, the ineffectiveness of Independents in Parliament, his underground support from the press and so on. Thus, as the *Lincolnshire Echo* pointed out, nobody ever questioned that Taverne had been a good MP for Lincoln: this did not mean that he *had* been a good MP, but simply that his supporters said so and his opponents did not disagree. A spoiling campaign could have been fought by Dilks or by Guinness, but neither appears to have considered it seriously; it is perhaps only in retrospect that it looks preferable to the campaigns which they actually fought, for it could hardly have been less successful. Both were of course swayed by considerations other than mere tactics. A Conservative candidate had to identify mainly with the government, and despite many deviations Guinness did so; Dilks had no difficulty identifying with the Labour Party and its policies. Both Guinness and Dilks saw politics through the issues of the two-party system, and Taverne simply did not fit into their frames of reference. An article in *Labour Weekly*, by Joe Ashton, MP, on 9 March made exactly this point: after listing all the damaging facts about Taverne that could have been made known during the campaign (including his foreign parentage and his possession of an expensive catamaran!), Ashton concluded: 'We were just too bloody honest.' It might be suggested, though, that Labour and Conservatives were 'too bloody honest' just because they believed that honesty would pay.

It is in this context that the changed character of the campaign in its last week must be seen. By the time Gallup published its first campaign poll, on 22 February, the Labour and Conservative parties were both well on with canvassing. Whether because of Gallup's findings or because of their canvass, both the major parties changed course. It was just not working to ignore Taverne, and so both Guinness and Dilks were reluctantly drawn into Taverne's campaign and away from their own. At a meeting on 23 February, Dilks announced that Labour had so far fought a clean campaign but that he could no longer remain silent while his friends and supporters in the Lincoln Labour Party were under constant attack from Taverne. His attack on Taverne was echoed by Guinness at a press conference the next day; according to Dilks, Taverne was a traitor, and according to Guinness, Taverne was now attacking the two-party system because he had been too incompetent to keep his place in it. These charges and others were repeated with increasing force over the last few days of the campaign, and Taverne countered by describing Guinness as a 'crank' and Dilks as a mere puppet of a party caucus. Even in the midst of personal vituperation, both Dilks and Guinness continued to make their points within the two-party framework: Dilks accused Taverne of being 'just a Tory' (the word was spat out with a particular venom), and Guinness remarked that Taverne was still a Socialist and a member of the Labour Party. Both these views were no doubt intended to convince the candidates' wavering supporters that in voting for Taverne they would be tampering with the evil one. Both of them were also untrue or at least wildly misleading: Taverne was in no sense a Conservative and had made it quite clear that he wished to rejoin a moderate Labour Party; and although he was technically still a member of the Labour Party, it was wholly unrealistic to state that fact out of context. Even in abusing Taverne, his opponents had to relate their attacks to the two-party system, for the alternative would have released their supporters from the constraints of party loyalty altogether. All the same, it is hard to believe that the personal bitterness of the last few days of campaigning helped anyone but Taverne. More attention was focused on the rival personalities and this could only be to his advantage, both because his was essentially a personality campaign anyway, and because he was so much more impressive than his rivals on a personal comparison. This last fact was not particularly related to the potential abilities of the rivals as Members of Parliament but to their images as candidates. Taverne was fighting his sixth election campaign, his fifth in Lincoln, and his previous career at the Oxford Union and at the Bar had all combined to create an impressive politician. He exuded self-control and self-confidence to an extent that made him a formidable opponent, alongside which both Guinness and Dilks appeared as political lightweights. Most important of all, Taverne adopted a posture of studied moderation, apparently rebuking his erstwhile supporters of the Lincoln Labour Party more from sorrow than from anger; he even managed to be abusive in an overtly moderate way, as with the way in which his criticisms were always of 'Grafton House' and never of individuals. The criticisms were no less effective, but the image of moderation was not lost. Dilks came across as just too committed, too earnest, too tense and too easily rattled by an unexpected heckle.[18] Conversely, Guinness seemed to lack the element of steel which is expected from the character of a politician, and his campaign was characterised by too little seriousness rather than too much. He could be extremely witty in the right circumstances, but was not very effective in putting a basic message across to the voters. Taverne had said at the beginning of the campaign that *he* was the issue in the campaign, and the only issue; this apparently arrogant statement obscured one simple fact – that unless he was the real issue, then he had no chance of winning. In comparison with his rivals, if Taverne *was* the issue, then there was only one possible result. Having decided first that they must ignore him and second that they could not ignore him, Dilks and Guinness were ill-equipped to beat him on his own ground. The attempt to divert attention away from him failed and the attempt to discredit him had perhaps little chance of success but was in any case tried rather too late.

Labour made a great effort to hold all three seats which polled on 1 March, but clearly recognised that a special effort would be required in Lincoln. No fewer than five members of the Shadow Cabinet visited Lincoln to speak for Dilks, as did a much larger number of MPs and trade union leaders.[19] At times, 15 or more MPs were working for Dilks, and the size of Labour's effort was shown by the sudden rise in the government's parliamentary majorities. In a debate on Scottish unemployment, presumably arranged by the oppositon to impress the voters of Dundee, the government's majority of 63 was more than double its normal margin of safety because so many Labour MPs were absent. A meeting with a national speaker was organised in each of Lincoln's ten wards, and the

[18] At one meeting, Dilks was protesting that he was no puppet of any caucus and that he would be just as independent as any MP, when a loud shout of 'Well, you'll be out then' prompted an outburst of laughter which was greatly increased by Dilks's obvious discomposure.

[19] The Shadow Cabinet members were Denis Healey, Judith Hart, Anthony Crosland, Anthony Wedgwood Benn and Michael Foot (twice).

overall impression was of a party stressing its national position to draw attention away from local difficulties. Attendances were not always commensurate with effort: only thirty people assembled to hear Denis Healey (many being journalists) on the same evening as Taverne attracted eighty people to hear him speaking without any support at all. Even when attendances went up later in the campaign, Labour's meetings contained a large number of 'plants' (Conservative and Taverneite) as well as journalists and Labour activists who might have been better employed elsewhere.

Canvassing presented special problems, which they were unable to solve within the format of a traditional campaign. There were plenty of canvassers and the returns apparently showed Labour in a strong position: from a canvass aimed at Labour voters and doubtfuls, canvassers found that only 10 per cent of normal supporters would defect to Taverne. However, this left two questions unanswered: how well was Taverne doing among Conservative voters, and how reliable were Labour's canvass returns anyway? The second was much more important than the first, for if Labour's position was as strong as it looked to be, then they would win anyway. More important was the fact that they might not be succeeding in identifying defectors from the ranks of their supporters, and in retrospect it can be seen that this was the case. It is well known among political organisers that third-party voters are especially difficult to identify even when known to exist in large numbers: this is always true of Liberal voters, and Pat Mulligan's experience of Nationalists in Scotland had proved the same. It was, however, one thing to be aware of the problem and another to solve it. Overall, Labour seems to have remained convinced of its impending victory despite the evidence of all opinion polls to the contrary.

There was a weakening of Labour's confidence during the last week, perhaps as a result of the opinion polls and of the fact that several known Labour voters were seen to be displaying Taverne's posters. The reaction, apart from attacks to brand Taverne as a 'Tory', was a curious one: volunteer canvassers were given the rather unrewarding task of visiting houses which displayed a Taverne poster in order to inform the occupants that Taverne was not the Labour candidate. A greater effort was made to get Labour posters out on display, with the caption 'John Dilks, *the* Labour Candidate'. In effect, the campaign organisers at last realised that many Labour voters in Lincoln regarded Taverne as a Labour candidate just as much as Dilks was; to many, Taverne was the Labour candidate while Dilks was the candidate of Grafton House. This was at once a testament to the efficiency of Taverne in selling himself and discrediting Grafton House, and to the isolation of Grafton House from the voters. It may have been clear to activists that, according to the party constitution, Taverne had no connection with the Labour Party, but it was not clear to the voters. It is worth considering what could have been done to convince Labour voters of the need for party unity. The only credible method of doing this would have been to demonstrate that the party, nationally as well as locally, *was* united. In terms of local unity, much was done – as when every Labour councillor but one signed a letter supporting Dilks – but the national picture was less clear.

Spectacular by their absence from Lincoln were the Jenkinsite group, which had counted Taverne as an enthusiastic member before his resignation from Parliament. It is certain that none of them supported his decision to fight a by-election,[20] and once he embarked on that course, they remained outside the battle. The Labour Committee for Europe was reported to be working hard for the return of the (pro-Market) Labour candidate in Chester-le-Street, while Jenkins himself spoke in Chester-le-Street and in Dundee. Why, then, did they remain aloof from Lincoln? The explanation which was most current was popularly attributed to Roy Hattersley: in the army, it was said, the deserter's friends are not asked to form the firing-squad, and so, although they did not support Taverne's campaign, neither would they assist in his coming humiliation. This of course assumed that Taverne's defeat was inevitable and that the Jenkinsites could play no special role in making the inevitable more likely. However, in view of Taverne's stance as the voice of moderation in the Labour Party, and in view of Dilks's image as a machine-man and left-winger, Jenkins's

[20] Later, Taverne remarked that only Roy Jenkins of his parliamentary friends had believed that he could win a by-election (*Sunday Times*, 11 Mar 1973).

intervention on Dilks's behalf could have been very effective. Taverne frequently said that nothing substantial separated him from Roy Jenkins; the illusion that he was a sort of Jenkinsite candidate could only have been shattered by Jenkins himself. The front-benchers who did visit Lincoln were all left-wingers or centrists in the party: Anthony Crosland was probably the most pro-Market of them all, but – as Leo Beckett reminded listeners at Crosland's meeting, – 'Tony Crosland is above all a party man'. The fact which did separate Taverne from the Jenkinsites was that they too wished to be seen as loyal to the party while he had abandoned it; once again, only the Jenkinsites themselves could have made the distinction clear. One incident illustrated the almost schizo-phrenic attitude of the Jenkinsites to Lincoln, caught between loyalty to a friend and loyalty to their party. Philip Whitehead, MP for Derby North, campaigned for Dilks – his local party leader in Derby – although a friend of Taverne. Dilks mentioned this support at an open meeting, and Taverne immediately revealed that Whitehead had previously apologised to him by telephone and had explained that unless he came to support Dilks his own seat in Derby would be in danger. A great deal of laughter and applause greeted this abuse of a confidence and, although Whitehead later reaffirmed his support for Dilks in a message to the local press, he did not deny Taverne's story. Perhaps the most interesting aspect of the whole affair was the fact that it was not reported in the national press, although a number of journalists were present. The press had been pro-tecting the Jenkinsites from embarrassing news of this sort for some time, and it did not pass unremarked (although only by *Tribune*) that, although Jenkins was not in Lincoln, his press adviser, John Harris, was. The impression of the Jenkinsites' ambiguity of approach was strengthened by their reaction to the result: Taverne had no difficulty in finding Labour sponsors for his reintroduction into the House of Commons, and Jenkins made a speech the following week remarking on the disastrous performance of the party and blaming it on control by the Left. On television the next week, William Rodgers was asked whether he had been glad to see the official candidate defeated at Lincoln; it is significant that he avoided the ques-tion altogether. None of this is to suggest that even the most active of campaigns by the Jenkinsites on behalf of Dilks could have reversed the tidal wave which was sweeping Taverne back to Westminster. But that too is clear only with the benefit of hindsight: when most observers were predicting a close finish at Lincoln, the Jenkinsites remained in their tents.

In the last week of the campaign Labour tried to exploit two particular issues which were intended to concentrate attention on national and economic problems rather than personalities. During the weekend before polling, a large number of copies of *Labour Weekly* were circulated in Lincoln, including a story about the impending closure of a Lincoln engineering works and the consequent loss of 400 jobs. The firm in question first said that no decision had been taken and later denied the story absolutely: if all this had any effect on the voters it can only have helped to demonstrate Labour's increasing panic and to confirm local distrust of Grafton House. There was also a good deal of discussion of the projected delegation which was to be sent from Lincoln to the Department of Trade and Industry in order to discuss the employment position in Lincoln. This had been planned to take place just two days before polling in the by-election, but was postponed by the Minister, Christopher Chataway, so that the new MP could be included in the delegation at a later date. Labour tried hard to present this as evidence of governmental indifference to the real efforts being made by Lincoln's Labour council; had it occurred, it would also have been useful evidence of what the local Labour Party and its council group could achieve without an MP. In any case, it was hardly the sort of issue to switch many votes in the last days of a hard campaign.

The Conservative campaign was much more straightforward than Labour's, as Lewis Chester summed it up in the *Sunday Times*: 'The Tory strategy is simple enough: turn out the traditional vote and slip into office through the Labour divide.' Thus, Guinness held only one factory-gate meeting and did very little open campaigning in the centre of the city. This had the double advantage of leaving the two Labour candidates to slog it out in the open, and of not exposing Guinness to a form of electioneering for which he was not well fitted. He therefore spent most of his time canvassing Conservative areas, and naturally formed the impression that he was about to win. This view was theoretically justified by canvass returns, as he remarked in dismissing the importance of opinion polls: 'The Gallup Poll works on a very small sample. We have a sample of the 30,000 people we have canvassed, and I am going to win this seat – unless more people are telling more lies than, in a Cathedral city, is conceivable.' In fact, Conservative canvass returns gave little ground for optimism: taken at face value and ignoring doubtfuls, they gave a chance of victory if the other two candidates had split evenly. If the normal criteria for assessing canvass figures were applied (to count all doubtfuls as hostile and to discount about 20 per cent of firm promises), then the same figures demonstrated the near-certainty of defeat. Moreover, Conservatives faced the same problem as Labour, in being unable to identify those Conservatives who were going to defect to Taverne. An attempt was made to identify 'Conservatives for Taverne' in order to send them a special letter from Guinness, but only a few hundred could be found of the many thousands who existed. Once again, the problem was known to be there but was simply unidentifiable and unquantifiable. For the Conservatives, it was compounded by the dangerous influence that the opinion polls might exert in squeezing their votes. Many voters had no doubt simply lied to the canvassers, but many more who had really meant to vote for Guinness could reasonably change their minds when he could be seen to have no chance of winning. Of course, political organisers are in business not to predict results but to maximise their votes, and the Conservatives could hardly have done more to achieve that end.

There was no truth in the *Spectator*'s charge that the Conservatives did not want to win,[21] as the visits of Peter Walker, Sir Keith Joseph, Sir Geoffrey Howe and Joseph Godber showed. Guinness was used in the way least likely to expose his defects as a candidate, and when he had to be exposed at an open meeting, he was efficiently protected by 'plants' in the audience: when he was visibly worried by heckling, an organised shout of 'Give him a chance' arose from all sides of

[21] Oddly, it was also the *Spectator* which erred in describing the arrival of the Conservative 'efficiency machine' in Lincoln when only one agent was there, part-time, in the autumn.

the room. In the last week of the contest, Guinness's statements and advertisements in the local press all concentrated on pointing out that Taverne was a Socialist, doubtless in order to steady the Conservative ranks. The basic strategy of a low-key campaign was forced on the Conservatives even more than on Labour because their candidate rapidly came to be treated by the press as something of a joke figure. His most-quoted remark was the suggestion that convicted murderers should be provided with razor-blades, so that they could relieve the state of the cost of maintaining them for the rest of their lives. This was significant not so much for itself as for the basic lack of seriousness which characterised Guinness's entire campaign. There was, however, no question of Guinness's lack of seriousness being assumed for the purpose of losing the election.

Overall, the Conservatives tried as hard as possible to win the seat, but were perhaps more easily convinced than Labour that they would not do so. But then they had so much less at stake.

There were three minor candidates in the Lincoln campaign: Jean Justice, who campaigned on the issue of Taverne's attitude to the A6 murder; Reginald Simmerson, who stood as an Independent Conservative against the Common Market; and Malcolm Waller, who campaigned for majority rule by the use of the referendum. None of these made a great deal of impact on the voters or on the other candidates, and Waller and Simmerson were unable even to campaign in Lincoln for very long. None had much chance of saving his deposit, for any independent votes in Lincoln were clearly going to go to Taverne. It was suggested early that Justice, Simmerson and Waller would be doing well if they amassed a thousand votes between them; the result showed that this estimate erred greatly on the side of generosity.

Press and television

The press and television impact on Lincoln was much less than might have been expected in view of the build-up in the autumn of 1972. The most obvious influence was in fact a reverse one: Lincoln attracted more coverage from the media than any other by-election can ever have done. There were thirteen different camera crews in Lincoln during the campaign, including two from Germany, and it was virtually impossible to cross the High Street without seeing filming in progress. Similarly, journalists flooded into Lincoln from London, and wrote standard pieces about the social divisions and picturesque history of the city. Almost all of this was for consumption outside the city and outside the campaign. Anglia and Yorkshire Television networks both did a good deal of filming, but very few television sets in Lincoln could receive their programmes: the most intensive filming was by the BBC's *Midweek* programme, but their 'The Battle for Lincoln' was not shown until after the close of the polls. Similarly, most of the journalists in Lincoln were writing for papers that were never read by Lincoln voters, or for national papers whose circulations in the city were relatively small.

The actual press coverage was mostly balanced and fair, probably as much through the real confusion found by reporters in Lincoln as through any deliberate editorial line. Until the last few days of the campaign most of the news stories and comments were clearly hedging bets to allow for any victory from three.[22] It was only in the light of advance news of the NOP poll, scooped by the *Daily Mail* on 27 February, that the press began to predict a Taverne victory. On polling day itself, almost every paper gave its prediction of a Taverne win, but by that time the findings of NOP and Gallup (and the rumoured findings of private Conservative polls) had all predicted Taverne's easy victory. If the press as a whole had an influence on the result, it was in the style of their reporting rather than in its actual content. It is always easier to make news from the clash of personalities than from detailed arguments about policy: 'Labour candidate attacks Heath Government' or 'Conservative denounces strikes' do not make headlines as effective as 'Dick's got glamour, but will he win?', or 'Not all green men in Lincoln', or 'The machines close in on

[22] It is important to stress that, as late as the last week before polling day, many observers still expected a close three-way fight. In a carefully researched article in the *Sunday Times* (25 Feb), Lewis Chester wrote that 'what once looked like a triumphal canter for Taverne is now a real race'. The *Guardian* report on Lincoln on the eve of poll was headed 'Guinness threatens quietly confident Taverne'.

Lincoln's Lochinvar'. However fair their reports, the national press was giving Taverne a bonus by simply reporting the campaign in the terms on which he was trying to fight it. *The Times*, which from previous from might have been expected to intervene most actively, did not do so until the last week of the campaign. It ran only one editorial on Lincoln, its Lincoln reports by Christopher Warman were a model of fair reporting, and David Wood's Political Editor's column (on 26 February) ignored the by-elections altogether. However, in the last few days *The Times* more than made up for its previous restraint: Bernard Levin wrote about electoral affairs for the first time in 1973 with two trenchant articles urging support for Taverne; a long leader on Willi Brandt's success as a Social Democrat turned out in the last paragraph to be no more than a puff for Taverne; finally, on 28 February, there was a front-page story about private Conservative polls. This last was of particular interest: it was a piece by 'Our Political Editor'[23] which reported that private polls conducted for the Conservative Party had shown that they would do badly in all three by-elections the next day. This story was in fact partly untrue and wholly misleading, for no poll had ever been conducted in Chester-le-Street, and the polls in Lincoln and Dundee had been conducted several weeks earlier. There had been a similarly anonymous story in *The Times* on 22 February (by 'Our Political Staff'), which stated that the reports from by-election constituencies to Conservative Central Office had given no hopes of victory. In the case of Lincoln at least, this story too was untrue. Within the Conservative Party, in London and in the by-election constituencies, there was a deal of annoyance occasioned by the printing of both stories. Both had been based on unreliable leaks, both had been at least partly untrue, and both had the obvious intention of persuading wavering Conservatives that they would waste their votes by voting Conservative. Since so few copies of *The Times* are sold in Lincoln (and presumably even fewer in Chester-le-Street or Dundee), its influence on the voters cannot have been very great. Indirectly, though, it may have affected the line taken by other newspapers, especially because

[23] Unusually, it did not also have the name of the Political Editor, David Wood, attached to it – perhaps for copyright reasons.

its stories conformed with what was actually coming out of the published opinion polls.

The local press presented a different picture altogether: one local paper, the *Lincolnshire Echo*, presented a fair and balanced picture, refusing to take sides, and attempting to present the election in terms of issues as well as personalities. The other, the *Lincoln Weekend Chronicle*, was frankly campaigning for Taverne from the start. Since these two papers had such a wide circulation in the city,[24] and since they naturally included more by-election news and comment than all the national press added together, their influence was presumably more than that of the national press. During the campaign the *Echo* used a double column of each day's issue on the front page to keep readers up to date with the activities of the three major candidates, and the allocation of space was always equal. The more partisan approach of the *Chronicle* may be summarised by quoting the advice to voters which was included in its final editorial:

> FLOATING VOTERS: If you are impressed by the present government's performance, VOTE CONSERVATIVE. If you are impressed by the kind of Government the Labour Party could provide, VOTE LABOUR. If you are impressed by Taverne's service to Lincoln – or feel strongly against the way he was rejected by the Labour Party (the national executive even ignored a recommendation by their own sub-committee in so doing), then vote Taverne.
>
> A consoling word for the voter who selects Taverne. You are not necessarily voting into a void – it is not always a waste to vote for an independent candidate. Sir Stafford Cripps, Nye Bevan, Winston Churchill were all at some stage rejected by their party!

The most notorious of hanging judges could hardly have summed up in a more prejudicial way. This front-page advice was presumably read by many thousands of Lincoln voters in the weekend before polling day. The *Echo*'s more sober and balanced presentation of the issues and the candidates may

[24] The *Lincolnshire Echo* was estimated to reach over 80 per cent of households in the city, and the *Lincoln Weekend Chronicle* also had a large local circulation.

have helped to increase interest in the campaign and knowledge of it, but it would not push voters towards any one candidate.

All in all, only *The Times* and the *Lincoln Weekend Chronicle* can be said to have indulged in the sort of interventionist campaign that had been anticipated. Television was not in a position to do so anyway, for its procedure in covering elections specifically requires equal coverage for all candidates.

Results and reactions

By polling day there was little reason to doubt that Taverne was going to win, and to win by a considerable margin. Both the Gallup Poll in the *Daily Telegraph* and the NOP poll in the *Daily Mail* gave him the hope of an easy victory, while the report in *The Times* indicated that private Conservative polls had found the same result. Labour and Conservatives had increasing difficulty in keeping up the claims that they would win. Other impartial evidence pointed in the same direction: a count of posters undertaken the previous weekend had shown far more posters for Taverne than for all the others combined. Despite all this, the size of Taverne's majority came as a justifiable shock to everyone involved – not excluding Taverne himself. The bitterness of Labour scrutineers and the apathy of Conservatives were witness to their shock. Taverne's victory speech was almost drowned by cries of 'Tory' and 'Traitor', and it required police intervention to return him safely to the counting-hall.[25]

Reactions to the result conformed exactly to what might have been expected. *The Times* rejoiced with 'Didn't he do well!' while the *Lincoln Weekend Chronicle* spread its front page with the banner headline 'Taverne crushes Grafton House'. Rather sourly, *Tribune* commented that 'Mr Taverne's victory would be funny if it were not so tragic'. The only comment worth quoting at length was the more irreverent one from *Private Eye*:

> The fresh clean wind of decency and integrity is blowing through British public life today.

[25] The leaders of the Lincoln Labour Party again played into Taverne's hands by the rough treatment given to his supporters after the declaration. Several Labour councillors and local party officers were actively involved in this demonstration.

That was the message from Lincoln Racecourse this morning as Sir William Haley Mogg's DICK TAVERNE (Blessed Mervyn Stockwood up) romped home 50 lengths ahead of his nearest rival party hack, Mr Wedgwood Benn's DILKS.

Decent men and women can hold their heads up high again this morning. Not since St George (25–1) defeated the controversial odds-on favourite the Dragon has a greater blow been struck for honour, courage, chivalry, integrity, peace. . . .

Comment on Lincoln was inevitably bracketed with Chester-le-Street (where Labour held the very safe seat by a much-reduced margin from the Liberals) and Dundee East (where Labour held on narrowly from the SNP). In all three contests Labour had been hard pressed in seats that had never been lost since the war, and in all three the Conservative had come third. Indeed, in all three the Conservative vote had been squeezed by the knowledge that a third candidate had more chance of beating Labour, and it was in Dundee, where the Conservative seemed to have the best chance, that his vote held up best. In Chester-le-Street, where the Conservative clearly had no chance whatever, his vote faded away almost entirely. In Lincoln, Taverne seems to have secured a clear majority of Labour voters and of Conservative voters, but this masks a very important distinction: some Conservatives no doubt voted for him through admiration for his stand, but many clearly voted for Taverne to vote against Labour. Labour voters, on the other hand, were presumably voting about the sort of party that they wanted. In other words, Labour Taverneites were voting *for* Taverne while Conservative Taverneites were voting *against* Dilks. Overall, at Lincoln as in the other contests, the proportion of Conservative defections was about the same as Labour defections. It makes very little sense in theory to calculate a Labour/Conservative swing for any of the contests of 1 March, but it is interesting to note that in all the contests there was little or no relative change between the major parties. This could give little comfort to the Conservatives but even less to Labour: they, after all, had lost the last general election, and yet with unemployment and inflation simultaneously high, they could make up no ground on the government. In that sense, the results of 1 March confirmed those of the autumn of 1972.

However, all this is a long way from theories about third or new parties: Roy Jenkins categorically rejected any such ideas in the week after Lincoln and *The Times* regretfully accepted his view. In fact, the by-elections had given no indication of any positive desire for a new party, and in a negative sense had shown the strength of two-party attitudes. The Liberals did very well at Chester-le-Street, but lost their deposit at Dundee East and could claim no credit for Taverne's win. Moreover, the Liberals who did well at Chester-le-Street and the Scottish Nationalists who did well at Dundee had little in common with each other, and even less in common with Taverne. The only credible theory is one which says that voters were unhappy with the existing parties but unsure about a new one – in other words, that they were in a state of dis-illusion and had not yet settled on a new illusion. This has to be set against British politics in the long term, for ever since the modern two-party system evolved in the 1920s, the voters have regularly been accused of disillusion. Such disillusion has only been manifested in by-elections because it is only then that it appears to have any real point, and opinion polls have assisted it because they help minor party candidates to break through the credibility gap. What the by-elections of 1 March did not show was evidence of unusual disillusion with the major parties in the middle of a Parliament, only that in these contests there appeared to be a real chance to make feelings of disillusion known.

If an explanation of the Lincoln result is required, it must be this: that Taverne profited from the natural sympathy for an underdog and an individualist, and that he was able to establish his claim to this position because the others chose not to question it. (Joe Ashton later remarked: 'We fought Ted Heath and the Tories fought the unions but nobody fought Taverne.') Taverne was crusading on the easy ground of personal consistency at a time when both major parties had been forced to change position by external circumstances. In all this, the Lincoln contest was, as Taverne said, simply about Taverne, but superimposed on this was the impact of the opinion polls. These would persuade Conservatives that they might as well vote for Taverne to keep Dilks out, and would persuade Labour voters that they had a perfectly free vote between two Labour candidates and with no risk of letting in the Conservatives. In view of Taverne's standing and the unpopularity of Grafton House, there was little doubt what the choice would be.

Lincoln as testing-ground for a new party was always a dubious proposition, and the personal nature of Taverne's victory ruled it out completely. The case for a centre party or a 'third force' in British politics could only be tested properly when personal factors and local rivalries did not complicate the position beyond recognition. It was so tested on 12 April 1973, when the new county councils of England and Wales were elected on one day. When all the voters were given a chance to go to the polls – a unique mid-term 'general' election – they responded by electing 1,772 Conservatives and 1,835 Labour councillors. Only 782 seats in the new authorities were awarded by the 'disillusioned' voters to any but the 'discredited' major parties. Perhaps these results put Taverne's victory in its proper electoral context.[26]

However, perhaps the best commentary on 'the Lincoln affair' and the furore that it stirred up in the media was the reply of one Lincoln lady when canvassed by Taverne: 'Whatever happened to that nice Mr de Freitas?' she asked. Mr de Freitas last stood for election in Lincoln in 1959.

APPENDIX I: LINCOLN POLLS

1. Richard Jay, Department of Government, University of Essex. Published 15 June 1972. Postal questionnaire. Random sample 800.

Question 1: 'Dick Taverne has publicly expressed strong support for entry into the Common Market. His party, locally and nationally, are opposed to entry on present terms. Do you think he was right to vote in accordance with his views, or should he have voted with his party?'

---

[26] The results on 7 June in Lincoln however were as follows:

	Votes	Seats	Candidates
Conservative	13,811	6	23
Labour	14,953	1	29
Democratic Lab.	22,860	20	25
Ind. Con.	2,719	3	4

Coun. Fred Allen became new Leader of Lincoln City Council.

Question 2: 'Do you approve or disapprove of Dick Taverne as your MP?'

Replies were received from the original questionnaire and a reminder.

		Questionnaire	Reminder	Total
Qu. 1.	Thought right	73·1%	66·9%	71·3%
	Thought wrong	20·8%	21·7%	21·1%
	Don't knows	6·1%	11·4%	7·6%
Qu. 2.	Approve	82·4%	71·3%	79·2%
	Disapprove	12·0%	13·8%	12·5%
	Don't knows	5·6%	14·9%	8·3%
	Numbers	432	175	607

2. *Lincolnshire Chronicle*. Published 23 June 1972. Doorstep interviews by local sociology students. Concentration on heavily Labour areas of the city.

Question 1: 'Do you normally support the Labour candidate at elections?'

Question 2: 'Lincoln Labour Party has decided to ask Dick Taverne to resign as Lincoln MP before the next election. Do you approve of the move?'

	Approve	Disapprove	Don't know	Numbers
Labour voters	17%	76%	7%	812
'Conservative' voters	17%	66%	17%	343
All voters	17%	73%	10%	1,155

3. Opinion Research Centre. Published *Lincolnshire Chronicle*, 13 October 1972. Sample 600.

Question 1: 'Who will you vote for in the by-election?'

Question 2: 'Has Taverne done a good job or a bad job as MP?'

Question 3: 'Do you agree with Lincoln Labour Party's decision not to adopt Taverne?'

Qu. 1.	Taverne	49%
	Official Labour	14%
	Conservative	16%
	Other	2%
	Undecided	19%
Qu. 2.	Good job	82%
	Bad job	2%
	Neither good nor bad	5%
	Don't know	11%
Qu. 3.	Agree	10%
	Disagree	77%
	Neither agree nor disagree	5%
	Not heard about	8%

4. Gallup. Published *Daily Telegraph*, 22 February 1973. Random sample 466, taken 17–20 February.

Voting intentions:

Democratic Labour	37·5%
Labour	35·5%
Conservative	26·5%
Other parties	0·5%

Question: 'Who would you vote for if you thought that your party were going to be badly beaten?'

35% Conservative voters said Taverne
41% Labour voters said Taverne

5. National Opinion Polls. Published *Daily Mail*, 1 March 1973. Interviews 25–27 February.

Question: 'How do you think you will vote at the by-election?'

Taverne (Democratic Labour)	50%
Dilks (Labour)	30%
Guinness (Conservative)	19%
Other Independents	1%

After pollsters' conclusions that voters were confused over party labels, a mock ballot paper was presented to respondents. The results of this were:

Taverne	54·5%
Dilks	26·6%
Guinness	17·9%
Other Inds.	1·0%

6. Gallup. Published *Daily Telegraph*, 1 March 1973. Random sample 672, taken 24–27 February.

Voting intentions:

Democratic Labour	49·5%
Labour	27·5%
Conservative	22·0%
Others	1·0%

Asked whether, when they went to vote, they were voting mainly for the person or the party, respondents replied:

Person	30%
Party	56%
Both or undecided	14%

Of Taverne supporters:

Person	57%
Party	30%
Both or undecided	13%

Question: 'If an MP finds his own views on an issue, like joining the Common Market, differ from those of the majority of his constituents, what should he do when the issue is debated in Parliament – vote according to his own views or according to his constituents' views?'

	Con.	Lab.	Dem. Lab.	Total
Own views	59%	28%	59%	48%
Constituents' views	29%	61%	30%	40%
Don't know	12%	11%	11%	12%

Comments

1. Taverne's claim that his electorate would support him on an 'independence of the MP' platform can be backed up from the results of the first three polls. However, it is noteworthy that when 'acting in accordance with one's constituents' views' replaces 'acting in accordance with one's party's views', Taverne's support for the Common Market becomes somewhat less justifiable.

2. Investigations have shown that poll 4 (Gallup), taken around ten days before the election, may have given a somewhat misguided impression. Respondents were asked only which *party* they intended to support, with no mention of candidates' names. In both later polls, when names were included, a more accurate prediction of the result (although one still undervaluing Taverne's support) was obtained. Note that Taverne's support a few days before the election wellnigh exactly replicates his support the previous October.

On the other hand, the Gallup Poll of 22 February is interesting. If we add the 'second preferences' of Labour and Conservative voters to Taverne's support, the figure closely corresponds to Taverne's final result, though it somewhat overestimates eventual Labour and underestimates Conservative votes.

APPENDIX II: NOTE ON SOURCES

The printed material available to the instant historian is very large but rather unvaried. During the by-election most of the national newspapers, local press and political weeklies were read; in the circumstances, *The Times* and the local press provided most of the information used, but other national and provincial newspapers provided background. This was of course supplemented by interviews and by observation. The authors would like to express particular thanks for co-operation to Mr Tony Elkington, Mr Joe Ghose, Mr Pat Mulligan, Mr Dick Taverne, Mr Ernest Ward and Mrs Clodagh Wilkinson.

11. Towards an Economic Theory of By-Elections since the War

By MATTHEW OAKESHOTT

Why do we need an economic theory of by-elections since 1945? Why do we need any theory of by-elections at all? Rhetorical questions tend to have answers treading eagerly on their heels, and these are no exception. Put at its simplest, the broad sweep of by-election results has been considerably less favourable to governments in the later part of this period than in its first decade. The possible explanations for this phenomenon are as varied as they are individually intriguing. Sadly, the ingenuity of their formulation is almost always outweighed by their inherent implausibility or immaturity.

To avoid a similar charge, one important proviso about the basis for an economic theory of by-election results is required. One is not discounting the importance of the familiar influences such as class, heredity and religion on the electorate; but many of the swings in by-elections since 1945, and especially in the last few years, have clearly been far too large for these familiar influences to explain on their own. The solid floor of party allegiance is still there; indeed, it is quite likely that the floor of basic Labour support is sloping very slightly upwards over the years, while the floor in the Conservative corner tilts gently down. But the by-election dances on that same floor are performed to more transitory tunes; by-election voters and non-voters are affected very significantly by short-term stimuli. In so far as it is possible to isolate one principal source of these stimuli, this essay contends that there is substantial – albeit incomplete – evidence that this source is economic: the government's economic performance and the electorate's view of that performance.

One fashionable 'explanation' of by-election results which

can be laid to rest immediately is 'volatility' *tout court*. It is frequently suggested that electors are becoming more volatile. This, however, is a description of a phenomenon rather than even a partial explanation. If they are becoming more volatile, the description does not solve the problem of finding the stimuli to which they are responding with increased volatility. Nevertheless, these criticisms cannot fairly be levelled at the fascinating study by Goodhart and Bhansali[1] of the relationships between economic fluctuations and the British Government's standing in the opinion polls between 1947 and 1968. The basic question which they ask is how far swings in political popularity have been affected by economic circumstances, and the answer can be crudely summarised as 'very significantly'. They find that

> the response of the electorate to economic developments – at least as represented by the two variables chosen [the level of unemployment six months previously and the rate of price inflation] – has been both more marked and more volatile in the years since 1959 than in the earlier years. The influence of economic events upon the popularity of the government of the day has thus apparently been steadily growing.

How closely can this interwoven pattern be seen in by-elections since 1945? And, if the pattern is established, what framework of analysis is necessary to provide a coherent account of why the electorate behaves in this way at by-elections? In the period since 1945, with the battle-lines in the two-party system reasonably clearly drawn and the shares of the total votes cast going to the two main parties fluctuating within fairly narrow limits, the pattern of by-elections has been superimposed on a base free from either substantial long-run changes in party allegiance or the tactical switches of large blocks of votes in by-elections of the inter-war period with its three- and two-and-a-half-party systems. (There are in fact some traces of systematic economic influence in by-elections in the two-party system before the First World War, but comparison with by-elections after 1945 is complicated by the problems of a very

[1] C. A. E. Goodhart and R. J. Bhansali, 'Political Economy', *Political Studies*, XVIII (1970) 43–106.

different class and sex composition of the electorate as well as differences in voters' expectations of a government's economic policy; there was also widespread doubt at that time about the possibility of governments controlling the 'hidden hand'.)

On any feasible indication, however, whether swing figures[2] or more complicated measures of political behaviour are used, the results of by-elections have become considerably less favourable to the government party over this period; the by-election trough was deep in the later years of the Conservative Government which was defeated in 1964, and appeared almost bottomless for much of the life of the 1966–70 Labour Government. The 1945–50 Labour Government lost only one by-election (although there was a considerable amount of luck in this achievement, since only one by-election – Heywood and Radcliffe in early 1946 – occured in a marginal seat where the Labour majority at the general election had been under 12 per cent). Nevertheless, a government elected with the highest parliamentary majority and largest lead in popular votes which Labour has ever achieved experienced only five by-elections in which the two-party swing against it since the general election reached double figures (Bexley, Liverpool Edge Hill, Glasgow Gorbals, Edmonton and Leeds West; South Kensington is excluded since Labour did not contest the by-election).

The 1951–5 Conservative Government also suffered no serious by-election reverses; the heaviest anti-government swing, at Dundee East in 1952, was only 7·4 per cent, and the Conservatives gained Sunderland South from Labour in 1953. After the 1955 general election, pro-government swings in by-elections grew very rare, and Leeds North-East in February 1956 provides the only example of a pro-government swing between 1955 and 1959 in a by-election free from a strong Liberal intervention. Nevertheless, even including seats where the by-election results were not strictly comparable with the general election, there were only four double-figure swings against the 1955–9 Conservative Government. Once the electoral bonus of the antics of the Labour Party in 1960 was used up, the government started suffering far more serious and

[2] All swing figures quoted in this chapter are calculated as Steed swing (see p. 359).

sustained by-election swings from the spring of 1961, with adverse swings frequently over 10 per cent whether a Liberal candidate was standing or not. After the protracted 1964–6 general election campaign, the Labour Government's by-election performance was simply disastrous. Throughout 1968 and 1969 the only by-elections in which the two-party swing could even appear to be under 10 per cent were those for which no swing figure can meaningfully be calculated because of a large increase in the Nationalist vote – Caerphilly and Glasgow Gorbals.

On any plausible method of calculation, governments in the 1960s were considerably less popular than in the late 1940s and early 1950s. The really substantial swings against the government in 1962–3 and after the 1966 election coincided with serious economic problems in the first case and a prolonged crisis in the second. Unemployment in both cases was far higher than the average for the 1950s, as was inflation after the 1967 devaluation. Unemployment, inflation and the balance of payments were all more serious in the 1960s than in the 1950s after the Korean war crisis; the growth rate of national income was roughly the same, but considerable expectations about an increase were undoubtedly raised by the Labour campaign leading up to the 1964 general election and the National Plan period immediately afterwards. The phrase 'rising expectations' can be used in attempts to explain the greater degree of disillusion with governments now apparent in by-election results; this description, however, only obscures the basic question 'rising expectations about what?' If it is rising expectations about the economy, this is not a counter-argument to the economic theory but merely a reason for predicting rather greater fluctuations in government electoral support from the same set of changes in economic circumstances.

If voters and non-voters at by-elections are responding, in part at least, to economic conditions, it is also necessary to consider whether differing swings at by-elections reflect different economic conditions in each region. The most important proviso is that the economic conditions at the time of a by-election must be compared with the conditions *at the previous general election in that area*. For example, Goodhart and Bhansali say (p. 67) that 'the finding of the considerable impact of unemployment on political popularity in the years since 1959 implied that high unemployment appeared to cause many voters not themselves directly threatened or personally involved to switch their voting habits (also the swing against the government was rarely much less in by-elections in areas with low than in those with high unemployment)'. There is a serious gap in their argument here: one might find that Scottish unemployment at the time of every Scottish by-election since the war has been higher than unemployment in London at the time of every London by-election, but that would not in itself be a reason for expecting a higher swing against the government from the previous general election result.

The three economic indicators which have been used in most 'politico-econometric' studies so far have been unemployment and the growth of retail prices and personal incomes. These three variables are clearly not independent of each other, but there is a strong case for considering them separately since the relationships between them can change significantly over a period as short as two or three years, as the recent experience of many Western industrial economies has shown. Unemployment figures in Britain, for example, no longer correspond in any predictable way to the growth rate of either prices or national income at a particular point in the economic cycle. Such evidence as is available suggests that, although there are noticeable and measureable differences in the consumer price *level* between different regions of Britain, there has been no significant difference in recent years in the rates of *increase* of prices in different regions of the country. If, then, voters in by-elections are responding to the rate of price increase, it seems reasonable to assume that the response in different regions is to a single national rate.

Changes in real personal income have been found by Gerald Kramer[3] to be an important influence on American congressional elections between 1896 and 1964. 'In analysis-of-variance terms, economic fluctuations can account for something like half the variance of the congressional vote, over the period considered. (Presidential elections, however, are substantially less responsive to economic conditions)'. American

---

[3] G. Kramer, 'Short Term Fluctuations in US Voting Behaviour', *American Political Science Review* (Mar 1971).

congressional elections may be considered to fit into the logical framework at a point midway between British by-elections and British general elections. To the extent that American congressional election outcomes are 'in response to objective changes occurring under the incumbent party', and if this response is more marked in congressional than in presidential elections, when voters in practice consider they are choosing a new government, there are close parallels with the theory that in Britain voters react to economic conditions in by-elections but that the pattern is far more confused in general elections. Goodhart and Bahansali find that changes in personal incomes do not provide a good fit with government popularity, but they point out that 'one reason for this could well be that quarterly changes in personal incomes are hard to calculate with accuracy, and the variations in unemployment could well have been a better index of the cyclical movements in most people's earnings than the aggregated statistics for personal incomes'. This relationship no longer holds, but the problems of calculating short-period changes in personal incomes remain; as it would be even more difficult to calculate regional changes in personal income, this is not a promising research avenue for an economic theory of British by-elections.

A fourth economic variable which has not so far been considered explicitly in politico-econometric studies is taxation, net of social security benefits (which may be regarded for this purpose as a form of negative taxation). The omission is understandable. Extreme caution would be necessary in estimating any relationship between government popularity and aggregate measures of changes in taxation and benefits: some taxes are obviously far less popular than others which raise the same amount of revenue, and few realistic political observers would argue that a government would improve its performance in by-elections and the opinion polls by an increase of £100 million in the total disbursed in family allowances, as compared with the same increase in old-age pensions.

An economic theory of by-elections must take account of regional variations in economic conditions; it can also be developed to allow for the differential impact of economic changes and economic policies on different classes and even occupational groups. Unfortunately the lack of voting figures in

Britain for any voting unit smaller than the constituency makes it very hard to produce more than general impressions of the political effect of fluctuations in particular industries. Nevertheless, there have occasionally been instances since the war of government economic policy giving sharply differing benefits to social groups in different economic circumstances. The combination of increased social service and welfare charges with very substantial tax concessions to the better off in November 1970 and the 1971 budget provide perhaps the clearest example, and it may not be completely fanciful to see some reflection of these measures in the by-elections held two days after the 1971 budget in Arundel and Shoreham and Liverpool Scotland, constituencies separated by a very wide gap indeed in the economic position of their electors. There was a wide variation in the swing, with the electors of Arundel and Shoreham returning a pro-government swing, while Liverpool Scotland swung appreciably to Labour, in spite of the intervention of a maverick Independent Labour candidate.

To give some weight to this theory it is not necessary to hold an idealised view of the electorate and place the voter on a pedestal on which he reads the *Financial Times*, studies the latest business forecasts and carefully analyses the government's attempts to control the rate of inflation or unemployment. There *may* be voters who go through this exercise before casting their vote in by-elections; but it is hardly likely that they exist in sufficient numbers to affect a swing figure calculated to only one decimal point, even in the unlikely event of their economic expertise being unaccompanied by firm political affiliation. It is not even necessary to postulate a voter who is aware of the rate of price increase in the last year or of the simple total of unemployed. One needs only to assume that a significant number of people feel satisfied or dissatisfied with the government for some reason or set of reasons which are related systematically to the course of the economy. The theory probably needs to make a very limited assumption that these electors either think the government has some degree of control over the economy or that it should do something to help them when 'business is going badly', but it does not need to show that these electors have a carefully formulated set of beliefs or any particular interest in politics or economic conditions generally.

In the longer term a relationship between economic conditions and by-election swings may be affected by changes in expectations; clearly, the electorate in ten or fifteen years' time may not 'expect' the same economic performance from a government that it does today, and the swings predicted from a particular rate of unemployment or inflation may therefore change. This shift in the relationship can stem from two causes: first, the electorate is changing, with older cohorts dying and younger ones entering; neither of these groups is likely to have identical economic expectations, or to react to changing economic conditions in the same way as the electorate as a whole. For example, Butler and Stokes,[4] in using survey data to examine the links between changes in support for the parties and perceived changes in economic well-being, found that

> an interesting aspect of these findings is that the trends that were above and the trends that were below the average for the electorate as a whole were disproportionately the result of younger electors' responding to their perceived economic conditions. Not only were younger electors more likely than older ones to see their condition as having improved, as we have noted; they were also more likely to be *moved* by such perceptions whether they were of an improvement or worsening of their condition.

This finding by itself does not provide conclusive evidence that the electorate as a whole is becoming either more volatile generally or more responsive politically to changes in economic conditions; to be able to say that, one would need to compare changes over time in *differential* volatility and responsiveness to economic fluctuations between the different age groups as well as the changes in the numbers of electors in each age group. But the relationship found by Butler and Stokes is a strong one, and the enfranchisement of the 18–21-year-olds in 1969 provides a clear example of a large extra block of voters which is very likely to have increased the volatility and the 'econoresponsiveness' of the total electorate. Second, those who have been members of the electorate throughout the period may none the less experience a change in their perceptions and reactions as

[4] D. E. Butler and D. Stokes, *Political Change in Britain* (1969) pp. 403–404.

they live through differing economic circumstances. This may very well not be a conscious reappraisal of the performance of governments or their handling of the economy; it may be much nearer the familiar everyday process of becoming readier to accept a situation as normal the longer that situation persists.

A further argument for the importance of economic factors in by-elections is the argument from perceived salience. If politicians and journalists think the electorate is concerned with economic conditions, then the focus of political debate and political effort tends to switch towards the economic arena. The concentration on the economy may not be quite so intense as during some periods of the 1964–70 Labour Government, when the only concern of politicians, press, television and radio appeared at times to be the size of each month's balance-of-payments deficit. But for most of the term of that government the rather broader economic question of prices and incomes was so widely and hotly debated, and so generally assumed to be an important determinant of the mood of the electorate, that one would expect this public focus to increase the 'econo-responsiveness' of electors independently of the effect of changes in the economy or the age or class structure of the electorate. It is always tempting to try to undermine a widely held theory of how electors behave; but in politics, if a large enough number of people in influential positions believe a theory firmly enough for long enough – and if they act on that theory – then the theory may to some extent justify itself by producing evidence on which it should not have been based originally because the evidence did not then exist.

In the case of balance-of-payments figures, the argument from perceived salience is particularly relevant. Goodhart and Bhansali point out that 'the authorities' concern, and therefore also that of much of the press, was frequently directly with the health of our balance of payments. One wondered whether this concern had filtered down to the general populace.' Whether one uses data on the balance of monetary movements or even the crude trade figures, these clearly have less direct personal effect on voters than prices, incomes or unemployment; one would not expect a series of balance-of-payments indicators themselves to show a systematic relationship with either by-election swings or opinion-poll ratings, since the commentaries in the newspapers, television and radio are the only significant channels of causation by which the balance of payments influences electors month by month. These comments, at times when the balance of payments is considered newsworthy, are usually of the form 'the figures are worse/better than expected'; a large deficit can, at times, thus be presented as a reasonable achievement. To derive a correlation would be practically impossible since one would have to compare the outturn of the chosen balance-of-payments indicator with some index of informed expectations about that indicator. This is not to say that the balance of payments, or – more precisely – beliefs and comments about the balance of payments, are unimportant in the economic influences on the government's standing in opinion polls or its performance in by-elections; it is just that unfortunately this cannot be demonstrated in a systematic and satisfactory way since there is a cushion of other more immediate economic variables between the balance of payments and the economic facts of life for the great majority of electors.

If electors react in by-elections to economic conditions, is it a valid objection to the theory if they are not shown to react in the same way at general elections? There is a split-level reply to this argument.

On a theoretical plane, the most familiar explanation of this apparent contradiction is also the most plausible: that the vision of an alternative government does not normally appear to the by-election voter or non-voter; he is reacting to the recent performance of the government as he sees it, and he is not so concerned with the credibility of the opposition's policies or personalities. At the general election, however, in what may seem to the political theorist a muddled and inchoate process, he will make some comparison with the prospect of life under the alternative government (and the retrospect over their previous terms of office, if he is old enough). He may also react to the performance of the existing government over at least the most recent year or two, rather than just to the past three or six months as he appears to do in by-elections. A general election does not concentrate most electors' minds wonderfully, but it is hard to argue that it fails to concentrate them a little more than a mid-term by-election or opinion poll.

This theory of the invisible opposition at by-elections does not always hold; on economic grounds alone, one would have expected the Conservative Governments to have fared considerably worse than they did in by-elections held in 1960 and 1972. But the contortions of the Labour Opposition in each case proved too frenzied for them not to cause some stir even within the usual thick cocoon of elector indifference between general elections. A theory of an opposition which is invisible (or visible only in isolated and exceptional circumstances) at by-elections also fits neatly with the findings of Butler and Stokes[5] on the relationship between voting intention and voters' perceptions of the government's economic performance and the opposition's ability to handle the economy. They point out that

> It is at once apparent from the contrast of these figures that perceptions of the *government's* [my italics] economic performance are much more variable and match more closely the movements of party strength. If party bias and the accidents of sampling accounted for the agreement of the series in the earlier figure, the party lead in votes ought to provide an equally good match with each of the two series showing the changing approval of the economic performance of the government and the opposition. The fact that the agreement with approval of the government is much the closer of the two is evidence that we are tapping changes which have genuine influence on party strength and is at the same time evidence that it is the government's performance that is of greater salience for the electorate.

The practical reply is that there is insufficient evidence of general elections for anyone to be able to say whether the theory holds for them as well. Whereas there have been 299 by-elections between July 1945 and the end of 1972, there have only been eight general elections in the same period, and only nineteen this century. In March 1968 the then Prime Minister was reported[6] as saying that 'All political history shows that the standing of a government and its ability to hold the confidence of the electorate at a General Election depend on the success of its economic policy'. Any statement beginning 'all political history shows' is a strong candidate for the butcher's

---

[5] Butler and Stokes, *Political Change in Britain*, pp. 413–14.
[6] *Financial Times*, 8 Mar 1968.

slab, and the second half of this one looks easier meat than most. It is not clear, for example, that on the normal economic evidence the 1955–9 Conservative Government's economic policy was more successful than that of its predecessor between 1951 and 1955, yet there was a swing to the Conservatives between 1955 and 1959. It requires even more ingenuity to argue Harold Wilson's case[7] for 1945, 1923, 1922, 1918, 1910, 1906 or 1900.

Of course, the timing and treatment of the *news* of more personally relevant economic policy changes as well as the longer-term effects of those changes can affect by-election results. It is arguable that Labour would have lost Bassetlaw (majority on 31 October 1968: 740 votes) had the by-election been held a week later (or if the hire-purchase restrictions had been announced a day earlier). A similar case occurred in February 1956 when Harold Macmillan announced hire-purchase restrictions and price increases for bread and milk just after the Conservatives had held Taunton by 657 votes, Gainsborough by 1,006 and Hereford by 2,150. The difference in political effect between news about changes in the balance of payments and news about changes in price and unemployment is perhaps similar to the difference between water being pumped through a pipe and into a tank. Surges of water into both the balance-of-payments pipe and the prices and unemployment tank have a short-run effect on the standing of the government; but while news flows through the pipe and into oblivion, the water in the tank after the initial surge does not settle back to its earlier level.

If a government's standing *between* general elections (as shown in by-election results and opinion polls) is thus determined very largely by changes in economic conditions, then a government's performance in by-elections may in practice be affected significantly by luck – by the luck of inheriting a particular set of economic problems at a particular time; whether one regards the relationship between changing economic conditions and by-elections throughout a Parliament as politically healthy also depends on whether one considers that such economic changes as may in practice take place should be ascribed more to luck than to judgement. If a government's

[7] On the assumption that he was for once not misquoted by the press.

economic policy is 'blown off course', its by-election candidates are usually blown off course as well; and governments with majorities of 5 or 17 clearly have thresholds of by-election salience which are considerably lower than those of governments wielding majorities of 93 or 100.

The impact on economic policy of parliamentary majorities small enough to be vulnerable to by-election losses is even less comfortably traceable than the effect of the economy on the by-elections and thus on the parliamentary majority. A case can be made out to support the view that the Conservative Government elected with a narrow majority in 1951 was content to coast along on a favourable terms-of-trade tide and was unwilling to initiate necessary structural reforms in the fields of price and income determination, fiscal or regional policy, for example, because of a fear that by offending powerful groups it might lose vital votes in by-elections as well as in the next general election. This case, however, would be stronger had the accretion of Conservative seats in 1955 led to vigorous reforming policies thereafter when the threat of by-election losses was much less serious. There is perhaps more evidence to support the theory that the economic policies of the 1964 Labour Government were more significantly influenced by the prospect of the majority vanishing in the space of first three and then two by-elections. Again, this line of argument would be stronger had that government taken decisive economic action after the 1966 election: for example, by devaluing the pound – a decision that was eventually taken for, rather than by, the government. In this case, however, it seems possible that the economic policy arguments used so often during the days of a narrow majority had convinced many of their users of their universal and perpetual validity, with the result that it took over a year before it dawned that both the parliamentary and the economic situation had changed. Thus the economic policy (or lack of policy) stemming from short-run by-election fears in 1964–6 may have contributed powerfully to the disastrous by-election results for the government later in the 1966–70 Parliament.

If it is accepted that economic fluctuations have been a significant influence on both opinion-poll ratings and by-election results, this does not imply that governments should attempt to base their economic policies on this relationship in either their own electoral interest or in the interests of the 'elector–consumer'; observed correlation is not an unbreakable chain of causation, as those who believed in a stable Phillips curve and argued for the economy to be run with a higher unemployment level have discovered. But in a very basic form an economic theory of by-elections does provide the only available explanation of the broad trends of government performance at British by-elections between 1945 and 1972 which is neither implausible in principle nor untestable in practice.

12. Features of Electoral Behaviour at By-Elections

By STAN TAYLOR and CLIVE PAYNE

Introduction[1]

A by-election is held to select a Member of Parliament when a vacancy has occurred between general elections. It provides an opportunity for the electorate to pass judgement upon a government's performance, and thus by-election results reflect the translation of opinion changes within the electorate into voting behaviour.[2] This chapter attempts to examine a number of propositions about the behaviour of the electorate at a by-election using elementary statistical methods.

The approach adopted was to examine by-election behaviour of electors in terms of the choice made from the various alternatives of voting for one of the parties standing or abstaining. We were interested in how the choice made depends upon a number of factors: for example, who the elector voted for at the previous general election, the marginality of the seat, which party was in power and the number and type of alternatives available. By-elections were considered as unique political events with their own special characteristics influencing the electors' choices more or less independently of the historical period in which the by-election occurred. In particular, by-

[1] The authors would like to thank Mrs Jean Nicholls and Mrs Barbro Noman for assistance with the coding and card-punching, and Miss Jenny Barton and Mrs Margaret Bett for editorial help.

[2] One of Frey and Garbers's criticisms of the Goodhart and Bhansali attempt to test the 'rational voter' model of electoral behaviour is that poll responses did not necessarily reflect voting intentions. The by-election series, of course, are actual votes. See C. A. E. Goodhart and R. J. Bhansali, 'Political Economy', *Political Studies*, xviii (1970) 43–106, and B. Frey and H. Garbers, 'Politico-Econometrics: On Estimation in Political Economy', *Political Studies*, xix (1971) 317.

elections were seen primarily as a test of a government's performance so that the electors' choice lay between voting for the government or the opposition party rather than between Conservative and Labour.

The propositions examined are grouped into four categories. First, we examined turnout, the degree of elector participation in the by-elections compared with general elections. Second, we investigated the relationship between changes in the government and opposition shares of the votes cast. The third aspect concerned the performance of minor party candidates. Finally, we have attempted to estimate the magnitude of the components of change in party support that have taken place at by-elections. Before beginning the substantive discussion we set out our policy of selecting by-elections for analysis and describe the methods of analysis used.

Methodological preliminaries

The analysis set. Data were collected on all 808 by-elections over the period February 1919 to April 1972.[3] We interpreted our task as the description of electoral behaviour at 'normal' by-elections, and therefore excluded 'abnormal' results from the analysis set. There were eight categories of exclusions:

1. All by-elections 1918–23. The low turnout at the general election of 1918 (at 58·9 per cent the lowest this century) meant that there were dramatic increases in turnout in subsequent by-elections. The confusion of party labels during the Coalition and its disintegration made interpretation of behaviour very difficult.

2. All by-elections 1939–45. The war years were atypical because of the party truce and very low turnouts.

3. Double-Member constituencies. The double-Member constituency was a feature of British elections up to 1950. However, it is difficult to compare these with single-Member constituencies because of 'plumping' and the diversity of candidatures.

4. University constituencies. There were 7 of these, returning

[3] The source of our data was the invaluable reference books of F. W. S. Craig, *British Parliamentary Election Results, 1918–49* and *1950–70* (1969, 1971).

12 Members, from 1918 to 1949. Four constituencies elected
more than one Member on a system of proportional representation and in all seats there was a highly specialised and
atypical electorate.

5. Irish seats. Irish seats contested before 1920 and Ulster
seats contested since have been excluded because of differences
in behaviour among the electorate and in the nature of the
party system.[4]

6. Unopposed contests. All seats where a member was
returned unopposed at the by-election or previous general
election were excluded as there was no basis for comparison
between the two elections.

7. Seats where one of the major parties did not fight either
the preceding general election or the by-election. For a variety
of reasons several seats were not fought by one or other of the
major parties at a by-election and therefore the calculation of
change in government or opposition share of the vote was
impossible. Examples include the Speaker's seat at Southampton Itchen in 1971 where the Conservatives had not opposed in
1970, or Bristol South-East in 1963 where the Conservative
candidate stood down in favour of Anthony Wedgwood Benn.

8. Contests involving National Government candidates. The
formation of the National Government of 1931 and the splits
in the Labour and Liberal parties meant that by-election
candidatures were difficult to compare with those at the
previous general election, and shifts in votes difficult to appor-
tion. Where it was obvious that the party division at the by-
election corresponded with that of the general election, the
contest was included. However, in several seats, for example
Kilmarnock and Ashford in 1933, Ross and Cromarty in 1936,
it proved impossible to match candidatures and votes with
those of the previous general election, and such seats were
excluded.

These eight categories reduced the analysis set to 459 by-
elections (57 per cent of the total from 1918 to 1972). If we
take the periods 1924–39 and 1945–72, and exclude University,
Irish and unopposed seats, we have included 91 per cent of

[4] See R. Rose, *Governing without Consensus: An Irish Perspective* (1971) for
the best description of the political and social differences between Britain
and Ulster.

by-elections which may be regarded as adequate for an examination of general behaviour.[5]

Measures of electoral change. We then had to decide upon appropriate measures of electoral change with which to conduct our general analysis. It is possible to distinguish two sources of electoral change. First, there are movements among the parties and abstention among electors who were resident in a constituency at the time of both the by-election and the general election. The second source is the entry of new electors on to the register (voters too young to vote at the previous general election and immigrants into the constituency) and the exit of other electors (those who have died or migrated from the constituency).[6] While recognising the importance of changes in the composition of the electorate in the period between a by-election and a general election, we were unable to derive estimates of the net effect upon government and opposition fortunes. Therefore we have assumed that all movements took place within a constant electorate.

The set of possible movements within the electorate where there are straight fights between government and opposition on each occasion are represented by the cells of the matrix below.

		By-election			
		Govt. (1)	Opp. (2)	Abstentions (3)	
	Govt. (1)	V_{11}	V_{12}	V_{13}	G_G
Preceding general election	Opp. (2)	V_{21}	V_{22}	V_{23}	O_G
	Abstentions (3)	V_{31}	V_{32}	V_{33}	A_G
		G_B	O_B	A_B	E

[5] The reader who is especially interested in the periods we have excluded should see the chapters in this book on Newport and the by-elections in the war years, Chapters 2 and 7.

[6] For an attempt to estimate the magnitude of these various sources of electoral change, see D. E. Butler and D. Stokes, *Political Change in Britain* (1969) pp. 275–92.

The choices available to the elector at the preceding general election were: (1) to vote for the party that becomes the government; (2) to vote for the party that becomes the Opposition; or (3) to abstain. At the by-elections the elector had the same range of choices, except, of course, that he knew which party was the government and which the opposition. The column marginals G_G, O_G and A_G are the numbers of electors voting for the government party, opposition party or abstaining at the general election respectively. The row marginals G_B, O_B and A_B are the numbers voting for the government or opposition or abstaining at the by-election. Each cell represents the number of electors fulfilling the specifications of the particular combination of row and column. For example, V_{11} is the number of electors voting for the government party at both the general election and the by-election, V_{12} the number who voted for the government at the general election and then for the opposition at the by-election. For other types of contest we may add rows and columns as appropriate to the matrix to represent the larger set of possible movements: for example, if the Liberals intervened at the by-election an additional column would be added. The matrix may be converted to proportions by dividing by the row sums. Each cell may then be interpreted as the proportion of electors who, having made a particular choice (row) at the general election, make a subsequent choice (column) at the by-election. These proportions give complete information on the changes that have taken place within the electorate. Ideally, we should like this information for each by-election; we could then investigate in detail how these proportions were related to various factors such as the safeness of the seat or the stage in the life of the Parliament. Such data are not available and we have only the row and column totals for each election. Given this, there are two possible approaches to the analysis of electoral change.

The first is to compute a summary measure from the marginals, and in this category we include the family of measures known as 'swing'. The measures of swing used in the Nuffield election studies are 'two-party' and 'total vote' swing, which take one-half of the difference between the two major parties' proportions of the vote at successive elections as the measure of change.[7] There are two major criticisms of 'swing'. First, net movement between the parties and abstention are weighted and included in a final figure purporting to measure change between the parties.[8] If net movements in abstention are in the same ratio as party proportions of the total vote at the previous election, then the computation of swing reflects changes between major party supporters but does not take account of the fact that some of the electorate have moved to abstention. If abstentions are disproportionate compared with the ratio between the parties at previous elections, then the change is included as a gain of a one-half vote to the party whose supporters have abstained less than proportionately. Given that data on all the marginals are available, it is better to utilise all this information and not produce a summary measure which distorts the movements to and from abstention unnecessarily. Further, in by-election situations where the abstention choice is especially important, we feel that movements to and from abstention should be treated separately from movements between the parties. The second criticism derives from the substantive implications of these considerations. Swing may be excellent as a 'predictive' measure, in the sense of indicating the proportion of major party supporters who must change sides for a seat to be lost by its holder, but it is not a 'behavioural' measure in the sense of measuring the change in the distribution of electoral choices between two elections unless very restrictive assumptions are made.[9] For these reasons we have used all the information available and have not used any of the traditional summary indices. Thus we have used three indicators of electoral change for each by-election: the change

[7] See R. B. McCallum and A. Readman, *The British General Election of 1945* (1947); H. G. Nicholas, *The British General Election of 1950* (1951); D. E. Butler, *The British General Election of 1951* (1952); D. E. Butler, *The British General Election of 1955* (1955); D. E. Butler and R. Rose, *The British General Election of 1959* (1960); D. E. Butler and A. King, *The British General Election of 1964* (1965); D.E. Butler and A. King, *The British General Election of 1966* (1966); D. E. Butler and M. Pinto-Duschinsky, *The British General Election of 1970* (1971).

[8] For a fuller explanation of the treatment of abstention in measure of swing, see M. Steed, in Butler and King, *The British General Election of 1964*, pp. 337–8.

[9] W. Miller, 'Measures of Electoral Change Using Aggregate Data', *Journal of the Royal Statistical Society*, series A (General), cxxxv (1972) 123–4.

in the government's, opposition's and abstention's share of the electorate between the preceding general election and the by-election. We have investigated separately the relationship of these indicators to a number of factors. Usually this was done in a fairly crude way without any attempt to control for the simultaneous effect of other factors. We were often precluded from controlling because an insufficient number of contests was available for detailed analysis.

The second methodological approach in examining electoral change is to attempt to estimate the proportions in the cells of the matrix by regression methods using methods described by Hawkes[10] and Miller.[11] In the following sections we use the marginals as indicators, at the aggregate level, of the processes of change within the electorate between the two elections. In the final section we shall attempt to estimate the actual cell proportions, thus providing a check on our earlier conclusions and, we hope, illuminating the process of electoral change at by-elections.

In conducting our analysis we must distinguish between types of by-election contest which offer different sets of choices to the elector; associated with each will be a matrix of components of change. We shall consider five such types:

1. Straight fights between Conservative and Labour at both general election and by-election (155 contests).
2. Three-cornered fights between Conservatives, Liberals and Labour at both the previous general election and the by-election (123 contests).
3. Liberal withdrawals, where the Liberals did not fight the by-election but stood at the previous general election (34 contests).
4. Liberal interventions, where Liberals did not fight the previous general election but stood at the by-election (82 contests).
5. All seats where the main 'other' or Independent candidate gained more than 5 per cent of the electorate (65 contests).

[10] A. G. Hawkes, 'An Approach to the Analysis of Electoral Swing', *Journal of the Royal Statistical Society*, series A (General), CXXXII (1969) 68–79.
[11] Miller, op. cit.

The main problem encountered in this classification was categorising 'other' and 'Independent' candidates. To produce a fully comprehensive classification would have required a large number of classes with a small number of contests in each. Therefore it was decided to assign seats where 'others' and Independents had less than 5 per cent of the electorate to the main categories and to create a separate category for seats where such candidates were a significant factor in the by-election, that is, received more then 5 per cent of the electorate.

This completes the methodological preliminaries; the next step is to examine turnout at by-elections.

Turnout at by-elections

A by-election does not normally decide the fate of a government. For this reason it was expected that electors at by-elections would be less likely to vote than at a general election. To use King's phrase, by-elections are 'low salience' elections.[12] Further, some electors may use abstention as a form of protest against their 'normal' party. For these reasons we should expect that turnout would generally be lower in by-elections than at the previous general election. In 91 per cent of our selected by-elections turnout fell, with a mean fall of 12·1 per cent and a range of + 13·1 to − 41·9 per cent. Those by-elections where turnout rose either provided an alternative to the major parties in the form of Liberal or Independent intervention, or were fought on single major issues which had achieved national prominence. An example of Independent intervention increasing turnout (through a greater range of choice to the electorate and improved major party organisation to stave off the challenge) was provided by Hamilton in 1967 where the Scottish Nationalists stood and won the seat. The Macclesfield by-election of 1970, which was purportedly fought on the issue of entry into the European Common Market, provided an example of issues influencing turnout, again in part through increased party activity. Conversely we should expect that, in a general election, with the choice of government at stake, turnout would rise from the by-election

[12] A. King, 'Why All Governments Lose By-Elections', *New Society*, 21 Mar 1968, pp. 413–16.

level; the mean turnout increase between by-elections and following general election, in those seats where it was possible to measure such change, was + 10·4 per cent.[13] This lower rate of turnout recovery reflects the 10 per cent decline in general election turnout in the post-war period. In general, the evidence on turnout change supports the 'salience' theory of by-elections. Following from this, it was expected that factors influencing the importance of the by-election would also influence the level of turnout.

We investigated the influence of two such factors. First, the 'safeness' or 'marginality' of the seat. Recent survey evidence has shown that electorate is aware of the possibility that a seat may or may not change hands at an election.[14] This suggests that the electorate in seats which were 'marginal' for the major parties would show greater interest in the election and vote in greater numbers than electors in 'safe' seats. Table 12.1 presents mean turnout change by 'safeness' or 'marginality' of the seats, the latter being defined in terms of the majority of the winning party over the major opposition party at the previous general election as a proportion of the total vote. This shows clearly that the safer the seat, the more turnout fell.

TABLE 12.1

Mean Turnout Change in By-Elections by Winning Party's Majority over Major Opposition Party at Previous General Election

Winning party's majority over major opposition party	Mean turnout change	N
0% but less than 5%	−6·7%	49
More than 5% but less than 10%	−9·9%	31
More than 10%	−13·0%	376

The next proposition which we examined concerned the relation between type of contest and turnout. The larger the number of candidates, the wider the set of choices available to the elector, and the more likely it was that a wide range of

[13] We could measure this only where there had been no boundary changes between the by-election and the general election. The boundary revisions of 1948 and 1954 excluded 93 cases from the analysis.

[14] See forthcoming second edition of Butler and Stokes, *Political Change in Britain.*

opinions were represented. Thus it may be expected that where third parties intervene at the by-election some abstainers at the general election would then vote. Furthermore, major party supporters, disillusioned with their own party, may switch to a third party rather than abstain. Conversely, where a minor party candidate withdraws, it would be expected that turnout would fall as certain opinions in the electorate are no longer represented and deserting major party supporters do not have a third alternative. Table 12.2 shows that turnout fell more in

TABLE 12.2

Mean Turnout Change in By-Elections Compared with Previous General Elections by Structure of Contest

	Contest type				
	Straight fight	*Three-cornered*	*Liberal withdraws*	*Liberal intervenes*	*Significant Independent*
Mean turnout change	-14.7%	-11.1%	-15.5%	-9.6%	-9.0%
Number of contests	154	123	12	82	63

straight fights than in three-cornered contests, but fell most in seats where Liberals withdrew in the by-election. Where a Liberal intervened, turnout fell 5·1 per cent less than in a straight fight. The lowest fall in turnout occurred when a significant third party or Independent stood. It seems plausible to argue that Liberal or other intervention increased turnout by providing an alternative to non-voters at the previous election as well as providing an outlet for the protest vote. We have not attempted a breakdown of turnout change by type of contest and marginality jointly as the number of marginal seats is too small to allow this comparison.

Movements between the parties and abstention influence the parties' shares of the electorate. It was expected that government supporters would be more likely to choose to abstain than opposition supporters because of government unpopularity. Thus, the proposition examined was that government supporters were more likely to protest because of unfulfilled expectations of government outputs than opposition supporters, abstention being one means of protest. Table 12.3 sets out the correlation coefficients[15] of the change in abstention and change in government and opposition shares of the electorate by structure of contest. The correlation between change in opposition proportion of the electorate and change in turnout was slightly

TABLE 12.3

Correlation Coefficients of Change in Government and Opposition Share of the Electorate between General Elections and By-Elections by Turnout Change and Structure of Contest

Contest type	Correl. coeff. of change in government proportion and change in turnout	Correl. coeff. of change in opposition proportion and change in turnout
Straight fights	0·74	0·77
Three-cornered fights	0·69	0·73

higher than the comparative figure for change in government vote in both types of contest. This suggests that, overall, the opposition party was slightly more likely to suffer from abstention than the governing party – a surprising result. How can this be accounted for? Labour was the opposition party for most of our period. Therefore it might be expected that the relationship was indirectly caused by higher proportions of Labour voters abstaining in by-elections; in other words, that party loyalty rates among Labour partisans were much lower than among Conservative partisans. In this case a higher correlation

TABLE 12.4

Correlation Coefficients of Change in Government and Opposition Share of the Electorate between General Elections and Turnout Change when Labour is in Government and Opposition

	Correl. coeff. of change in government share of electorate and change in turnout				Correl. coeff. of change in opposition share of electorate and change in turnout			
	Straight fights	N	Three-cornered	N	Straight fights	N	Three-cornered	N
Labour in government	0·79	(31)	0·58	(40)	0·58	(31)	0·74	(40)
Conservative in government	0·71	(123)	0·78	(70)	0·78	(123)	0·54	(70)

[15] The correlation coefficient used was Pearson's *R*.

between the change in the Labour share of the electorate and change in abstention when Labour was in office or in opposition was expected than the comparative correlation for change in Conservative shares of the electorate.

In straight fights, when Labour was in power or in opposition, the correlation between change in turnout and change in Labour's share of the electorate is, as Table 12.4 shows, higher than the comparable coefficient for the Conservatives. In three-cornered contests, with a Labour Government in power, the correlation coefficient for the change in the Conservative share of the electorate was higher, suggesting that Conservative supporters are more likely to abstain and Labour supporters to go to the Liberals. However, in terms of the majority of contests it seems that Labour supporters were less likely to turn out for their party at by-elections, and this may be the explanation of our finding that differential turnout appears to affect the opposition more than the government.

To summarise our findings on turnout, we can say that, in almost every by-election in our period, turnout fell and recovered at the following general election. This fall varies in magnitude and is related to the 'safeness' or 'marginality' of the seat, and to the structure of the contest. The impact of turnout change upon by-election results appeared that the opposition was more affected than the government. This has been attributed to some extent to lower party loyalty rates among Labour supporters than among Conservatives. We can interpret these findings plausibly using the 'rational choice' model of electoral behaviour.[16] By-elections are 'low salience' because they do not normally change the government. To the individual voter the probability of his vote having an influence upon governmental outputs is lower than at a general election, though there is still a probability of changing existing policies, particularly where the government faces a revolt from its own

---

[16] For the first comprehensive statement of these models, see A. Downs, *An Economic Theory of Democracy* (New York, 1967). For a summary of the critique of the Downsian model, see B. Barry, *Sociologists, Economists and Democracy* (New York, 1970). For an attempt to overcome the criticisms and still retain the basic precepts of the model, see Davis, Hinch and Ordeshook, 'An Expository Development of a Mathematical Model of the Electoral Process', *American Political Science Review*, LXIV (1971).

electors.[17] The probability of having an impact is greater in marginal seats, the actual loss of a seat causing concern to a party, or in seats where third parties stand an increase in their vote causes concern, as for example the Liberal revival of the early-1960s or the Nationalist interventions of the mid-1960s. To Labour stalwarts, particularly after the loss of the three elections in the 1950s, the probability of influencing governmental outputs must have seemed small; therefore they were more likely to abstain. Likewise, when the 1964–70 Labour Government showed itself willing, in its early years, to neglect the views of its supporters, they abstained. The difference between Conservative supporters and Labour supporters when their respective parties are in power may be explained through the level of expectations of governmental outputs which, partly through the promises made by the competing parties, rose exponentially over the period of the 1960s. We continue the development of this model in our next section on the behaviour of government and opposition votes in our period.

Major party support at by-elections

We discuss this in terms of 'government' and 'opposition' party votes, for, despite the differences we have just outlined, we believe that there are elements common to these groupings and related to the experience of governing and being in opposition, rather than to the specific party. First, we examine general aspects of change in government and opposition share of the electorate at by-elections. Given that by-elections are 'low salience' elections and that government supporters were likely, when the government was unpopular, to switch to the oppo-

[17] Barry raises the problem that, for any individual, the probability of influencing the election result is so small that, if the decision to vote is calculated as a multiple of it, nobody would vote. However, in this situation it is always worthwhile for the nth person to vote: he can determine the election. It is countered to this that no voter knows whether or not he is the nth person and, on the other hand, there is a probability that the nth person will decide the election against the individual's preference or interests. It is this uncertainty, the probability of a decision being taken against his interests, that influences his decision to vote, as well as citizen duty and other factors, and therefore we feel justified in using the language of the Downsian model. See Barry, *Sociologists, Economists and Democracy*, pp. 19–23.

sition, we expected that the government's share of the electorate would fall at by-elections compared with previous general
elections. The government party in fact increased its share of
the electorate in only 15 of our 459 by-elections (3 per cent).
Four of these exceptions were three-cornered fights at the
general election where the government party had improved
at the expense of the Liberals, and 7 of the remaining 11 were
straight fights where turnout increased and both government
and opposition improved their shares of the electorate. The mean
fall in the government's proportion of the electorate was 11·5
per cent. The mean fall in the opposition's share of the electorate was 2·9 per cent, implying that, on average, the opposition did 8·6 per cent better than the government in retaining its
share of the electorate. The opposition, without the problem
of satisfying supporters' expectations and with greater freedom
of criticism, could expect to gain votes from supporters of the
government and it would be expected to do relatively better
at by-elections than the government party; therefore its share
of the electorate would fall less or rise more from the previous
general election to the by-election. In 84·8 per cent of cases the
opposition did relatively better than the government.

The exceptions may be explained by three factors. First,
contest structure. The intervention or withdrawal of Liberals
at by-elections seemed to hurt the government party more than
the opposition. Where the Liberals intervened in the by-
election, government party supporters were more likely to
switch to the Liberals than opposition party supporters; or,
conversely, where Liberals withdrew in the by-election, previous
Liberal voters were more likely to switch to the opposition

TABLE 12.5

*Proportion of Contests in which the Government did Better than the Opposition by
Contest Type*

	Structure of contest						
	Straight fight	N	Three-cornered	N	Liberal withdraws	N	Liberal intervenes	N
% of contests in which govt. did relatively better than opposition	19·5	(154)	16·4	(110)	15·9	(34)	16·1	(82)

party than to the government party. Table 12.5 outlines the proportion of seats in which the government did relatively better than the opposition by contest type. The government improved relatively to the opposition more in straight-fight situations than where the Liberals intervened.

A second factor influencing the relative performance of the government and opposition derives from the Labour victory of 1945, where Labour won more than its 'normal' class share.[18] A third of by-elections where the government did relatively better than the opposition were in 1945–50 and 1951–5: in the first case the movement to Labour continuing and then a switch in the early 1950s to more 'normal' rates of class shares for the respective parties.

A third cause appears to be related to the safeness or marginality of the seat. Table 12.6 sets out the proportion of seats where the government did better than the opposition, by safeness or marginality of seat at the previous general election.

TABLE 12.6

Proportion of Seats where the Government did Better than the Opposition by Safeness or Marginality of the Seat at the Previous General Election

		Safeness of seat		
Labour safe	Labour marginal	Conservative marginal	Conservative safe	N
25·5	13·9	6·8	8·9	424

This shows clearly that the government was more likely to do better than the opposition in Labour seats than in Conservative seats, particularly in safe Labour seats. This agrees with our earlier finding that Labour voters were more likely to abstain whether their party is in opposition or government, and abstention was greater in safe seats as the chances of influencing the result, either nationally or locally, or of being able to 'push' the government, were much smaller. The Conservative vote was more loyal, in either government or opposition, and fell less in most kinds of seats.

It is then possible to attribute the phenomenon of the government doing relatively better than the opposition to contest structure, the switch back to the Conservatives in the late 1940s and early 1950s, and the greater propensity of

[18] See Butler and Stokes, *Political Change in Britain*, p. 109.

Labour voters to abstain in by-elections, especially in safe Labour seats.

Our next concern was with the development of our model of by-election behaviour over the life of Parliaments. We assume that a party entering office after a general election will plan over its period of office to maximise votes at the following general election. Second, we suppose that the government has some control over the economy during its period of office. It is apparent that this is a post-Keynesian model derived from post-war experience.[19] Therefore the aim of the government is to create the best possible economic conditions before the following general election, assuming that economic issues are the most salient dimension in the individual's decision on choice of party. It will therefore, given a reasonable majority, prefer to take unpopular economic decisions in the early years of its life, accepting the cost of unpopularity in return for the long-term gain of electoral support from a boom prior to the election. We should then expect that, after its initial popularity after an election, unpopular measures would be taken in the middle years of a government's life and, as these put the economy on a more stable footing, allow a boom to develop in the immediate pre-election period with a consequent increase in popularity. At the level of the individual elector, we can recast the model as follows. After the election of a government there is a 'honeymoon' period when the level of expectations derived from the party's election promises are not expected to be fulfilled immediately: the government is given a chance. However, as the government moves into its middle years, expectations are still unfulfilled, and the government's performance becomes unacceptable to its supporters, who switch votes or abstain. As the election approaches, there are three sets of influences upon the voter to 'home' on his 'normal' party. First, improvements in the economic conditions fulfil, in part, the expectations, which may have been influenced in their level by his experiences in the earlier years of a government's life, that is, revised downwards. Second, the probability of his vote actually influencing the national result of the election is greater than at a

---

[19] Demand management has only been a feature of the post-war period, following the government's acceptance of responsibility for full employment in 1944.

by-election; and third, there are what we may describe as
psychological costs in terms of sanctions of relations, friends
and workmates if he votes for his 'non-normal' party.Therefore
he is encouraged to return to his normal party to minimise
these costs and because his party differential in view of the
government's performance is now revised. To test adequately
this cyclical model of electoral behaviour, we would require
detailed time series at aggregate level, comparable data on the
economy (and unfortunately by-elections are a highly discrete
time series whereas economic data are often a continuous
series), as well as survey data. The opinion polls certainly
seemed to follow this sort of cycle. We tried to test this model
with our by-election data by examining the relative performance of government and opposition over the life-cycle of
post-war Parliaments, our indicator being the differences
between the changes in the opposition share of the electorate
and the changes in the government share of the electorate. A
positive value signifies by how much the government did worse
than the opposition in terms of the change in relative shares of
the electorate, a negative the converse. Table 12.7 presents
these mean differences for post-war Parliaments and governments' year of office.

TABLE 12.7

*Differences between Changes in Opposition Share of Electorate and Changes in
Government Share of Electorate, 1945–72*

Parliament	Party in government	Year of office of government				
		1	2	3	4	5
1945–50	Labour	1·0	11·0	9·3	11·3	–
1950–1	Labour	7·2	6·3	–	–	–
1951–5	Conservative	3·2	3·3	– 2·6	0·8	–
1955–9	Conservative	3·4	10·2	11·2	3·4	–
1959–64	Conservative	5·5	2·3	9·2	8·1	9·0
1964–6	Labour	2·5	– 2·9	–	–	–
1966–70	Labour	10·4	16·7	17·3	13·1	–
1970–	Conservative	6·4	7·0			

The pattern we have described is complete only in the cases
of the Parliaments of 1955–9 and 1966–70, the opposition doing
relatively better in the middle years of the life-cycle of the
government than at either end. However, in four of the five
Parliaments which ran for more than two years, the opposition

did relatively better in the second year of the Parliament than in the first, and in three better in the third than in the second year of office. In three the opposition advantage over the government in its final year of office was less than that in its third year. In both of the two-year Parliaments the opposition did relatively worse in the election year than in the previous year. It therefore seems that, though the complete cycle only exists for two parliaments, there are elements of the cycle in others. Indeed, we can interpret this in terms of the development of demand-management politics in the post-war period, the cycle appearing for the first time in the 1955–9 period in its entirety, being modified in the 1959–64 Parliament by the Labour split in 1960 and the continuance of the Conservatives into a third period of office, and then reappearing in 1966–70, perhaps the classic case of the cycle. The signs are that this will be followed in the 1970 Parliament, though of course we have the impact of the Common Market to contend with in terms of the unknown nature of economic difficulties this is likely to create. Turning to the inter-war period, we should not expect the cycle to operate as governments were generally pessimistic about the efficacy of intervention in the economy, and of course had not accepted the responsibility for full employment and for rising living standards which has created a revolution of expectations. We should, however, anticipate that by-election results would broadly follow the trend of economic distress, as electors turned from Conservative to Labour and then to the National Government as a solution to the economic situation. We present similar data to the post-war period for the pre-war period in Table 12.8.

TABLE 12.8

Differences between Changes in Opposition Share of Electorate and Changes in Government Share of Electorate, 1923–39

Parliament	Party in government	Year of office of government				
		1	2	3	4	5
1923–4	Labour	− 0·7	−	−	−	−
1924–9	Conservative	7·4	9·5	8·7	11·5	15·8
1929–31	Labour	2·7	6·7	14·8	−	−
1931–5	National Government	17·6	25·8	22·2	29·9	−
1935–9	National Government	7·0	8·4	8·2	6·1	−

The 1923–4 Labour Government did slightly better than the Conservatives, but it was of course a minority government in the first place. The Conservatives up to 1929 did steadily worse as the economy went deeper into the mire, and though the Labour Government of 1929 started with a fund of goodwill this steadily evaporated as they proved unable to halt the downslide in the economy. The apparent dramatic slide in the fortunes of the National Government is in part a reflection of Labour's collapse in 1931. Only those who would vote Labour under almost any conceivable circumstances (in model terms, those whose preference functions ranked Labour very high and the Conservatives very low on all dimensions of partisan issues) voted Labour in 1931, so that is was very difficult for their vote to decrease, whereas the National Government share, with an artificially high proportion of the electorate, could decrease much more. After 1935, with a more even party balance, the opposition did less well and the approach of the impending 1940 general election was marked by an improvement in the National Government's fortunes.

Thus it is possible, on an impressionistic basis, to interpret by-election results in terms of the economic models of party and electoral behaviour. It would be desirable to have a 'politico-econometric' model of the inter-war years using the economic indicators and a form of spectral analysis to iron out the overall trends in partisanship in the period (the decline of the Liberals and the growth of the Labour Party), but our data were not sophisticated enough to attempt this.

We now address ourselves to a consideration of the volatility of by-election behaviour. The 'volatility' argument derives from the 'trench warfare' model of the electorate, that there are two main armies of approximately equal strength who occupy entrenched positions on the political battlefield. Their leaders are fighting for the electoral 'no-man's-land' in the middle, the floating voter. The volatility argument refers to the changes in the relative size of the three groups, 'solid' Conservative voters, 'solid' Labour voters and 'floaters', to change over time. If volatility increases, the solid cores of major party support are smaller, and a larger proportion of the electorate is willing to 'float'. In terms of the 'mover–stayer' model of change, a higher proportion of the electorate can be classified as 'movers'. We should expect that such movements would be reflected in our indicator of government and opposition changes in by-elections, so that in periods when there was a good deal of switching between the parties, the value of the relative performance indicator would be higher. An examination of Tables 12.7 and 12.8 shows that there were two periods when there is a very high positive difference between the change in the opposition and government share of the electorate, 1931–5 and 1966–70. Analysis of these illustrates the major differences between pre-war and post-war politics. Over the 1931–5 period Labour was recovering from its collapse in 1931 at the expense of a National Government labouring under very high unemployment and balance-of-payments problems, these two factors inducing greater switching within the electorate than previously. In 1966–70 unemployment was much lower by comparison, and balance-of-payments problems much less acute, but expectations of government outputs had changed very considerably in the interim. It is interesting, in terms of our model of voting, to point out that the greatest volatility has occurred when, compared with earlier periods, the economy has been going badly. There are, however, signs that in the 1970s some adjustment of the level of expectations of electors has been made, with a much lower difference between the relative performance of the two major parties than under the previous Labour Government.

The Liberal Party and Independents in by-elections

We now turn to the performance of parties other than Conservatives and Labour at by-elections, Liberal and Independent candidates. The Liberals, over the whole period, contested just over one-half of the selected by-elections, 229 out of 459. In the majority of contests (136) they fought at both the by-election and the previous general election; in the other 93 they intervened at the by-election. This illustrates the value of by-elections to the Liberals, intervention giving them the chance to capitalise on protest against the major parties and to gain publicity from the media's concentration upon a single event. The Liberal Party, in all seats where they stood at by-elections, won an average of 14·8 per cent of the electorate.

Their mean vote in seats where they intervened at the by-election was 10·9 per cent, compared with 17·5 per cent in those seats fought at the previous general election. The mean change in the Liberals' share of the electorate between previous general election and by-election was −2·3 per cent, slightly less than the mean fall in the major opposition party vote of −2·9 per cent. It seems that the Liberal vote held up well at by-elections, but this was probably due in large measure to defections of other major party supporters to the Liberals. Voting Liberal is a reasonable alternative for government supporters. It enables them to express a protest against the government while not incurring the possible psychological costs of voting for the opposition. We should therefore expect a higher correlation between change in government vote and change in Liberal vote (or absolute level of Liberal vote at by-elections where the Liberals intervened) than between change in opposition vote and change in Liberal vote. The correlation coefficients for the Liberal change in vote and major party votes are presented in Table 12.9. This shows that, in three-cornered fights, the correlation of change in government share

TABLE 12.9

Correlation Coefficients between Change in Liberal Share of the Electorate and Government and Opposition Shares of the Electorate by Contest Type

	Coeff. of change in Liberal proportion with change in government proportion	Coeff. of change in Liberal proportion with change in opposition proportion	N
Three-party contests	0·58	0·44	110
Liberal interventions	0·22	0·33	82

of the electorate and change in Liberal share was greater than for change in opposition share and change in Liberal share. This suggests that the Liberals benefited more from desertions from the government party than from desertions from the opposition. This finding may reflect other factors which we have been unable to control for. However, where Liberals intervened, the relationship was reversed, suggesting that the Liberals have taken more from the opposition than from the government. We can offer the tentative explanation that, as Liberals have tended to intervene in safe Conservative seats, Labour voters, aware that their party cannot win, were willing to turn to the Liberals.

With the exception of Nationalist candidates, the performance of Independents at by-elections was difficult to compare with previous general elections as many only stood at the by-election to gain publicity from media concentration on one constituency. For this reason we have confined ourselves to examining the sources of their support. Candidates from other than the three major parties stood in 145 of our selected by-elections, 32 per cent of the total. The mean share of the electorate of Independents and others was 6·1 per cent. Table 12.10 presents a frequency distribution of proportion of the electorate gained by other candidates. In 83·4 per cent of

TABLE 12.10

Frequency Distribution of Proportions of the Electorate Gained by Independents and Others in By-Elections

Proportion of the electorate	N	Cumulative frequency as % of total
0–5%	86	59·3
5–10%	35	83·4
10–15%	7	88·3
15–20%	6	92·4
20–25%	2	93·8
25–30%	4	96·6
30–35%	4	99·3
35% +	1	100·0

contests, Independent and other candidates collectively failed to get more than 10 per cent of the electorate. In 65 per cent of contests, the main Independent or other candidate failed to gain more than 5 per cent of the electorate ($N = 50$), and in only 7 per cent of cases did the main other candidate get more than 20 per cent of the electorate ($N = 10$). Of these 10 contests, 7 were in the period 1966–70 and were related to the resurgence of Welsh and Scottish Nationalism. There are signs that this may be becoming a permanent protest in by-elections, with the Scottish Nationalists gaining 21 per cent of the electorate in Stirling in 1970 and Plaid Cymru gaining 29 per cent in Merthyr in 1972.

We then analysed the origin of Independent and other votes at by-elections by examining the correlation coefficients of the relationship between Independent change in government party vote and change in opposition party vote. Both correlations are very low, as Table 12.11 shows, but the correlation of the change in government vote with change in Independent vote

TABLE 12.11

Correlation Coefficients of Change in Other and Independent Share of Electorate and Change in Government and Opposition Shares

Coefficient of Independent and other share of electorate with change in government share	*Coefficient of Independent and other share of electorate with change in opposition share*
0·30	0·13

is greater than the correlation with change in opposition vote, the implication being that, overall, the Independent vote is composed more of government than of opposition defectors.

Our conclusion is that Other candidates and Liberals over the period have been a 'safety-valve' for discontented government supporters rather than for opposition supporters, a means of putting pressure upon the government during its term of office. The individual elector was making a 'strategic vote', voting for a third party or Independent to express his disapproval of government performance. It is a purely temporary vote which generally evaporates at the following general election when the probability of influencing the result, and the importance of the result, are greater.

Movement within the electorate at by-elections

We have also attempted to disaggregate the components of electoral change, using a recently developed technique described by Miller.[20] This technique is a modified regression method by which direct estimates of the cell proportions can be obtained. We call these proportions 'rates' as they measure the rate of movement between choices. A group of contests must be selected which are assumed to be homogeneous in the

[20] Miller, op. cit.

sense that the matrix of rates is statistically equal across them: in other words, that individual deviations around the mean rates estimated for the whole group are random. In practical terms this means that the types of contest must be treated separately, for there is associated with each type a different matrix of rates. Furthermore, we are making strong assumptions in applying this technique to a group of contests which may be spread over a long period of time. However, it was felt that the special characteristics of the by-election situation, with important factors operating independently of time, allow a cautious use of the ridge regression technique. Inferences have been made on the basis of a comparison of the relative magnitude of the rates, rather than on their specific values.

The basic equations for estimating the rates for straight fights are:

$$g_b = p_{11}g_E + p_{21}o_E + p_{31}a_E$$
$$o_b = p_{12}g_E + p_{22}o_E + p_{32}a_E$$
$$a_b = p_{13}g_E + p_{23}o_E + p_{33}a_E$$

where g_B, o_B and a_B are the known proportions of the electorate voting for the government, voting for the opposition and abstaining respectively at the by-election, and g_E, o_E and a_E are the corresponding known proportions at the preceding general election. The p's are the rates to be estimated as shown in the matrix on p. 333 above.

Miller points out that the technique can be applied as long as the rates do not depend upon the variables in the equation (here, the proportions choosing the various alternatives at the general election). He suggested that the basic model is inadequate because the rates are likely to depend upon the degree of partisanship. Similarly, our basic equations are refined by the inclusion of a variable measuring the marginality of the contest as it was felt that the rates are likely to differ in marginal seats from those in safe seats in a by-election situation.

Following Miller, the first equation for the refined model is[21]

$$g_B = (p_{11} + p^1_{11}M)g_E + (p_{21} + p^1_{21}M)o_E + (p_{31} + p^1_{31}M)a_E$$

[21] The model as now presented includes high intercorrelations and the ridge regression method is necessary in order to get stable estimates of the rates. The application of the technique is most satisfactory when other evidence of the magnitude of the rates is available. We have none here, another reason for cautious interpretation.

with similar equations for o_B and a_B. M, the marginality variable, was defined to have value 1 if the contest is marginal (a difference of less than 10 per cent between the government and opposition shares of the total vote at the general election). In this formulation, p_{11}, p_{21}, p_{31} are the rates of movement from electors to the government at the by-elections from the government party, opposition party and abstentions in safe seats, and p^1_{11}, p^1_{21} and p^1_{31} are the increments in the rates associated with marginal seats. The estimates for the rates for straight fights are presented separately for safe seats and marginal seats in the following section.

We have applied the ridge regression technique only to straight-fight contests. The three-cornered situation is much more difficult to deal with and the assumptions of the method are much more likely to be unreasonable. In particular, there are several important reasons why this was not attempted. First, the attraction of the Liberals has varied considerably over the time period. Second, there are likely to be complex dependences of the rates on such factors as the chances of the Liberals winning the seat and marginality, and an insufficient number of contests are available for such an investigation.

Party loyalty rates were higher for both the government and the opposition in general elections, as Table 12.12 demonstrates. In safe seats there was little difference between the loyalty rates. However, the opposition gained more from government supporters switching than vice versa. Opposition supporters were more likely to move to abstention, but this was compensated to some extent by higher rates of movement from abstention to the opposition than to the government. In marginal seats, previous voters were more likely to turn out than in safe seats. Opposition party supporters are more loyal than government party supporters, though still slightly more likely to switch to abstention. There was much greater switching between the parties in marginal seats but a higher rate of switching to the opposition than from the opposition. There was slightly more movement between previous abstention and voting at the by-election than in safe seats, the opposition benefiting from this. Overall, this supports our earlier proposition that the opposition was more likely to be hurt by differential abstention but more likely to

TABLE 12.12

Rates of Electoral Movement in Straight Fights Controlling for 'Safeness' and 'Marginality' of Seat[a]

		'Safe' seats By-election					'Marginal' seats By-election		
		Govt.	Opp.	Abst.			Govt.	Opp.	Abst.
General election	Govt.	74	5	(21)		Govt.	77	13	(10)
	Opp.	0	73	(27)	General election	Opp.	6	81	(13)
	Abst.	-2	9	(93)		Abst.	-1	10	(91)

[a] (Ridge regression parameter $K = 0.10$.) Note that the matrices include negative values for rates of movement from abstention to the government. This is partly caused by the over-representation of the true number of abstentions in election results as some electors on the electoral roll will have left the constituency or died by the time of the by-election.

gain from switching from the government party and from abstention.

Conclusions on the behaviour of the electorate at by-elections

We have tried, using aggregate data, to indicate some aspects of the behaviour of the electorate in by-elections over the past half-century. Our account of such behaviour has been cast in terms of the 'rational choice' model of political behaviour which, at macro-level, provides a plausible interpretation of our findings. A by-election was less salient to the elector than a general election. This was reflected in a lower turnout. The salience of the election was influenced by the marginality of the seat and the candidatures of minor parties. The by-election allows government supporters to register their approval or disapproval of government policy and disapproval is expressed in switching to the opposition or to minor parties. Opposition supporters were more likely to switch to abstention. Governments generally did worse than the opposition at by-elections and this was related, after 1945, to the life-cycle of the government, while generally following economic trends before the war. Liberal and minor parties were able to cash in on protest against the government, as well as attracting some of those who had previously abstained.

We are well aware of the dangers of making inferences about individual behaviour from aggregate data, and must hope that survey work will further test some of the implications for individual behaviour which we have proposed on the basis of our analysis. However, we do feel that this analysis has shown that there is much of interest to the political scientist in by-election behaviour, particularly in the translation of opinion into voting during the life-cycle of a government, which has so far been a neglected area of electoral sociology.

Appendixes

The Results of Contested By-Elections

The following is a list of all contested by-elections from 1919 to March 1973, excluding only Irish, University and double-Member constituencies. Irish seats (1919–22) and Ulster seats (from 1923) are not comparable because of the different structure of parties; University seats and double-Member seats are not comparable because of different voting systems. Nor were any of these categories in themselves a continuous run of comparable results covering the whole period of the book. The seats excluded are listed in chronological order on p. 386.

For actual numbers of votes cast, for an explanation of party allegiances and for the results of succeeding general elections, information can be found in F. W. S. Craig's *British Parliamentary Election Results, 1918–1970*, 2 vols. (1969, 1971).

In the following table, only official Labour, Conservative and Liberal candidates are listed in these columns. Coalition Liberals (1918–23), National Liberals (1931–45), National candidates (1931–45), Scottish and Welsh Nationalists, Communists and all minor party candidates or Independents are list as 'Others'. Where the votes of more than one candidate are aggregated in the 'Others' column, a superior numeral shows the actual number of other candidates. Where a seat changed hands at the by-election, it is marked *, and where the by-election was a second contest in the same seat in a single Parliament it is marked †.

All swing figures are calculated between Conservative and Labour candidates only, a plus figure being a swing to Conservative and a minus figure being a swing to Labour. Whenever Conservative and Labour were not first *and* second at both the preceding general election and at the by-election, the swing figure is printed in italics.

Butler swing (also called 'conventional swing') is calculated from the mean shares of total votes cast at the preceding general election and at the by-election which were cast for Conservative and Labour candidates. *Steed swing* (also called 'two-party swing') is calculated from the mean shares of the Conservative and Labour votes cast at the preceding general election and at the by-election which were cast for the Conservative and Labour candidates. *Goguel swing* (also called 'electorate swing') is calculated from the mean shares of the total electorate at the preceding general election and at the by-election who voted for the Conservative and Labour candidates.

It is possible, and relatively easy, to calculate a Butler swing between any two parties that contested both the preceding general election and the by-election, from the figures printed below. This is done using the following formula:

Where X_1 is the percentage gained by X at the preceding general election, X_2 the percentage gained by X at the by-election, Y_1 the percentage gained by Y at the preceding general election, and Y_2 the percentage gained by Y at the by-election:

$$\text{Percentage swing from } X \text{ to } Y = \frac{(X_1 - X_2) + (Y_2 - Y_1)}{2}\%.$$

For example, at Manchester Rusholme on 7 October 1919 the swing from Conservative to Liberal was:

$$\frac{(65\cdot1 - 47\cdot7) + (19\cdot1 - 19\cdot3)}{2} = 8\cdot6\%.$$

In the same by-election the swing from Labour to Liberal was:

$$\frac{(15\cdot6 - 31\cdot2) + (19\cdot1 - 19\cdot3)}{2} = -7\cdot9\%.$$

By-Election and Date	Previous Gen. Election Con. %	Lab. %	Lib. %	Others %	Turnout %	By-Election Result Con. %	Lab. %	Lib. %	Others %	Turnout %	Swing to Con. Butler	Steed	Goguel
Liverpool, West Derby 26 Feb 19	67·4	32·6	–	–	55·1	56·5	43·5	–	–	34·3	−10·9	−10·9	−7·4
*Leyton, West 1 Mar 19	67·5	–	32·6	–	49·9	42·7	–	57·3	–	42·5	–	–	–
*Kingston-upon-Hull, Central 29 Mar 19	80·1	–	19·9	–	54·9	47·2	–	52·8	–	51·9	–	–	–
*Aberdeenshire, Central & Kincardine 16 Apr 19	52·6	–	47·4	–	47·3	36·1	26·4	37·5	–	50·2	–	–	–
Swansea, East 10 July 19	–	36·4	–	63·6	64·1	–	46·9	–	53·1	64·0	–	–	–
*Lanarks, Bothwell 16 July 19	50·9	49·1	–	–	69·2	–	68·8	–	31·2	71·9	–	–	–
*Lancs, Widnes 30 Aug 19	59·6	40·5	–	–	63·0	47·7	52·3	–	–	71·1	−11·8	−11·8	−7·6
Yorks, Pontefract 6 Sep 19	–	37·1	–	62·9	45·6	–	46·0	–	54·0	61·5	–	–	–
Manchester, Rusholme 7 Oct 19	65·1	15·6	19·3	–	62·9	45·7	31·2	19·1	4·0	67·5	−17·5	−21·2	−10·7
Durham, Chester-le-Street 13 Nov 19	–	Unop.	–	–	–	–	77·1	–	23·0	63·7	–	–	–
Croydon, South 14 Nov 19	71·8	28·2	–	–	55·0	55·2	–	44·8	–	45·5	–	–	–
Kent, Isle of Thanet 15 Nov 19	Unop.	–	–	–	Unop.	57·9	–	42·1	–	52·8	–	–	–
Plymouth, Sutton 15 Nov 19	66·0	20·6	13·5	–	59·7	51·9	33·3	14·8	–	72·5	−13·4	−15·3	−6·8
Herts, St Albans 10 Dec 19	Unop.	–	–	–	Unop.	45·8	42·4	11·8	–	62·8	–	–	–
Bromley 17 Dec 19	79·5	–	20·5	–	52·0	52·5	47·5	–	–	48·9	–	–	–
Yorks, Spen Valley 20 Dec 19	–	44·4	–	55·6	49·4	–	39·4	33·8	26·8	76·5	–	–	–
Ashton-under-Lyne 31 Jan 20	58·3	–	–	41·7	68·4	43·2	39·6	17·1	–	82·3	–	–	–
*Shrops., Wrekin 7 Feb 20	–	–	–	Unop.	–	–	38·4	–	61·6[2]	71·0	–	–	–
Paisley 12 Feb 20	–	33·5	34·0	32·5	57·6	12·5	39·1	48·4	–	77·6	–	–	–
Lincs, Horncastle 25 Feb 20	54·3	–	45·7	–	68·2	44·5	18·8	36·7	–	77·1	–	–	–
Argyll 10 Mar 20	–	–	–	100·0[2]	52·0	–	35·0	–	65·0	50·2	–	–	–
*Kent, Dartford 27 Mar 20	–	28·6	–	71·4	47·9	15·6	50·1	16·8	17·5[2]	61·3	–	–	–
Camberwell, N.-West 31 Mar 20	36·1	–	23·0	63·9	36·5	–	32·1	23·0	44·9	47·9	−5·9	−2·7	−2·9
Hants, Basingstoke 31 Mar 20	64·1	35·9	–	–	55·2	44·2	27·8	28·0	–	60·0	–	–	–
Northampton 1 Apr 20	–	37·4	62·7	–	62·5	–	44·4	–	55·6	67·2	–	–	–

By-Election and Date	Previous Gen. Election					By-Election Result					Swing to Con.		
	Con. %	Lab. %	Lib. %	Others %	Turnout %	Con. %	Lab. %	Lib. %	Others %	Turnout %	Butler	Steed	Goguel
Edinburgh, North — 9 Apr 20	63·0	—	37·0	—	53·0	44·8	17·1	38·1	—	62·3	—	—	—
Edinburgh, South — 9 Apr 20	75·0	—	25·0	—	61·8	57·8	—	42·3	—	59·3	—	—	—
*Lincs., Louth — 3 June 20	54·5	—	45·5	—	60·3	42·7	—	57·3	—	63·1	—	—	—
Nelson & Colne — 17 June 20	—	62·0	38·0	—	52·3	30·1	49·6	20·4	—	65·2	—	—	—
*Norfolk, South — 27 July 20	—	35·7	64·3	—	55·8	—	45·7	19·8	34·5	58·5	—	—	—
Suffolk, Woodbridge — 28 July 20	55·9	—	44·2	—	51·0	53·2	46·8	—	—	61·4	—	—	—
Ilford — 25 Sep 20	60·8	19·5	13·7	—	58·3	54·4	22·9	22·7	—	66·2	−7·9	−7·1	−3·4
†Shrops., Wrekin — 20 Nov 20	—	Unop.	—	—	—	—	42·1	—	57·9	78·3	—	—	—
Mon., Abertillery — 21 Dec 20	—	Unop.	—	—	—	—	66·4	—	33·6	70·8	—	—	—
Rhondda, West — 21 Dec 20	—	—	—	—	—	41·5	58·5	—	—	70·2	—	—	—
Herefs., Hereford — 11 Jan 21	75·8	24·2	—	—	54·6	56·6	—	43·4	—	62·5	—	—	—
*Kent, Dover — 12 Jan 21	68·7	—	31·3	—	46·6	43·7	—	—	56·3	71·0	—	—	—
Cardiganshire — 18 Feb 21	—	Unop.	—	—	—	—	—	42·7	57·3	80·1	—	—	—
*Woolwich, East — 2 Mar 21	—	—	—	—	—	51·3	48·7	—	—	78·5	—	—	—
*Dudley — 3 Mar 21	60·2	39·9	—	—	60·4	49·3	50·7	—	—	79·9	−10·8	−10·8	−6·7
*Kirkcaldy Burghs — 4 Mar 21	—	—	—	—	—	—	53·4	—	46·6	65·6	—	—	—
*Yorks., Penistone — 5 Mar 21	36·2	24·4	39·4	—	58·4	—	36·2	33·7	30·1	71·7	—	—	—
Somerset, Taunton — 8 Apr 21	72·4	27·6	—	—	60·4	61·1	39·0	—	—	73·5	−11·3	−11·3	−5·4
Worcs., Bewdley — 19 Apr 21	Unop.	—	—	—	—	89·6	—	10·4	—	63·8	—	—	—
Beds., Bedford — 23 Apr 21	—	—	—	100·0[2]	45·2	—	40·3	—	59·7	73·3	—	—	—
Hastings — 4 May 21	75·9	24·1	—	—	59·2	54·7	24·5	19·9	—	78·0	−11·3	−7·7	−3·9
Cumberland, Penrith & Cockermouth — 13 May 21	Unop.	—	—	—	—	50·1	—	49·9	—	74·0	—	—	—
*Westminster, St George's — 7 June 21	90·2	—	9·8	—	39·9	42·5	—	—	57·5	39·8	—	—	—
*Lancs., Heywood & Radcliffe — 8 June 21	—	32·4	—	67·6	52·2	—	41·7	17·6	40·7	80·9	—	—	—
Herts., Hertford — 16 June 21	—	9·1	—	90·9[2]	57·4	31·1	—	—	69·0	55·2	—	—	—

–	54·8	45·2	–	64·0	Glam., Caerphilly	24 Aug 21	–	54·3	–	45·7[2]	73·2	–	–	–
Unop.	–	–	–	–	Westminster, Abbey	25 Aug 21	43·6	–	21·5	34·9	38·5	–	–	–
Unop.	–	–	–	–	Lewisham, West	13 Sep 21	39·0	–	25·6	35·4	59·3	–	–	–
54·5	–	45·5	–	60·3	†Lincs., Louth	22 Sep 21	38·3	19·5	42·2	–	72·1	–	–	–
–	63·9	36·1	–	61·6	Lancs., Westhoughton	5 Oct 21	–	57·8	–	42·2	84·7	–	–	–
Unop.	–	–	–	–	Hornsey	10 Nov 21	53·4	–	46·6	–	65·7	–	–	–
–	27·4	–	72·6	36·1	*Southwark, South-East	14 Dec 21	–	57·0	–	43·0[2]	38·5	–	–	–
Unop.	–	–	–	–	Warwicks., Tamworth	17 Jan 22	68·8	31·2	–	–	60·0	–	–	–
61·6	38·4	–	–	57·5	*Manchester, Clayton	18 Feb 22	43·0	57·1	–	–	73·7	−18·7	−18·7	−11·9
58·0	21·0	21·0	–	39·2	*Camberwell, North	20 Feb 22	46·1	53·9	–	–	50·8	*−22·4*	*−27·3*	*−9·2*
58·4	–	41·6	–	69·1	*Cornwall, Bodmin	24 Feb 22	43·6	–	56·5	–	74·8	–	–	–
56·8	43·3	–	–	63·3	Wolverhampton, West	7 Mar 22	54·9	45·1	–	–	80·0	−1·9	−1·9	−0·4
75·3	24·7	–	–	61·0	Cambridge	16 Mar 22	48·7	31·1	20·2	–	80·4	−16·5	−14·3	−8·3
–	–	–	100·0[2]	37·3	Inverness	16 Mar 22	–	–	49·0	51·0	50·1	–	–	–
80·7	19·3	–	–	48·0	Surrey, Chertsey	24 Mar 22	55·5	–	44·6	–	55·4	–	–	–
–	27·1	–	72·9	65·6	*Leicester, East	30 Mar 22	–	52·9	14·4	32·8	71·3	–	–	–
65·7	19·4	–	14·9	49·5	Nottingham, East	29 June 22	52·3	27·3	20·4	–	66·3	−10·7	−11·5	−3·2
–	54·8	45·2	–	62·2	Glam., Gower	20 July 22	–	57·5	–	42·5	73·1	–	–	–
1·1	42·8	–	56·1	68·3	*Glam., Pontypridd	25 July 22	–	57·0	–	43·0	72·9	–	–	–
–	–	–	100·0[2]	55·4	*Hackney, South	18 Aug 22	50·2	49·8	–	–	56·3	–	–	–
–	41·0	–	59·0[2]	62·2	*Newport	18 Oct 22	40·0	33·8	26·2	–	79·2	–	–	–
68·7	–	31·3	–	73·7	Portsmouth, South	13 Dec 22	62·9	–	–	37·1	57·7	–	–	–
–	43·2	30·0	26·9	73·7	Newcastle-upon-Tyne, East	17 Jan 23	26·8	45·7	27·6	–	76·4	–	–	–
22·4	40·2	37·4	–	64·1	Stepney, Whitechapel	8 Feb 23	–	57·0	42·1	0·9	60·5	–	–	–
49·7	33·8	16·5	–	88·0	Darlington	28 Feb 23	56·6	43·4	–	–	85·4	−1·4	−2·9	−1·4
65·0	–	35·0	–	52·7	*Surrey, Mitcham	3 Mar 23	34·1	38·0	15·2	12·7	66·2	–	–	–
52·8	–	47·2	–	58·4	*Willesden, East	3 Mar 23	39·4	–	60·6	–	60·2	–	–	–
59·8	–	40·2	–	70·5	*Liverpool, Edge Hill	6 Mar 23	47·3	52·6	–	–	58·1	–	–	–
–	54·2	–	45·8	80·5	*Anglesey	7 Apr 23	16·2	30·5	53·3	–	76·4	–	–	–
66·4	–	–	33 7	71·6	Shrops., Ludlow	19 Apr 23	55·0	7·8	37·2	–	73·0	–	–	–

By-Election and Date	Previous Gen. Election					By-Election Result					Swing to Con.		
	Con. %	Lab. %	Lib. %	Others %	Turnout %	Con. %	Lab. %	Lib. %	Others %	Turnout %	Butler	Steed	Goguel
*Northumberland, Berwick-upon-Tweed 31 May 23	—	—	38·1	61·9	66·2	55·0	18·2	26·8	—	74·9	—	—	—
*Devon, Tiverton 21 June 23	46·9	6·6	46·5	—	80·1	48·1	2·1	49·8	—	88·1	2·9	8·3	4·2
Morpeth 21 June 23	19·5	48·4	32·2	—	72·1	—	60·5	39·5	—	76·9	-8·0	—	—
Leeds, Central 26 July 23	50·1	27·8	22·2	—	66·1	47·6	41·4	11·0	—	64·3	-8·0	-10·8	-5·3
†Portsmouth, South 13 Aug 23	68·7	—	31·3	—	73·7	54·9	—	45·1	—	54·9	—	—	—
Somerset, Yeovil 30 Oct 23	61·8	38·3	—	—	73·0	46·6	28·7	24·8	—	80·8	-2·8	0·1	-1·4
Rutland & Stamford 30 Oct 23	46·8	32·9	—	20·3	81·2	57·1	42·9	—	—	71·5	0·2	-1·6	-0·5
Burnley 28 Feb 24	31·8	37·8	30·4	—	87·3	41·6	58·4	—	—	82·4	-5·4	-4·1	-4·3
Westminster, Abbey 19 Mar 24	Unop.				—	35·9	27·0	1·3	35·8	61·6	—	—	—
*Liverpool, West Toxteth 22 May 24	50·3	49·7	—	—	66·1	45·7	54·3	—	—	76·2	-4·6	-4·6	-3·5
Glasgow, Kelvingrove 23 May 24	42·9	39·0	18·1	—	68·2	55·3	39·8	4·9	—	70·5	5·8	5·7	4·1
*Oxford 5 June 24	43·9	—	56·1	—	83·5	47·8	13·1	39·1	—	80·3	—	—	—
Sussex, Lewes 9 July 24	59·6	40·4	—	—	58·1	52·0	33·2	14·8	—	67·3	-0·2	1·5	0·8
*Lincs, Holland-with-Boston 31 July 24	45·9	54·1	—	—	68·8	39·6	37·1	23·3	—	77·2	5·3	5·7	3·8
Carms, Carmarthen 14 Aug 24	30·1	24·8	45·1	—	78·3	27·2	28·8	44·0	—	78·9	-3·5	-6·3	-2·7
Walsall 27 Feb 25	37·9	28·7	31·8	1·6	86·2	38·2	30·0	31·8	—	83·4	-0·5	-0·9	-0·6
Ayr Burghs 12 June 25	62·3	37·7	—	—	73·5	46·3	35·2	18·6	—	71·0	-6·7	-5·4	-5·1
Sussex, Eastbourne 17 June 25	67·9	16·0	16·1	—	77·6	58·4	16·9	24·7	—	65·5	-5·2	-3·4	-6·5
Gloucs., Forest of Dean 14 July 25	46·9	53·2	—	—	70·0	35·9	48·4	15·7	—	80·9	-3·1	-4·3	-2·9
Galloway 17 Nov 25	53·1	—	46·9	—	76·8	43·4	16·9	39·7	—	83·3	—	—	—
Suffolk, Bury St Edmunds 1 Dec 25	63·1	—	36·9	—	81·8	62·8	—	37·2	—	74·0	—	—	—
Yorks., Ripon 5 Dec 25	Unop.				—	59·0	—	41·0	—	74·6	—	—	—

Constituency	Date																
Dunbartonshire	29 Jan 26	55·8	44·2	—	—	75·6	48·0	43·9	8·1	—	75·0	-3·7	-3·6	-2·8
Renfrewshire, East	29 Jan 26	55·7	44·3	—	—	83·5	52·0	48·0	—	—	75·2	-3·7	-3·7	-3·2
*Darlington	17 Feb 26	53·8	46·2	—	—	86·1	43·3	44·4	12·3	—	87·6	-4·4	-4·5	-3·8
Lanarks., Bothwell	28 Mar 26	43·7	56·3	—	—	79·3	35·2	59·7	5·1	—	74·2	-5·9	-6·6	-4·1
*East Ham, North	29 Apr 26	39·4	35·8	—	24·6	77·6	34·5	40·6	24·9	—	71·7	-4·9	-6·6	-3·6
Yorks., Buckrose	5 May 26	56·0	—	—	44·0	82·3	48·7	8·8	42·5	—	81·7	—	—	—
*Hammersmith, North	28 May 26	54·1	45·9	—	—	74·2	38·6	53·3	8·0	—	72·2	-11·4	-12·1	-8·3
Wallsend	21 July 26	47·6	52·4	—	—	85·4	30·1	57·7	12·2	—	82·9	-11·4	-13·3	-9·4
Cumberland, North	17 Sep 26	54·2	10·9	—	34·9	86·0	47·5	15·1	37·1	—	82·0	-5·3	-7·2	-5·2
Yorks., Howdenshire	25 Nov 26	Unop.	—	—	—	—	54·2	11·8	34·0	—	73·6	—	—	—
*Kingston-upon-Hull, Central	29 Nov 26	45·9	—	54·1	—	77·1	37·6	52·9	9·5	—	82·8	—	—	—
Essex, Chelmsford	30 Nov 26	54·7	10·0	35·3	—	77·1	47·9	22·0	30·2	—	70·5	-9·4	-16·0	-8·1
Smethwick	21 Dec 26	47·7	52·3	—	—	78·2	33·7	57·1	9·2	—	78·6	-9·4	-10·6	-7·4
*Worcs., Stourbridge	23 Feb 27	39·5	34·8	25·7	—	83·7	34·0	41·9	24·1	—	79·8	-6·3	-8·3	-5·1
Leith	23 Mar 27	—	40·4	59·6	—	70·5	15·7	42·0	42·4	—	73·9	—	—	—
*Southwark, North	28 Mar 27	17·9	43·9	38·3	—	71·5	19·2	36·9	43·9	—	62·8	4·2	5·3	3·7
*Leics., Bosworth	31 May 27	34·9	31·5	33·6	—	80·8	24·5	37·3	38·2	—	84·6	-8·1	-12·9	-6·8
Wilts., Westbury	16 June 27	44·2	18·1	37·7	—	84·9	40·1	20·4	39·5	—	84·6	-3·2	-4·6	-2·8
Lambeth, Brixton	27 June 27	56·6	25·9	17·5	—	69·4	48·1	28·0	30·9	—	53·9	-5·3	-5·4	-5·2
Southend-on-Sea	19 Nov 27	62·5	8·4	29·1	—	79·3	54·7	12·3	30·7	2·4	73·2	-5·9	-6·5	-6·0
Kent, Canterbury	24 Nov 27	70·3	—	29·7	—	65·9	57·3	—	42·7	—	60·8	—	—	—
*Northampton	9 Jan 28	40·0	37·2	23·3	—	87·0	36·1	37·5	23·7	2·7	84·2	-1·9	-2·5	-1·6
Kent, Faversham	25 Jan 28	46·9	29·9	23·2	—	73·9	41·6	36·2	18·6	3·5	72·4	-5·8	-7·7	-4·4
Bristol, West	2 Feb 28	79·0	21·0	—	—	75·1	57·2	26·0	16·8	—	67·6	-13·4	-10·2	-11·2
*Lancs., Lancaster	9 Feb 28	47·8	17·5	34·8	—	82·9	38·2	18·1	43·7	—	82·7	-5·1	-5·4	-4·3
Ilford	23 Feb 28	58·4	21·7	19·9	—	74·8	44·8	21·9	33·4	—	67·5	-6·9	-5·8	-6·0
*Cornwall, St Ives	6 Mar 28	53·0	—	47·0	Unop.	69·1	39·4	18·1	42·6	—	77·4	—	—	—
Middlesbrough, West	7 Mar 28	—	—	—	—	—	27·8	36·0	36·3	—	82·2	—	—	—
*Linlithgowshire	4 Apr 28	51·1	48·9	—	—	80·0	31·5	49·1	19·4	—	81·5	-9·9	-12·0	-8·1
Stoke-on-Trent, Hanley	23 Apr 28	47·0	53·1	—	—	73·5	26·3	60·2	13·5	—	69·9	-13·9	-16·6	-9·6
St Marylebone	30 Apr 28	73·5	26·5	—	—	65·5	56·2	29·4	14·5	—	43·1	-10·1	-7·8	-9·6

	Previous Gen. Election					By-Election and Date		By-Election Result					Swing to Con.		
	Con. %	Lab. %	Lib. %	Others %	Turnout %			Con. %	Lab. %	Lib. %	Others %	Turnout %	Butler	Steed	Goguel
Holborn	75·5	24·6	–	–	55·1	Holborn	28 June 28	59·7	21·0	19·3	–	39·0	−6·1	−1·5	−6·5
*Carms., Carmarthen	–	31·5	68·5	–	67·9	*Carms., Carmarthen	28 June 28	29·1	35·4	35·5	–	76·6	–	–	–
Surrey, Epsom	79·5	20·5	–	–	67·1	Surrey, Epsom	4 July 28	60·3	16·8	23·0	–	51·2	−7·8	−1·3	−8·7
*Halifax	–	–	Unop.	–	–	*Halifax	13 July 28	26·4	42·9	30·8	–	78·7	–	–	–
Sheffield, Hallam	63·7	36·3	–	–	77·8	Sheffield, Hallam	16 July 28	53·7	30·8	15·5	–	54·7	−2·2	−0·1	−4·4
Aberdeen, North	39·2	60·8	–	–	64·4	Aberdeen, North	16 Aug 28	23·1	52·5	11·5	12·9	56·8	−3·9	−8·6	−1·4
Cheltenham	56·6	–	43·4	–	82·7	Cheltenham	26 Sep 28	49·5	18·8	31·7	–	80·3	–	–	–
Devon, Tavistock	52·8	–	47·2	–	77·7	Devon, Tavistock	11 Oct 28	45·2	10·3	44·5	–	77·3	–	–	–
*Ashton-under-Lyne	39·5	32·8	27·7	–	88·3	*Ashton-under-Lyne	29 Oct 28	30·3	40·5	29·1	–	89·1	−8·4	−11·8	−7·5
*Midlothian, North	55·2	44·8	–	–	79·2	*Midlothian, North	29 Jan 29	36·9	42·0	16·6	4·5	66·0	−7·8	−9·9	−5·8
*Battersea, South	57·7	42·3	–	–	76·5	*Battersea, South	7 Feb 29	43·4	45·6	11·1	–	57·7	−8·8	−8·9	−6·5
Durham, Bishop Auckland	–	55·1	44·9	–	80·9	Durham, Bishop Auckland	7 Feb 29	13·0	57·2	29·9	–	74·4	–	–	–
Northumberland, Wansbeck	47·2	52·9	–	–	79·4	Northumberland, Wansbeck	13 Feb 29	27·3	58·0	14·7	–	65·3	−12·5	−15·1	−7·7
Liverpool, East Toxteth	60·0	24·6	15·5	–	76·4	Liverpool, East Toxteth	19 Mar 29	43·2	29·2	27·6	–	61·7	−10·7	−11·3	−9·2
*Cheshire, Eddisbury	54·1	–	45·9	–	86·9	*Cheshire, Eddisbury	20 Mar 29	46·6	–	53·4	–	80·6	–	–	–
Bath	55·8	13·6	30·6	–	84·6	Bath	21 Mar 29	45·1	25·7	29·3	–	70·1	−11·4	−16·7	−11·1
*Lincs, Holland-with-Boston	47·5	32·8	19·7	–	75·9	*Lincs, Holland-with-Boston	21 Mar 29	24·2	27·3	38·1	10·4	75·6	−8·9	−12·1	−6·7
*Lanarks., North	53·9	46·1	–	–	79·9	*Lanarks., North	21 Mar 29	33·4	57·5	9·1	–	82·3	−16·0	−17·2	−13·1
Leeds, South-East	24·8	75·2	–	–	62·6	Leeds, South-East	1 Aug 29	–	95·8	–	4·2	25·9	–	–	–
Middx., Twickenham	48·5	34·8	16·7	–	69·8	Middx., Twickenham	8 Aug 29	47·7	46·1	6·2	–	49·5	−6·1	−7·4	−4·4
Ayrshire, Kilmarnock	30·4	48·2	21·4	–	77·8	Ayrshire, Kilmarnock	27 Nov 29	40·0	55·7	–	4·4	71·7	1·1	3·2	1·3
Warwicks., Tamworth	67·4	32·6	–	–	73·6	Warwicks., Tamworth	2 Dec 29	64·8	35·2	–	–	60·3	−2·6	−2·6	−3·9
Sheffield, Brightside	26·8	55·2	18·0	–	77·3	Sheffield, Brightside	6 Feb 30	34·6	46·4	14·7	4·4	52·4	8·3	10·1	7·9

Constituency	Date														
*Fulham, West	6 May 30	71·3	38·7	44·9	16·4	—	50·4	49·6	—	—	63·6	3·4	4·0	2·4
Nottingham, Central	27 May 30	77·4	41·8	33·2	25·1	—	54·3	28·8	16·9	—	61·1	8·5	9·6	4·5
Glasgow, Shettleston	26 June 30	76·9	39·6	60·4	—	—	43·8	45·5	—	10·7[2]	55·8	9·5	9·4	7·5
Norfolk, North	9 July 30	78·0	41·4	47·5	11·1	—	49·7	50·3	—	—	75·0	2·8	3·2	2·2
Bromley	2 Sep 30	73·1	47·2	18·7	34·1	—	32·5	15·1	28·4	24·1	53·4	-5·5	-3·3	-5·8
*Paddington, South	30 Oct 30	—	Unop.	—	—	—	34·3	26·6	—	39·1[2]	57·3	—	—	—
*Yorks, Shipley	6 Nov 30	85·0	31·2	42·3	26·6	—	36·0	32·1	30·2	1·7	80·0	7·6	10·6	6·4
Renfrewshire, East	28 Nov 30	77·8	52·2	47·8	—	—	53·6	33·4	—	13·1	69·0	7·9	9·4	5·3
Stepney, Whitechapel	3 Dec 30	60·3	16·0	63·1	20·8	—	17·1	39·2	34·1	13·1	59·0	12·5	10·2	7·7
Bristol, East	16 Jan 31	78·2	—	65·8	34·2	—	25·4	61·7	12·9	9·6	66·6	—	—	—
Liverpool, East Toxteth	5 Feb 31	75·5	48·0	26·9	25·2	—	75·4	24·5	14·6	—	45·6	14·9	11·3	3·6
Islington, East	19 Feb 31	66·4	34·1	38·0	27·9	—	23·5	34·7	14·6	27·2	50·0	-3·6	-6·9	-1·5
Hants, Fareham	20 Feb 31	68·0	54·2	22·1	23·7	—	65·6	22·1	12·3	—	50·3	5·7	3·7	-0·0
Wilts, Salisbury	11 Mar 31	81·9	47·3	13·4	39·3	—	53·9	13·4	32·7	—	71·1	3·3	2·1	0·5
Westminster, St George's	19 Mar 31	53·3	78·1	21·9	—	—	59·9	—	—	40·1	53·1	—	—	—
Glam., Pontypridd	19 Mar 31	82·0	10·1	53·1	36·8	—	15·9	59·9	24·2	—	73·6	-0·5	5·0	1·5
Woolwich, East	15 Apr 31	75·6	36·8	63·2	—	—	43·3	56·7	—	—	66·6	6·5	6·5	5·5
*Ashton-under-Lyne	30 Apr 31	85·9	33·0	44·5	22·6	—	44·5	39·5	—	16·0	80·2	8·3	10·5	7·0
Yorks., Scarborough & Whitby	6 May 31	79·7	48·3	10·8	40·9	—	52·7	—	47·3	—	75·5	—	—	—
Glasgow, St Rollox	7 May 31	72·0	36·3	61·8	—	2·0	39·0	45·2	—	15·8	54·1	9·6	9·3	7·5
Glam., Ogmore	19 May 31	82·8	10·3	56·7	29·2	3·8	—	78·8	—	21·2	50·8	—	—	—
Gloucs., Stroud	21 May 31	81·6	44·5	26·1	29·5	—	49·6	30·0	20·4	—	71·4	0·6	-0·8	-0·5
Lanarks., Rutherglen	21 May 31	75·7	36·5	52·2	8·8	2·5	48·7	51·4	—	—	69·6	6·5	7·5	5·0
Gateshead	8 June 31	73·9	21·6	52·5	19·1	6·8	48·4	51·6	—	—	60·8	13·9	19·4	10·5
Manchester, Ardwick	22 June 31	72·0	39·7	60·3	—	—	49·5	50·5	—	—	64·1	9·8	9·8	7·1
Liverpool, Wavertree	23 June 31	78·1	40·0	32·2	27·8	—	65·1	35·0	—	—	51·7	11·1	9·6	4·7
Croydon, South	9 Feb 32	68·3	80·3	19·7	—	—	67·6	32·5	—	—	38·2	-12·8	-12·8	-14·0
Hants, New Forest & Christchurch	9 Feb 32	71·9	83·3	16·7	—	—	82·0	18·0	—	—	48·0	-1·3	-1·3	-8·6

By-Election and Date	Previous Gen. Election Con. %	Lab. %	Lib. %	Others %	Turnout %	By-Election Result Con. %	Lab. %	Lib. %	Others %	Turnout %	Swing to Con. Butler	Steed	Goguel
Oxon., Henley — 25 Feb 32	72·3	11·5	16·3	—	68·6	69·9	—	30·1	—	48·9	—	—	—
Dunbartonshire — 17 Mar 32	63·6	36·4	—	—	82·8	43·5	35·6	—	20·9[2]	70·5	−9·6	−8·6	−8·5
*Wakefield — 21 Apr 32	57·4	42·6	—	—	85·5	49·4	50·6	—	—	83·0	−8·1	−8·1	−6·9
St Marylebone — 28 Apr 32	86·7	13·3	—	—	63·5	52·3	—	—	47·7	30·8	—	—	—
Camberwell, Dulwich — 8 June 32	71·5	15·6	12·9	—	70·7	61·0	19·3	19·8	—	47·1	−7·1	−6·1	−10·0
Montrose Burghs — 28 June 32	—	23·0	77·0	—	74·6	—	41·4	46·9	11·8	56·7	—	—	—
Cornwall, North — 22 July 32	45·3	5·6	49·2	—	85·7	47·6	—	52·4	—	80·8	—	—	—
*Wednesbury — 26 July 32	54·5	45·5	—	—	89·0	45·3	54·7	—	—	78·0	−9·2	−9·2	−7·7
Middx., Twickenham — 16 Sep 32	74·0	26·0	—	—	71·3	56·2	43·8	—	—	51·9	−17·8	−17·8	−13·9
Cardiganshire — 22 Sep 32	—	24·0	76·0	—	67·5	32·1	19·2	48·7	—	70·4	—	—	—
Liverpool, Exchange — 19 Jan 33	68·8	31·2	—	—	69·0	55·1	45·0	—	—	55·2	−13·8	−13·8	−10·2
Fife, East — 2 Feb 33	—	—	—	Unop.	—	—	22·0	7·6	70·4[3]	65·6	—	—	—
*Rotherham — 27 Feb 33	50·8	49·2	—	—	82·6	31·0	69·1	—	—	73·5	−19·9	−19·9	−14·7
Kent, Ashford — 17 Mar 33	58·7	—	—	41·3	75·9	47·7	18·4	33·9	—	70·9	—	—	—
Rhondda, East — 28 Mar 33	—	68·1	—	31·9	73·7	—	47·4	26·3	26·3	67·3	—	—	—
Herts, Hitchin — 8 June 33	75·7	24·3	—	—	71·2	58·4	41·6	—	—	51·3	−17·2	−17·2	−13·9
Cheshire, Altrincham — 14 June 33	Unop.	—	—	—	—	52·2	16·8	32·0	—	63·4	—	—	—
Derbys., Clay Cross — 1 Sep 33	35·4	64·6	—	—	74·6	19·9	69·3	—	10·8	71·2	−10·1	−13·1	−6·7
*Fulham, East — 25 Oct 33	68·7	26·1	5·2	—	66·1	42·1	57·9	—	—	59·5	−29·1	−30·3	−18·7
Ayrshire, Kilmarnock — 2 Nov 33	—	40·4	—	59·6	79·5	34·8	27·4	—	37·8[2]	77·3	—	—	—
Yorks., Skipton — 7 Nov 33	68·2	31·8	—	—	80·3	43·0	33·5	21·8	1·7	82·7	−13·5	−12·1	−10·7
Rutland & Stamford — 21 Nov 33	71·9	28·1	—	—	75·3	53·3	46·7	—	—	77·2	−18·7	−18·7	−14·0
Manchester, Rusholme — 21 Nov 33	69·3	17·7	13·0	—	80·4	50·7	40·2	9·1	—	60·8	−20·6	−23·9	−17·5
Leics, Harborough — 28 Nov 33	74·5	25·5	—	—	78·1	50·9	32·9	16·2	—	72·3	−15·4	−13·9	−12·6
Cambridge — 8 Feb 34	73·2	26·8	—	—	75·6	51·2	41·9	7·0	—	67·8	−18·5	−18·2	−14·4
Suffolk, Lowestoft — 15 Feb 34	67·8	32·3	—	—	70·8	47·9	42·1	10·0	—	67·9	−14·9	−14·5	−10·6
Portsmouth, North — 19 Feb 34	68·4	31·6	—	—	74·5	59·6	40·4	—	—	55·7	−8·7	−8·7	−8·3
Hants, Basingstoke — 19 Apr 34	69·7	12·2	18·1	—	74·2	53·7	15·5	30·8	—	64·4	−9·6	−7·5	−9·0

(1)	(2)	(3)	(4)	Poll	Constituency	Date	(1)	(2)	(3)	(4)	Poll	(a)	(b)	(c)
59·2	37·3	—	3·6²	69·6	*Hammersmith, North	24 Apr 34	41·9	55·7	—	2·4	56·7	−17·8	−18·4	−11·5
58·5	41·5	—	—	70·4	*West Ham, Upton	14 May 34	40·1	56·4	—	3·5	50·5	−16·7	−16·9	−10·1
—	69·4	—	30·6	80·8	Merthyr Tydfil, Merthyr	5 June 34	—	51·9	28·9	19·3²	81·2	—	—	—
70·9	29·2	—	—	78·0	Mon., Monmouth	14 June 34	65·0	35·0	—	—	69·2	−5·8	−5·8	−5·9
74·0	26·0	—	—	71·3	†Middx., Twickenham	22 June 34	56·1	43·9	—	—	55·5	−17·9	−17·9	−13·7
85·7	14·4	—	—	71·8	Somerset, Weston-super-Mare	26 June 34	61·5	16·6	21·9	—	57·3	−13·2	−6·9	−12·7
72·1	27·9	—	—	77·8	Notts., Rushcliffe	26 July 34	48·8	38·0	13·2	—	56·5	−16·7	−15·9	−14·2
—	34·9	65·1	—	64·6	*Lambeth, North	23 Oct 34	—	57·9	25·5	16·6	52·6	—	—	—
55·9	44·1	—	—	85·5	*Wilts., Swindon	25 Oct 34	46·6	53·4	—	—	81·8	−9·3	−9·3	−7·8
81·6	18·4	—	—	66·3	Wandsworth, Putney	28 Nov 34	54·7	45·3	—	—	57·5	−26·9	−26·9	−18·2
77·9	22·1	—	—	75·2	*Liverpool, Wavertree	6 Feb 35	51·0	35·4	9·5	23·9	72·3	−30·0	−31·0	−22·5
81·0	19·0	—	—	63·9	Lambeth, Norwood	14 Mar 35	51·0	40·5	—	8·5	53·4	−22·8	−22·6	−17·0
50·2	9·7	—	—	81·4	Perthshire, Perth	16 Apr 35	68·7	31·3	13·1	—	53·0	−1·6	−15·2	−6·6
71·2	28·8	—	—	79·2	Edinburgh, West	2 May 35	53·0	33·9	—	—	51·2	−11·6	−10·2	−11·9
83·7	16·3	—	—	75·8	Aberdeen, South	21 May 35	66·0	34·0	—	—	56·6	−17·6	−17·6	−16·5
57·9	42·1	—	—	76·2	*Liverpool, West Toxteth	16 July 35	39·1	60·9	—	—	53·9	−18·9	−18·9	−11·9
—	22·3	77·7	—	77·6	Dumfriesshire	12 Sep 35	—	39·7	60·3	—	58·8	—	—	—
50·3	23·3	—	26·4	50·8	Ross & Cromarty	10 Feb 36	13·4	33·0	4·1	49·5	65·2	—	—	—
—	42·0	—	7·8	80·5	*Dunbartonshire	18 Mar 36	45·7	48·1	—	6·2	63·6	−5·3	−5·8	−4·2
—	Unop.	—	—	—	Carms., Llanelly	26 Mar 36	—	66·8	—	33·2	68·4	—	—	—
51·3	48·7	—	—	64·8	*Camberwell, Peckham	6 May 36	49·8	50·2	—	—	56·6	−1·5	−1·5	−1·0
70·0	30·0	—	—	66·4	Sussex, Lewes	18 June 36	66·0	34·0	—	—	40·6	−4·0	−4·0	−6·4
62·9	37·1	—	—	61·8	Wandsworth, Balham & Tooting	23 July 36	53·7	46·3	—	—	49·2	−9·2	−9·6	−6·2
78·4	21·6	—	—	61·2	Sussex, East Grinstead	23 July 36	79·6	20·5	—	—	45·5	1·1	1·1	−4·0
58·3	37·4	—	4·3	65·5	Birmingham, Erdington	20 Oct 36	56·5	43·5	—	—	64·7	−4·0	−4·4	−2·7
25·4	74·6	—	—	73·6	Derbys., Clay Cross	5 Nov 36	24·9	75·1	—	—	72·4	−0·6	−0·6	−0·1

By-Election and Date	Previous Gen. Election Con. %	Lab. %	Lib. %	Others %	Turnout %	By-Election Result Con. %	Lab. %	Lib. %	Others %	Turnout %	Swing to Con. Butler	Steed	Goguel
*Greenock, 26 Nov 36	—	44·0	—	56·0²	84·4	—	53·4	—	46·6	83·3	—	—	—
St Pancras, North, 4 Feb 37	53·7	42·3	4·0	—	68·3	50·6	49·4	—	—	50·9	−5·2	−5·4	−3·6
Manchester, Gorton, 18 Feb 37	44·1	55·9	—	—	77·7	42·3	57·7	—	—	66·8	−1·8	−1·8	−0·6
Richmond-upon-Thames, 25 Feb 37	73·5	26·5	—	—	69·8	72·7	27·3	—	—	47·3	−0·8	−0·8	−5·7
Kent, Tonbridge, 23 Mar 37	61·3	24·6	14·1	—	68·2	56·9	24·7	18·4	—	58·2	−2·2	−1·6	−3·1
Surrey, Farnham, 23 Mar 37	78·5	21·5	—	—	59·8	66·7	25·3	—	8·0²	50·0	−7·8	−6·0	−6·7
Cheshire, Stalybridge & Hyde, 28 Apr 37	55·5	44·5	—	—	78·7	50·4	49·6	—	—	74·6	−5·1	−5·1	−4·1
Birmingham, West, 29 Apr 37	64·4	35·7	—	—	63·6	56·6	43·4	—	—	56·0	−7·8	−7·8	−5·4
*Wandsworth, Central, 29 Apr 37	58·6	41·4	—	—	65·0	49·0	51·0	—	—	63·2	−9·6	−9·6	−6·2
York, 6 May 37	57·0	43·0	—	—	82·5	55·1	44·9	—	—	74·2	−2·0	−2·0	−2·0
Glasgow, Hillhead, 10 June 37	68·2	31·8	—	—	73·2	60·1	29·8	—	10·1²	56·1	−3·0	−1·3	−4·8
Bucks., Buckingham, 11 June 37	58·0	42·0	—	—	75·1	52·6	37·6	9·8	—	71·4	−0·5	0·3	−0·7
Plymouth, Drake, 15 June 37	58·3	41·7	—	—	74·8	58·8	41·2	—	—	54·6	0·6	0·6	1·4
*Cheltenham, 22 June 37	70·5	29·5	—	—	70·4	38·8	21·2	—	40·1	69·3	−11·7	−5·8	−8·3
Herts., Hemel Hempstead, 22 June 37	62·5	15·4	22·1	—	69·4	57·7	14·1	28·3	—	55·0	−1·7	0·2	−4·3
Lincs., Holland-with-Boston, 24 June 37	—	34·5	—	65·5	63·6	—	40·0	—	60·0	59·4	—	—	—
Worcs., Bewdley, 24 June 37	Unop.	—	—	—	—	63·9	—	36·1	—	60·6	—	—	—
Ilford, 29 June 37	63·1	36·9	—	—	64·0	61·2	38·8	—	—	37·3	−2·0	−2·0	−4·2
Cornwall, St Ives, 30 June 37	—	—	—	Unop.	—	—	—	49·6	50·4	66·1	—	—	—
Kingston-upon-Thames, 1 July 37	67·5	20·5	12·0	—	65·5	66·6	33·4	—	—	38·1	−6·9	−10·1	−9·1
Surrey, Chertsey, 2 July 37	71·4	—	28·6	—	60·0	64·8	—	35·2	—	39·2	—	—	—
Dorset, North, 13 July 37	50·1	5·2	37·9	6·8	79·7	51·1	—	48·9	—	73·4	—	—	—
Glasgow, Springburn, 7 Sep 37	36·9	63·1	—	—	71·1	37·4	62·6	—	—	50·9	0·5	0·5	2·9
*Islington, North, 13 Oct 37	54·4	45·6	—	—	59·7	47·5	52·5	—	—	40·4	−7·0	−7·0	−3·7

1935 %	1935 %			Constituency	Date	By-election %				Turnout	Swing	Swing	Swing
69·0	31·0	—	—	Hastings	24 Nov 37	62·1	37·9	—	—	65·3	–6·9	–6·9	–4·7
39·5	51·7	—	8·8	Lancs., Farnworth	27 Jan 38	40·9	59·1	—	—	77·9	–3·0	–2·4	–2·0
—	Unop.	—	—	Glam., Pontypridd	11 Feb 38	—	59·9	—	40·1	78·3	—	—	—
57·3	42·7	—	—	*Ipswich	16 Feb 38	47·0	53·0	—	—	82·8	–10·3	–10·3	–8·5
53·4	43·3	3·3	54·8	*Fulham, West	6 Apr 38	47·8	52·2	—	—	65·5	–7·3	–7·5	–5·0
—	46·2	31·6	—	*Staffs., Lichfield	5 May 38	—	50·9	—	49·1	57·8	—	—	—
57·4	11·0	—	—	Bucks., Aylesbury	19 May 38	54·1	19·1	26·8	—	63·1	–5·8	–10·1	–5·3
Unop.	—	—	—	Derbys., West	2 June 38	48·6	32·5	18·9	—	79·4	1·2	1·2	—
56·4	43·6	—	41·1	Staffs., Stafford	9 June 38	57·6	42·4	—	—	77·2	—	—	0·8
—	58·9	—	—	Barnsley	16 June 38	—	64·4	—	35·6	72·7	–4·8	–5·7	–4·5
57·8	35·0	7·3	—	Willesden, East	28 July 38	56·6	43·4	—	35·6	39·3	—	—	—
62·8	37·2	—	—	Oxford	27 Oct 38	56·1	—	—	43·9	76·3	–4·2	–4·2	–2·9
51·8	48·2	—	—	*Kent, Dartford	7 Nov 38	47·6	52·4	—	—	68·5	—	—	—
—	39·4	—	60·6²	Walsall	16 Nov 38	38·7	42·9	—	57·1	75·9	–3·7	–3·7	–2·6
42·4	57·7	—	—	Yorks., Doncaster	17 Nov 38	38·7	61·3	—	—	75·4	—	—	—
56·9	19·8	—	23·4	*Somerset, Bridgwater	17 Nov 38	46·8	—	—	53·2	82·3	–7·6	–7·6	–5·2
64·7	35·3	—	—	Lewisham, West	24 Nov 38	57·1	42·9	—	—	58·4	–7·6	–7·6	–5·2
70·8	29·2	—	39·8	Lancs., Fylde	30 Nov 38	68·4	31·6	—	—	64·8	–2·4	–2·4	–3·0
60·2	—	39·8	—	Kinross & Perthshire, West	21 Dec 38	52·9	—	—	47·1	66·6	—	—	—
—	—	—	—	Norfolk, East	26 Jan 39	—	37·1	—	62·9	53·1	—	—	—
53·6	31·2	24·9	—	Yorks., Holderness	15 Feb 39	39·4	21·4	25·7	13·5	66·3	–7·1	–6·6	–5·6
77·2	21·5	—	—	Yorks., Ripon	23 Feb 39	69·5	30·5	—	—	57·3	–7·7	–7·7	–7·5
46·4	22·8	—	—	Batley & Morley	9 Mar 39	44·6	55·4	—	—	72·6	–1·8	–1·8	–1·1
55·9	53·6	44·1	—	Aberdeenshire, West	30 Mar 39	52·7	58·0	47·3	—	71·4	—	—	—
42·4	57·6	—	—	Ayrshire, South	20 Apr 39	42·0	58·0	—	—	74·5	–0·4	–0·4	0·0
67·3	32·7	—	—	Sheffield, Hallam	10 May 39	61·7	38·3	—	—	57·9	–5·6	–5·6	–5·6
68·8	31·2	—	50·3	Birmingham, Aston	17 May 39	66·3	33·7	—	—	45·0	–2·6	–2·6	–4·9
—	49·8	—	—	*Southwark, North	17 May 39	—	57·4	—	42·6	38·9	—	—	—
77·5	22·5	—	—	Westminster, Abbey	17 May 39	67·4	—	—	32·6	30·3	—	—	—
51·1	48·9	—	—	*Lambeth, Kennington	24 May 39	39·9	60·1	—	—	40·6	–11·2	–11·2	–4·7
23·8	76·3	—	—	Glam., Caerphilly	4 July 39	32·0	68·0	—	—	68·4	8·3	8·3	6·7

	Previous Gen. Election					By-Election and Date	By-Election Result					Swing to Con.		
	Con. %	Lab. %	Lib. %	Others %	Turnout %		Con. %	Lab. %	Lib. %	Others %	Turnout %	Butler	Steed	Goguel
	48·7	—	51·3	—	79·9	Cornwall, North — 13 July 39	47·8	—	52·2	—	79·3	—	—	—
	63·9	—	36·1	—	68·3	Hythe — 20 July 39	54·2	—	43·2	2·6	62·4	—	—	—
	63·4	36·6	—	—	76·8	Mon., Monmouth — 25 July 39	60·1	39·9	—	—	58·2	—	—	-4·4
	25·8	39·5	30·6	4·1	76·0	Yorks., Colne Valley — 27 July 39	25·4	48·6	26·0	—	63·7	-3·3	-3·3	-2·2
	52·6	47·4	—	—	84·3	*Brecon & Radnor — 1 Aug 39	46·6	53·4	—	—	79·9	-4·8	-5·2	-4·9
	39·0	42·2	14·4	4·5	76·3	Stirlingshire, East & Clackmannan — 13 Oct 39	—	93·7	—	6·4	35·4	-6·0	-6·0	—
	64·4	35·6	—	—	72·5	Lancs., Stretford — 8 Dec 39	79·8	15·1	—	5·2	36·6	17·9	19·7	1·4
	—	53·3	—	46·7	57·2	Southwark, Central — 10 Feb 40	—	64·3	—	35·7[2]	24·7	—	—	—
	19·0	81·0	—	—	53·4	West Ham, Silvertown — 22 Feb 40	—	92·8	—	7·2[2]	40·1	—	—	—
	52·1	47·9	—	—	77·3	Northants., Kettering — 6 Mar 40	73·0	—	—	27·0	37·8	—	—	—
	64·8	35·2	—	—	66·1	Leeds, North-East — 13 Mar 40	97·1	—	—	2·9	35·0	—	—	—
	53·6	—	46·4	—	56·6	Argyll — 10 Apr 40	62·8	—	—	37·2	47·9	—	—	—
	41·3	58·7	—	—	63·5	Battersea, North — 17 Apr 40	—	92·6	—	7·4	25·1	—	—	—
	72·1	27·9	—	—	70·1	Glasgow, Pollok — 30 Apr 40	88·1	11·9	—	—	44·5	16·0	16·0	1·5
	55·6	34·0	—	10·4	76·0	Renfrewshire, East — 9 May 40	80·7	19·3	—	—	43·4	19·9	18·7	5·1
	61·1	38·9	—	—	74·6	Lancs., Middleton & Prestwich — 22 May 40	98·7	—	—	1·3	49·0	—	—	—
	77·0	23·1	—	—	70·3	*Newcastle-upon-Tyne, North — 7 June 40	28·8	—	—	71·2	22·0	—	—	—
	23·0	77·0	—	—	59·5	Poplar, Bow & Bromley — 12 June 40	—	95·8	—	4·2	32·4	—	—	—
	67·1	32·9	—	—	64·6	Croydon, North — 19 June 40	90·7	—	—	9·3	18·3	—	—	—
	51·5	48·5	—	—	79·6	Northampton — 6 Dec 40	93·4	—	—	6·6	30·0	—	—	—
	50·3	42·0	—	7·8	80·5	†Dunbartonshire — 27 Feb 41	—	85·0	—	15·0	38·7	—	—	—
	56·8	43·2	—	—	74·6	Birmingham, King's Norton — 8 May 41	86·9	—	—	13·1[2]	35·0	—	—	—
	64·9	22·0	13·2	—	67·0	Hornsey — 28 May 41	72·8	—	—	27·2	21·1	—	—	—

Constituency	Date	(1)	(2)	(3)	(4)	(5)	(6)	(7)	(8)	(9)	(10)	(11)	(12)
Dudley	23 July 41	75·3	54·8	45·2	—	56·2	—	—	43·9	34·7	—	—	—
Yorks, Scarborough & Whitby	24 Sep 41	74·7	53·9	7·4	38·7	60·8	—	—	39·2	35·9	—	—	—
Shrops., Wrekin	26 Sep 41	79·1	57·9	42·1	—	53·2	—	—	46·8[2]	40·5	1·9	1·5	-5·5
Lancs., Lancaster	15 Oct 41	79·0	53·7	20·0	26·3	56·9	19·5	23·6	—	41·9	—	—	—
Hampstead	27 Nov 41	59·0	73·2	18·1	8·8	67·4	—	—	32·6[3]	17·3	14·7	14·4	0·1
Middx., Harrow	2 Dec 41	64·4	62·7	37·3	—	80·9	—	—	19·1	10·7	—	—	—
Edinburgh, Central	11 Dec 41	64·5	54·0	41·4	4·7	71·0	29·1	—	—	20·0	10·8	19·1	-1·0
*Lincs., Grantham	25 Mar 42	74·2	58·1	41·9	—	49·2	—	—	50·8	42·6	—	—	—
Cardiff, East	13 Apr 42	73·1	53·4	37·8	8·7	—	24·8	—	75·2	33·1	—	—	—
Glasgow, Cathcart	28 Apr 42	74·3	62·1	37·9	—	59·6	13·8	—	26·6[2]	39·1	—	—	—
*Wallasey	29 Apr 42	66·1	67·4	32·6	—	31·7	—	—	68·3[2]	34·2	—	—	—
*Warwicks., Rugby	29 Apr 42	73·9	61·5	38·5	—	48·2	—	—	51·8	38·5	—	—	—
Wandsworth, Putney	8 May 42	68·5	65·2	31·9	—	74·9	—	—	25·1	23·0	—	—	—
Sussex, Chichester	18 May 42	59·5	78·3	21·7	3·0	58·1	—	—	41·9[2]	29·2	—	—	—
Glam., Llandaff & Barry	10 June 42	77·0	51·3	48·8	—	56·9	—	—	43·2[2]	41·5	—	—	—
*Essex, Maldon	25 June 42	73·8	53·3	28·9	17·7	31·3	—	—	68·8[2]	44·4	—	—	—
Berks., Windsor	30 June 42	Unop.	Unop.	Unop.	—	58·4	—	—	41·6	27·9	—	—	—
Wilts., Salisbury	8 July 42	66·2	71·5	28·5	—	67·8	—	—	32·2[2]	39·7	—	—	—
Poplar, South	12 Aug 42	55·3	26·8	73·2	—	—	86·2	—	13·8	9·3	—	—	—
Manchester, Clayton	17 Oct 42	77·0	46·3	53·7	—	—	93·3	—	6·7	20·8	—	—	—
Lanarks., Hamilton	29 Jan 43	74·0	34·3	65·7	23·2	69·7	81·1	—	18·9	36·8	—	—	—
Kent, Ashford	10 Feb 43	73·6	59·2	17·6	—	51·9	—	—	30·3	27·7	—	—	—
Midlothian, North	11 Feb 43	74·3	62·9	37·1	15·5	54·2	—	—	48·1	34·6	—	—	—
Norfolk, King's Lynn	12 Feb 43	71·7	50·0	34·5	—	59·7	—	—	45·8	39·8	—	—	—
Portsmouth, North	16 Feb 43	64·9	66·6	33·4	—	52·1	—	—	40·3	21·9	—	—	—
Bristol, Central	18 Feb 43	72·8	52·5	47·5	—	53·9	—	—	47·9[3]	32·9	—	—	—
Herts., Watford	23 Feb 43	63·6	65·4	34·6	—	—	—	—	46·1	32·4	—	—	—
*Cheshire, Eddisbury	7 Apr 43	—	—	—	Unop.	45·8	—	15·3	84·7[2]	56·1	—	—	—
Northants., Daventry	20 Apr 43	76·0	63·8	36·3	—	64·0	—	20·8	33·4[2]	48·8	—	—	—
Hartlepools	1 June 43	83·0	47·8	37·1	15·2	—	—	—	36·0[3]	39·5	—	—	—

Previous Gen. Election					By-Election and Date	By-Election Result					Swing to Con.		
Con. %	Lab. %	Lib. %	Others %	Turnout %		Con. %	Lab. %	Lib. %	Others %	Turnout %	Butler	Steed	Goguel
62.4	37.6	—	—	69.9	Notts., Newark 8 June 43	44.8	—	10.8	44.4[2]	44.4	—	—	—
68.8	31.2	—	—	64.7	Birmingham, Aston 9 June 43	72.5	—	—	27.5[2]	22.2	—	—	—
53.3	12.2	34.5	—	77.5	Wilts., Chippenham 24 Aug 43	50.6	—	49.4	—	41.4	—	—	—
56.6	43.4	—	—	80.8	Northants., Peterborough 15 Oct 43	52.4	—	—	47.6	44.2	—	—	—
58.7	41.3	—	—	75.8	Woolwich, West 10 Nov 43	65.2	27.2	—	7.6	20.8	10.4	11.9	-2.6
58.5	41.5	—	—	67.8	Middx., Acton 14 Dec 43	60.3	28.1	—	11.6[2]	17.1	7.6	9.7	-3.0
41.1	20.9	38.0	—	89.6	Lancs., Darwen 15 Dec 43	50.2	—	49.8	—	45.0	—	—	—
56.2	43.8	—	—	79.6	*Yorks., Skipton 7 Jan 44	44.0	—	—	56.0[2]	54.9	—	—	—
43.7	56.3	—	—	79.9	Kirkcaldy Burghs 17 Feb 44	—	51.6	—	48.4[2]	37.2	—	—	—
Unop.	—	—	—	—*	†Derbys., West 17 Feb 44	41.5	—	—	58.5[2]	65.4	—	—	—
Unop.	—	—	—	—	Suffolk, Bury St Edmunds 29 Feb 44	56.2	—	43.8	—	50.8	—	—	—
32.8	64.7	—	2.5	55.6	Camberwell, North 30 Mar 44	—	79.8	—	20.3	11.2	—	—	—
25.4	74.6	—	—	73.6	†Derbys., Clay Cross 14 Apr 44	—	76.3	—	23.7[2]	40.3	—	—	—
62.6	29.4	8.0	—	69.8	Manchester, Rusholme 8 July 44	53.2	—	—	46.8[2]	34.7	—	—	—
51.2	48.8	—	—	36.3	Wolverhampton, Bilston 20 Sep 44	50.9	—	—	49.1	32.6	—	—	—
49.0	—	51.0	—	76.0	Northumberland, Berwick-on-Tweed 17 Oct 44	—	—	87.4	12.6	24.5	—	—	—
49.3	50.7	—	—	75.9	*Lanarks., Motherwell 12 Apr 45	—	48.6	—	51.4	54.0	—	—	—
33.4	—	66.6	—	77.4	Carnarvon Boroughs 26 Apr 45	—	—	75.2	24.8	58.8	—	—	—
70.8	29.2	—	—	65.4	*Essex, Chelmsford 26 Apr 45	42.5	—	—	57.5	54.1	—	—	—
—	Unop.	—	—	—	Glam., Neath 15 May 45	—	79.3	—	20.7[2]	58.0	—	—	—
51.7	48.3	—	—	79.4	Newport 17 May 45	54.5	45.5	—	—	50.0	2.8	2.8	0.9
34.1	65.9	—	—	72.4	Smethwick 1 Oct 45	31.2	68.9	—	—	65.4	-3.0	-3.0	-0.8
43.6	56.4	—	—	78.6	Ashton-under-Lyne 2 Oct 45	35.1	54.0	10.9	—	70.5	-3.1	-4.3	-1.7

					Constituency	Date								
37·3	56·4	—	6·3	69·4	Edinburgh, East	3 Oct 45	38·4	61·6	—	—	51·0	-2·0	-1·4	0·7
51·9	48·1	—	—	72·0	Mon., Monmouth	30 Oct 45	52·7	47·3	—	—	66·7	0·7	0·7	0·4
44·9	34·1	21·0	—	71·0	Bromley	14 Nov 45	49·6	39·1	11·3	—	60·6	-0·2	-0·9	-0·7
55·5	21·7	22·9	—	71·2	Bournemouth	15 Nov 45	46·9	33·7	19·5	—	56·5	-10·3	-13·7	-8·3
69·8	18·9	11·3	—	67·9	Kensington, South	20 Nov 45	81·7	—	18·3	—	36·8	—	—	—
28·2	71·8	—	—	70·3	Tottenham, North	13 Dec 45	36·4	63·6	—	—	39·5	8·2	8·2	10·0
38·7	61·3	—	—	75·0	Ayrshire, South	7 Feb 46	36·4	63·6	—	—	69·0	-2·2	-2·2	-0·9
58·8	41·2	—	—	67·6	Glasgow, Cathcart	12 Feb 46	52·5	37·1	—	10·4	55·6	-1·2	-0·3	-1·7
49·0	51·0	—	—	76·4	Lancs., Heywood & Radcliffe	21 Feb 46	49·5	50·5	—	—	75·6	0·5	0·5	0·4
—	76·4	—	23·6²	75·6	Glam., Ogmore	4 June 46	—	70·6	—	29·4	33·7	—	—	—
29·8	56·9	13·3	—	76·7	Bexley	22 July 46	47·5	52·5	—	—	62·6	11·1	13·2	8·9
22·7	77·3	—	—	77·0	Mon., Pontypool	23 July 46	26·8	73·2	—	—	65·8	4·0	4·0	5·7
26·1	73·9	—	—	70·9	Battersea, North	25 July 46	29·6	69·0	—	1·5	57·1	4·2	3·9	5·7
33·6	66·4	—	—	58·2	*Glasgow, Bridgeton	29 Aug 46	21·6	28·0	—	50·4³	53·3	13·2	9·9	7·8
20·9	79·1	—	—	68·1	Bermondsey, Rotherhithe	19 Nov 46	9·7	65·0	22·6	—	50·9	1·4	-7·9	5·7
37·1	61·2	11·0	1·7	71·0	Paddington North	20 Nov 46	43·2	55·6	—	1·2	53·9	5·8	6·0	5·2
46·7	42·3	—	—	71·9	Aberdeen, South	26 Nov 46	54·8	45·2	—	—	65·6	2·6	2·4	1·6
15·7	84·3	—	—	76·1	Merthyr Tydfil, Aberdare	5 Dec 46	11·7	68·3	—	20·0	65·8	5·9	-1·2	7·5
40·6	59·4	—	—	76·1	Ayrshire, Kilmarnock	5 Dec 46	32·5	59·7	4·4	7·8	68·4	-4·2	-5·3	-2·1
15·7	84·3	—	—	79·9	Yorks., Normanton	11 Feb 47	17·8	79·8	16·0	2·4	54·6	3·3	2·5	10·5
34·0	66·0	—	—	76·0	Durham, Jarrow	7 May 47	37·5	59·3	—	3·2	73·4	5·1	4·8	4·2
35·1	64·9	—	—	66·1	Liverpool, Edge Hill	11 Sep 47	42·6	52·0	10·5	1·0²	62·7	10·2	10·0	6·9
26·2	73·8	—	—	60·1	Islington, West	25 Sep 47	26·6	57·1	10·1	0·2	51·4	8·5	5·6	6·5
35·3	52·5	12·2	—	74·5	Kent, Gravesend	26 Nov 47	48·2	51·8	7·5	—	77·3	6·8	8·0	5·0
55·9	29·2	14·9	—	71·1	Yorks., Howdenshire	27 Nov 47	64·0	25·5	1·2	10·5	67·0	5·9	5·9	3·4
37·3	56·4	—	6·3	69·4	†Edinburgh, East	27 Nov 47	34·3	50·5	—	5·0	63·0	1·5	0·6	1·5
49·9	37·8	12·2	—	74·6	Surrey, Epsom	4 Dec 47	61·1	31·5	—	—	70·5	8·8	9·1	5·9
42·3	57·7	—	—	65·0	*Glasgow, Camlachie	28 Jan 48	43·7	42·1	—	13·0³	56·8	8·5	8·6	5·5
32·7	55·6	10·0	1·7	73·9	Paisley	18 Feb 48	—	56·8	—	43·2	76·0	—	—	—

	Previous Gen. Election					By-Election and Date	By-Election Result					Swing to Con.		
	Con. %	Lab. %	Lib. %	Others %	Turnout %		Con. %	Lab. %	Lib. %	Others %	Turnout %	Butler	Steed	Goguel
	31·8	68·2	–	–	80·4	Wigan · 4 Mar 48	35·7	59·1	–	5·3²	81·4	6·5	5·8	5·1
	41·1	40·1	18·8	–	73·2	Croydon, North · 11 Mar 48	54·0	36·6	9·4	–	74·8	8·2	9·0	6·1
	41·1	58·9	–	–	74·6	Lincs, Brigg · 24 Mar 48	45·4	54·6	–	–	77·1	4·3	4·3	3·1
	28·1	71·9	–	–	62·6	Southwark, Central · 29 Apr 48	34·6	65·4	–	–	48·7	6·5	6·5	6·2
	20·0	80·0	–	–	56·8	Glasgow, Gorbals · 30 Sep 48	28·6	54·6	–	16·9	50·0	17·0	14·4	10·5
	43·9	56·1	–	–	71·5	Stirling & Falkirk Burghs · 7 Oct 48	42·8	49·1	–	8·2	72·9	3·0	2·7	2·1
	29·0	68·2	–	2·8	69·0	Edmonton · 13 Nov 48	46·6	53·4	–	–	62·7	16·8	16·8	11·4
	58·6	33·6	7·9	–	65·8	Glasgow, Hillhead · 25 Nov 48	68·4	31·6	–	–	56·7	5·9	4·8	2·2
	28·4	58·1	13·5	–	80·8	Batley & Morley · 17 Feb 49	40·7	59·3	–	–	81·3	5·6	7·8	4·4
	42·0	58·0	–	–	65·7	Hammersmith, South · 24 Feb 49	47·2	52·8	–	–	60·6	5·2	5·2	3·6
	34·7	63·8	–	–	71·0	St Pancras, North · 10 Mar 49	39·5	57·5	–	3·0	65·1	5·5	5·5	4·5
	30·9	50·8	18·3	–	81·9	Yorks, Sowerby · 16 Mar 49	46·9	53·1	–	–	80·7	6·9	9·1	5·7
	27·7	59·0	13·3	–	75·2	Leeds, West · 21 July 49	44·8	55·2	–	–	65·1	10·5	12·9	8·4
	33·1	52·5	14·4	–	76·7	Bradford, South · 8 Dec 49	42·4	51·3	6·3	–	74·4	5·3	6·6	4·1
	27·2	72·8	–	–	83·8	Sheffield, Neepsend · 5 Apr 50	26·8	70·8	–	2·3	62·9	0·8	0·3	5·3
	47·8	49·3	–	2·9	85·5	Dunbartonshire, West · 25 Apr 50	49·6	50·4	–	–	83·9	0·4	0·4	0·3
	47·8	52·2	–	–	88·0	Yorks, Brighouse & Spenborough · 4 May 50	49·5	50·5	–	–	85·4	1·7	1·7	1·5
	33·3	56·5	9·5	–	85·8	Leicester, North-East · 28 Sep 50	42·1	57·9	–	–	63·0	3·7	5·0	5·0
	46·5	46·0	5·0	2·6	84·6	Glasgow, Scotstoun · 25 Oct 50	50·9	47·3	–	1·9	73·7	1·5	1·5	1·1
	46·9	40·6	11·6	0·8	84·9	Oxford · 2 Nov 50	57·5	42·5	–	–	69·3	4·4	4·0	2·6
	50·6	39·2	10·3	–	83·1	Birmingham, Handsworth · 16 Nov 50	60·7	38·1	–	1·2	62·2	5·6	5·1	2·4
	26·8	62·6	9·5	1·1	85·0	Bristol, South-East · 30 Nov 50	35·2	56·7	8·1	–	61·1	7·1	8·3	8·6
	13·0	87·1	–	–	84·6	Mon., Abertillery · 30 Nov 50	13·5	86·5	–	–	71·1	0·5	0·5	5·4
	58·9	30·0	11·1	–	82·4	Bristol, West · 15 Feb 51	81·4	18·6	–	–	53·6	16·9	15·1	4·9

					Constituency	Date								
66·3	33·7	—	—	83·9	Lancs, Ormskirk	5 Apr 51	71·5	26·5	—	2·0	64·7	6·2	6·7	0·9
58·5	29·5	12·0	—	86·7	Harrow, West	21 Apr 51	72·0	28·0	—	—	68·0	7·5	5·5	2·4
33·0	61·6	3·5	2·0[2]	83·3	Woolwich, East	14 June 51	39·3	60·7	—	—	66·8	3·6	4·4	4·8
37·7	62·3	—	—	88·2	Lancs, Westhoughton	21 June 51	39·6	60·4	—	—	76·5	1·8	1·8	2·8
63·3	25·1	11·6	—	80·8	Bournemouth, East & Christchurch	6 Feb 52	61·9	23·4	10·1	4·7	63·8	0·1	1·0	-3·2
60·2	24·8	15·0	—	77·7	Southport	6 Feb 52	62·0	28·5	9·5	—	61·0	-0·9	-2·3	-3·5
39·5	60·5	—	—	84·4	Leeds, South-East	7 Feb 52	36·8	63·2	—	—	55·7	-2·7	-2·7	1·5
46·2	53·8	—	—	87·2	Dundee, East	17 July 52	35·6	56·2	—	8·2[2]	71·5	-6·5	-7·4	-4·0
45·2	54·8	—	—	85·1	Yorks, Cleveland	23 Oct 52	45·9	54·1	—	—	71·4	0·7	0·7	1·2
51·7	48·3	—	—	86·2	Bucks, Wycombe	4 Nov 52	52·0	48·0	—	—	83·9	0·4	0·4	0·3
30·9	63·4	5·7	—	77·2	Birmingham, Small Heath	27 Nov 52	33·0	67·0	—	—	46·6	-0·7	0·3	4·6
40·8	59·2	—	—	86·8	Lancs, Farnworth	27 Nov 52	40·1	59·9	—	—	71·0	-0·7	-0·7	1·0
61·1	31·0	7·9	—	80·1	Kent, Canterbury	12 Feb 53	67·1	32·9	—	—	49·2	2·1	0·8	-3·6
61·6	38·4	—	—	78·0	Kent, Isle of Thanet	12 Mar 53	61·3	38·7	—	—	58·7	-0·3	-0·3	-2·4
17·3	69·7	13·0	—	77·2	Barnsley	31 Mar 53	27·1	72·9	—	—	58·0	3·4	7·3	7·0
28·6	71·4	—	—	83·8	Stoke on Trent, North	31 Mar 53	24·5	75·5	—	—	50·5	-4·1	-4·1	5·1
35·2	64·8	—	—	82·2	Hayes and Harlington	1 Apr 53	36·2	63·8	—	—	44·8	1·0	1·0	6·0
49·7	50·3	—	—	82·2	*Sunderland, South	13 May 53	48·6	46·1	5·3	—	72·7	1·6	1·6	1·7
55·5	44·5	—	—	80·0	Berks, Abingdon	30 June 53	53·2	39·7	7·1	—	75·9	1·3	1·8	0·8
64·3	35·7	—	—	76·1	Birmingham, Edgbaston	2 July 53	67·6	32·4	—	—	50·2	3·4	3·4	-2·0
27·3	72·7	—	—	84·1	Notts, Broxtowe	17 Sep 53	25·9	74·1	—	—	63·5	-1·4	-1·4	3·8
71·0	29·1	—	—	79·8	Crosby	12 Nov 53	68·1	26·7	—	4·3	62·5	-0·7	0·2	-4·1
67·4	32·6	—	—	78·7	Lancs, Ormskirk	12 Nov 53	65·4	34·6	—	—	54·1	-2·0	-2·0	-5·4
45·8	50·2	4·0	—	73·7	Holborn & St Pancras South	19 Nov 53	45·6	52·1	2·3	—	56·2	-1·1	-1·1	-0·2
44·3	55·7	—	—	81·0	Paddington, North	3 Dec 53	44·3	53·8	—	0·9	60·3	1·4	1·4	2·0
55·5	38·0	6·5	—	84·8	Ilford, North	3 Feb 54	55·5	32·3	7·9	—	45·4	5·0	5·6	-1·2
58·9	41·1	—	—	78·8	Essex, Harwich	11 Feb 54	59·1	40·9	—	—	58·8	0·2	0·2	-1·7

Previous Gen. Election Con. %	Lab. %	Lib. %	Others %	Turnout %	By-Election and Date	By-Election Result Con. %	Lab. %	Lib. %	Others %	Turnout %	Swing to Con. Butler	Steed	Goguel
58·1	41·9	—	—	82·8	Kingston-upon-Hull, Haltemprice — 11 Feb 54	61·8	38·2	—	—	45·7	3·7	3·7	−1·3
65·5	34·5	—	—	77·7	Bournemouth, West — 18 Feb 54	69·7	30·3	—	—	45·1	4·2	4·2	−3·2
67·4	32·6	—	—	78·0	Sussex, Arundel & Shoreham — 9 Mar 54	68·5	31·5	—	—	54·2	1·2	1·2	−3·5
70·6	29·4	—	—	78·7	Yorks., Harrogate — 11 Mar 54	70·8	29·2	—	—	55·3	0·2	0·2	−4·7
45·9	54·1	—	—	83·8	Edinburgh, East — 8 Apr 54	42·4	57·7	—	—	61·8	−3·6	−3·6	−1·3
42·8	57·3	—	—	84·7	Lanarks., Motherwell — 14 Apr 54	39·3	56·4	—	4·3	70·5	−1·3	−1·7	0·1
58·8	41·2	—	—	84·2	Croydon, East — 30 Sep 54	56·6	35·4	8·0	—	57·5	1·8	2·7	−1·3
27·4	72·6	—	—	73·2	Shoreditch & Finsbury — 21 Oct 54	21·8	78·2	—	—	40·7	−5·6	−5·6	5·1
41·7	58·3	—	—	85·3	Wakefield — 21 Oct 54	41·9	58·1	—	—	68·6	0·2	0·2	1·5
60·3	39·7	—	—	77·8	Hants., Aldershot — 28 Oct 54	60·1	39·9	—	—	58·7	−0·3	−0·3	−2·1
15·4	78·6	—	6·1	86·1	Aberdare — 28 Oct 54	14·5	69·5	—	16·0	69·7	4·1	0·9	8·1
62·8	37·2	—	—	81·7	Sutton & Cheam — 4 Nov 54	66·6	33·5	—	—	55·6	3·8	3·8	−1·2
28·1	71·9	—	—	85·5	Northumberland, Morpeth — 4 Nov 54	28·7	71·3	—	—	73·0	0·6	0·6	3·2
51·6	48·4	—	—	80·3	Liverpool, West Derby — 18 Nov 54	53·2	46·9	—	—	58·9	1·6	1·6	0·6
64·5	35·5	—	—	69·3	Inverness — 21 Dec 54	41·4	22·6	36·0	—	49·2	−5·2	0·1	−5·5
54·5	45·5	—	—	82·4	Norfolk, South — 13 Jan 55	51·5	48·5	—	—	66·2	−3·0	−3·0	−2·7
62·7	37·4	—	—	82·0	Kent, Orpington — 20 Jan 55	65·8	34·2	—	—	55·4	3·2	3·2	−1·6
62·1	37·9	—	—	81·3	Twickenham — 25 Jan 55	64·0	36·0	—	—	47·3	2·0	2·0	−3·2
58·8	41·2	—	—	80·0	Edinburgh, North — 27 Jan 55	59·4	40·6	—	—	46·4	0·6	0·6	−2·7
54·2	45·8	—	—	84·2	Stockport, South — 3 Feb 55	54·3	45·7	—	—	64·6	0·1	0·1	−0·8
34·9	61·5	—	3·6	84·8	Denbighs., Wrexham — 17 Mar 55	30·8	57·9	—	11·3	62·4	−0·2	−1·4	2·9
34·7	65·3	—	—	72·5	Gateshead, West — 7 Dec 55	33·5	66·5	—	—	42·3	−1·2	−1·2	4·1
48·6	51·4	—	—	77·9	Greenock — 8 Dec 55	46·3	53·7	—	—	75·3	−2·3	−2·3	−1·7
60·4	25·4	14·2	—	75·5	Torquay — 15 Dec 55	51·0	25·3	23·8	—	62·6	−4·6	−3·5	−5·1

					Constituency	Date								
33·5	66·5	—	80·7	—	Durham, Blaydon	2 Feb 56	30·1	69·9	—	56·5	—	-3·5	-3·5	2·0
61·5	38·6	—	73·1	—	Leeds, North-East	9 Feb 56	63·2	36·8	—	39·9	—	1·7	1·7	-3·1
51·8	23·4	24·8	78·8	—	Herefs., Hereford	14 Feb 56	44·3	19·3	36·4	61·5	—	-1·7	0·8	-3·5
55·8	44·2	—	76·8	—	Lincs., Gainsborough	14 Feb 56	40·8	37·6	21·6	62·0	—	-4·2	-3·7	-3·4
52·1	39·5	8·4	85·5	—	Somerset, Taunton	14 Feb 56	50·8	49·2	—	75·0	—	-5·5	-6·0	-4·7
34·3	65·7	—	72·5	—	Walthamstow, West	1 Mar 56	20·0	64·7	14·7	54·0	0·4	-6·6	-10·5	-1·4
60·4	39·6	—	75·5	—	Kent, Tonbridge	7 June 56	52·0	48·0	—	60·6	—	-8·4	-8·4	-6·7
46·3	53·7	—	81·6	—	Newport	6 July 56	39·9	56·3	—	72·1	3·8	-4·5	-4·8	-2·9
23·7	76·3	—	79·6	—	Durham, Chester-le-Street	27 Sep 56	19·2	80·8	—	65·0	—	-4·5	-4·5	0·9
56·7	31·6	11·7	77·9	—	Cheshire, City of Chester	15 Nov 56	51·7	36·2	12·1	71·5	—	-4·8	-5·3	-4·2
60·9	39·1	—	81·0	—	Leics., Melton	19 Dec 56	53·3	46·7	—	56·5	—	-7·6	-7·6	-7·0
54·0	46·0	—	77·9	—	*Lewisham, North	14 Feb 57	46·5	49·5	—	70·8	4·0	-5·4	-5·5	-4·1
39·6	60·4	—	72·9	—	Wednesbury	28 Feb 57	28·0	62·2	—	60·0	9·9	-6·8	-8·6	-2·7
—	42·7	49·5	85·1	7·8	*Carms., Carmarthen	28 Feb 57	—	47·3	41·2	87·5	11·5	—	—	—
75·3	24·7	—	74·6	—	Bristol, West	7 Mar 57	70·2	29·8	—	61·1	—	-5·0	-5·0	-6·5
64·5	35·5	—	78·8	—	Warwicks., Warwick & Leamington	7 Mar 57	52·3	47·7	—	77·9	—	-12·2	-12·2	-9·7
69·0	31·0	—	76·5	—	Beckenham	21 Mar 57	62·9	37·1	—	64·7	—	-6·0	-6·0	-6·2
63·8	36·2	—	77·6	—	Newcastle-upon-Tyne, North	21 Mar 57	60·2	39·8	—	64·1	—	-3·6	-3·6	-4·2
67·5	32·5	—	77·2	—	Edinburgh, South	29 May 57	45·6	30·9	23·5	65·8	—	-10·2	-7·9	-8·7
40·9	59·1	—	74·9	2·6	East Ham, North	30 May 57	29·5	56·3	—	57·3	14·3²	-4·3	-6·5	-0·8
60·2	37·2	—	76·3	—	Hornsey	30 May 57	53·5	46·5	—	63·0	—	-8·0	-8·4	-6·6
52·1	15·5	32·4	82·2	—	Dorset, North	27 June 57	45·1	18·3	36·1	75·8	0·5	-4·9	-5·9	-4·9
49·1	50·9	—	80·9	—	Gloucester	12 Sep 57	28·6	51·3	20·1	71·0	—	-10·5	-13·3	-7·4
47·1	52·9	—	80·5	—	Ipswich	24 Oct 57	32·7	45·9	21·5	75·6	—	-3·7	-5·5	-2·6
64·2	35·8	—	78·5	—	Leicester, South-East	28 Nov 57	61·0	39·0	—	56·4	—	-3·3	-3·3	-5·0
63·5	36·5	—	71·0	—	Liverpool, Garston	5 Dec 57	49·2	35·6	15·2	49·7	—	-6·7	-5·5	-6·2
51·5	48·5	—	82·8	—	*Rochdale	12 Feb 58	19·8	44·7	35·5	80·2	—	-14·0	-20·8	-11·2
55·4	44·6	—	67·6	—	*Glasgow, Kelvingrove	13 Mar 58	41·6	48·0	35·5	60·5	10·4²	-8·6	-9·0	-5·6

| Previous Gen. Election | | | | | By-Election and Date | By-Election Result | | | | | Swing to Con. | | |
Con. %	Lab. %	Lib. %	Others %	Turnout %		Con. %	Lab. %	Lib. %	Others %	Turnout %	Butler	Steed	Goguel
65·1	35·0	—	—	69·2	*Devon, Torrington 27 Mar 58	37·4	24·6	38·0	—	80·6	-8·7	-4·8	-5·3
39·7	60·4	—	—	64·7	Islington, North 15 May 58	29·3	67·7	—	3·0	35·6	-8·9	-9·4	-0·1
59·6	30·9	9·6	—	77·9	Ealing, South 12 June 58	50·3	32·5	17·2	—	64·5	-5·5	-5·1	-5·4
35·7	64·3	—	—	73·5	St Helens 12 June 58	35·3	64·7	—	—	54·6	-0·4	-0·4	2·5
32·2	64·4	—	3·4	80·3	Wigan 12 June 58	26·5	71·0	—	2·5	70·3	-6·1	-6·1	-2·7
62·7	37·3	—	—	73·8	Somerset, Weston-super-Mare 12 June 58	49·3	26·2	24·5	—	72·2	-1·1	2·6	-1·0
67·6	32·4	—	—	66·6	Argyll 12 June 58	46·8	25·7	27·5	—	67·1	-7·1	-3·1	-4·7
71·2	28·8	—	—	74·4	Lancs., Morecambe & Lonsdale 6 Nov 58	65·3	34·7	—	—	63·9	-5·9	-5·9	-6·0
70·8	29·2	—	—	71·8	Sussex, Chichester 6 Nov 58	70·9	29·1	—	—	51·8	0·1	0·1	-4·1
27·1	72·9	—	—	77·1	Mon., Pontypool 10 Nov 58	21·5	68·5	—	10·0	61·7	-0·6	-3·2	3·2
68·5	31·5	—	—	59·8	Aberdeenshire, East 20 Nov 58	48·6	27·1	24·3	—	65·9	-7·8	-4·3	-4·0
26·6	73·5	—	—	61·6	Shoreditch & Finsbury 27 Nov 58	24·0	76·0	—	—	24·9	-2·6	-2·6	-8·0
64·2	20·8	15·0	—	74·1	Southend, West 29 Jan 59	55·8	20·2	24·2	—	42·9	-4·0	-2·2	-8·5
54·4	45·6	—	—	82·6	Harrow, East 19 Mar 59	52·8	46·2	—	1·0	69·0	-1·1	-1·1	-1·4
49·7	50·3	—	—	82·6	Norfolk, South-West 25 Mar 59	46·4	51·0	—	2·6	75·2	-2·0	-2·0	-1·5
66·9	33·1	—	—	69·1	Galloway 9 Apr 59	50·5	23·9	25·7	—	72·8	-3·6	1·0	-2·0
37·7	62·3	—	—	80·0	Yorks., Penistone 11 June 59	35·9	64·1	—	—	65·0	-1·8	-1·8	0·7
42·0	58·0	—	—	63·8	Cumberland, Whitehaven 18 June 59	41·4	58·6	—	—	79·2	-0·6	-0·6	-0·1
70·9	29·1	—	—	79·2	Harrow, West 17 Mar 60	55·8	18·2	21·4	4·7	61·6	-2·1	4·5	-5·0
50·0	50·1	—	—	85·5	*Yorks, Brighouse & Spenborough 17 Mar 60	50·8	49·3	—	—	82·4	0·8	0·8	0·7
64·0	36·0	—	—	73·9	Edinburgh, North 19 May 60	54·2	30·3	15·5	—	53·8	-2·1	0·1	-3·9
52·8	47·2	—	—	81·0	Bolton, East 16 Nov 60	37·8	36·2	24·8	1·2	68·2	-2·0	-1·7	-1·7
46·8	35·4	17·8	—	84·5	Mid-Bedfordshire 16 Nov 60	45·4	29·3	24·8	0·6	71·1	2·4	3·9	0·9

Station	Date										
Shrops., Ludlow	60·3	39·7	—	16 Nov 60	46·4	26·3	27·4	—	63·6	−0·3	3·5	−1·5
Devon, Tiverton	55·6	25·2	19·2	16 Nov 60	45·7	17·6	36·7	—	68·4	−1·2	3·4	−2·7
Surrey, Carshalton	54·0	30·5	15·5	16 Nov 60	51·7	20·7	27·6	—	54·2	·3·7	7·5	−1·3
Hants., Petersfield	60·9	21·3	17·8	16 Nov 60	54·4	16·6	29·0	7·0	53·6	−0·9	2·5	−4·5
Mon., Ebbw Vale	19·0	81·0	—	17 Nov 60	12·7	68·8	11·5	—	83·8	3·0	0·0	0·0
Blyth	25·4	74·6	—	24 Nov 60	21·7	68·9	—	9·5	54·1	1·0	−1·5	7·6
Worcester	57·7	42·3	—	16 Mar 61	39·7	30·2	30·1	—	64·2	−2·9	−0·9	−3·1
Essex, Colchester	51·6	35·9	12·5	16 Mar 61	47·2	33·1	19·7	—	64·9	−0·8	−0·2	−1·9
Derbys., High Peak	46·0	34·0	20·0	16 Mar 61	37·4	32·1	30·6	—	72·5	−3·4	−3·7	−3·1
Cambridgeshire	57·9	42·1	—	16 Mar 61	45·9	30·1	24·0	—	62·4	0·0	2·5	−1·2
Birmingham, Small Heath	42·6	57·4	—	23 Mar 61	28·8	59·2	12·0	—	42·6	−7·8	−9·9	−1·6
Warrington	43·7	52·3	—	20 Apr 61	31·6	55·8	12·5	—	56·7	−5·8	−7·6	−2·1
Paisley	42·7	57·3	—	20 Apr 61	13·2	45·4	41·4	—	68·1	−18·8	−20·1	−5·2
Bristol, South-East	43·8	56·2	—	4 May 61	30·5	69·5	—	—	56·7	−3·2	−13·2	−6·0
Manchester, Moss Side	62·3	37·7	16·1	7 Nov 61	41·1	25·8	27·8	5·2	48·7	−4·6	−0·8	−4·9
Shrops., Oswestry	55·9	28·0	—	8 Nov 61	40·8	28·0	28·4	2·8	60·8	−7·6	−7·3	−6·5
Fife, East	70·0	30·1	—	8 Nov 61	47·4	26·4	26·1	—	67·3	−9·4	−5·7	−7·9
Glasgow, Bridgeton	36·6	63·4	—	16 Nov 61	20·7	57·5	—	21·8[2]	41·9	−5·0	−10·1	1·5
Lincoln	44·9	55·1	—	8 Mar 62	30·2	50·5	18·2	1·2	75·0	−5·0	−7·5	−3·3
Blackpool, North	57·9	21·6	20·6	13 Mar 62	38·3	26·4	35·3	—	55·2	−12·2	−13·7	−10·3
*Kent, Orpington	56·6	22·2	21·2	14 Mar 62	34·7	12·4	52·9	—	80·3	−6·0	1·9	−5·3
Middlesbrough, East	38·5	61·5	—	14 Mar 62	15·0	61·7	23·3	—	51·3	−11·8	−18·9	−3·2
Pontefract	23·6	76·4	—	22 Mar 62	19·4	77·3	—	3·4	63·3	−2·6	−3·6	3·9
Stockton-on-Tees	46·3	53·7	—	5 Apr 62	27·8	45·2	26·9	—	81·5	−5·0	−8·3	−4·0
Derby, North	47·2	52·8	—	17 Apr 62	22·5	49·5	25·4	2·7	60·6	−10·7	−15·9	−6·0
Montgomeryshire	31·3	26·6	42·0	15 May 62	21·9	20·6	51·3	6·2	85·1	−1·7	−2·5	−1·4
*Middlesbrough, West	54·9	35·5	9·7	6 June 62	33·7	39·7	25·8	0·8[2]	72·2	−12·7	−14·8	−10·4
Derbys., West	61·3	38·7	—	6 June 62	36·0	27·3	32·5	4·2	79·4	−6·9	−4·4	−5·8
West Lothian	39·7	60·3	—	14 June 62	11·4	50·8	10·8	26·9[2]	71·1	−9·4	−21·4	−6·0
Leicester, North-East	48·1	51·9	—	12 July 62	24·2	41·5	34·3	—	60·9	−6·7	−11·2	−3·8
*Glasgow, Woodside	49·3	43·1	7·7	22 Nov 62	30·1	36·1	21·7	12·1[3]	54·7	−6·1	−7·8	−4·0

Previous Gen. Election					By-Election and Date	By-Election Result					Swing to Con.		
Con. %	Lab. %	Lib. %	Others %	Turnout %		Con. %	Lab. %	Lib. %	Others %	Turnout %	Butler	Steed	Coguel
49·8	34·7	15·6	—	78·8	*Dorset, South — 22 Nov 62	31·8	33·5	21·7	13·0[4]	70·2	−8·4	−10·3	−6·6
52·1	31·0	16·9	—	80·3	Wilts., Chippenham — 22 Nov 62	36·8	29·1	32·5	1·6[3]	68·0	−6·7	−6·9	−5·8
57·0	43·0	—	—	82·7	Northants., South — 22 Nov 62	41·2	38·6	19·3	0·9	69·0	−5·7	−5·4	−4·9
50·4	34·8	14·9	—	79·9	Norfolk, Central — 22 Nov 62	37·7	37·1	22·5	2·8[2]	60·2	−7·5	−8·7	−6·1
29·9	44·3	25·8	—	84·2	Yorks., Colne Valley — 21 Mar 63	15·4	44·5	39·5	0·7	78·9	−7·4	−14·6	−5·4
37·2	62·8	—	—	78·9	Rotherham — 28 Mar 63	28·4	69·3	—	2·3	56·3	−7·6	−8·1	−1·4
22·0	67·5	—	10·5	80·1	Swansea, East — 28 Mar 63	7·4	61·1	15·8	15·7[3]	55·9	−4·2	−13·9	3·2
31·0	58·6	10·4	—	79·0	Leeds, South — 20 June 63	20·1	62·9	14·7	2·2	60·5	−7·7	−10·5	−2·1
38·1	62·0	—	—	69·3	Deptford — 4 July 63	19·2	58·3	22·6	—	44·1	−7·6	−13·3	−0·3
42·6	57·4	—	—	72·6	West Bromwich — 4 July 63	23·6	58·7	17·6	—	55·2	−10·2	−13·9	−4·3
68·5	31·5	—	—	76·9	Warwicks., Stratford — 15 Aug 63	43·6	34·1	21·0	1·4[2]	69·4	−13·7	−12·4	−10·9
43·8	56·2	—	—	81·4	†Bristol, South-East — 20 Aug 63	—	79·7	—	20·3[3]	42·2	—	—	—
55·1	44·9	—	—	82·5	*Luton — 7 Nov 63	39·5	48·0	11·4	1·1	74·0	−9·4	−10·0	−7·4
68·2	16·8	—	15·0	71·0	Kinross & Perthshire, West — 7 Nov 63	57·4	15·2	19·5	7·9[4]	76·1	−4·6	−1·2	−2·2
48·3	49·6	—	2·1	82·9	Dundee, West — 21 Nov 63	39·4	50·6	—	10·0[2]	71·6	−4·9	−5·5	−3·4
53·0	33·0	14·0	—	81·1	Suffolk, Sudbury & Woodbridge — 5 Dec 63	49·6	37·0	13·4	—	70·5	−3·7	−4·4	−3·7
39·8	60·2	—	—	76·0	Manchester, Openshaw — 5 Dec 63	29·2	65·9	—	4·9	46·1	−8·2	−9·1	−0·7
64·5	23·6	11·9	—	65·5	St Marylebone — 5 Dec 63	55·0	31·8	13·3	—	44·2	−8·9	−9·9	−8·3
58·4	41·6	—	—	77·4	Dumfriesshire — 12 Dec 63	40·8	38·5	10·9	9·8	71·7	−7·2	−6·9	−5·7
58·8	41·3	—	—	78·6	Suffolk, Bury St Edmunds — 14 May 64	49·0	43·5	7·5	—	74·6	−6·0	−5·8	−4·9
51·4	41·9	6·7	—	79·2	Wilts., Devizes — 14 May 64	46·9	42·9	10·3	—	75·8	−2·8	−2·9	−2·3
52·1	47·9	—	—	85·9	*Lanarks., Rutherglen — 14 May 64	44·5	55·5	—	—	82·0	−7·6	−7·6	−6·3
67·3	32·7	—	—	76·7	Hants., Winchester — 14 May 64	52·2	34·6	13·2	—	68·7	−8·5	−7·2	−7·2
49·7	50·3	—	—	83·8	Kent, Faversham — 4 June 64	44·1	·155	—	0·8	74·8	−5·2	−5·3	−3·9

38·2	61·8	—	—	62·5	11 June 64	Liverpool, Scotland	25·7	74·3	—	—	42·0	−12·5	−12·5	−2·8
29·1	52·8	18·1	—	80·1	21 Jan 65	Warwicks., Nuneaton	34·9	48·9	16·1	—	60·8	4·9	6·1	5·2
33·5	50·4	16·2	—	70·2	21 Jan 65	*Leyton	42·9	42·4	14·0	0·8[2]	57·7	8·7	10·4	6·1
46·8	28·0	25·2	—	81·2	4 Feb 65	Altrincham & Sale	50·0	29·1	19·4	1·6	62·0	1·1	0·7	−1·1
53·2	19·9	27·0	—	78·0	4 Feb 65	Sussex, East Grinstead	55·0	13·5	31·5	—	64·5	4·1	7·5	0·4
48·3	34·4	17·3	—	78·6	4 Feb 65	Wilts., Salisbury	48·2	37·4	12·9	1·5	69·1	−1·5	−2·1	−1·7
49·3	37·5	13·3	—	82·4	23 Mar 65	Essex, Saffron Walden	48·5	39·6	11·9	—	76·1	−1·4	−1·7	−1·5
42·8	15·9	38·9	2·5	82·2	24 Mar 65	*Roxburgh, Selkirk & Peebles	38·7	11·3	49·2	0·9	82·2	0·2	4·5	0·2
14·1	85·9	—	—	75·5	1 Apr 65	Mon., Abertillery	14·3	79·0	—	6·7	63·2	3·6	1·2	6·7
55·5	31·8	15·6	—	75·8	6 May 65	Birmingham, Hall Green	54·9	28·8	16·4	—	52·4	2·7	3·4	−1·0
68·4	31·6	—	—	69·6	22 July 65	Hove	62·2	20·6	16·9	0·3	58·5	2·4	6·7	−0·6
58·4	30·6	11·1	—	59·7	4 Nov 65	Cities of London & Westminster	59·5	32·9	6·3	1·3	41·8	−0·6	−1·2	−2·7
32·5	53·1	14·4	—	79·6	11 Nov 65	Erith & Crayford	37·5	55·4	7·2	—	72·0	1·3	2·4	1·8
40·8	43·3	15·9	—	77·2	27 Jan 66	Kingston-upon-Hull, North	40·8	52·2	6·3	0·7[3]	76·3	−4·5	−4·7	−3·4
11·6	46·2	26·1	16·1	83·0	14 July 66	*Carms., Carmarthen	7·1	33·1	20·8	39·0	74·9	4·3	−2·5	4·6
31·6	54·0	14·5	—	79·7	9 Mar 67	Warwicks., Nuneaton	32·7	42·1	17·6	7·6[2]	66·1	6·5	6·9	5·8
7·8	76·1	—	16·1[2]	80·3	9 Mar 67	Rhondda, West	4·3	49·0	—	46·7[2]	82·2	11·8	−1·3	9·0
47·6	52·4	—	—	79·0	9 Mar 67	*Glasgow, Pollok	36·9	31·2	1·9	30·0[2]	75·7	5·3	6·6	4·1
54·4	26·8	18·9	—	78·6	16 Mar 67	Devon, Honiton	57·0	20·4	22·6	—	72·7	4·5	6·6	2·4
51·2	48·8	—	—	79·0	24 Apr 67	Staffs., Brierley Hill	53·8	36·2	7·8	2·2	68·0	7·6	8·6	5·0
43·4	45·5	10·2	0·9	80·0	21 Sep 67	*Cambridge	51·6	36·6	11·8	—	65·8	8·6	9·7	5·8
24·8	61·2	14·1	—	71·0	21 Sep 67	*Walthamstow, West	37·1	36·7	22·9	3·4[2]	54·0	18·4	21·4	13·0
41·4	58·7	—	—	74·0	2 Nov 67	*Leicester, South-West	51·6	35·9	12·5	—	57·5	16·5	17·7	10·9
39·9	60·1	—	—	72·6	2 Nov 67	Manchester, Gorton	44·5	45·9	5·9	3·7[2]	72·4	9·4	9·3	6·8
28·8	71·2	—	—	73·3	2 Nov 67	*Lanarks., Hamilton	12·5	41·5	—	46·0	73·7	6·7	−5·7	4·8

	Previous Gen. Election						By-Election Result					Swing to Con.		
By-Election and Date	Con. %	Lab. %	Lib. %	Others %	Turnout %		Con. %	Lab. %	Lib. %	Others %	Turnout %	Butler	Steed	Goguel
Derbys., West — 23 Nov 67	49·6	37·2	13·2	—	83·4		56·7	18·4	19·8	5·2	64·6	13·0	18·4	7·2
Kensington, South — 14 Mar 68	65·1	19·9	15·1	—	58·1		75·5	8·6	12·6	3·4[2]	40·0	10·8	13·2	0·3
*Dudley — 28 Mar 68	41·0	59·1	—	—	73·9		58·1	34·0	7·9	—	63·5	21·2	22·2	14·4
Warwicks., Warwick & Leamington — 28 Mar 68	51·6	36·1	12·3	—	78·9		68·3	16·5	15·2	—	58·5	18·1	21·7	9·0
*Warwicks., Meriden — 28 Mar 68	46·4	53·6	—	—	85·7		64·8	35·2	—	—	66·0	18·5	18·5	12·9
*Acton — 28 Mar 68	42·3	57·7	—	—	74·0		48·7	33·9	11·4	6·0[3]	59·7	15·1	16·6	10·1
*Oldham, West — 13 June 68	38·8	61·2	—	—	70·9		46·5	33·6	6·7	13·2	54·7	17·7	19·3	11·5
Sheffield, Brightside — 13 June 68	21·3	75·9	—	2·8	66·2		34·8	55·2	—	10·0[3]	49·8	17·1	16·7	13·0
*Nelson & Colne — 27 June 68	37·0	49·3	—	13·7	81·0		48·9	38·4	9·0	3·7	74·2	11·4	13·1	8·8
Glam., Caerphilly — 18 July 68	14·6	74·3	—	11·1	76·7		10·4	45·7	3·6	40·4	75·9	12·2	2·1	9·5
Notts., Bassetlaw — 31 Oct 68	38·4	61·6	—	—	73·4		47·9	49·6	—	2·4	68·0	10·8	10·8	8·0
Hants, New Forest — 7 Nov 68	51·2	26·8	22·1	—	74·2		66·3	13·8	19·9	—	55·9	14·0	17·1	5·6
*Walthamstow, East — 27 Mar 69	42·3	47·8	9·8	—	80·1		63·2	36·9	—	—	51·2	15·9	16·2	8·9
Brighton, Pavilion — 27 Mar 69	58·1	41·9	—	—	70·3		70·5	18·6	10·8	—	45·1	17·8	21·0	6·0
Somerset, Weston-super-Mare — 27 Mar 69	52·1	28·8	19·1	—	78·5		65·7	14·6	19·7	—	60·8	13·9	17·4	6·4
Sussex, Chichester — 27 May 69	57·2	25·1	17·7	—	73·2		74·2	12·2	13·6	—	53·4	15·0	16·4	4·8
*Birmingham, Ladywood — 26 June 69	17·4	58·9	23·7	—	59·7		16·8	25·5	54·3	3·4[2]	51·9	16·5	17·0	10·2
Paddington, North — 30 Oct 69	32·3	58·5	9·3	—	66·4		48·3	51·7	—	—	46·3	11·4	12·7	7·9
Islington, North — 30 Oct 69	30·7	59·5	9·9	—	54·2		38·9	49·2	10·2	1·7	32·8	9·2	10·1	6·1
Glasgow, Gorbals — 30 Oct 69	22·8	73·1	—	4·1	61·7		18·6	53·4	—	28·0[3]	58·6	7·7	2·1	5·3
Newcastle-under-Lyme — 30 Oct 69	38·2	61·8	—	—	79·9		44·4	46·6	6·4	2·6	71·5	10·7	10·6	8·6
*Swindon — 30 Oct 69	36·7	61·4	—	2·0	73·5		41·7	40·5	15·3	2·4[2]	69·8	12·9	13·3	9·5
*Northants., Wellingborough — 4 Dec 69	47·6	52·4	—	—	86·5		54·4	39·8	—	5·8	69·7	9·7	10·1	7·1

Constituency	Date													
Lincs., Louth	4 Dec 69	46·4	36·9	16·8	—	75·0	58·0	19·9	17·8	4·4	44·7	14·3	18·8	5·0
Somerset, Bridgwater	12 Mar 70	44·4	38·1	17·5	—	80·2	55·5	31·9	12·6	—	70·3	8·6	9·6	5·7
Ayrshire, South	19 Mar 70	32·8	67·3	—	—	75·1	25·6	54·1	—	20·4	76·3	3·0	-0·6	2·1
St Marylebone	22 Oct 70	62·1	29·3	8·6	—	59·6	63·5	27·0	6·0	3·4	35·3	1·9	2·2	-3·3
Enfield, West	19 Nov 70	57·9	26·2	12·8	3·1	71·3	57·2	26·1	12·4	4·4	49·9	-0·3	-0·1	-3·5
Liverpool, Scotland	1 Apr 71	25·3	74·8	—	—	50·7	18·4	71·3	—	10·3	37·7	-1·7	-4·8	-2·6
Sussex, Arundel & Shoreham	1 Apr 71	60·8	22·9	16·3	—	72·0	64·1	20·9	14·7	0·4	53·1	2·6	2·8	-2·2
*Worcs., Bromsgrove	27 May 71	58·5	41·5	—	—	76·6	48·4	51·6	—	—	67·0	-10·1	-10·1	-7·6
Yorks., Goole	27 May 71	39·8	60·2	—	—	69·5	31·1	68·9	—	—	55·6	-8·7	-8·7	-3·4
Southampton, Itchen	27 May 71	—	67·2	—	32·8[2]	54·2	31·6	55·4	5·4	7·6	50·1	—	—	—
Hayes & Harlington	17 June 71	41·2	57·7	—	1·1	67·2	25·3	74·7	—	—	42·3	-16·5	-16·4	-5·0
Greenwich	8 July 71	36·3	57·3	6·4	—	64·0	28·0	66·7	—	5·3	39·2	-8·9	-9·3	-0·9
Stirlingshire, Stirling & Falkirk	16 Sep 71	34·8	50·7	—	14·5	73·1	19·0	46·5	—	34·6	60·9	-5·8	-11·7	-2·6
Lancs., Widnes	23 Sep 71	42·3	57·7	—	—	68·8	30·9	69·1	—	—	46·2	-11·5	-11·5	-3·6
Cheshire, Macclesfield	30 Sep 71	52·1	33·3	14·6	—	76·4	44·7	42·7	10·7	1·9	76·6	-8·4	-9·9	-6·4
*Merthyr Tydfil	13 Apr 72	9·9	28·7	—	61·5[2]	77·9	7·4	48·5	2·4	41·7[2]	77·6	-11·2	-12·4	-8·6
Southwark	4 May 72	28·2	67·3	—	4·5	48·2	18·1	79·3	—	2·6	29·4	-11·1	-11·0	0·4
Kingston-upon-Thames	4 May 72	56·7	31·7	11·7	—	69·1	52·3	31·0	11·3	5·4	53·3	-1·9	-1·4	-3·0
*Rochdale	26 Oct 72	28·0	41·6	30·4	—	72·9	17·7	31·1	42·3	8·9	69·0	0·1	-4·1	0·3
Uxbridge	7 Dec 72	49·3	41·7	9·0	—	74·9	39·8	36·8	10·2	13·2[4]	56·2	-2·3	-2·1	-2·0
*Sutton & Cheam	7 Dec 72	58·1	27·3	14·6	—	67·6	31·9	8·7	53·6	5·9[2]	56·2	-3·8	10·4	-3·4
*Lincoln	1 Mar 73	39·0	51·0	—	10·0	74·5	17·5	23·3	—	59·2[4]	72·6	3·1	-0·3	2·4
Dundee, East	1 Mar 73	42·4	48·3	—	9·3[2]	76·1	25·2	32·7	8·3	33·8[3]	70·6	-0·8	-2·8	-0·6
Chester-le-Street	1 Mar 73	28·4	71·6	—	—	73·7	8·4	53·0	38·6	—	71·4	-0·8	-14·7	0·9

Contests excluded above (see p. 359)

Londonderry, North	(4 Mar 19)
Oxford University	(19 Mar 19)
*Antrim, East	(27 May 19)
Stockport (double by-election)	(27 Mar 20)
Sunderland	(24 Apr 20)
City of London	(19 May 22)
City of London	(1 Feb 24)
Dundee	(22 Dec 24)
Oldham	(24 June 25)
*Stockport	(17 Sep 25)
*Combined English Universities	(8–12 Mar 26)
Combined Scottish Universities	(26–29 Apr 27)
*Preston	(31 Aug 29)
*Sunderland	(26 Mar 31)
Combined Scottish Universities	(7–12 Mar 34)
Fermanagh & Tyrone	(27 June 34)
†Combined Scottish Universities	(17–22 June 35)
Combined Scottish Universities	(27–31 Jan 36)
*Derby	(9 July 36)
Preston	(25 Nov 36)
*Oxford University	(23–27 Feb 37)
*Combined English Universities	(15–19 Mar 37)
†Combined Scottish Universities	(21–25 Feb 38)
*Cambridge University	(19–24 Feb 40)
University of Wales	(25–29 Jan 43)
Belfast, West	(9 Feb 43)
Antrim	(11 Feb 43)
Brighton	(3 Feb 44)
*‡Combined Scottish Universities	(9–13 Apr 45)
City of London	(31 Oct 45)
Preston	(31 Jan 46)
*Combined English Universities	(13–18 Mar 46)
*Down	(6 June 46)
*Combined Scottish Universities	(22–27 Nov 46)
Armagh	(5 Mar 48)
Belfast, West	(29 Nov 50)
Belfast, South	(4 Nov 52)
Mid-Ulster	(12 Aug 55)
†Mid-Ulster	(8 May 56)
Belfast, East	(19 Mar 59)
*Mid-Ulster	(17 Apr 69)

Summary Tables

TABLE I

Turnout and Swing by Year

Year	Government	Contests[a]	Mean turnout	Mean turnout change	Mean swing to Conservative Butler	Steed	Goguel	n[b]
1919	Con./Lib.	13	58·3	+2·3	−12·0	−12·7	−7·3	3
1920	Con./Lib.	15	64·0	+7·9	−7·9	−7·1	−3·8	1
1921	Con./Lib.	14	68·1	+14·1	−11·2	−9·9	−5·3	3
1922	Con./Lib.	13	68·8	+11·2	−11·9	−11·6	−5·9	4
1922–3[c]	Con.	16	70·4	−1·3	−3·0	−3·8	−2·1	4
1924	Lab.	7	76·1	+3·2	−0·2	−0·8	−0·2	5
1925	Con.	6	76·3	−1·3	−4·9	−4·9	−4·0	2
1926	Con.	12	77·9	−2·4	−6·9	−7·6	−5·3	8
1927	Con.	8	71·7	−4·0	−5·8	−6·9	−5·2	2
1928	Con.	17	68·9	−5·4	−7·6	−7·9	−6·4	10
1929[d]	Con.	9	73·4	−6·6	−12·9	−13·1	−9·1	4
1929	Lab.	4	51·8	−19·1	−2·5	−2·3	−2·3	3
1930	Lab.	9	63·3	−12·0	+6·9	+8·0	+5·2	7
1931	Lab.	17	62·1	−13·4	+10·1	+10·5	+6·4	8
1932	Nat. (Con.)	12	58·7	−16·3	−9·8	−9·6	−9·9	6
1933	Nat. (Con.)	12	68·3	−7·2	−17·6	−18·1	−13·2	9
1934	Nat. (Con.)	14	62·5	−11·2	−15·3	−15·3	−11·5	10
1935	Nat. (Con.)	7	57·0	−18·6	−20·8	−20·6	−16·0	5
1936	Nat. (Con.)	9	56·8	−10·4	−3·4	−3·5	−3·5	7
1937	Nat. (Con.)	22	56·9	−12·6	−4·0	−3·9	−3·7	17
1938	Nat. (Con.)	16	69·0	−3·8	−4·7	−4·7	−3·7	9
1939	Nat. (Con.)	19	57·5	−13·3	−1·2	−1·1	−2·5	10
1940	Nat.	13	34·6	−32·2	+18·0	+17·3	+3·3	2
1941	Nat.	10	29·6	−42·3	+14·7	+14·4	+0·1	1
1942	Nat.	12	33·0	−37·0	−	−	−	0
1943	Nat.	16	34·3	−39·4	+9·4	+10·8	−2·8	2
1944	Nat.	7	33·6	−33·6	−	−	−	0
1945[e]	Nat.	4	54·2	−20·3	+2·8	+2·8	+0·9	1
1945	Lab.	8	55·9	−15·7	+0·1	−0·1	+1·3	6
1946	Lab.	13	59·8	−12·6	+2·3	+2·5	+2·5	9
1947	Lab.	8	65·0	−6·5	+6·3	+5·8	+5·5	8
1948	Lab.	10	65·7	−3·6	+8·4	+8·1	+5·8	9
1949	Lab.	6	71·2	−4·0	+6·5	+7·9	+5·1	6

TABLE I—*continued*

Year	Government	Contests	Mean turnout	Mean turnout change	Mean swing to Conservative Butler	Steed	Goguel	n
1950	Lab.	9	70·3	− 14·7	+ 2·9	+ 3·0	+ 3·6	9
1951	Lab.	5	65·9	− 19·0	+ 7·2	+ 6·7	+ 3·2	5
1952	Con.	8	65·6	− 17·6	− 1·3	− 1·4	− 0·3	8
1953	Con.	13	58·2	− 21·6	+ 0·1	+ 0·5	+ 0·5	13
1954	Con.	17	57·0	− 23·8	+ 0·8	+ 0·8	− 0·7	15
1955ᶠ	Con.	6	57·1	− 25·3	+ 0·4	+ 0·2	− 1·3	6
1955	Con.	3	60·0	− 15·3	− 2·7	− 2·3	− 0·9	3
1956	Con.	11	61·3	− 17·1	− 4·7	− 5·3	− 2·9	10
1957	Con.	15	66·7	− 11·0	− 6·6	− 7·0	− 5·4	13
1958	Con.	14	61·0	− 10·5	− 4·3	− 3·9	− 1·4	11
1959	Con.	6	67·3	− 11·4	− 1·4	− 1·4	− 0·6	4
1960	Con.	11	65·0	− 15·5	+ 1·7	+ 1·3	+ 2·1	6
1961	Con.	12	58·7	− 17·3	− 5·4	− 5·4	− 2·8	9
1962	Con.	17	68·1	− 12·3	− 6·6	− 8·3	− 4·4	8
1963	Con.	15	61·1	− 16·1	− 8·1	− 9·0	− 4·8	10
1964	Con.	6	69·6	− 8·2	− 7·1	− 6·9	− 4·6	6
1965–6ᵍ	Lab.	13	64·3	− 12·8	+ 1·5	+ 1·9	+ 0·9	11
1966–7	Lab.	12	69·4	− 8·8	+ 10·3	+ 11·4	+ 7·4	7
1968	Lab.	11	60·6	− 13·3	+ 16·2	+ 17·4	+ 11·0	8
1969–70ʰ	Lab.	14	58·8	− 15·1	+ 11·3	+ 12·2	+ 6·7	10
1970–1	Con.	12	51·2	− 15·8	− 6·2	− 6·6	− 3·3	10
1972	Con.	6	56·9	− 11·3	− 5·1	− 4·8	− 1·8	3

Notes:

ᵃ Number of contests is the number used for the calculation of turnout, and excludes the seats excluded from Appendix A.

ᵇ This is the number of contests for which a Conservative/Labour swing is calculable and meaningful. It includes all swing figures from Appendix A, except those printed in italics.

ᶜ Portsmouth South (13 Dec 22) included with 1923 as the only 1922 by-election after the general election of that year.

ᵈ 1929 divided at the general election.

ᵉ 1945 divided at the general election.

ᶠ 1955 divided at the general election.

ᵍ 1966 divided at the general election: Kingston-upon-Hull North included with 1965 and Carmarthen included with 1967.

ʰ 1970 divided at the general election: Bridgwater and South Ayrshire included with 1969; St Marylebone and Enfield West included with 1971.

TABLE 2

Turnout and Swing by Parliament

Parliament	Government	Contests[a]	Turnout	Turn-out change	Butler swing	n[b]	Butler[c] swing-back	n
1918–22	Con./Lib.	55	64·7	+9·0	−11·4	11	+4·9	12
1922–3	Con.	16	70·4	−1·3	−3·0	4	−	0
1923–4	Lab.	7	76·1	+3·2	−0·2	5	−0·8	3
1924–9	Con.	52	73·1	−4·2	−7·7	26	+0·9	31
1929–31	Lab.	30	61·1	−13·3	+6·7	18	+11·7	17
1931–5	Nat. (Con.)	45	62·2	−12·6	−15·8	30	+4·4	32
1935–9[d]	Nat. (Con.)	64	60·7	−9·5	−3·9	42	−9·9	40
1939–45	Nat.	64	34·6	−36·1	+12·8	7	−26·2	8
1945–50	Lab.	45	62·9	−8·9	+4·9	38	−	0[e]
1950–1	Lab.	14	68·8	−16·2	+4·4	14	−3·1	14
1951–5	Con.	44	58·9	−22·2	+0·1	42	+1·1	5[f]
1955–9	Con.	49	63·5	−12·5	−4·7	41	+5·4	40
1959–64	Con.	61	64·1	−14·4	−5·5	39	+1·7	39
1964–6	Lab.	13	64·3	−12·8	+1·5	11	−4·2	11
1966–70	Lab.	37	62·4	−12·3	+12·0	25	−6·9	26

Notes:

[a] Number of contests is the number used for the calculation of turnout, and excludes the same categories of seat as in Table 1 above, and Appendix A.

[b] The *n* figures in this column are the number of seats where swing calculations were realistic: this therefore gives an indication of the reliability of the figures.

[c] Butler swing-back is the swing in by-election constituencies between the by-election and the next general election.

[d] The 1935–45 Parliament is divided at the outbreak of war; Labour did not enter the National Government until May 1940, but an electoral truce was implemented in September 1939.

[e] Swing-back figures cannot be calculated in 1950 because of the re-distribution of seats.

[f] Few swing-back figures calculable because of a partial redistribution of seats.

Bibliography

Where books have been found particularly useful for single chapters, they have been acknowledged in footnotes or in bibliographical notes. This list is therefore of a more general nature; it includes only items which are not listed elsewhere in the book and items of general and methodological interest. All books listed were published in London unless stated otherwise.

I. REFERENCE WORKS

F. W. S. Craig (ed.), *British Parliamentary Election Statistics, 1918–1970*, 2nd ed. (Chichester, 1971).

F. W. S. Craig (ed.), *British Parliamentary Election Results, 1918–1970*, 2 vols. (Chichester, 1969, 1971).

F. W. S. Craig (ed.), *British Parliamentary Constituency Boundaries* (Chichester, 1972).

M. Kinnear, *The British Voter* (1968).

B. R. Mitchell and K. Boehm, *British Parliamentary Election Results, 1950–1964* (Cambridge, 1966).

Census of 1966: Parliamentary Constituency Tables (1969).

T. Erskine May, *Parliamentary Practice*, 18th ed., edited by Sir B. Cocks (1971).

Parker's Election Agent and Returning Officer, 6th ed. (1959).

A. N. Schofield, *Parliamentary Elections*, 3rd ed. (1959).

II. COMMENTARIES

A. J. Allen, *The English Voter* (1964).

A. Booth, *British Hustings, 1924–1950* (1956).

J. C. Brown, 'Local Party Efficiency as a Factor in the Outcome of British Elections', *Political Studies* (June 1958).

D. E. Butler, *The Electoral System in Britain since 1918*, 2nd ed. (Oxford, 1963).

D. E. Butler, *The British General Election of 1951* (1952).

D. E. Butler, *The British General Election of 1955* (1955).

D. E. Butler and R. Rose, *The British General Election of 1959* (1960).

D. E. Butler and A. King, *The British General Election of 1964* (1965).

D. E. Butler and A. King, *The British General Election of 1966* (1966).

D. E. Butler and M. Pinto-Duschinsky, *The British General Election of 1970* (1971).

D. E. Butler and D. Stokes, *Political Change in Britain* (1969).

J. P. Dunbabin, 'British Elections: A Psephological Note', *English Historical Review* (1966).

C. A. E. Goodhart and R. J. Bhansali, 'Political Economy', *Political Studies* Mar 1970).

R. T. Holt and J. E. Turner, *Political Parties in Action* (1968).

T. L. Humberstone, *University Representation* (1951).

D. Kavanagh, *Constituency Electioneering in Britain* (1970).

A. King, 'Why all Governments Lose By-Elections', *New Society*, 21 Mar 1968.

R. L. Leonard, *Elections in Britain*, 2nd ed., (1968).

E. G. Lewis, *British By-Elections as a Reflection of Public Opinion* (Berkeley, 1943).

R. B. McCallum and A. Readman, *The British General Election of 1945* (1947).

J. P. Mackintosh, *The Government and Politics of Britain* (1970).

H. G. Nicholas, *The British General Election of 1950* (1951).

J. K. Pollock, 'British By-Elections between the Wars', *American Political Science Review* (1941).

P. G. Pulzer, *Political Representation and Elections in Britain* (1967).

S. F. Rae, 'The Oxford By-Election: A Study in the Straw-Vote Method', *Political Quarterly* (1939).

R. Rose, *Influencing Voters* (1967).

R. Rose, 'Money and Election Law', *Political Studies* (1959).

G. N. Sanderson, 'The Swing of the Pendulum', *Political Studies* (1966).

R. M. Scammon, 'British By-Elections, 1950', *American Political Science Review* (1951).

R. M. Scammon, 'British By-Elections, 1952', *American Political Science Review* (1953).

R. M. Scammon, 'British By-Elections, 1951–5, *Journal of Politics* (1956).

Index of Outstanding Results

The following list gives the results of all by-elections between February 1919 and March 1973 where the seat changed hands, where there was an abnormally large swing, or where for other reasons the by-election has been mentioned in the book. Swing figures are quoted as 'conventional swing' (see p. 359) and all swing figures which are quoted as plus figures are swings to the party which retained the seat with an increased majority.

Aberdeen, South: Con. held seat but 17·6% swing to Lab. (21 May 35)

Aberdeenshire, Central & Kincardine: Lib. gain from Con. (16 Apr 19)

Acton: Con. gain from Lab. (28 Mar 68) *p.* 250

Anglesey: Lib. gain from Ind. Lab. (7 Apr 23) *p.* 46

Antrim, East: Ind. Unionist gain from Unionist (27 May 19)

Ashton-under-Lyne: (1) Lab. gain from Con. (29 Oct 28) *p.* 74

    (2) Con. gain from Lab. (30 Apr 31) *p.* 78

Ayrshire, South: Lab. hald seat from Con. and SNP (19 Mar 70) *p.* 261

Bassetlaw: Lab. held seat but 10·8% swing to Con. (31 Oct 68) *p.* 255, 327

Battersea, South: Lab. gain from Con. (7 Feb 29)

Belfast, West: Eire Lab. gain from Unionist (9 Feb 43) *p.* 169

Berwick-upon-Tweed: Con. gain from Lib.; winning Con. was wife of the Lib. MP unseated on petition (31 May 23)

Bexley: Lab. held seat, but 11·1% swing to Con. (22 July 46)

Birmingham, Ladywood: Lib. gain from Lab. (26 June 69) *p.* 258

Blackpool, North: Con. held seat narrowly from Lib. (13 Mar 62) *p.* 206

Bodmin: Lib. gain from Coalition Con. (24 Feb 22)

Bolton, East: Con. held seat narrowly from Lab. and Lib. (16 Nov 60) *p.* 218

Bosworth: Lib. gain from Con. (31 May 27)

Bothwell: Lab. gain from Coalition Con. (16 July 19) *p.* 18

Brecon & Radnor: Lab. gain from Con. (1 Aug 39)

Bridgwater: (1) Ind. Progressive gain from Con. (17 Nov 38) *p.* 116, 140–164

    (2) Con. held seat with +8.6% swing (12 Mar 70)

Brighouse & Spenborough: Con. gain from Lab. (17 Mar 60)

Brighton: Con. held seat from Ind. (3 Feb 44) *p.* 171

Brighton, Pavilion: Con. held seat with +17·8% swing (27 Mar 69)

Bristol, Central: Con. held seat from Ind. Lab. (18 Feb 43) *p.* 183

Bristol, South-East: (1) seat awarded to Con. after Lab. MP disqualified as a peer (4 May 61)

(2) A. Wedgwood Benn re-elected after disclaiming peerage; no Con. candidate (20 Aug 63)

Bristol, West: (1) Con. held seat but 13·4% swing to Lab. (2 Feb 28)
    (2) Con. held seat with +16·9% swing (15 Feb 51)

Bromley: (1) Coalition Con. held seat narrowly from Lab. (17 Dec 19) *p.* 18
    (2) Con. held seat narrowly from Lib. after intervention by Empire Crusade (2 Sep 30) *p.* 76
    (3) H. Macmillan returned to Parliament after defeat at 1945 general election (14 Nov 45)

Bromsgrove: Lab. gain from Con. (27 May 71)

Burnley: A. Henderson, Home Sec., returned to Parliament after defeat at 1923 general election (28 Feb 24) *p.* 50

Bury St Edmunds: Con. held seat from Ind. Lib. (29 Feb 44) *p.* 186, 189

Caerphilly: (1) Lab. held seat from Con. (4 July 39) *p.* 158
    (2) Lab. held seat narrowly from Plaid Cymru (18 July 68) *p.* 255

Camberwell, North: Lab. gain from Coalition Con. (20 Feb 22)

Camberwell, Peckham: Lab. gain from Con. (6 May 36)

Cambridge: (1) Con. held seat but 18·5% swing to Lab. (8 Feb 34)
    (2) Con. gain from Lab. (21 Sep 67) *p.* 246

Canterbury: Con. held seat but 13·0% swing to Lib. (24 Nov 27)

Carmarthen: (1) Lib. held seat from Lab. (14 Aug 24) *p.* 69
    (2) Lab. gain from Lib. (28 Feb 57) *p.* 194
    (3) Plaid Cymru gain from Lab. (14 July 66) *p.* 230

Chelmsford: Common Wealth gain from Con. (26 Apr 45) *p.* 169, 186

Cheltenham: Ind. Con. gain from Con. (22 June 37) *p.* 116

Chichester: Con. held seat from Ind. (18 May 42) *p.* 187

Chippenham: (1) Con. held seat narrowly from Ind. Lib. (24 Aug 43) *p.* 186
    (2) Con. held seat narrowly from Lib. and Lab. (22 Nov 62) *p.* 218

City of London: Con. held seat from Lib. (1 Feb 24) *p.* 50

Clay Cross: A. Henderson returned to Parliament after defeat at 1931 general election (1 Sep 33) *p.* 132

Colne Valley: Lab. held seat narrowly from Lib. (21 Mar 63) *p.* 218

Darlington: Lab. gain from Con. (17 Feb 26)

Dartford: (1) Lab. gain from Coalition Lib. (27 Mar 20) *p.* 17, 18
    (2) Lab. gain from Con. (7 Nov 38) *p.* 149

Darwen: Con. held seat narrowly from Ind. Lib. (15 Dec 43) *p.* 186

Daventry: Con. held seat from Common Wealth (20 Apr 43) *p.* 168

Derby: Lab. gain from National Lab. (9 July 36)

Derby, North: Lab. held seat from Lib. and Con. (17 Apr 62) *p.* 214

Derbyshire, West: (1) Ind. Lab. gain from Con. (17 Feb 44) *p.* 183
    (2) Con. held seat narrowly from Lib. (6 June 62) *p.* 214

Doncaster: Lab. held seat from National Lib. (17 Nov 38) *p.* 149

Dorset, North: Con. held seat from Lib. (27 June 57) *p.* 195

Dorset, South: Lab. gain from Con. after intervention of Anti-Common Market candidate (22 Nov 62) *p.* 13

Dover: (1) Ind. gain from Coalition Con. (12 Jan 21)
    (2) Con. re-elected after being unseated (12 Mar 24) *p.* 50
Down: Unionist gain from Ind. Unionist (6 June 46)
Dudley: (1) Lab. gain from Coalition Con., Sir A. Griffith-Boscawen,
    seeking re-election as Minister of Agriculture (3 Mar 21) *p.* 21
    (2) Con. gain from Lab. (28 Mar 68) *p.* 250
Dunbartonshire: Lab. gain from Con. (18 Mar 36)
Dundee, East: (1) Lab. held seat from Con. (17 July 52) *p.* 193
    (2) Lab. held seat narrowly from SNP (1 Mar 73) *p.* 310

East Ham, North: Lab. gain from Con. (29 Apr 26)
Eddisbury: (1) Lib. gain from Con. (20 Mar 29)
    (2) Common Wealth gain from Con. (7 Apr 43) *p.* 168, 184
Edinburgh, South: (1) Coalition Con. held seat but 17·3% swing to Lib.
    (9 Apr 20)
    (2) Con. held seat but 10·2% swing to Lab. after Lib. intervention
    (29 May 57)
Edmonton: Lab. held seat but 16·2% swing to Con. (13 Nov 48) *p.* 192
English Universities: (1) Con. gain from Lib. (8–12 Mar 26)
    (2) Ind. Progressive gain from Con. (15–19 Mar 37) *p.* 116
    (3) Con. gain from Ind. (13–18 Mar 46)

Fulham, East: Lab. gain from Con. (25 Oct 33) *p.* 113, 118–139
Fulham, West: (1) Con. gain from Lab. (6 May 30) *p.* 78
    (2) Lab. gain from Con. (6 Apr 38) *p.* 162

Gainsborough: Con. held seat narrowly from Lab. (14 Feb 56) *p.* 327
Gateshead: Lab. held seat but 13·9% swing to Con. (8 June 31) *p.* 78
Glasgow, Camlachie: Con. gain from Lab./ILP (28 Jan 48)
Glasgow, Gorbals: (1) Lab. held seat, but with much-reduced majority,
    after Comm. intervention (30 Sep 48) *p.* 192
    (2) Lab. held seat from SNP (30 Oct 69) *p.* 260
Glasgow, Kelvingrove: Con. held seat with +5·8% swing (23 May 24) *p.*
    64
Glasgow, Pollok: Con. gain from Lab. after SNP intervention (9 Mar 67)
    p. 237
Glasgow, Shettleston: Lab. held seat but 9·5% swing to Con. (26 June 30)
Glasgow, Woodside: Lab. gain from Con. (22 Nov 62)
Gloucester: Lab. held seat with +10·5% swing after Lib. intervention
    (12 Sep 57)
Grantham: Ind. gain from Con. (25 Mar 42) *p.* 174
Greenock: Lab. gain from Con. (26 Nov 36)

Hackney, South: Coalition Con. gain after Ind. MP expelled from House
    of Commons; no Ind. candidate (18 Aug 22) *p.* 18
Halifax: Lab. gain from Con. (13 July 28)
Hamilton: SNP gain from Lab. (2 Nov 67) *p.* 13, 239
Hammersmith, North: (1) Lab. gain from Con. (28 May 26)
    (2) Lab. gain from Con. (24 Apr 34)

Harborough: Con. held seat but 15·4% swing to Lab. (28 Nov 33) *p.* 132
Harrow: Con. held seat from Ind. (2 Dec 41) *p.* 173
Hereford: Con. held seat narrowly from Lib. (14 Feb 56) *p.* 327
Heywood & Radcliffe: Lab. gain from Coalition Lib. (8 June 21) *p.* 19
High Peak: Con. held seat narrowly from Lab. and Lib. (16 Mar 61)
Hitchin: Con. held seat but 17·2% swing to Lab. (8 June 33)
Holland-with-Boston: (1) Con. gain from Lab. (31 July 24) *p.* 68
    (2) Lib. gain from Con. (21 Mar 29)
Hornsey: Con. held seat from Ind. (28 May 41) *p.* 166, 171
Hull, Central: (1) Lib. gain from Coalition Con. (29 Mar 19) *p.* 18
    (2) J. Kenworthy, MP, re-elected on transfer from Lib. to Lab. (29 Nov 26) *p.* 72
Hull, North: Lab. held seat with +4·5% swing (27 Jan 66) *p.* 228
Hythe: Con. held seat from Lib. (20 July 39) *p.* 159

Ilford: Con. held seat but 13·6% swing to Lib. (23 Feb 28)
Ilford, North: Con. held seat with +5·0% swing (3 Feb 54) *p.* 193
Ipswich: Lab. gain from Con. (16 Feb 38)
Islington, East: Lab. held seat from Empire Crusade and Con. (19 Feb 31) *p.* 76, 87
Islington, North: (1) Lab. gain from Con. (13 Oct 37)
    (2) Lab. held seat but 9·2% swing to Con. (30 Oct 69) *p.* 260

Kilmarnock: National Lab. held seat from Lab. (2 Nov 33) *p.* 132
King's Lynn: Con. held seat narrowly from Ind. Lab. (12 Feb 43) *p.* 183
Kirkcaldy Burghs: (1) Lab. gain from Coalition Lib. (4 Mar 21) *p.* 18
    (2) Lab. held seat narrowly from SNP (17 Feb 44)
Kinross & Perthshire West: (1) Duchess of Atholl, MP, not re-elected on transfer from Con. to Ind. Con.; the official Con. elected (21 Dec 38) *p.* 116, 161
    (2) Sir A. Douglas-Home, Prime Minister, elected after disclaiming peerage (7 Nov 63)

Lambeth, Kennington: Lab. gain from Con. (24 May 39)
Lambeth, North: Lab. gain from Lib. (23 Oct 34)
Lambeth, Norwood: Con. held seat with reduced majority (14 Mar 35) *p.* 114
Lanarkshire, North: Lab. gain from Con. (21 Mar 29)
Lancaster: Lib. gain from Con. (9 Feb 28)
Leeds, North-East: Con. held seat from Lab. (9 Feb 56)
Leeds, West: Lab. held seat but 10·5% swing to Con. (21 July 49)
Leicester, East: Lab. gain from Coalition Lib. (30 Mar 22)
Leicester, North-East: Lab. held seat with increased majority after Lib. intervention (12 July 62) *p.* 214
Leicester, South-West: Con. gain from Lab. (2 Nov 67) *p.* 247
Leith: Lib. held seat narrowly from Lab. (23 Mar 27)
Lewes: Con. held seat from Lab. (9 July 24) *p.* 67
Lewisham, North: Lab. gain from Con. (14 Feb 57)

Lewisham, West: (1) Con. held seat narrowly from Ind. (13 Sep 21)
    (2) Con. held seat from Lab. (24 Nov 38) *p.* 159
Leyton: Con. gain from Lab. (21 Jan 65) *pp.* 223–7
Leyton, West: Lib. gain from Coalition Con. (1 Mar 19) *p.* 18
Lichfield: Lab. gain from Con. (5 May 38)
Lincoln: Dick Taverne, MP, re-elected overwhelmingly after transfer from
    Lab. to Democratic Labour (1 Mar 73) *pp.* 264–315
Linlithgowshire: Lab. gain from Con. (4 Apr 28)
Liverpool, East Toxteth: (1) Con. held seat but 10·7% swing to Lab. (19
    Mar 29)
    (2) Con. held seat with +14·9% swing (5 Feb 31)
Liverpool, Edge Hill: (1) Lab. gain from Con. (6 Mar 23) *p.* 46
    (2) Lab. held seat but 10·2% swing to Con. (11 Sep 47)
Liverpool, Scotland: (1) election of D. Logan, Lab., after death of T. P.
    O'Connor, MP, Irish Nationalist (14 Dec 29) *p.* 75
    (2) Lab. held seat with +12·5% swing (11 June 64)
Liverpool, Wavertree: (1) Con. held seat with +11·1% swing (23 June 31)
    p. 78
    (2) Lab. gain from Con. after Ind. Con. intervention (6 Feb 35)
Liverpool, West Derby: Coalition Con. held seat but 10·9% swing to Lab.
    (26 Feb 19)
Liverpool, West Toxteth: (1) Lab. gain from Con. (22 May 24) *p.* 62
    (2) Lab. gain from Con. (16 July 35)
Louth: (1) Lib. gain from Coalition Con. (3 June 20) *p.* 18
    (2) Lib. held seat from Con. (22 Sep 21) *p.* 18
    (3) Con. held seat with +14·3% swing (4 Dec 69)
Lowestoft: Con. held seat but 14·9% swing to Lab. (15 Feb 34)
Luton: Lab. gain from Con. (7 Nov 63)

Macclesfield: Con. held seat narrowly from Lab. (30 Sep 71)
Maldon: Ind. Lab. gain from Con. (25 June 42) *p.* 176
Manchester, Ardwick: Lab. held seat but 9·8% swing to Con. (22 June 31)
    p. 78
Manchester, Clayton: Lab. gain from Con. (18 Feb 22)
Manchester, Gorton: Lab. held seat but 9·4% swing to Con. (2 Nov 67)
    p. 247
Manchester, Rusholme: (1) Coalition Con. held seat but 17·5% swing to
    Lab. (7 Oct 19)
    (2) Con. held seat but 20·6% swing to Lab. (21 Nov 33) *p.* 132
Melton: Con. held seat but 7·6% swing to Lab. (19 Dec 56)
Meriden: Con. gain from Lab. (28 Mar 68) *p.* 250
Middlesbrough, East: Lab. held seat from Lib. (14 Mar 62)
Middlesbrough, West: (1) Lib. held seat narrowly from Lab. (7 Mar 28)
    (2) Lab. gain from Con. (6 June 62) *p.* 218
Midlothian, North: (1) Lab. gain from Con. (29 Jan 29)
    (2) Con. held seat narrowly from Common Wealth (11 Feb 43)
Montgomeryshire: Lib. held seat from Con. (15 May 62) *p.* 218
Motherwell: SNP gain from Lab. (12 Apr 45) *p.* 189

Nelson & Colne: Con. gain from Lab. (27 June 68) *p.* 255
Newcastle-under-Lyme: Lab. held seat but 10·7% swing to Con. (30 Oct 69) *p.* 260
Newcastle-upon-Tyne, North: Ind. Con. gain from Con. (7 June 40) *p.* 170
Newport: Con. gain; seat previously Coalition Lib. (18 Oct 22) *pp.* 14–43
Norfolk, South: Lab. gain from Lib. (27 July 20)
Northampton: Lab. gain from Con. (9 Jan 28)
Nuneaton: Lab. held seat from Con. (9 Mar 67) *p.* 234

Oldham, West: Con. gain from Lab. (13 June 68) *p.* 255
Orpington: Lib. gain from Con. (14 Mar 62) *pp.* 198–222
Oxford: (1) Con. gain from Lib. (5 June 24) *p.* 66
    (2) Con. held seat from Ind. Progressive (27 Oct 38) *p.* 116, 140–64
Oxford University: Ind. gain from Con. (23–27 Feb 37)

Paddington, North: Lab. held seat but 11·4% swing to Con. (30 Oct 69) *p.* 260
Paddington, South: Empire Crusade gain from Con. (30 Oct 30) *p.* 76, 84
Paisley: H. Asquith, Lib. leader, returned to Parliament after defeat at 1918 general election (12 Feb 20)
Penistone: Lab. gain from Lib. (5 Mar 21) *p.* 19
Peterborough: Con. held seat narrowly from Ind. Lab. (15 Oct 43) *p.* 182
Pontypridd: Lab. gain from Coalition Lib. (25 July 22) *p.* 36
Portsmouth, South: Sir L. Wilson, Con. Chief Whip, returned to Parliament after defeat at 1922 general election (13 Dec 22) *p.* 44
Preston: W. A. Jowitt, MP, re-elected on transfer from Lib. to Lab. (31 July 29) *p.* 75

Renfrewshire, East: (1) Con. held seat narrowly from Lab. (29 Jan 26)
    (2) Con. held seat from ILP (9 May 40) *p.* 170
Rhondda, West: Lab. held seat narrowly from Plaid Cymru (9 Mar 67) *p.* 234
Ripon: Con. held seat from Lab. (23 Feb 39) *p.* 159
Rochdale: (1) Lab. gain from Con., Lib. close second (12 Feb 58) *p.* 195
    (2) Lib. gain from Lab. (26 Oct 72) *p.* 269
Ross & Cromarty: M. J. MacDonald, Colonial Secretary, returned to Parliament after defeat at 1935 general election (10 Feb 36) *p.* 114
Rotherham: Lab. gain from Con. (27 Feb 33)
Roxburgh, Selkirk & Peebles: Lib. gain from Con. (24 Mar 65) *p.* 237
Rugby: Ind. gain from Con. (29 Apr 42) *p.* 173, 174
Rushcliffe: Con. held seat but 16·7% swing to Lab. (26 July 34)
Rutherglen: (1) Lab. held seat from Con. (21 May 31) *p.* 78
    (2) Lab. gain from Con. (14 May 64)
Rutland & Stamford: Con. held seat but 18·7% swing to Lab. (21 Nov 33) *p.* 132

St Albans: Coalition Con. held seat narrowly from Lab. (10 Dec 19) *p.* 18
St Ives: Lib. gain from Con. (6 Mar 28)
St Marylebone: Con. held seat narrowly from Ind. Con. (28 Apr 32)

Scarborough & Whitby: (1) Con. held seat narrowly from Lib. (6 May 31) *p.* 78

(2) Con. held seat from Ind. (24 Sep 41) *p.* 172

Scottish Universities: (1) J. R. MacDonald, Lord President, returned to Parliament after defeat at 1935 general election (27–31 Jan 36)

(2) Ind. gain from National Lib. (9–13 Apr 45)

(3) Con. gain from Ind. (22–27 Nov 46)

Sheffield, Brightside: Lab. held seat but 17·1% swing to Con. (13 June 68)

Shipley: Con. gain from Lab. (6 Nov 30) *p.* 78

Skipton: (1) Con. held seat but 13·5% swing to Lab. (7 Nov 33) *p.* 132, 135

(2) Common Wealth gain from Con. (7 Jan 44) *p.* 185.

Southwark, North: (1) Lib. gain from Lab.: L. Haden-Guest, MP, not re-elected on transfer from Lab. to Constitutionalist (28 Mar 27)

(2) Lab. gain from National Lib. (17 May 39)

Southwark, South-East: Lab. gain from Coalition Lib. (14 Dec 21)

Spen Valley: Lab. gain from Coalition Lib. (20 Dec 19) *p.* 17, 19

Stalybridge & Hyde: Con. held seat narrowly from Lab. (28 Apr 37)

Stockport: (1) Coalition Government held both seats in double-Member by-election (27 Mar 20) *p.* 17

(2) Lab. gain from Con. (17 Sep 25)

Stockton-on-Tees: Lab. held seat from Con. and Lib. (5 Apr 62) *p.* 214

Stourbridge: Lab. gain from Con. (23 Feb 27)

Stratford-on-Avon: Con. held seat, but 13·7% swing to Lab. after resignation of J. Profumo, MP (15 Aug 63)

Stretford: Con. held seat from ILP (8 Dec 39) *p.* 170

Stroud: Con. held seat from Lab. (21 May 31) *p.* 78

Sunderland: Con. gain from Lab. (26 Mar 31) *p.* 78

Sunderland, South: Con. gain from Lab. (13 May 53) *p.* 193

Sutton & Cheam: Lib. gain from Con. (7 Dec 72) *p.* 270

Swansea, East: Coalition Lib. held seat, but 10·5% swing to Lab. (10 July 19)

Swindon: (1) Lab. gain from Con. (25 Oct 34) *p.* 113

(2) Con. gain from Lab. (30 Oct 69) *p.* 260

Tamworth: Con. held seat from Lab. (2 Dec 29) *p.* 76

Taunton: (1) Coalition Con. held seat but 11·3% swing to Lab. (8 Apr 21)

(2) Con. held seat narrowly from Lab. (14 Feb 56) *p.* 327

Tiverton: Lib. gain from Con. (21 June 23)

Tonbridge: Con. held seat, but 8·4% swing to Lab. (7 June 56)

Torrington: Lib. gain from Con. (27 Mar 58) *p.* 195, 199

Twickenham: (1) Con. held seat narrowly from Lab. (8 Aug 29) *p.* 75

(2) Con. held seat, but 17·8% swing to Lab. (16 Sep 32)

Ulster, Mid: (1) Unionist gain from Sinn Fein, after Sinn Fein MP disqualified (12 Aug 55)

(2) Ind. Unionist gain from Unionist, after Unionist MP disqualified (8 May 56)

(3) Ind. gain from Unionist (17 Apr 69)

Wakefield: Lab. gain from Con. (21 Apr 32)

Wallasey: Ind. gain from Con. (29 Apr 42) *p.* 167, 175

Walsall: National Lib. held seat from Lab. (16 Nov 38) *p.* 149

Walthamstow, East: Con. gain from Lab. (27 Mar 69)

Walthamstow, West: Con. gain from Lab. (21 Sep 67) *p.* 246

Wandsworth, Central: Lab. gain from Con. (29 Apr 37)

Wandsworth, Putney: Con. held seat but 26·9% swing to Lab. (28 Nov 34) *p.* 137

Warwick & Leamington: (1) Con. held seat, but 12·2% swing to Lab. after resignation of Sir A. Eden (7 Mar 57)

(2) Con. held seat with +18·1% swing, (28 Mar 68) *p.* 250

Watford: Con. held seat from Common Wealth (23 Feb 43)

Wednesbury: Lab. gain from Con. (26 July 32)

Wellingborough: Con. gain from Lab. (4 Dec 69) *p.* 260

West Bromwich: Lab. held seat with +10·2% swing (4 July 63)

West Ham, Upton: Lab. gain from Con. (14 May 34)

Westminster, Abbey: (1) Coalition Con. held seat narrowly from Anti-Waste League (25 Aug 21) *p.* 53

(2) Con. held seat narrowly from W. Churchill, standing as Constitutionalist (19 Mar 24) *pp.* 53–61

(3) Con. held seat from Ind. Progressive (17 May 39) *p.* 159

Westminster, St George's: (1) Anti-Waste League gain from Coalition Con. (7 June 21) *p.* 53, 86

(2) Con. held seat from Ind. (19 Mar 31) *pp.* 79–108

Widnes: Lab. gain from Coalition Con. (30 Aug 19) *p.* 18

Willesden, East: Lib. gain from Con. (3 Mar 23)

Wolverhampton, West: Coalition Con. held seat from Lab. (7 Mar 22) *p.* 18

Woolwich, East: (1) Coalition Con. gain from Lab., J. R. MacDonald (2 Mar 21) *p.* 16

(2) Lab. held seat but 6·5% swing to Con. (15 Apr 31)

Wrekin: (1) Ind. gain from Coalition Lib. (7 Feb 20)

(2) Ind. held seat from Lab. (20 Nov 20)

Index of Persons